GUIDE MAP FOR TO[URISTS]

——— ROUTE 1 ——— ROUTE 2

A traveller's companion to

Southern Africa

A traveller's companion to

Southern Africa

Mike Crewe-Brown

SOUTHERN
BOOK PUBLISHERS

ISBN 1 86812 119 4

First edition, first impression 1990

Published by
Southern Book Publishers (Pty) Ltd
PO Box 548, Bergvlei 2012
Johannesburg

Cover design by Insight Graphics, Pretoria

Maps compiled and drawn by Ingrid Booysen, Pretoria

Set in 9 on 10 pt Hanover
by Unifoto, Cape Town
Printed and bound by CTP Book Printers, Cape

Foreword

Accurate information is an obvious prerequisite for the traveller who wishes to make the right decisions on where to go, what to see and do, and how to reach his or her destination.

The South African Tourism Board welcomes the publication of this comprehensive South African travel book by Mike Crewe-Brown, who has a keen insight into his subject. The book fills a gap in the existing library of local travel publications and provides a broad spectrum of travel-oriented data. It encompasses snippets of history and geography, suggested itineraries, accommodation, the best times of the year to visit each region, route descriptions, coach tours, sports facilities and maps. The section on useful tips will be of special interest to tourists from overseas.

I hope that this publication will contribute in a meaningful way to the maintenance and improvement of standards in our hospitality industry. I hope also that *The Traveller's Companion to southern Africa* will prove to be an invaluable travel guide — one which will ensure that the holiday-maker obtains the maximum benefit from his leisure time and value for money, and that it will enhance his appreciation of this lovely many-faceted land.

DANIE HOUGH

Acknowledgements

To compile a book of this magnitude, I needed the advice, time, assistance and encouragement of a number of people. I wish to thank one and all for their help. Although they are too numerous to name individually, I would, however, like to thank the following people individually for their assistance:

Sam and Alida for their encouragement in getting me to turn a dream into reality.

Cilla, who spent long hours in the car (while heavily pregnant) taking notes and reading maps. She also spent countless hours sorting, labelling and framing thousands of slides, and even more hours typing, retyping and editing drafts, while running a happy home.

Marion, who also spent long hours in the car, taking notes and reading maps, as well as being a constant source of information.

Crewe, who drove me through Zululand and Swaziland for two weeks.

The members of our family who gave us encouragement and hospitality when we needed it.

The staff of the South African Tourism Board and the SWA Directorate of Tourism, who were faithful colleagues and always ready to help with information and advice.

And lastly, the whole South African Tourism plant, who helped in numerous ways, with advice, information and accommodation.

The following writers' works were used as sources of reference for checking facts and figures, and for inspiration. They are also books well worth getting if you wish to delve deeper than the superficial surface of southern Africa:

Maxwell Leigh, *Touring in South Africa*; T.V. Bulpin *Discovering southern Africa* and *Illustrated guide to southern Africa*; Denis Conolly, *Conolly's guide to southern Africa*; Geoffrey Jenkins and Eve Palmer, *The companion guide to South Africa*; Anthony Bannister and René Gordon, *The national parks of South Africa*; Richard Hilton and Leslie Richfield, *Wining, dining and where to stay*; Glynis van Rooyen, *South Africa on R10 and R20 a day*; Monica Fairall, *When in Durban*; Heather Johnston and Judy Rowe, *Johannesburg alive*; and *An illustrated history of South Africa* (edited by Trewhella Cameron and S.B. Spies). A number of publications by the South African Tourism Board were also used as sources of reference.

Contents

PART 2
The Routes

PART 3
Useful Addresses and Information

List of maps

PART 1
General Information

How to use the guide

This book tries to present the person travelling through southern Africa with a concise reference guide to the worthwhile hotels, restaurants and tourist attractions along the most popular routes.

South Africa's modern history began when the Dutch arrived at the Cape in 1652. Gradually the settlement expanded and European settlements spread north. The book has been designed to guide the traveller along a route which follows the discovery and settlement of the interior by European settlers: starting in Cape Town, the oldest city in the country, and ending in Johannesburg, a modern city just over a hundred years old. Along the way there is a wide variety of historical landmarks, each depicting an important feature of South Africa's make-up. All the places referred to in the book have been visited by the author and have also been recommended by a number of visitors. These places can easily be reached with a normal motor vehicle and are open to the general public. The photographs in the book were taken by the author with ordinary 35 mm camera equipment, from public vantage points which are easily accessible along the route.

This guide can be used in a number of ways, as it is a grand tour route-planner, a guide between centres and a destination guide:

A GRAND TOUR ROUTE-PLANNER

This aspect of the guide is ideal for those with three or more weeks on their hands, and who wish to tour from Cape Town to Johannesburg through the most scenic sections of the country. There is a choice of two routes: along the coast (*route 1*), following the most popular route through South Africa; or along the mountain ranges (*route 2*), passing over the most spectacular passes. These routes meet at various points along the way and therefore the tourist can travel a section of *route 1* followed by a section of *route 2*, or the other way around.

The tourist is given information on accommodation facilities, restaurants, the best routes, and the most interesting sights along the way.

A GUIDE BETWEEN CENTRES

If one wishes to travel from, say, East London to Durban over a period of days, all one needs to do is turn to East London and follow the route description to Durban. All the recommended tourist attractions, accommodation establishments and restaurants are clearly listed.

A DESTINATION GUIDE

Once the traveller has arrived at his or her destination, for instance, Oudtshoorn, he or she can use the list of recommended accommodation establishments, restaurants, sights and sporting activities.

A number of itineraries have been especially designed (see page 33) to assist the traveller in planning trips along the various routes.

History

Many people believe that the history of southern Africa began in 1488, when Bartholomew Dias rounded the Cape, and are unaware that Africa features prominently in the evolution of man on earth. From recent archaeological findings it has been determined that early man established himself in the area over three million years ago.

EVOLUTION OF MAN

It is generally accepted today that man evolved from one of the ape species. Darwin, the great scientist who developed the theory of evolution, wrote in his book *The descent of man* (published in 1871) that "... it is somewhat more probable that our early progenitors lived on the African Continent than elsewhere ..." He was speculating on the basis of what he knew then.

It was not until 1924 that the first evidence substantiating Darwin's theories emerged when the *Taung* skull was discovered near Kimberley. This skull was that of a child, and classified as *Australopithecus africanus,* one of the very early ancestors of man. In 1936 fossils of adults of the same species were found at Sterkfontein, near Johannesburg. Since then many more skeletons have been found in Africa, some more than 5 million years old.

Over one million years ago possibly two distinct kinds of hominid lived in Africa: *Homo* and *Australopithecus Homo habilis* and *Australopithecus robustus* coexisted in the Transvaal and *Homo habilis* and *Australopithecus boisei* were East African contemporaries. Later *Homo erectus* existed side by side with *Australopithecus robustus.* About one million years ago these small-brained hominids became extinct – possibly as a result of fierce competition for food. The more versatile *Homo erectus* survived.

Between 700 000 and 125 000 years ago, departures from the original *Homo erectus* skeleton began to take place, giving rise to four distinctive *Homo sapiens* subspecies: two found in Africa, one in Java and one in Europe and Asia. Of the two subspecies found in Africa, one, *Homo sapiens rhodensiensis,* was found throughout southern Africa and is probably the direct ancestor of the Negro people who inhabited various parts of Africa, including southern Africa, some 8 000 years ago.

ORIGINS OF THE ETHNIC COMMUNITIES

The earliest known modern human occupants of southern Africa were the Khoisan, who can be divided into the San (Bushmen) and the Khoikhoi (Hottentots). It is generally believed that these groups were originally hunter-gatherers, who occupied central Botswana for over eight thousand years. About two thousand years ago a gradual southward migration began, and along the way a number of groups started herding cattle which they had somehow acquired from the black tribes. They usually moved in large groups, grazing their cattle on common ground until the pasture was depleted. Then they would split up into smaller groups in search of new grazing. If a group's cattle was destroyed, they would become hunter-gatherers again. Their nomadic lifestyle allowed for flexible political structures. The San groups continued their stone-age existence more or less undisturbed until the arrival of the first European traders. The Cape Khoikhoi societies disintegrated rapidly, but Khoikhoi communities are still to be found in Namibia, as are San groups.

Evidence has been found of Iron Age Negroid communities in both Natal and the northern Transvaal dating back to A.D. 300. They established themselves in villages, kept livestock (cattle, goats and sheep), cultivated crops, made pottery and developed other crafts. It is accepted that the first route to South Africa was down the eastern coastal belt, reaching the eastern Transvaal lowveld and Natal coast before A.D. 300. These Early Iron Age communities confined themselves to the savannah areas which were already inhabited by Stone Age people.

By A.D. 800 over-arching political and economic structures began to emerge in the Limpopo Basin, eastern Botswana, far northern Transvaal and southern Zimbabwe. Little is known of the transition made from Early to Late Iron Age cultures by these communities. However, they seem to have been the forerunners of the Great Zimbabwe Tradition and were the first to have long-distance trade links with Indian Ocean trading system.

Elsewhere in South Africa the Late Iron Age saw important changes, such as the starting of metal production, despite the fact that most communites remained small and their economies remained based on subsistence farming. Towards 1400, expansion from the savannah areas to the open grasslands took place. By 1552 survivors of Portuguese shipwrecks described settlements of black people on the Cape and Natal coasts.

THE ARRIVAL OF THE EUROPEAN TRADERS

The first European explorers to round the Cape of Good Hope, in the latter part of the fifteenth century, were Portuguese explorers looking for an alternative trade route to the spice islands of the East. Once the route had been found, they were followed by the British and Dutch who all rounded the Cape en route to the East. For the next two hundred-odd years the occasional ship laid anchor along the South African coast to replenish water supplies and occasionally barter with black tribes for meat and fruit, but no permanent settlement took place.

THE DUTCH OCCUPATION

In 1652 the fate of southern Africa changed. The Dutch East India Company (Vereenigde Oost-Indische Compagnie) decided to establish a half-way station at the Cape, with a hospital for ailing crew and a garden where fresh produce could be grown to replenish the passing ships.

From this point South African history can be documented in chronological order:

1652   On 6 April Jan van Riebeeck lands at the Cape and establishes the first settlement.

1657   The first free burghers start farming at Rondebosch.

1658   About 400 slaves are imported from West Africa.

1659   On 2 February the first wine is pressed in the Cape. Soon after, wine is exported to Batavia.

1666   Building of the Castle at Cape Town commences.

1679   Stellenbosch is founded by Simon van der Stel.

1688   The arrival of the first Huguenot settlers.

1778   Fish River is declared the eastern boundary.

1781   The first British attempt to annex the Cape. French troops land to protect the Cape against the British, and are withdrawn in 1784.

BRITISH ANNEXATION

1795 – 1803   The first British occupation of the Cape.

1803 – 1806   The Cape is returned to the Batavian Republic.

1806   The Second British occupation of the Cape.

1814   Holland cedes the Cape to Britain.

1819   Cape boundary is extended to Keiskama River.

1820   The arrival of 5 000 British settlers.

1828   Death of the Zulu ruler Chaka. English becomes the official language. Passes for Hottentots abolished. All free coloureds in Cape placed on political level of whites.

1834   Slavery is abolished and many colonists are ruined.

1835   Durban is founded.

1836   Great Trek from the Cape Colony.

1837   Matabele, defeated by the Voortrekkers and cross the Limpopo into Zimbabwe. Retief treks to Natal.

1838   Retief negotiates a treaty with Dingane, successor to Chaka. Massacre of Boers under Retief by Dingane. Andries Pretorius wins the battle of Blood River. Dingane is overthrown. Republic of Natal is founded.

1839   Temporary British occupation of Durban.

1843   Natal proclaimed a British Colony.

1844   Majority of Voortrekkers leave Natal under British rule.

1845   Natal separated from Cape Colony.

1847   East London is founded. British rule is extended over Kaffraria (Ciskei).

1848   British sovereignty proclaimed between Orange and Vaal Rivers. Skirmish between British and Boers at Boomplaats (southern O.F.S.).

1852   Britain recognises independence of Transvaal in Sand River Convention.

1854   Britain recognises independence of Orange Free State (O.F.S) in Convention of Bloemfontein. First Cape Parliament in session.

1855   Pretoria is founded.

1856   Natal is made a separate colony.

1857-1859   Settlement of the "German Legion" in Kaffraria.

1860   The first railway, a link of 3 km between the Point and Port Natal, comes into operation. (Rail development in the Cape was started in 1857, but the first line, from Cape Town to Eerste Rivier — a distance of 30 km — was completed only in 1862.) The first stretch of telegraph line, between Cape Town and Simonstown, comes into operation.

1867   The first diamond discovered near Hopetown.

1869   Diamonds discovered near Kimberley.

1870   The diamond fields annexed by Britain.

1871   Gold discovered at Eersteling, Pietersburg.

1872   Responsible parliamentary government is granted to Cape Colony.

1873   Gold discovered in Lydenburg district.

1875   Formation of *Die Genootskap van Regte Afrikaners* (Association of True Afrikaners) in the Cape, with the aim of striving for the full recognition of the Afrikaans language.

1877   Transvaal is proclaimed British territory.

1878   Walvis Bay is proclaimed British territory.

1879   Zulu War: Cetewayo is exiled and Britain occupies Zululand. On 31 July South Africa is linked by cable with Europe, via Aden.

1880   Formation of *Afrikaner Bond*. First War of Independence in the Transvaal.

1881   Transvaal regains independence under British suzerainty. Use of Dutch in Cape Parliament is permitted.

1883   Paul Kruger becomes President of South African Republic (Transvaal).

1884   German protectorate established over South-West Africa (SWA). Barberton gold-fields opened. Treaty of London (27 February) grants Transvaal full independence with exception of the right to make treaties with foreign states.

1886   Johannesburg founded with the discovery of gold on the Witwatersrand.

1889   Defence alliance between O.F.S. and Transvaal.

1890   Cecil Rhodes becomes Prime Minister of the Cape Colony.

1892   The railway between Cape Town and Johannesburg completed.

1893   Natal is granted self-government.

1896   Resignation of Rhodes as Prime Minister of Cape Colony after the abortive Jameson Raid which attempted to overthrow the Transvaal government.

1898   Paul Kruger is elected President of the Transvaal for the fourth time.

1899-1902   Anglo-Boer War between Great Britain and the two Boer republics.

1902   Peace Treaty of Vereeniging (31 May). Transvaal and OFS are made British colonies. Death of Cecil Rhodes. Start of Premier Diamond Mine.

1904   Death of President Kruger at Clarens, Switzerland. Chinese labourers are imported to work on gold mines of Transvaal.

THE BIRTH OF A UNION

1910   The establishment of the Union of South Africa (31 May) with Lord Gladstone as Governor-General and Gen. Louis Botha as Prime Minister. Laying of foundation stone of Union Buildings, Pretoria, by the Duke of Connaught.

1913   Miners' strikes and riots on the Witwatersrand.

1914   Grave industrial disturbances on Witwatersrand and elsewhere and proclamation of martial law. General Hertzog
founds the National Party (NP). On outbreak of World
War 1, the defence of South Africa is taken over by the
Union Government and imperial troops are released for
service in Europe. On 10 September Parliament decides
by 91 votes against 12 in favour of participation in war.

1915   Surrender of German forces in SWA to Gen. Botha. Union
Government raises a volunteer contingent for service in
Europe.

1916   Union expeditionary force under Gen. Smuts dispatched
to German East Africa.

1919   Union granted mandate over SWA protectorate. Conclu-
sion of peace with Germany (Treaty of Versailles) on 28
June; Generals Botha and Smuts are signatories on behalf
of the Union. Death of Gen. Botha. Gen. Smuts appointed
Prime Minister.

1920   Strike by black workers on the Rand. General election
(10 March) and a new Cabinet is appointed under Gen.
Smuts.

1922   Strike by white workers on the gold and coal mines,
followed by widespread violence. Referendum in southern
Rhodesia on joining the Union (27 October); Union Government's terms rejected (8 744 votes against 5 989).

1924   National Party, with Gen. Hertzog as Prime Minister
gains power in general election (17 June).

1925   Afrikaans is recognised as official language, parallel with
English and Dutch.

1930   Enfranchisement of white women.

1934   South African Party and National Party fuse to form
United Party (UP).

1936   Native Trust and Land Act passed, forming the basis of
the future development for the black homelands.

1939   Start of World War II. Resignation of Gen. J.B.M. Hertzog
after arguing that Union should remain neutral and being
defeated in Parliament. New Cabinet is formed under
Gen. J.C. Smuts as Prime Minister. South Africa declares
war on Germany (6 September).

1943   Parliamentary election: UP 89, NP 43, Labour Party 9,
Dominion Party 7, Independents 2, Native Representa-
tives 3, Gen. Smuts remains Prime Minister.

1948   General election: NP in coalition with Afrikaner Party
obtains majority. Dr D.F. Malan elected Prime Minister.

1951   Group Areas Act comes into operation. Union withdraws
from UN temporarily. Abolition of Natives' Representative Council. Black Authorities Act is passed.

1956   Joint sitting of both Houses of Parliament adopts a bill
placing coloured voters on a separate voters' roll.

1958   General election: NP 103, UP 53. Dr H.F. Verwoerd (Minister of Native Affairs since 1950) is elected sixth Prime
Minister of the Union.

1960   At Sharpeville (21 March) about 15 000 angry blacks
gather around a police station. Police fire, killing 69.
Riots on the same day at Langa in the Cape. The government reacts by ordering the arrest of the leaders. In a
referendum (5 October) 850 458 vote in favour and 775 878
against South Africa becoming a republic.

INDEPENDENCE AS A REPUBLIC

1961   New decimal coinage system is introduced. On 15 March at the Conference of Commonwealth Prime Ministers in London, Dr Verwoerd withdraws South Africa from the Commonwealth as a republic. Republic of South (RSA) established (31 May). Mr C.R. Swart is sworn in as the first State President.

1962   On 23 January the Prime Minister announces in Parliament that the government is to grant self-government to Transkei.

1966   Dr Verwoerd is assassinated in the House of Assembly by Dimitri Tsafendas, a parliamentary messenger. Mr B.J. Vorster is elected Prime Minister.

1967   The first heart transplant by Prof. Chris Barnard is performed on Mr Louis Washkansky at the Groote Schuur Hospital in Cape Town.

1970   Census taken, population exceeds 21 million.

1973   Territories of Gazankulu and Venda become self-governing.

1976   In June unrest begins in black residential areas and lasts until February 1977. The cause is the insistence that Afrikaans be placed on an equal footing with English as a medium of instruction in black high schools.

1980   Parliament votes to establish a President's Council.

1982   The President's Council submits its first constitutional proposals: one central parliament comprising three chambers — one each for whites, coloured and Indians. Each chamber is to have autonomy in only the matters pertaining to the population group concerned, while the three chambers are to assume joint responsibility for all matters of common concern, including legislation which must be approved by all three chambers sitting separately. The functions of President and Prime Minister are to be combined in the President, who can appoint members of his Cabinet from among the ranks of the three chambers.

1983   The White electrorate give a massive "yes" to the above constitutional proposals in a referendum held on 2 November.

The Swartberg Pass

"Oom Samie se Winkel" in Dorp Street, Stellenbosch

Above: Windsurfing in Cape Town

Right: *Oudtshoorn is famous for its ostriches*

Below: *A lioness and her cubs in Mala Mala*

Geography

South Africa lies between the latitudes 22° and 35° south, on Africa's southern tip. The country is bordered by Namibia, Botswana and Zimbabwe in the north, and by Mozambique and Swaziland in the north-east. The east and west coasts are flanked by the Indian and Atlantic oceans respectively.

The Republic covers an area of 1 123 226 km² (433 678 square miles), five times the size of Great Britain, or larger than Germany, France and the Benelux together. The distance from Cape Town to Johannesburg is equal to that between Amsterdam and Rome.

The country consists of four provinces, Cape Province, Transvaal, Orange Free State and Natal. The four principal cities are (in order of population size): Johannesburg, Cape Town, Durban and Pretoria.

GEOLOGY

South Africa forms part of the southern African subcontinent, which is largely composed of very old and stable parts of the earth's crust. The country's rocks range in age from some of the very oldest known on earth to very recently formed ones.

The old stable portions of the crust (cratons or shields) form the ancient foundation of the subcontinent. The oldest rocks in the world are Swazian in age and include granite and gneiss as well as the rocks of the Barberton and Murchison sequences. The latter are more than three thousand million years old. These Swazian rocks are overlain by younger, less deformed rocks of the Randian Era. The Swazian and Randian rocks are of great economic importance since they include the famous goldbearing rocks such as those of the Murchison and Barberton ranges and the Witwatersrand.

Younger than the above are the rocks of the Vaalian, Mokolian and Namibian Era. The Transvaal contains rich iron and manganese deposits. The Bushveld Igneous Complex is of prime importance by virtue of its platinum and chrome deposits.

Geological formations of the Palaeozoic and Mesozoic Eras cover very large parts of the country. These formations include the strata of the Cape Supergroup and the Karoo Sequence, the latter being the country's only source of coal (as well as a potential source of uranium. Kimberlite pipes of the Cretaceous Era provide most of South Africa's diamonds.

TOPOGRAPHY AND VEGETATION

The surface of South Africa can be divided into three distinct areas: the coastal belt, the escarpment and the interior plateau.

The *coastal belt* varies in width from 16 km in the southern Cape to over 200 km in Zululand. Vegetation in the area also varies greatly. In the south-western Cape (Cape Town area) the Mediterranean climate and winter rainfall gives rise to a wide variety of chaparral-like vegetation known as scherophyllous bush or *fynbos*, which is resistant to summer droughts. Species include the beautiful proteas and ericas which bloom in profusion in the area.

Bordering on the Mediterranean area is the coastal strip of tall evergreen hardwood forests between George and Humansdorp. The area is part of an all-year rain belt where forests of such well-known species as yellowwood and stinkwood can be found. Some trees tower up to 45 m.

From Port Elizabeth to Transkei patches of subtropical coastal forests occur; and from Transkei northwards various palm species also appear, while mangroves are commonly found in swamp areas. Natal has subtropical vegetation.

The *escarpment area* forms a great barrier between the coastal belt and the interior plateau, and runs parallel to the coast from the western Cape right around to the northern Transvaal. It is referred to as the Drakensberg Range in the Transvaal and Natal and reaches a height of 2 316 m (at Mt. Anderson) in the Transvaal, and 3 376 m (at Champagne Castle) in Natal.

The *interior plateau*, which covers the greatest area of South Africa, can be compared to a giant saucer. It is slightly higher on the eastern boundary, where it rests on the escarpment. In total, the plateau varies in height between 1 800 m on the highveld (Johannesburg area) and 900 m in the north-western Karoo. Vegetation varies greatly as well: the highveld is predominantly covered by savanna-type vegetation and temperate grasslands, while the Karoo is covered extensively by semi-desert perennial shrubs.

CLIMATE

The climate in South Africa is temperate and agreeable, with warm summers (November to April) and mild winters. (See "Times to visit" on page 32.)

South Africa can be divided into two main climatic regions:

The Cape coastal belt runs from Cape Town to Port Elizabeth. In Cape Town and the western and southern Cape (up to Mossel Bay) the climate is Mediterranean in nature. Summers are dry and sunny, while rain is common in winter. Further along the coast, up to Port Elizabeth, rainfall is distributed evenly throughout the year. Frost is rare in the region, and snow falls only occasionally on the high mountain peaks.

Natal and interior — that is, most of the country — has a summer rainfall climate. In the Transvaal rain falls mainly in the late afternoon, in thundershowers, which help to cool down the evenings after hot days. Winters are dry, with light frost. In Natal rain tends to be more prolonged, often lasting for a day or two, and summer days can be very humid. Winters are mild but still perfect for bathing along the coast.

Useful information

(For a comprehensive up-to-date booklet on useful tips see the SATOUR Publication, *Travel Digest.*)

ACCOMMODATION

A wide range of accommodation can be found in South Africa, from the luxurious ultra-modern five-star hotels in downtown Johannesburg to the rustic huts on the shores of Lake St. Lucia. The accommodation establishments in this guide have been selected either for their convenience, their suitability within a category or simply because I find them to be charming and relaxing places. After all, is relaxation not the whole point of a vacation? Each accommodation establishment listed in this book is described as follows:

Name   Telephone number
Physical (postal) address   Marketing organization
Description of recreational amenities (and facilities at caravan and camping sites)
Description of establishment

(For a full list of accommodation possibilities refer to the official *Tourism Board Guide.*)

Hotels

All registered hotels in South Africa are graded by the Tourism Board according to a system of stars that indicates their facilities. One-star hotels are usually comfortable family-run establishments with limited facilities, while five-star hotels are on a par with the best in the world.

A plaque, displayed at the entrance to a hotel, indicates the star rating of the hotel as well as the liquor and residential status of the hotel. The code is:

T   More than half the occupancy is transitory.
R   More than half the occupancy is residential.
Y   Licensed to sell wine and beer only with meals.
YY   Licensed to sell only wine and beer.
YYY Licensed to sell all alcoholic beverages.

The Law prohibits the levying of service charges in hotels, but beware, telephone calls are exempt. This means that telephone costs are often twice that of metered unit costs.

A large range of hotel chains exist in S.A. One organisation —*Southern Sun/Holiday Inns* — owns a large number of the five-star hotels, as well as a range of four- and three-star hotels. *Protea Hotels and Inns* on the other hand have a few four- and five-star flagships and a large number of ex-family run one- to three-star hotels for the budget-conscious traveller. One other organisation worth mentioning is *Portfolio of Country Places.*

They represent a selection of fine country houses, hotels and game lodges in southern Africa. Each property has been selected because of its individual charm and character, personal service, and peaceful setting. Most are small and owner-run.

A full list of hotel chain addresses can be found at the back of this book on page 286. Most of the hotel chains have special voucher systems. These entitle the tourist to reduced rates when travelling through South Africa on condition that more than seven nights are spent in that chain's hotels. Remember to make enquires from your travel agent when booking.

Many of the smaller country hotels fill up during mid-week —with commercial visitors — while coastal hotels and those in scenic areas are usually full during school holidays and week-ends. It is always advisable to book in advance.

Ungraded accommodation

Under this heading comes a variety of establishments:

CHARACTER COUNTRY HOUSES There are a large number of country retreats with individual charm and character in South Africa. In the strict sense of the word they should be classified as guest houses, but the high standard of the accommodation and superb cuisine place these establishments in a different category. The majority of these establishments are represented by *Portfolio of Country Places.*

GUEST HOUSES These are usually hotel-type establishments with no star rating that offer inexpensive accommodation at often basic levels.

BED AND BREAKFAST By staying in one of these private homes you are really able to sample the South African way of life. Standards are generally high; and each room has its own private bathroom (see page 286).

YOUTH HOSTELS YMCA and YWCA Youth hostels can be found in Johannesburg, East London, Cape Town (two) and Kimberley (page 286). The YMCA and YWCA offer accommodation to members only (page 286).

Self-catering

This type of accommodation includes holiday flats, small bunga-lows, or thatched huts. Facilities vary greatly, so always check what you need to take along when making your bookings. The majority of places in this guide provide kitchen utensils and bedding.

Caravan and camping parks

The facilities offered by South African parks vary greatly. All the parks mentioned in this book maintain a high standard and include security, clean ablution facilities and a constant supply of water. Most have beautiful natural surroundings and swim-ming facilities are often within walking distance. With South Africa's sunny climate a caravan or a camping holiday will always be successful and enjoyable. *Club Caraville* represents some of the top resorts in South Africa (see page 286 for the address). Campers can also be hired (see pages 67 & 242).

BANKING AND CURRENCY

Currency

The currency unit in S.A. is the rand (R) R1 = 100 cents. Banknotes in circulation are R5, R10, R20 and R50; nickel (silver) coins are R2, R1, 50c, 20c, 10c, 5c; and copper coins are 2c and 1c.

Banking

Banking practices are similar to those in other Western countries. The following banks have branches throughout South Africa:
— First National Bank Ltd. (previously Barclays Bank)
— Nedbank Ltd.
— The Standard Bank of Africa Ltd.
— The Trust Bank of Africa Ltd.
— Volkskas Ltd.
Most of these banks also have representation abroad. Many major overseas banks are represented in South Africa by one of the above banks.
Business hours are as follows:
Major centres: 09h00 to 15h30 — Monday to Friday
08h30 to 11h00 — Saturdays
Other centres: 09h00 to 12h45 and 14h00 to 15h30 — Monday to Friday
08h30 to 11h00 — Saturdays
Jan Smuts Airport: 24 hour service
Cape Town Airport (D.F. Malan): 09h30 to 12h30 and 12h45 to 15h30 — Monday to Friday
09h30 to 11h00 — Saturdays
Durban Airport (Louis Botha): during arrival and departure of International flights
All branches of the above banks, have traveller's cheques and foreign currency exchange facilities.

Credit Cards

Most international credit cards (*Visa, Access, American Express* and *Diners Club*) can be used extensively in South Africa. It is always best, though, to check before you order a service. Petrol can not be bought on standard credit cards. Credit cards are not widely accepted in Namibia.

Traveller's Cheques

Traveller's cheques can be exchanged at all banks and most four- and five-star hotels if you are a resident. Rates are always better at banks. Most major currency traveller's cheques are accepted. It is also possible to buy traveller's cheques in rands from South African represented banks outside South Africa. These cheques are very useful as they are treated as cash in hotels as well as in most large shops and restaurants within South Africa and no further commission needs to be paid when they are exchanged for cash.

CLOTHING

It never gets very cold in South Africa; so clothing for a temperate climate would be suitable. If you are in South Africa between June and September, a light coat is sometimes useful. Otherwise you would just need a jersey and jacket or windbreaker. In the game parks and at the coastal resorts dress is very casual. In larger hotels and restaurants, evening dress is more formal, and men often wear ties and jackets.

EATING AND DRINKING

Once a roof over your head has been found, it's time to satisfy your hunger. South Africa offers a wide range of culinary delights and excellent wines and South Africans are renowned for their hospitality and their ability to entertain. Don't be surprised if you bump into somebody in a pub and are invited home for a meal — or very often a barbecue under the stars (called *braai* and pronounced *bry*) — in South Africa.

Over the last three hundred-odd years, immigrants have arrived from all over the world to settle in South Africa. They, together with the indigenous population, have a wonderful selection of ingredients and recipes, which have been blended together to create a mouth-watering and imaginative range of traditional dishes. In the early years of colonisation most of the settlers came from the Dutch East Indian colonies of Malaysia and Indonesia, bringing their slave cooks and recipes with them. These spicy foods have formed the basis of many South African dishes, intermingled with local ingredients. Later came immigrants from France, Germany, India, Britain, Greece, Portugal and Italy, all of whom added a bit of their own character to South African cuisine. Even the British roast beef and Yorkshire pudding have found their way onto our Sunday lunch tables.

With the abundance of wildlife, the nomadic lifestyle of the first settlers and the failure of the first crops, South Africans became great meat-eaters. Nowadays meat still forms a large part of most diets. Boerewors, a type of spiced sausage, which is most flavoursome cooked over an open fire, is by itself a delight worth visiting South Africa for.

South African wines are also very good. Over 1 500 different labels are now available in South Africa in a spectrum of red and white of varying degrees of sweetness. Most of the well-known cultivars are grown locally. Only a foolish snob would drink foreign wines while in South Africa. Here are a few personal favourites:

Wine

WHITE WINES *Zonneblom Premier Grand Crû:* a dry refreshing wine.
Backsberg Chenin Blanc: a dry fruity wine, soft on the palate.
Boschendal Chenin Blanc: an off-dry soft fruity wine.
Autumn Harvest Grand Crû: a dry value-for-money wine.
Cellar Cask Premier Light: a fruity and crisp off-dry wine in a five-litre box.
Cellar Cask Late Harvest: a semi-sweet wine in a five-litre box.

Nederburg Fonternel: a semi-sweet, and pleasantly fruity wine.
Nederburg Special Late Harvest: a sweet golden after-dinner wine.
Bellingham Noble Late Harvest: one of the most pleasant after-dinner wines.

ROSÉ WINES   *Zonneblom Blanc de Noir:* a light dry wine (usually listed under white wines).
Boschendal Blanc de Noir: a light dry wine (usually listed under white wines).

SPARKLING WINES   *Fleur de Cap Premier Grand Crû:* dry and crisp.
Here XVII: off-dry.

RED WINES   *Meerlust Cabernet Sauvignon:* a light bodied top-quality wine.
Meerlust Rubicon: full-bodied yet smooth.
Nederburg Baronne: full-flavoured.
Nederburg Pinotage: full-bodied and fruity.
Fleur de Cap Cabernet Sauvignon: a medium-bodied wine.
Tassenberg: dry and light; best value-for-money every-day table wine.
Cellar Cask Dry Red: five-litre box dry wine.

This list is by no means even the tip of the best, so be adventurous. Good value at a large gathering or outdoor party is always the five-litre box of wine which, owing to its special packaging keeps perfectly sealed even once tapped.

A variety of other beverages are also produced in South Africa. The South African sherries and fortified wines became famous long before the wines. A good 10- or 25-year-old KWV brandy compares favourably with any cognac. *South African Breweries* produce a variety of beers of the lager variety, mainly in tins or bottles. Tapped beer is not often found in a pub.

Another type of drink which is unique to South Africa is the *Appletiser* fruit juices. *Appletiser* itself is a type of sparkling fresh apple juice, which is delicious when well chilled. They also make a variety of fresh fruit juices marketed under the name of Liquifruit, all based on fresh apple and/or grape juices, with no preservatives added. They are available in 125 ml and one-litre packs. The smaller packs are ideal for travelling.

Restaurants

Cuisine from nearly every nationality is enjoyed in South Africa. Owing to South Africa's liquor laws, not all restaurants serve liquor. Restaurants are divided into those that are fully licensed; those that have wine and malt licences; and those that are not licensed at all. To the last group you may take your own liquor. Check on the liquor status when you book. Booking is always advisable. As with hotels, licensed restaurants are prohibited by law from charging for service. Unlicensed restaurants may, however, charge whatever they wish, as long as it is clearly stated on their menus. Apart from international cuisine, a large number of restaurants in South Africa specialise in traditional food, which includes the following:

SEAFOOD

Galjoen   This fish has a layer of fat just under the skin and thus remains moist when cooked. It is best grilled on an open fire.

Snoek   This is a large fish with firm oily flesh and can be eaten fried, grilled, smoked or dried. Smoorsnoek is a traditional Cape dish.

Kingklip   This firm fleshy fish lends itself very well to frying or grilling.

Perlemoen   Abalone, as it is otherwise known, can be grilled, fried or cooked in a stew.

Crayfish   It is the size of a lobster, but has no pincers. It is best when still fresh and served grilled with garlic butter.

MEAT

Ostrich   Ostrich is the largest bird in the world. They are farmed like cattle in the Oudtshoorn district. Their meat is very tasty and is served in many restaurants either as steaks or in stew.

Boerewors   This type of sausage is made of mixed meats and spices. Best cooked on an open fire or grilled.

Sosatie   A sosatie is a kebab made up of curried, spiced lamb, mixed with fresh fruit and vegetables, and then grilled.

Bredie   *Wateruintjies* are a type of water flower which grows wild on the marshlands. They make a delicious stew, with mutton, called *Waterblommetjiebredie*.

Karoo lamb   Mutton from the Karoo has a very delicate, but distinctive flavour because the sheep feed on the Karoo bush, which is a type of herb. Karoo lamb is usually served roasted.

Venison   An increasing number of farmers in South Africa are realising that farming with indigenous antelope is most rewarding. These animals are naturally adapted to their habitat and are therefore less prone to illnesses or likely to overgraze. This has meant that venison has become more readily available. Many restaurants now serve it in various forms. Favourites are steaks, venison stew and spit roast.

Indian curry   South Africa has a large Indian population, concentrated in Natal. Their various curry dishes have become firm favourites within South Africa, and are found on many menus, especially in Natal.

VEGETABLES   In general, South Africa has an abundance of vegetables, which are cooked in a variety of ways or eaten fresh, in salads.

DESSERT

Fresh fruit   South Africa has a wide variety of fruits, from the exotic guava to the well-known orange. There is no better way to end off a meal than with a bowl of fresh fruit-salad. Check that it is fresh when ordering as a few restaurants will serve canned fruit out of season.

Melktert   Milk tart is a flaky pastry shell with a type of baked milk custard filling.

Koeksisters   These are made from a plaited dough which has been deep fried and then coated with a flavoured syrup.

Tipsy tart   This has a similar texture to Boston loaf, but is soaked in brandy, which makes it much more moist.

The steakhouse is a very popular type of restaurant which serves mainly grilled food, plain and marinated meats, chicken, fish, hamburgers and salads and relies on a fast turnover. The best of the steakhouse chains is *Mike's Kitchen*, which offers a hearty meal at a reasonable price, and a choice of over fifty fresh salads. Another feature is that they cater for children by way of smaller portions and provide high chairs for babies. The various carvery/buffets offered by many of the hotels and a few restaurants are value for money. For a set fee you are able to help yourself to an unlimited amount off the hot and cold buffet (often including many traditional dishes), and from the carvery, which always has at least two different joints of meat.

Bars, Pubs and Lounges

The S.A. liquor laws that govern the times during which liquor can be sold, are largely based on the British system. However, South Africa has a few peculiarities:
- Pubs are open from 10h00 to midnight, six days a week.
- On Sundays liquor can be served (even in public areas of hotels) only in conjunction with meals. For this reason many of the "open" pubs charge an entrance fee on a Sunday, which covers the cost of a meal. Most of these meals are fairly basic, i.e. curry and rice, or fish and chips, but helpings are large and tasty. This insures that all those present have paid for a meal. Whether they eat it or not is up to them, but they are entitled to drink as much as they wish.
- South Africa is one of the last outposts of true male chauvinism: They have created the Bar, where only men are allowed to enter and drink to their hearts' content. A few of these are fairly rough establishments where bar fights are not uncommon. So beware of what you are letting yourself in for when you enter one of these bars.
- A Ladies' Bar, on the other hand, is not a bar designed just for the female sex, but is a bar to which women are also admitted. Dress in these bars is also more formal — jeans and sandals are usually not allowed, while a shirt with a collar is usually required. Many of these establishments also feature live music of some kind.

Self-catering

Owing to the superb climate, picnics and barbequing have found a firm place in the hearts of tourists. Most camp and picnic sites have facilities for barbequing and wood or charcoal is readily available at most supermarkets, cafés and camping sites.

The best place to buy provisions is at one of the many supermarket chains to be found in most towns. (See paragraph on shopping, page 25.) They all provide a choice of products, including fresh vegetables and meat. The alternative is the local café — a type of corner general dealer — which stays open seven days a week from early morning to late evening. They sell most necessities, but are usually rather more expensive.

ELECTRIC POWER

The power throughout South Africa is 200/230 volts, A.C. at fifty cycles per second — except in Pretoria (250 volts) and Port Elizabeth (220/250 volts). The drawing, overleaf, depicts the

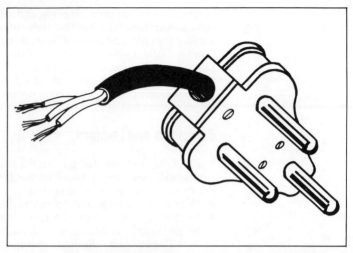

type of plug used in South Africa. It is best to buy an adaptor if you intend to use a power source.

ENTRY REQUIREMENTS

Visas

Valid visas are required by all visitors to South Africa, except nationals from the United Kingdom, the Republic of Ireland, Germany, Swaziland and Lichtenstein. They are issued free of charge by the local office of the diplomatic or consular representative of the South African Government. If there is no representative in your country, you can apply either to the representative closest to your country, or direct to The Director General, Home Affairs, Private X114, Pretoria 0001.

Points to remember when applying for a visa:
● Make sure your passport is valid for over six months after your return date.
● Use only the prescribed visa application form.
● If the prescribed form is not available, make sure you supply all the relevant information as requested on the visa form (see below).
● If you will be entering South Africa more than once during your journey (i.e. travelling through Swaziland, Transkei, Lesotho, etc.) you must apply for a *Multiple-entry Visa.*

Visas are also needed for Swaziland and Transkei (and most other countries in southern Africa not covered in this book).

Citizens from the following Commonwealth countries need visas for Swaziland: Bangladesh, India, Mauritius and Sri Lanka. Other Commonwealth citizens do not need visas, nor do citizens from the following countries: Belgium, Denmark, Finland, Greece, Iceland, Israel, Italy, Lichtenstein, Luxembourg, the Netherlands, Norway, Portugal, San Marino, South Africa, Sweden, Madagascar, Ireland, South Korea, U.S.A. and Uruguay. Visas for Swaziland can be applied for through any British Consultate in non-Commonwealth countries.

Visitors of all nationalities require visas for the Transkei. If, however, they plan to spend less than 24 hours in the country i.e.

if they are just passing through, visas are obtainable from the Transkei Consultate-General in Johannesburg, Durban, Port Elizabeth, Cape Town, Bloemfontein or East London. (See back of book for addresses.)

INFORMATION REQUESTED ON VISA APPLICATION FORM

1. Surname.
2. First names.
3. Maiden name (if applicant is or was a married woman).
4. Date of birth and in which city and country.
5. Sex and marital status.
6. Nationality; if acquired by naturalisation, state original nationality and where and when present nationality was obtained.
7. Passport number; issuing authority; date of expiry and whether the passport is valid for travel to South Africa.
8. Present address, telephone number and period of residence at this address.
9. Country of permanent residence and period of residence in that country.
10. Occupation or profession.
11. Name of your employer and/or university aid organisation, etc, to which you are attached; address; course being followed at university if applicable; if you contribute professionaly or otherwise to publications, radio, television or films, give details.
12. Expected date and port of arrival in South Africa.
13. The object of your visit.
14. Duration of intended stay (number of days, weeks or months).
15. Proposed residential address (no post-box numbers), including the full names of your host or hotel.
16. Names of firm, sponsor, institution, relatives, friends, etc., you will be contacting during your visit, address and nature of business or relationship.
17. If the object of your visit is medical treatment, a certificate from your doctor confirming the necessity for your treatment in South Africa, the nature of ailment and the dates of appointments with a South African doctor must be submitted. State the name, address and telephone number of the doctor, hospital or clinic you will visit; who will pay your medical expenses and hospital fees (proof must be submitted if paid by your medical scheme or employer); if you yourself will be paying the expenses and fees, submit proof of funds available.
18. Date of last visit to South Africa and where visa was obtained.
19. Name, date of birth, nationality of husband or wife (including her maiden name); his/ her occupation, name and address of employer.
20. Surname, first names, date of birth and place of birth of spouse and children endorsed on your passport. Separate forms must be completed in respect of persons over the age of 16 years and children under the age of 16 years travelling on their own passports.
21. State whether you at anytime applied for a permit to settle permanently in South Africa.

22. State whether you have ever been restricted or refused entry into South Africa.
23. State whether you have ever been deported from or ordered to leave South Africa.
24. State whether you have ever been convicted of any crime in any country.
25. State whether you suffer from tuberculosis, any other infections or contagious diseases or any mental or phisycal deficiency.
26. If you are a passenger in transit to a foreign country, state your destination after leaving South Africa; mode of travel to destination; whether you hold a visa or permit for permanent or temporary residence in the country of your destination (proof must be submitted), and intended date and port of departure from South Africa.
27. Two passport-type photographs must be attached to the application if the applicant requires a loose leaf visa or if the passport is not included. The reverse side of the photographs must bear the applicant's signature, full names and date of birth.

Entry

Proof of funds for maintenance during your stay could be requested by Passport Control before entry is granted. Prepaid travel arrangements will be considered as part of maintenance funds. You will also need to be in possession of a return ticket. If not, you may be requested to pay a refundable cash deposit to cover at least the cost of a single ticket back to the country of origin.

Customs

All used personal effects including recreational items are admitted duty-free. Adult visitors are also allowed the following duty-free articles: 1 litre spirits, 2 litres wine, 300 ml perfume, 400 cigarettes, 50 cigars and 250 g tobacco. Firearms need to be declared on entry, where permits will be issued on condition that: visitors can prove lawful ownership; and serial numbers are stamped into the metal. Permits are valid for 180 days.

No more than R200 per person in South African Reserve Bank notes may be taken in or out of the country. There is no limit on foreign currency.

It is a criminal offence to bring literature with the following themes into the country:

- pornography, as defined in the most conservative terms;
- writings of a Marxist of communist nature; and
- writings proclaiming the overthrow of the government in any form.

South African laws prescribe severe penalties for the possession of illegal drugs. Only bring in, take and use medication prescribed by your doctor. Also carry a copy of the prescriptions of the drugs that you are taking with you to avoid possible embarrassment.

LANGUAGES

English and Afrikaans are South Africa's official languages. About ten other languages are spoken by the people of South

Africa, but English is understood by the majority of the population. Most South Africans are patient and will always try to help a visitor with a poor command of the English language.

MEDICAL

Health Requirements

The most important health precaution you need to take is against malaria and then only when entering the Transvaal Lowveld (including the Kruger National Park) and Zululand in northern Natal. This can be done by taking tablets which are available from all South African pharmacies, without a doctor's prescription. If you are travelling from a yellow fever area to South Africa, a valid international certificate of vaccination against yellow fever is required. Bilharzia is still found in many of the slow moving rivers of the Transvaal, Natal and Swaziland. It is always advisable to enquire before swimming in any secluded stream or river.

Medical services

South Africa has no national health scheme: visitors are responsible for their own medical needs. It is advisable to take out medical insurance before departing for South Africa. Most hotels have a doctor on call. Otherwise, doctors will be found listed in the telephone directory under *medical* or *mediese*. Out-patient treatment can be obtained at provincial hospitals for a nominal fee. Chemists or pharmacies have fully qualified professionals dispensing medication in accordance with doctors' prescriptions. They also carry a variety of brands for general medication and other personal needs which may be obtained without prescription.

PUBLIC AND SCHOOL HOLIDAYS

Public holidays

New Year's Day	1 January
Second New Year's Day (Cape only)	2 January
Good Friday	Changeable date
Family Day	Changeable date
(same day as Easter Monday)	
Founders' Day	6 April
Workers' Day	First Friday in May
Ascension Day	Changeable date
Republic Day	31 May
Kruger Day	10 October
Day of the Vow	16 December
Christmas Day	25 December
Day of Goodwill	26 December

During public holidays the majority of shops and businesses are closed.

School holidays

The main summer holidays are from approximately 16 December until mid-January. This is also the end of the academic year for schools and universities. During this period many businesses close down. The majority of South Africans take their holidays then and usually stay in South Africa. It is thus imperative to book for this period. Also remember that you will be paying high-season prices. Schools in South Africa have four school holidays a year. They are:

Summer: six weeks between December and January
Autumn: two weeks over the Easter period
Winter: three weeks during June and July
Spring: one week during September/October

Remember, always book well in advance during school holidays.

PHOTOGRAPHY

Cameras

Equipment is not cheap in South Africa, but accessories for most makes are available in the major centres. Camera and accessory hire is available at very competitive rates in Johannesburg from: Cas Camera, tel. (011) 789-2720, cnr. Maxwell and Bordeaux Drive, Randburg.

Film

If you use professional film that is not always readily available, it is best to bring your own. If you are not fussy about the film you use, all major brands (except Kodak) are available throughout South Africa, although stocks are limited in smaller towns. Most souvenir shops at tourist attractions sell film of some description, though not always every brand. The perfect film for general photography in South Africa's light is ASA 50 or 100. It is, however, a good idea to have some ASA 200 or even 400 films for the game parks.

There are security x-ray machines at most of the airports in South Africa. Generally dosages are not high enough to damage film. If you want to be on the safe side, however, always ask for a hand inspection. Security officers are usually very helpful and willing to oblige.

Processing

Local film processing is generally of a high standard. For specialised processing work one of the following laboratories can be contacted:

Johannesburg: *Beith Process* (011) 802-8600
Cape Town: *Creative Colour* (021) 84-7424
Durban: *Creative Colour* (031) 23-1430

Restrictions

Installations, buildings and other objects relating to the defence and security of the country (including police stations and prisons) may not be photographed. Before photographing someone, ask their permission. If they refuse, respect their privacy. Some people believe it is bad luck to be photographed. It is prohibited to get out of your car in the national parks to take photos, except in demarkated areas. This includes climbing through windows or sun-roofs onto the top of the car.

SHOPPING

South Africa has many modern shops which offer excellent value for money, as well as exotic items which are peculiar to southern Africa.

Clothing

The clothing industry in South Africa is sophisticated and can boast exciting designers who often work with an African idiom. Small boutiques in the large centres offer specialist designer clothes, by South Africa's top designers. These are all mentioned under **shopping**. A worthwhile shop for good quality everyday clothing, is *Woolworths*. It offers the same line and quality of clothing as Marks and Spencers in the United Kingdom. The *Oriental Plaza* (closed between 12h00 and 15h00 on Fridays) in Johannesburg is worth a visit for those with half a day on their hands. The Plaza has a wide variety of goods, including clothing and materials. Most of the articles here can be bargained for. The various flea markets in Johannesburg, Durban and Cape Town also have pleasant clothing surprises.

Supermarkets

South Africa has a number of supermarket chains where onestop shopping can be done. The food outlets are *Checkers* (also open on Sundays); the *O.K. Bazaars*; *Pick 'n Pay* (generally the cheapest); *Spar* (linked to the international *Spar* organisation); *and Woolworths* (offering quality foods). *Dions* offers electrical gadgetry and sports and camping goods and a variety of other goods.

Curios and Souvenirs

There are curio shops in all of the major centres — they are listed separately. Things worth looking out for include beadwork, basket-work and carvings. The best places to buy these articles are Durban, Zululand and Swaziland. As Oudtshoorn is the centre of the ostrich industry it would be wise to buy ostrich leather goods there.

Johannesburg is the centre of the mining industry and beautiful jewellery can be bought there through reputable jewellers (see also Cape Town and Pretoria). Foreigners are usually given a substantial discount on presentation of their passports and return air tickets.

South African wines, brandy and liqueurs are also prized by visitors to South Africa. Many of the estates in the Western Cape have wine-tasting facilities. These wines can then be purchased at the estates and will often be despatched back home for the visitor.

Shopping Hours

Shops are generally open from 08h30 to 17h00 from Monday to Friday, and to 13h00 on Saturdays. They are closed on Sundays and public holidays. A few supermarkets have late-night shopping evenings and are open on Sundays.

TIME ZONES

South Africa is two hours ahead of Greenwich Mean Time. This puts the country one hour ahead of Central European Winter Time and seven hours ahead of Eastern Standard Winter Time. There is no time change for summer or winter.

TIPPING

It is customary to tip the following professions in South Africa: caddies, hotel and railway porters, room servants in accommodation, stewards and waiters, taxi drivers and tour guides. Tips should be appropriate to the kind of service rendered. The 10 per cent rule is always a safe compromise, but don't feel duty-bound if you honestly feel the service to be poor.

TOURIST INFORMATION

Information on tourist attractions can be obtained from three sources.

South African Tourism Board (SATOUR) Overseas offices

Satour has offices abroad in London, Frankfurt, Paris, Amsterdam, Milan, Zürich, Taipei, Tel Aviv, New York, Los Angeles (Beverley Hills), Tokyo, and Harare. These offices are able to supply a large variety of excellent literature free of charge. Most of the offices also have at least one South African staff member who has an intimate knowledge of the country and is always willing to help you plan your trip.

South African Tourism Board Regional Offices

Regional offices of the South African Tourism Board can be found in Cape Town, George, Port Elizabeth, East London, Kimberley, Bloemfontein, Durban, Johannesburg, Pretoria, Nelspruit, Pietersburg and at Jan Smuts Airport. These offices will be able to supply detailed information on the area in which they are situated, as well as information on the rest of the country. Full addresses can be found under the relevant towns in this book.

Information Bureaux

Most towns and cities have their own information bureaux, often linked to the town clerk's office. These bureaux are able to give more information on the town and its immediate environs. A few offer further facilities such as accommodation reservations. A full list of addresses and services can be found under the relevant towns.

TRANSPORT

Getting to South Africa

AIRLINES   *South African Airways (SAA)* is the national carrier. They fly a

modern fleet of Boeing 747s on direct scheduled flights between
South Africa and the major airports of Europe (London, Frankfurt, Lisbon, Amsterdam, Athens, Madrid, Paris, Rome, Zürich,
Tel Aviv, Vienna), South America (Rio de Janeiro), Hong Kong
and Taiwan.

The following airlines also have regular services to South
Africa: *Airolineas Argentinas* (Buenos Aires), *Alitalia* (Rome),
British Airways (London), *KLM* (Amsterdam), El Al (Tel Aviv),
Iberia (Madrid), *Lufthansa* (Frankfurt), *Luxavia* (Luxembourg),
Olympia (Athens), *Sabena* (Brussels), *Swissair* (Zürich), *TAP*
(Lisbon), *UTA* (Paris) and *Varig* (Rio de Janeiro).

From northern Europe the best value for direct services is via
Luxembourg, on *Luxavia*, which offers free bus transfers from a
number of points in the Netherlands, Belgium, northern Germany
and France. In general the cheapest way to fly to South Africa is
by using an airline which does not fly direct from your departure
point to South Africa i.e. from London via Lisbon to South
Africa on TAP. The disadvantage of these types of fares is that
your travelling time could be doubled, and that delays along the
way can cause you to miss a connection flight. The alternative is
SAA or the national carrier of your departure point i.e. *British
Airways* from London. Although in many cases the fares are
marginally higher, there are many advantages. You have no
change-overs to worry about; you know your baggage has a
much greater chance of reaching its destination; and flying time
is cut down to the bare minimum.

SHIPPING SERVICES The only regular sea connection is by way of the *R M St. Helena*,
which sails from Avonmouth in the UK via the Canary Islands,
Ascension and St. Helena to Cape Town, and then returns via
the same route. Booking can be done through *Curnow Shipping
Co. Ltd.,* The Shipyard, Portleven, Helston, UK (Tel: (03265)
63434; Telex 45654).

From time to time, cruise ships sail from various destinations
to South African ports. It is therefore best to contact your travel
agent for full information.

Internal Transport

AIRLINES There is a reliable network of internal airlines in South Africa.
South African Airways are state-funded, while the rest are
privately owned. All offer a high standard. Only routes relating
to the text are mentioned in this book.

South African Airways offer an efficient internal network of
services between all the main centres in Boeing 737s and Airbus
A300s. The traveller with limited time to spend touring through
South Africa would find the fly/drive packages, using the SAA
"Fly Pass" arrangement, convenient. This arrangement entitles
the traveller to fly from centre to centre at a greatly reduced rate.
(As regulations for the usage of the pass change periodically, it
is best to enquire at your travel agent as to the exact regulation
in force at the time of your booking.) (See page 291 for SAA
South African address.)

Air Cape have daily flights between Cape Town and Port
Elizabeth via Oudtshoorn, George and Plettenberg Bay. Their
flight from Cape Town to Oudtshoorn leaves early in the morn-

ing, and returns late afternoon, giving the tourist with limited time an exciting day to explore Oudtshoorn and its ostrich farms. Cars can be hired at all the airports. See the relevant towns for details on car hire.

Commercial Airways (Comair) fly daily between Johannesburg, Phalaborwa and Skukuza, bringing the Kruger Park as well as the private game parks within easy reach of Johannesburg. They also operate a fleet of touring vehicles in the Kruger Park and surrounding areas. Contact their office for more details (see page 291). Comair also offer flights between Johannesburg and Margate on the Natal South Coast.

Letaba Airways offer daily flights between Johannesburg, Pietersburg and Tzaneen.

Magnum Airlines operate daily flights between Johannesburg and Nelspruit and Pietersburg; as well as Durban and Nelspruit. Car hire is available from Nelspruit.

Apart from these services, all of the above private companies offer charter facilities to any one of the numerous airstrips in the country, including the private game parks.

Airport security

South Africa is justifiably proud of its high standard and good record of airport security. The credit must indeed go to the vigilant role played by airport security, which is firm but friendly. If you have legitimate reason to feel that the x-ray material will harm some kind of equipment, request that a hand search be done. They are always keen to oblige.

COACH/BUS TRANSPORT

This can be divided into:

Coach tours

These can be either day and half-day tours — with a duration of between four and eight and a half hours — or long-distance tours along the regular tourist routes. Tours are usually conducted by a driver/guide in English, Afrikaans, and often one foreign language. Most tours follow basically the same route, but occasionally use different hotels. For a full list of available tours contact either your travel agent, Satour, or the local information bureau in the town from which you wish to leave.

Inter-city bus transport

Inter-city buses are an upgraded version of the American Greyhound system and are a relatively new concept in South Africa. At the time of writing, all the major centres along the national roads, including Pretoria, Johannesburg, Nelspruit, Durban, Cape Town and Port Elizabeth are connected by this system. There are plans to expand the system. Details can be obtained from any Satour office. (See page 292 for tour arrangements; and a route using public transport is mapped out on page 42.)

Airport transfers

Transfers are offered from the major airports to the central railway stations of the respective cities.

City buses

The city bus services and other urban transport networks are less developed than those in most other Western countries. White South Africans rely mainly on private transport. If, however, you are forced to use the local bus services, it is best to contact the local information centre for a timetable and departure details. (See under various cities for the address of the information centre, or of the city bus department.)

TRAINS South Africa is known as one of the last strongholds of the steam engine, although diesel and electric trains have by now taken over on most of the main lines.

Commuter trains run on the Witwatersrand (Johannesburg, Pretoria, Krugersdorp, etc.), Cape Peninsula, and in Durban plus the coastal resorts. A commuter train also runs between Johannesburg and Durban. Most other trains have sleep coaches. These compartments serve as sitting-rooms by day and the seats convert to bunks by night. First class compartments accommodate four passengers and coupés, two. In second class, the accommodation is for six and three persons. First class carriages have communal showers and toilets, while second class carriages have communal toilets only. All compartments and coupés have wash basins. Up to 50 kg of personal luggage not needed on the journey, can be safely stored in the baggage van, but needs to be checked in one hour before departure.

Catering Most of the long-distance trains have dining saloons where passengers can order light snacks and beverages outside meal times. Very good full-course meals are served during meal times. Meal tickets can either be bought on the train from the chief steward who comes around to the compartments, or at the station before departure. (Catering trolleys also provide a corridor snack service.)

Bedding Free bedding is supplied in first class, and bedding tickets can be purchased at a nominal fee by second class passengers at the station before departure or on the train.

Reservations Reservations for train journeys are essential, and are usually made at the same time as purchasing your ticket. If travelling alone, you are placed in a compartment with three (in first class) or 5 (in second class) other people of the same sex. This is a great way of meeting South Africans. It is possible to make special arrangements for travelling alone or in a group, when purchasing your ticket. If your group does not fill a compartment, a supplementary charge will be made, depending on the amount of space not utilised. All seating arrangements are displayed on the departure platform on a notice-board.

All foreign passport-holders resident outside South Africa qualify for a discount on ordinary trains (at present it is 40 per cent). Reservations can be made at any station, or through the central reservation office in Johannesburg, London, or New York. (See telephone number on page 242).

Destinations The railways operate an extensive network throughout South Africa. However, although it is possible to travel between most large towns by train, it is not always practical. For instance, there is no continuous trainline along the coast between Cape Town and Durban. This means that if, for example, you wish to travel to East London from Port Elizabeth you would need to go inland, and change trains. Some changes between trains can take from several hours to a few days, as many trains travel only once or twice a week on their route. Most cities have a direct train link with Johannesburg – like Durban, East London, Port Elizabeth, Cape Town and some others. (See page 42 for a few suggestions on how to use public transport to tour South Africa.)

Special trains   *The Blue Train* is a luxury express train travelling between Pretoria, Johannesburg and Cape Town. The journey takes 25 hours and excellent food and service, luxurious accommodation with air-conditioning and wall-to-wall carpeting throughout is provided. Accommodation varies from a compartment for two or three persons (or coupé for one) with communal shower and toilet facilities, to a suite with separate bedroom, bathroom and lounge. The train has a separate lounge and diningcar.

Steam trains are still used regularly throughout South Africa. Because of public interest, some lines cater for tourists while carrying out their usual day-to-day schedules. The ones relevant to this book are:

- The Banana Express from Port Shepstone to Izingoloweni on a two-foot (0,6 m) gauge track (see page 162 for details).
- The Apple Express from Port Elizabeth to Loerie also on a two-foot (0,6 m) gauge track (see page 136 for details).
- The Outeniqua Choo Tjoe between George and Knysna (see page 118 for details).

TAXIS   Taxis (or cabs) do not cruise in South Africa but must be called from a rank. Ranks exist at all large airports and at many large hotels. They have set fares, but lower fares can be obtained on a quotation basis for long distances.

MOTORING   South Africa has an excellent road system. By far the best way to see the country is to drive through it yourself. In South Africa one drives on the left-hand side of the road. Driving is safe and in general South African drivers are courteous. Traffic build-up occurs in the large cities during rush hour, and on major routes during long week-ends, but otherwise it is very rare.

If you plan to take a motoring holiday through South Africa, it is just as well to bear the following points in mind:

A Driving Licence which is valid in any other country is accepted, provided that:

- it carries the signature and photograph of the holder as an integral part of the licence;
- it is printed in English, or is accompanied by a certificate of authenticity (in English).

If your licence does not comply with these regulations, you should obtain an international driving permit prior to your visit.

Speed limits and traffic laws are strongly enforced and offenders are heavily fined. Speed limits are generally signposted along most of the roads. In broad terms they are:

- 100 kph on country roads
- 120 kph on the freeway and major roads
- 60 kph in built-up areas

Petrol (gas) stations are found in all towns in South Africa and along major routes. As a rule, they are open from 07h00 to 18h00, but many, especially along the major routes, are open longer — some 24 hours a day.

Motoring clubs. The *Automobile Association* of South Africa offers maps, road information and general advice on motoring to all visitors who are members of overseas clubs affiliated to it. All that needs to be produced is a valid membership card of the club to which you belong. The *Automobile Association* of South Africa has its head office in Johannesburg (see address on page 242) and branch offices in all major towns.

Car hire　A wide range of cars can be hired in South Africa, such as a small Volkswagen Golf, a Microbus, an air-conditioned Mercedes Benz, or a Porche. The standard of the cars and service is high and tariffs are very reasonable. Avis, Budget, and Imperial Car Rental/Europa Car have branches throughout South Africa, including the national airports. One-way rentals are also available, without "drop-off" charges. Pick-up and delivery within city limits are also usually free. There are also a number of regional car-hire companies who offer car-hire at very competitive rates. They are ideal if you need a car only while in a particular town. (See the listings under each town and page 292.)

Camper hire　The temperate climate and fine weather in South Africa is ideal for caravanning and camping. All the caravan parks mentioned in this guide offer excellent facilities. In general, the campers are not any more difficult to drive than a microbus. Camper hire companies are found in Johannesburg, (page 242) and Cape Town (page 67). If a round trip is not made by camper, a "drop-off" fee is usually charged.

Times to visit

The South African year can be divided into five holiday periods, each with its own advantages and disadvantages for travellers.

December and January

This is the main summer holiday season, when most of South Africa seems to move to the coastal areas. Beaches are full, but very seldom over-crowded. There is an abundance of nightlife at every conceivable venue and most accommodation establishments are fully booked, as are inter-city buses, airlines and trains.

February to April

Things slowly unwind before picking up again for the Easter holiday break, when once again there is a mass migration towards the coast and eastern Transvaal. February and March are usually the most pleasant months of the year, when relatively little rain falls along the coast, and days are long and hot.

May and June

Autumn begins to set in, and trees lose their leaves. Days are still warm, but nights begin to cool down. It is the low season in the travel industry and many establishments offer special low season tariffs.

July to September

Winter has set in, and cold front after cold front moves across the southern Cape coastal region. The Transvaal and Free State have day after day of cloudless skies, warm days and cold nights. Snow occasionally falls on the Drakensberg and Cape mountains. The eastern Transvaal and Namibia are pleasantly warm, with grass low and vegetation minimal, making it an ideal time to visit the game parks and the surrounding tourist attractions. Durban is alive during the July school holidays, as many Transvalers move down for a week or two.

October and November

Cold fronts begin to decrease in frequency, and everything begins to warm up as spring sets in. The fields are covered with flowers, especially in the Cape coastal regions.

Itineraries

There are a variety of ways for the traveller to journey through southern Africa. Everything depends on budget, time available and needs. The itineraries below have been planned to suit various needs and are divided into two groups:
- complete tours of southern Africa and Namibia; and
- regional tours of southern Africa.

Each itinerary guides the traveller between points, giving an indication of the time required to explore the area adequately. As many of the people touring the country would leave from the Witwatersrand area, and most international flights arrive and depart from Johannesburg, the book offers several tours starting and finishing in Johannesburg. On the other hand, as European settlement radiated northwards from Cape Town, the detailed complete tours start from Cape Town and move northwards.

COMPLETE TOURS OF SOUTH AFRICA

To reach Cape Town, from the Witwatersrand (including Johannesburg), the traveller has one of four options:

Fly to Cape Town in two hours with South African Airways.

Take the **train** — the luxurious Blue Train (page 30) or the more economical Trans Karoo (see page 242) — and relax for 25 hours while the train speeds through the arid Karoo. Both trains depart in the late morning from both Johannesburg and Cape Town.

Drive. An excellent tar road (the N1 motorway) via Bloemfontein runs for the total of over 1 400 km, from Johannesburg to Cape Town through the Karoo. As the Karoo is rather flat (semi-desert), the road can become monotonous. It is therefore a good idea to split the journey over two days. The ideal place at which to break the journey is in or close to Colesberg (about 790 km from Cape Town and 635 km from Johannesburg). Comfortable accommodation at reasonable rates are offered at:

Hendrik Verwoerd Dam Motel   **TYYY   Tel. 0020 and ask for Verwoerd Dam 60
P.O. Box 20, Hendrik Verwoerd Dam, 9922
Swimming-pool, golf and tennis
Merino Inn Motel   **TYYY   Tel. 05852 and ask for 265
P.O. Box 10, Colesberg, 5980
Hendrik Verwoerd Dam Chalets **TYYY   Tel. 0020 and ask for Verwoerd Dam 45.
P.O. Box 20, Hendrik Verwoerd Dam, 9922
Swimming-pool, golf and tennis
Very well located and reasonably priced.

Inter-city coach services from Johannesburg to Cape Town are becoming increasingly popular, and are substantially cheaper than flying or travelling by train. They are, however, popular and it is a good idea always to book in advance. Two companies operate this route — Greyhound and Citi-Liner. Both leave in the late afternoon and arrive the next morning. They can both be booked through Computicket (see page 239). The coaches are comfortable, with reclining seats, on-board videos, toilets and refreshments.

Once in Cape Town, one of the itineraries which follows can be used as a guide-line for touring through southern Africa. (Distances in brackets are rough estimates.)

A grand tour of South Africa
(26 days, 3 360 km)

Route 1 starts in Cape Town and follows the above symbol throughout the book.

This four-week tour is especially recommended for those who are touring through South Africa for the first time. The tour starts in Cape Town and follows the most popular tourist route through South Africa (route 1 in the book). The route follows the coast for most of the way up to Zululand, where it swings inland, first towards Swaziland, then on to the Kruger National Park, and ends in Johannesburg. Most of it is along very good tarred roads. Of course, those with more time on their hands could spend more than the suggested amount of time at many of the overnight spots mentioned below, or could even overnight between these stops.

DAY 1: **Cape Town**
A morning walking tour of the city centre (page 67).
An afternoon trip up Table Mountain (page 71).

DAY 2: **Cape Town**
A full-day tour around the Cape Peninsula (page 74).

DAY 3: **Cape Town**
A full-day tour of the winelands (page 82).

DAY 4: **Cape Town to Arniston** *(288 km)*
Along the coast, stopping at Hermanus for lunch (page 93).

DAY 5: **Arniston**
Spend the day on the beach, or take a leisurely drive to Cape Agulhas (page 95).

DAY 6: **Arniston to Mossel Bay** *(323 km)*
Depart early in the morning for Swellendam and the Bontebok National Park (page 97). After lunch in Swellendam, head for Mossel Bay (page 98).

DAY 7: **Mossel Bay to Oudtshoorn** *(88 km)*
Leave late morning for Oudtshoorn, via the Robinson Pass (page 100). Stop along the way for lunch and visit an ostrich farm on the way into town (page 113).

DAY 8: **Oudtshoorn to Plettenberg Bay** *(225 km)*
Visit the Cango Croc Ranch and Cango Caves (page 113), before heading for the coast. Stop in George for lunch (page 114), before going on to Plettenberg Bay (page 125).

DAY 9: **Plettenberg Bay**
Spend the day on the beach, or in Knysna (page 123)

DAY 10: **Plettenberg Bay**
Relax on the beach, or visit sights nearby (page 127).

DAY 11: **Plettenberg Bay to Port Elizabeth** *(285 km)*
Leave fairly early, stopping at Storms River Mouth for an early lunch (page 129). Continue on to Port Elizabeth, exploring the town on arrival (page 134).

DAY 12: **Port Elizabeth to East London** *(368 km)*
(Add an extra day in here if the Addo Elephant Park is to be visited (page 137).)
Bypass the Addo Elephant Park and head for Settler country (page 138), stopping for lunch at Bathurst or Port Alfred (page 140).

DAY 13:   **East London to the Natal South Coast** *(513 km)*
          This is a rather long day's drive and therefore an adequate
          amount of time should be put aside. Try to pack a picnic lunch.
          Stay over in one of the coastal resorts on the Natal South Coast
          (page 160).

DAY 14:   **South Coast to Durban** *(119 km)*
          Leave after lunch for a leisurely drive up the coast (page 165).

DAY 15:   **Durban**
          Relax on the beach, visit the sights, or do some shopping
          (page 174).

DAY 16:   **Durban to Hluhluwe** *(282 km)*
          Leave early morning to arrive in Hluhluwe in time for lunch.
          Spend the afternoon at the False Bay Park (page 183).

DAY 17:   **Hluhluwe**
          Pack a picnic lunch and spend the day game viewing in Hluhluwe
          and Umfolozi Game Parks (page 182)

DAY 18:   **Hluhluwe to Ezulweni Valley — Swaziland** *(281 km)*
          Leave in the early morning, armed with a picnic lunch and stop
          off at Mkuzi Game Park (page 183). Leave at midday for Swazi-
          land (page 184).

DAY 19:   **Ezulweni Valley to the Kruger National Park** *(158 km)*
          Aim to reach the park by midday, leaving the afternoon free for
          game viewing (page 198).

DAY 20:   **Kruger Park to Sabi Sands private game parks** *(30 km)*
          (Spend the next two days in the Kruger Park if your budget does
          not permit you to stay in a private park.) Enjoy early morning
          game viewing in the Kruger Park, before leaving for a private
          park to arrive by midday (page 204).

DAY 21:   **Sabi Sands**
          Full day game viewing.

DAY 22:   **Sabi Sands to eastern Transvaal** *(90 km)*
          Leave mid-morning for one of the many resorts on the escarp-
          ment (page 206).

DAY 23:   **Eastern Transvaal**
          Spend the day exploring the area (page 209).

DAY 24:   **Eastern Transvaal to Johannesburg** *(398 km)*
          Take a leisurely drive to Johannesburg, stopping at the various
          sights along the way (page 215).

DAY 25:   **Johannesburg**
          Use the morning for shopping (page 248) or enjoying the sights
          (page 242), and spend the afternoon at Gold Reef City (page 245).

DAY 26:   **Johannesburg**
          Visit Cullinan and Pretoria (page 251).

DAY 27:   **Johannesburg**
          Take a day trip to Sun City (page 261).

2	# An alternative grand tour of South Africa
	(21 days, 3 042 km)

Route 2 starts in Cape Town and follows the above symbol throughout the book.

For those who have visited South Africa's popular tourist attractions and now wish to visit the less well-known areas, this route (route 2) offers the perfect alternative. The route winds its way back and forth along the mountain ranges of South Africa, crossing some of the country's most spectacular passes. A small part of the route is along dirt roads on which special care should be taken.

DAY 1: **Cape Town**
Relax on the beaches or visit a few of the sights (page 67).

DAY 2: **Cape Town**
Visit the winelands (page 78 or 82).

DAY 3: **Cape Town to Langebaan** *(125 km)*
A leisurely day's drive passing Mamre (page 101) along the way. The lagoon peninsula (page 101) is an ideal place on which to enjoy a picnic before continuing on to Langebaan or Velddrif (see page 101).

DAY 4: **Langebaan to Tulbagh** *(186 km)*
Leave mid-morning for Velddrif fishing village (page 104). The road from here swings inland through the wheatfields of the Western Cape to Tulbagh (page 104).

DAY 5: **Tulbagh to Matjiesfontein** *(263 km)*
A full day's tour, first passing over three of the most magnificent passes in the Western Cape (page 105) before reaching the pretty town of Worcester (page 106) where lunch can be enjoyed. Continue into the Great Karoo to Matjiesfontein (page 107).

DAY 6: **Matjiesfontein to Oudtshoorn** *(200 km)*
Leave mid-morning on this pleasant road which passes through an awe-inspiring gap in the towering Swartberg Mountains (page 108) and travel on to Oudtshoorn. Use the afternoon to explore the town (page 111).

DAY 7: **Oudtshoorn to Prince Albert** *(67 km)*
Heading for the Swartberg Pass, pause first at the Cango Caves (page 113) before ascending this magnificent pass, (page 147). Take a picnic lunch along. The rest of the afternoon can be spent exploring Prince Albert (page 147).

DAY 8: **Prince Albert to Graaff-Reinet** *(349 km)*
Traverse the Great Karoo before cutting back to the Little Karoo through Meirings Poort (page 150). From here the road is fairly straight, crossing the Swartberg once again before reaching Graaff-Reinet (page 150). Spend the afternoon exploring the town.

DAY 9: **Graaff-Reinet to the Mountain Zebra Park** *(152 km)*
It is a short drive to the park (page 154) and thus most of the day can be spent exploring the park.

DAY 10: **Mountain Zebra Park to Hogsback** *(185 km)*
Take a slow drive through to Hogsback (page 155), after a morning game drive.

DAY 11: **Hogsback**
Relax for the day.

DAY 12:   **Hogsback to Umtata** *(592 km)*
Leave early in the morning for this long day's drive. The route passes over some of the highest passes in the country and a large section is on gravel roads (page 156). Take a picnic lunch and warm clothing to wear on the pass as it is usually cold. The last section into Umtata (page 158) is tarred.

DAY 13:   **Umtata to Port St. Johns** *(101 km)*
Most of the road is in poor condition, so drive with care.

DAY 14:   **Port St. Johns**
Relax on the beach or enjoy one of the activities offered by the hotel (see page 188).

DAY 15:   **Port St. Johns to the southern Drakensberg** *(300 km)*
The section of road to Brooks Nek is in poor condition and care should be taken along it. Once in Underberg there are a number of resorts to choose from (page 191).

DAY 16:   **Underberg area**
Relax in the area for the day.

DAY 17:   **Northern Drakensberg** *(200 km)*
Head for Winterton from where a number of resorts can be visited (page 194).

DAY 18:   **Northern Drakensberg**
Relax for the day in the resort of your choice.

DAY 19:   **Northern Drakensberg to Johannesburg** *(323 km)*
Leave mid-morning for a drive straight up to Johannesburg.

DAY 20:   **Johannesburg**
Visit the sights in the city (page 242).

DAY 21:   **Johannesburg**
Visit Sun City (page 261).

South African highlights fly/drive tour
(14 days)

For those with limited time and who wish to see the highlights of South Africa, this is the perfect tour. The ideal way of doing this tour is to buy a round trip air ticket (page 27) and to hire a car at the various airports. Be sure to include the Johannesburg/ Cape Town flight in your ticket, if you are starting in Johannesburg.

DAY 1: **Cape Town**
Morning walking tour of the city (page 67), taking an afternoon trip up Table Mountain (page 71).

DAY 2: **Cape Town**
Day tour around the Cape Peninsula (page 74).

DAY 3: **Cape Town**
Tour the winelands (page 82).

DAY 4: **Fly Cape Town to George**
Drive from George (page 114) to **Oudtshoorn** *(59 km)* (page 111).

DAY 5: **Drive Oudtshoorn to Plettenberg Bay** *(165 km)*
Visit the sights in Oudtshoorn (page 111) before driving along the coast to Plettenberg Bay (page 125).

DAY 6: **Plettenberg Bay**
Spend the day on the beach or in Knysna (page 122).

DAY 7: **Drive Plettenberg Bay to Port Elizabeth** *(229 km)*; **fly to Durban.**
Leave Plettenberg Bay fairly early, stopping at Storms River (page 129) for an early lunch. Aim for the mid-afternoon flight to Durban (page 165).

DAY 8: **Durban**
Relax on the beach or visit some sights (page 174).

DAY 9: **Fly Durban to Nelspruit; drive to Sabi Sands private parks** *(110 km)*
This is a *Magnum Airways* flight (page 291). From Nelspruit take the R40 route to Hazy View via White River and then take the R538 route to one of the parks (page 204).

DAY 10: **Sabi Sands parks**
Relax for the day, game viewing.

DAY 11: **Drive Sabi Sands parks to eastern Transvaal resorts** *(approx. 90 km)*
Leave after the morning game drive for one of the eastern Transvaal resorts (page 208).

DAY 12: **Eastern Transvaal resorts**
Spend the day visiting the places of interest (page 209).

DAY 13: **Drive eastern Transvaal to Johannesburg** *(398 km)*
Take a leisurely drive to Johannesburg, stopping at places of interest along the way (page 215).

DAY 14: **Johannesburg**
Visit Gold Reef City (page 245) or Pretoria (page 251).

Three-week fly/drive tour of South Africa

(21 days)

For those with time on their hands, but who do not wish to drive long distances or change hotel rooms every night, this tour could be well worth considering. A lot of time is spent both in the southern Cape and the eastern Transvaal. Be sure to include the Johannesburg/Cape Town section of your ticket in the total tour (page 27).

DAYS 1-6: See the **South African highlights fly/drive tour (page 39).**

DAY 7: **Drive Plettenberg Bay to Storms River** *(66 km)*
Take a leisurely drive through to Storms River (page 129), stopping at the various places of interest along the way (page 128).

DAY 8: **Drive Storms River to Port Elizabeth** *(200 km)*; **fly to Durban**
After a leisurely drive to Port Elizabeth (page 131) and visiting sights in the city (page 134), take the mid-afternoon flight on to Durban (page 165).

DAY 9: **Durban**
Relax on the beach or visit some sights (page 174).

DAY 10: **Fly Durban to Johannesburg; drive to northern Transvaal** *(approx. 326 km)*
Take the early morning flight to Johannesburg and drive directly on to the northern Transvaal. (To reach the N1 take the R21 towards Pretoria; branch off onto the N1 towards Pietersburg, just before Pretoria.) A variety of resorts can be visited once you have reached Pietersburg (page 218, 220 & 221).

DAY 11: **Northern Transvaal**
Relax for the day at a resort, or tour the countryside (page 220).

DAY 12: **Drive northern Transvaal to Kruger National Park** *(approx. 251 km)*
Do not rush along this road, as there are many stray animals along the way. Aim to reach the park by lunch time (page 198). (An alternative route to the central Kruger National Park is via the R71 route, which enters the park through the Phalaborwa gate.) Spend the afternoon game viewing.

DAY 13: **Drive Kruger National Park**
Spend the day game-viewing, moving slowly south so as to spend the night no further north than Satara.

DAY 14: **Drive Kruger National Park to Sabi Sands private resorts**
Aim to reach one of the private resorts (page 204) by midday, spending the rest of the day game-viewing.

DAY 15: **Sabi Sands private resorts**
Enjoy the day game-viewing.

DAY 16: **Drive Sabi Sands private resorts to eastern Transvaal** *(approx. 90 km)*
After a morning game drive, head for one of the eastern Transvaal resorts (page 208).

DAY 17: **Eastern Transvaal**
Relax at a resort, or take a drive through the area (page 209).

DAY 18: **Drive eastern Transvaal to Johannesburg** *(approx. 398 km)* **fly to Sun City**
Leave the eastern Transvaal and head for Johannesburg, (page

215) to reach Jan Smuts Airport for the mid-afternoon flight to Sun City (page 261).

DAY 19:   **Sun City**
Relax for the day at the resort, or spend the day game-viewing at the Pilanesberg National Park (page 261).

DAY 20:   **Fly Sun City to Johannesburg**
Take the midday flight back to Johannesburg. Spend the afternoon at the Gold Reef City (page 245).

DAY 21:   **Johannesburg**
Spend the day at Heia Safari (page 247).

A budget tour through South Africa
(14 days)

With the ever-expanding inter-city coach services in South Africa, cheaper travel is fast becoming a reality. (See page 292 for addresses of companies running these coaches in South Africa.) This tour takes the traveller from Cape Town along the coast to Durban, and then up to Johannesburg.

DAY 1:   **Cape Town**
Take a walk through the city (page 67) and then a bus up to Table Mountain (page 71).

DAY 2:   **Cape Town**
Enjoy a train trip to Simonstown (page 78) or take a bus tour around the Peninsula (page 67).

DAY 3:   **Cape Town**
Join a bus tour to the wine estates (page 67).

DAY 4:   **Inter-city Cape Town to Mossel Bay**
Take the early-morning coach to Mossel Bay (page 98). Spend the rest of the day walking around the town, or on the beach.

DAY 5:   **Inter-city Mossel Bay to Oudtshoorn**
From Mossel Bay *Garden Route Tours* (page 118) offers excellent three-day tours of the area especially for inter-city travellers. They begin in Mossel Bay and end three days later in Knysna, taking in all the sights along the way. A shorter bus trip, into the Little Karoo at midday and to the Cango Caves in the afternoon, is another possibility.

DAY 6:   **Inter-city Oudtshoorn to George**
Hitch a ride to one of the ostrich farms (page 113) and back again, making sure that the early afternoon bus is not missed.

DAY 7:   **Train journey to Knysna**
The train leaves early every Monday to Saturday morning (page 118) and travels through spectacular scenery. (If this day falls on a Sunday continue to Knysna on day 6.)

DAY 8:   **Knysna**
Relax in the area: either walk around town or enjoy an oyster/champagne breakfast trip (page 122).

DAY 9:   **Inter-city Knysna to Port Elizabeth**
Relax in the coach enjoying the scenery along the way to Port Elizabeth (page 131). Find accommodation close to the station as the coach for the next stage leaves early in the morning.

DAY 10:   **Port Elizabeth**
Enjoy the city sights (page 134), or relax on the beach.

DAY 11:   **Inter-city Port Elizabeth to Durban**
A long day, with the coach leaving early in the morning and arriving in Durban (page 165) in the early evening.

DAY 12:   **Durban**
Relax at the beach or enjoy the city's sights (page 174).

DAY 13:   **Inter-city Durban to Johannesburg**
Another long day in the coach. Many of the Drakensberg resorts (page 191 & 194) will send staff to meet guests off the inter-city coaches in towns close to the resorts.

DAY 14:   **Johannesburg**

Take a trip to Gold Reef City (page 245) or Heia Safari (page 247) with one of the tour companies (page 239).

From Johannesburg a number of tour companies (page 292) offer exciting two- to seven-day tours of the Kruger National Park (page 198) and eastern Transvaal (page 209).

A circular tour of Namibia
(12 days, 2 674 km)

This arid desert area is fascinating and definitely worth a visit — especially for those who enjoy open spaces and a wide variety of wild life. About half the roads followed on this route are gravel roads and extra care should be taken when driving along them.

DAY 1:   **Windhoek**
Take a drive through the town. Stock up with all provisions needed along the way, as they are much cheaper here and more readily available. Also, check up on money matters as credit cards are not accepted in outlying areas.

DAY 2:   **Windhoek to Swakopmund** *(396 km)*
A long day's drive over some rough gravel roads, passing spectacular scenery (page 267). Fill your car with petrol and take along extra water.

DAY 3:   **Swakopmund** *(268 km return)*
Visit the seal colony at Cape Cross (page 271).

DAY 4:   **Swakopmund**
Visit the Namib-Naukluft Park (page 272).

DAY 5:   **Swakopmund**
Visit the Spitzkoppe (page 272).

DAY 6:   **Swakopmund to Khorixas** *(375 km)*
A fascinating day's drive along mostly gravel roads passing through the desert. Stop at Brandberg along the way (page 272), and then continue to Khorixas (page 274).

DAY 7:   **Khorixas**
Visit the sights in the area (page 274).

DAY 8:   **Khorixas to Okaukuejo** *(286 km)*
The first half of the road, to Outjo (page 275) is gravel (but is being tarred). From here the road leads to the Etosha National Park (page 275). The next four nights are spent at various camp sites inside the park.

DAY 9:   **Okaukuejo**
Spend the day game-viewing from the car or at the waterhole at the camp (page 277).

DAY 10: **Halali**
Spend the day game-viewing (page 277).

DAY 11: **Namutoni**
Spend the day game-viewing (page 277).

DAY 12: **Namutoni to Windhoek** *(627 km)*
A long day's drive, mostly along tarred roads, visiting various sights (page 278) along the way.

Regional tours of South Africa

The following regional tours all take between two and three weeks.

CIRCULAR TOUR OF GARDEN ROUTE FROM CAPE TOWN
(21 days, 1 797 km)

A leisurely tour through the western Cape and southern Cape, leaving Cape Town via *route 2* (up the west coast, before swinging east across the Great Karoo to the Garden Route. After one week on the Garden Route, the traveller returns via the south coast back to Cape Town *(route 1)*. This route is especially rewarding during spring when the countryside is ablaze with veld flowers.

DAY 1:   **Cape Town to Langebaan** *(125 km)*
A quiet drive via Mamre (page 101) to the lagoon peninsula and Churchhaven (page 101), which is an ideal place for a picnic. Continue from here on to Langebaan (page 101) or Velddrif (page 104).

DAY 2:   **Langebaan (or Velddrif)**
Relax on the beach or drive through the area (especially in spring).

DAY 3:   **Langebaan to Tulbagh** *(186 km)*
Leave Langebaan mid-morning; drive via Velddrif (page 104) and then inland through the wheatfields on to Tulbagh (page 104).

DAY 4:   **Tulbagh to Worcester** *(145 km)*
The road passes over three of the most magnificent passes in the western Cape (page 105) before reaching the pretty town of Worcester (page 106).

DAY 5:   **Worcester to Matjiesfontein** *(117 km)*
Visit the Farm Museum (page 107) before continuing on to Matjiesfontein (page 107).

DAY 6:   **Matjiesfontein to Oudtshoorn** *(200 km)*
After Laingsburg the road passes through the Seweweekspoort (page 108) — a narrow gap in the Swartberg Mountains — and continues on to Oudtshoorn. Use the afternoon to explore the town and ostrich farms (page 111).

DAY 7:   **Oudtshoorn** *(181 km)*
Take a leisurely drive over the Swartberg Pass (page 147) to Prince Albert (page 147). After lunch return to Oudtshoorn via De Rust (page 150).

DAY 8:   **Oudtshoorn to the Garden Route** *(approx. 225 km)*
From Oudtshoorn drive via George (page 114) to one of the many resorts along the Garden Route (page 119).

DAY 9 to 14:   **The Garden Route**
Spend these days exploring the area or just relaxing on one of the magnificent beaches.

DAY 15:   **Garden Route to Swellendam** *(approx. 226 km)*
          Leave via George on the N2 and drive on to Mossel Bay (page
          98). Explore the town; drive on to Swellendam and visit the
          museum in town (page 97).
DAY 16:   **Swellendam**
          Spend the day exploring the Bontebok National Park (page 97).
DAY 17:   **Swellendam to Arniston** *(103 km)*
          An easy morning drive to the coast, visiting places of interest
          (page 96) along the way. Spend the afternoon on the beach
          (page 95).
DAY 18:   **Arniston**
          Relax on the beach or explore the area around Cape Agulhas
          (page 95).
DAY 19:   **Arniston to Hermanus** *(142 km)*
          Drive via Elim (page 95) and Salmons Dam Nature Reserve
          (page 95) on to Hermanus (page 93).
DAY 20:   **Hermanus**
          Relax on the beach or explore the area (page 93).
DAY 21:   **Hermanus to Cape Town** *(146 km)*
          A relaxing drive via the coast (page 91) brings you back to Cape
          Town.

Circular tour of the Garden Route from Johannesburg

(20 days, 2 815 km)

The route takes the traveller from Johannesburg directly on to Graaff-Reinet and then winds slowly through the Karoo down to the Garden Route, where a week is spent exploring the area; from Port Elizabeth the traveller returns to Johannesburg via Cradock.

DAY 1: **Johannesburg to Graaff-Reinet** *(819 km)*
A long day's drive via the N1 through Bloemfontein and Coles-berg. From here take the R57 to Middelburg and then to Graaff-Reinet (page 150).

DAY 2: **Graaff-Reinet**
Explore the town and surroundings for the day (page 152).

DAY 3: **Graaff-Reinet to Prince Albert** *(349 km)*
From Graaff-Reinet to the R341 turn-off to De Rust (page 150) the road passes through the vast open plains of the Karoo. From De Rust drive via Meiringspoort to Prince Albert (page 147).

DAY 4: **Prince Albert to Oudtshoorn** *(67 km)*
Take a picnic lunch along and head up the Swartberg Pass (page 147) and then on to the Cango Caves. Spend the rest of the day at an ostrich farm (page 113).

DAY 5: **Oudtshoorn to Mossel Bay** *(88 km)*
Take an unhurried drive via the Robinson Pass to Mossel Bay and explore the town (page 98); or relax on the beach.

DAY 6: **Mossel Bay to Garden Route resorts** *(approx. 60 km)*
Drive via George (on to N2) to one of the Garden Route resorts (page 119).

DAYS 7 to 14: **The Garden Route**
Spend these days exploring the area or relaxing on a beach (page 122).

DAY 15: **The Garden Route to Port Elizabeth** *(approx. 285 km)*
Leave fairly early, stopping to explore Storms River Mouth (page 129) — or leave a day earlier and spend the night at the Mouth — before heading on to Port Elizabeth (page 131).

DAY 16: **Port Elizabeth**
Spend the day exploring the city (page 134).

DAY 17: **Port Elizabeth to Addo Elephant National Park** *(63 km)*
Leave early so as to have the day free to explore the park. (page 137)

DAY 18: **Addo to Mountain Zebra National Park** *(237 km)*
After a morning of game-viewing, depart for Paterson. Turn left onto the R32 and travel via Cookhouse and Cradock to the Mountain Zebra National Park (page 154).

DAY 19: **Mountain Zebra National Park**
Spend the day exploring the park.

DAY 20: **Mountain Zebra National Park to Johannesburg** *(847 km)*
Return to Cradock. From there take the R340 via Hofmeyer and Steynsburg to the N1; then travel via Bloemfontein to Johannes-burg.

Port Elizabeth to Johannesburg via the Natal Drakensberg

(19 days, 1 849 km)

This route which follows *route 1* to Umtata, and then *route 2* to Johannesburg, explores three areas of southern Africa. They are: 1820 Settler country from Port Elizabeth to Port Alfred; Transkei Wild Coast; and the Natal Drakensberg.

DAY 1: **Port Elizabeth to Addo Elephant National Park** *(63 km)*
Spend most of the day exploring Port Elizabeth (page 134) before moving on to the Addo Elephant National Park (page 137) in the afternoon.

DAY 2: **Addo Elephant National Park**
Take a leisurely morning and afternoon drive through the park.

DAY 3: **Addo Elephant National Park to Grahamstown** *(156 km)*
A pleasant drive via Alexandria and Salem (page 138) brings one to Grahamstown (page 138). Spend the rest of the day exploring the town.

DAY 4: **Grahamstown to Port Alfred** *(60 km)*
The road winds down to the coast via Bathurst (page 140). Spend the rest of the day exploring Port Alfred (page 141).

DAY 5: **Port Alfred to Coffee Bay** *(429 km)*
The road passes a number of coastal resorts before reaching East London (page 143). From here the road swings inland into Transkei (page 146). The turn-off for Coffee Bay (page 159) is 20 km before Umtata.

DAY 6 and 7: **Coffee Bay**
Relax on the beach or visit places of interest in the area.

DAY 8: **Coffee Bay to Port St. Johns** *(212 km)*
From Coffee Bay head inland to Umtata before heading towards the coast and Port St. Johns (page 188) or Umngazi Mouth (page 188).

DAY 9 and 10: **Port St. Johns**
Relax on the beach or explore the area.

DAY 11: **Port St. Johns to the southern Drakensberg** *(300 km)*
The road to Brooks Nek is in a poor condition and care should be taken when driving along it. A number of resorts can be reached from Underberg (page 191).

DAY 12 and 13: **Southern Drakensberg**
Relax in the area.

DAY 14: **Southern to northern Drakensberg** *(200 km)*
A slow drive to the northern resorts (page 194).

DAY 15 and 16: **Northern Drakensberg**
Relax at one of the resorts or join a hiking group.

DAY 17: **Northern Drakensberg to Golden Gate National Park** *(151 km)*
The road follows the edge of the mountain range before climbing over the Drakensberg to Golden Gate (page 196).

DAY 18: **Golden Gate National Park**
Enjoy the surroundings of the park.

DAY 19: **Golden Gate to Johannesburg** *(323 km)*
Drive directly up to Johannesburg.

Circular tour from Johannesburg via Durban, Zululand and The Eastern Transvaal

(21 days, 2 051 km)

The tour follows *route 2* in reverse from Johannesburg to Mooi River; it then goes to Durban and follows *route 1* from Durban up the coast to Zululand; from there it branches inland via Swaziland and the eastern Transvaal back to Johannesburg. The route passes through three of the major wilderness areas of southern Africa: the Natal Drakensberg, the Zululand Game Parks and the Kruger National Park.

DAY 1: **Johannesburg to Golden Gate National Park** (323 km)
Head south on the N3 from Johannesburg to Heidelberg and then on to Golden Gate National Park (page 196). Spend the rest of the day exploring the park.

DAY 2: **Golden Gate to Royal Natal National Park** (122 km)
A relaxing drive through magnificent scenery takes one on to the Royal Natal National Park (page 194).

DAY 3 and 4: **Royal Natal National Park**
Explore the area.

DAY 5: **Royal Natal National Park to Durban** (287 km)
Head for Mooi River then take the N3 to Durban (page 164).

DAY 6: **Durban**
Relax on the beach for the day or explore the bird park and botanical gardens (page 174).

DAY 7: **Durban to St. Lucia** (247 km)
Aim to arrive at St. Lucia (page 180) before lunch so as to be able to take part in the afternoon launch tour up the estuary.

DAY 8: **St. Lucia to Umfolozi** (72 km)
Explore St. Lucia in the morning, and aim to reach Umfolozi (page 182) just after lunch.

DAY 9: **Umfolozi**
Spend the day game-viewing.

DAY 10: **Umfolozi to Hluhluwe** (42 km)
After a morning drive head for Hluhluwe (page 182).

DAY 11: **Hluhluwe**
Spend the day game-viewing.

DAY 12: **Hluhluwe to Mkuzi Game Reserve** (66 km)
Aim to reach Mkuzi (page 183) just after lunch and spend the rest of the afternoon game-viewing.

DAY 13: **Mkuzi**
Spend the day game-viewing, or in a hide at one of the water-holes

DAY 14: **Mkuzi to Mlilwane Game Sanctuary** (229 km)
Leave mid-morning and head for Swaziland (page 184) and Mlilwane (page 185).

DAY 15: **Mlilwane**
Relax for the day in the area.

DAY 16: **Mlilwane to the Kruger National Park** (163 km)
Explore some of the towns on the way to the Kruger National Park (page 198).

DAY 17 and 18: **Kruger National Park**
                Spend the two days exploring the park.

DAY 19:   **Kruger National Park to the eastern Transvaal** *(approx. 100 km)*
                Head for one of the many resorts in the area (page 208).

DAY 20:   **Eastern Transvaal**
                Spend the day visiting some of the places of interest in the area
                (page 209).

DAY 21:   **The eastern Transvaal to Johannesburg** *(400 km)*
                Take a leisurely drive to Johannesburg, visiting some sights
                along the way (page 215).

Circular tour of Natal Drakensberg and Coast from Johannesburg

(14 days, 1 502 km)

The following tour allows you to spend one week at the beach resorts along the Natal coast and one week in the Drakensberg resorts.

DAY 1:   **Johannesburg to Durban** *(602 km)*
Drive directly to Durban (page 165) on the N3 motorway. Alternatively, Durban can be reached by air, train or inter-city coach (page 239) and a car can be hired (page 173) on arrival.

DAY 2 and 3:   **Durban**
Spend the days on the beach, or visiting the many attractions in the city (page 174).

DAY 4:   **Durban to Natal South Coast** *(130 km)*
Take an unhurried drive down the coast to one of the many resorts on the South Coast (page 160).

DAY 5 and 6:   **Natal South Coast**
Relax in the area.

DAY 7:   **Natal South Coast to southern Drakensberg** *(247 km)*
From the South Coast head on *route 1* (N2) (page 161) for Kokstad. From Kokstad follow *route 2* (page 190), the R394, for Underberg and stay at one of the resorts in the area (page 191).

DAY 8 and 9:   **Southern Drakensberg**
Spend the day exploring the area.

DAY 10:   **Southern to northern Drakensberg** *(approx. 200 km)*
Head for Winterton, from where a number of resorts can be visited (page 193).

DAY 10 to 13:   **Northern Drakensberg resorts**
Enjoy the wide variety of activities offered by the resorts.

DAY 14:   **Northern Drakensberg to Johannesburg** *(approx. 323 km)*
Leave for Johannesburg after lunch.

Circular tour from Johannesburg of Northern and Eastern Transvaal

(14 days, 1 111 km)

This is a tour especially designed for those who wish to enjoy the splendours of the Transvaal escarpment and Kruger National Park.

DAY 1: **Johannesburg to Warmbaths** *(95 km)*
Depart from Johannesburg via the N1 highway towards Pretoria and continue towards Pietersburg, taking the Warmbaths exit. Spend the rest of the day relaxing at the warm springs (page 224).

DAY 2: **Warmbaths to Haenertsburg/Tzaneen** *(257 km)*
Follow the N1 north to Pietersburg (page 223) and then on towards Tzaneen (page 221).

DAY 3 and 4: **Haenertsburg/Tzaneen area**
Spend the two days exploring the area.

DAY 5: **Tzaneen to Louis Trichardt** *(123 km)*
Take a slow drive on to Louis Trichardt (page 218).

DAY 6: **Louis Trichardt to Kruger National Park** *(136 km)*
Head for the park to arrive by early afternoon (page 198).

DAY 7 to 9: **Kruger National Park**
Spend the three days game-viewing, moving south slowly to reach one of the southern camps by the last day.

DAY 10: **Kruger National Park to eastern Transvaal** *(100 km)*
Leave the park during mid-morning and head for one of the many eastern Transvaal resorts (page 208).

DAY 11: **Eastern Transvaal**
Take your time to explore the area thoroughly (page 209).

DAY 12: **Eastern Transvaal to Johannesburg** *(400 km)*
Take a leisurely drive back to Johannesburg, visiting the various places of interest along the way (page 215).

PART 2
The Routes

Cape Town

Cape Town is affectionately known as the Mother City, and, like most mothers, she is beautiful, friendly, and serene. Sir Francis Drake described her location as "... the most stately thing, and the fairest cape we saw in the whole circumference of the earth".

Cape Town grew around the original site of the first European settlement of southern Africa, which was started in April 1652 when Jan van Riebeeck and his small party landed on the shores beneath Table Mountain. Their mission was to establish a refreshment station for the ships of the Dutch East India Company which were sailing between Europe and the spice islands of the East. A permanent settlement soon sprang up around the station: Company officials and Dutch adventurers settled first. They were followed by French Huguenots and slaves from the East.

In 1795 the first British arrived, after Holland was overrun by the French and the refugee Prince of Orange requested Britain to occupy the Cape. By this stage the whole of the Western Cape was settled by highly productive farms which were supplying produce to Europe and provisions for the trading ships sailing between the East Indies and Europe. Cape Town had become the centre of all the activity, with large warehouses, a strategic defensive garrison to protect the route and an active social life. In 1803, under the Treaty of Amiens, the Cape was once more handed over to Holland, but not for long.

The British again took control in 1806 and a stream of British settlers began to arrive. In 1867 diamonds were discovered at Kimberley, which boosted the Colony's economy. In 1910 the Union of South Africa came into being, and Cape Town became the legislative capital of South Africa, a position it still holds.

Today greater Cape Town covers an area of 187 200 hectares and has a population of over 1,7 million people of diverse cultures.

The Weather

The southern Cape coastal belt has a Mediterranean climate, with hot dry summers and cool wet winters.

January and February temperatures can reach up to 38 °C (100 °F), but are usually around 26 °C (78 °F) with low humidity. The kilometres of unpopulated beaches can be enjoyed to the full.

From **March to May** the summer winds die down and temperatures drop to around 23 °C (73 °F) making this one of the most pleasant times to visit the area. The days are long and warm, while the evenings are pleasantly cool. From early May the countryside is transformed by the golden colours of autumn and the sweet scent of ripened fruit.

June to September is the rainy season when the Cape takes on a lush green appearance. The countryside is clean and fresh, and the air is crystal clear. Temperatures range between 8 °C (46 °F) and 17 °C (63 °F).

October to December is the unpredictable time of the year, when howling storms alternate with hot bright summer days ranging in temperature from 10 °C (50 °F) to 21 °C (70 °F). This is also the best time to see the abundance of spring flowers in the various nature reserves and along the country roads.

In Cape Town the west side of the mountain (Sea Point and Clifton) has less rainfall and beaches are protected from the strong South-Easterly Wind which often blows during summer. It is said that the most beautiful girls can be found sun-tanning on the beaches situated on the Atlantic side of the Peninsula, but the water is at least 5 °C cooler than that of False Bay.

Accommodation

Although Cape Town is the second largest city in South Africa and therefore a major business centre, it is also regarded as one of the prime holiday resorts in the country. The standard of accommodation is therefore very high and varied.

An emergency Hotel and Accommodation Booking Centre is available to personal callers at the Visitors' Information Bureau (see address under *Useful Addresses*). This service is available from 09h00 to 17h00 on weekdays, and from 08h30 to 12h30 on Saturdays; and also on Sundays and Public Holidays during the Christmas and Easter season. A computer screen displays the availability of rooms after hours.

HOTELS
De Luxe

Mount Nelson Hotel *****TYYY Tel. (021) 23-1000
76 Orange Street, Cape Town, 8001
Swimming-pool, tennis, bowls, squash, 6-hole putting green
The "Nellie", as it is affectionately called, is one of the bastions of pure luxury and a relic of Cape Town's grand past. The spacious reception rooms are tastefully decorated with antiques. Rooms are also tastefully fitted out with antiques, but of course, all the modern comforts are also supplied. The three restaurants serve tasty food in the grand old English tradition. The hotel is located in large landscaped grounds beneath Table Mountain. It is ten minutes' walk through the tranquil gardens past the Houses of Parliament from the city centre. There is ample parking in the grounds.

The Cape Sun *****TYYY Tel. (021) 23-8844
Strand Street, Cape Town, 8001   Southern Sun
Small indoor pool, health studio
The Cape Sun is an ultra-modern newish hotel which makes clever use of a combination of old Cape Dutch interior designs and colours, and modern luxury. Rooms are spacious and comfortable with a choice of either a mountain or harbour view. The elegant Palm Court, on the ground floor, serves snacks and beverages to the soothing tunes of a pianist occasionally accompanied by a violinist. The hotel is centrally situated. One shortfall is the lack of parking; but the hotel does have a car valet service (although very slow at times) and there is a parking garage across the road from the hotel. Service in general does not always meet expectations.

The Capetonian Hotel ****TYYY Tel. (021) 21-1150
Pier Place, Heerengracht, 8001
Health studio

The rooms in the hotel were fairly recently converted from flatlets to standard rooms, giving very spacious well-furnished rooms. Most rooms have either a mountain or harbour view. The hotel is situated at the lower end of town, next to a parking garage.

The President Hotel   *****TYYY Tel. (021) 44-1121

Beach Road, Sea Point, 8001   Southern Sun

Pool, tennis, bowls, sauna, putt-putt

The hotel is on the sea-front at the end of Sea Point, a lively suburb of Cape Town. It has several restaurants and a bustling night-life. There are no bathing beaches in front of the hotel, but there are a number a short car or bus drive away. The best rooms in the hotel are situated in the new wing and are comfortable. Single rooms are very small. Grounds are spacious and there is ample parking.

Medium-priced   **Town House**   ***TYYY Tel. (021) 45-7050

60 Corporation Street,

Cape Town, 8001   Portfolio of Country Places

Squash, gymnasium, sauna, jacuzzi

Situated in the city centre, this gracious hotel has been tastefully furnished with antiques and country cottage items. The reception rooms have been finished off in face brick and wood. It is a truly elegant hotel. The hotel serves flavoursome seafoods and continental dishes.

Cape Town Holiday Inn   ***TYYY Tel. (021) 47-4060

Melbourne Road, Woodstock, 8001   Holiday Inns

Swimming-pool

Just off the Eastern Boulevard into town, this inn commands a fine view of the harbour. It is rated as one of the best Holiday Inns in South Africa. The Tavern restaurant serves an excellent carvery, while the Contented Sole is renowned as an outstanding fish restaurant. The hotel has ample parking.

Vineyard Hotel   ***TYYY Tel. (021) 64-4122

Colinton Road,

Newlands, 7700   Portfolio of Country Places

Swimming-pool

This historic hotel, originally built as a homestead in 1799, has recently been masterfully restored by the same family who owns the Town House in the city. The hotel is tastefully furnished throughout with period antiques. Dining in one of the hotel's restaurants is a culinary delight. There is ample parking in the hotel grounds.

Alphen Hotel   ***TYYY Tel. (021) 74-1011

Alphen Drive, Constantia, 7800

Swimming-pool

The Alphen is one of the old estates (still producing superb wines) situated in the famous Constantia Valley, a twenty-minute drive from the city centre or from the beach in the opposite direction. The grace and elegance of this hotel is true to its Georgian past. It is set in tranquil gardens and has ample parking.

St. James Protea Hotel   ***TYYY Tel. (021) 88-8931

Main Road, St. James, 7945   Protea Hotels and Inns

This charming seaside hotel was recently completely refurnished and modernised. Situated just across the road from the beach, it is ideally situated for those who are looking for a beach holiday location. The beach offers safe bathing with a walled-in paddling pool. There is also a regular train service to the city centre, and ample parking within the grounds.

Budget

Carlton Heights Hotel **TYY Tel. (021) 23-1260
88 Queen Victoria Street, Cape Town, 8001
This clean comfortable hotel is situated across the road from the public gardens and two minutes' walk from the city centre and the museums. The owners believe in service and a homely atmosphere. Food is basic, but good value for money. All rooms have private bathrooms.

Tudor Hotel *T Tel. (021) 24-1335
Greenmarket Square, Cape Town, 8001
A small comfortable hotel right in the centre of town facing Greenmarket Square, where a flea market is held every day from 07h00 to 16h00, except Sundays. Good food is served in the coffeeshop/restaurant. Half the rooms have private bathrooms. There is a parking garage just around the corner.

Metropole Hotel ***TYYY Tel. (021) 23-6363
38 Long Street, Cape Town, 8001
The hotel is an old family-run establishment with all the modern comforts, situated above the city centre. All rooms have bathrooms. The hotel restaurant serves good seafoods (see restaurants).

Carnaby Hotel *T Tel. (021) 49-7410
Main Road, Three Anchor Bay, 8001
Swimming-pool
This cosy family-run hotel is situated on the road to Sea Point in spacious grounds. Although it has no liquor licence, the hotel is willing to store your drinks and serve them when required. Not all rooms have bathrooms. There is ample parking in the grounds.

Winchester Mansions Hotel ***TYY
Tel. (021) 44-2351
Beach Road, Sea Point, 8001
It is an elegant hotel built in the Cape Dutch style, around a garden courtyard and is situated across the road from a large park and the seafront. Breakfasts are served in the rooms. All rooms have bathrooms.

Surfcrest Hotel **T Tel. (021) 44-8721
327 Beach Road, Sea Point, 8001
All rooms in this basic, but comfortable hotel have private bathrooms and refrigerators in which to store your drinks (the hotel is not licensed to sell alcohol). It is situated on the coast close to the famous Clifton beach. Parking is no problem here.

**UNGRADED
ACCOMMODATION
Character Country
Houses**

The Cellars Country House Tel. (021) 74-3468
Hohenort Avenue,
Constantia, 7800   Portfolio of Country Places
Swimming-pool, horse-riding, croquet, hiking
The Cellars is set high above the Constantia Valley and has a fine view of Table Mountain. It offers visitors a peaceful retreat in a rural setting, but is only twenty minutes' drive from the city centre and is close to the beaches. This house, which has been tastefully converted from three adjoining cellars, is furnished with Laura Ashley fabrics and antique furniture. Wholesome country-style food is served in an elegant setting. Wine is served with meals, but guests are requested to bring their own spirits.

The Greenmarket Square flea market in Cape Town

Windsurfing off Blouberg Strand with Table Mountain as a backdrop

The Cape Town City Hall and the Parade

A splash of colour on Table Mountain

Vista from Salmon's Dam

Fisherman's cottage at Arniston

One of the many beautiful wine farms in the Paarl district

Groot Moddergate Country House
Tel. (021) 790-1110
Hout Bay Main Road,
Hout Bay, 7800   Portfolio of Country Places
Swimming-pool, hiking
This charming historic Cape Dutch homestead is surrounded by
olive trees and oak-lined avenues close to the fishing village of
Hout Bay, close to the beaches and twenty minutes' drive from
the city centre. Guests are accommodated in the original homestead and in the tastefully renovated old slave quarters, where
rooms have balconies with sweeping views of the mountains
and valley. Traditional Cape dishes served with homemade
wholewheat nutty bread and superb wines are the order of the
day.

Guest Houses   **Ambleside**   Tel. (021) 45-2503
11 Forest Road, Oranjezicht, 8001
It is situated in a quiet street overlooking the city and is on a bus
route to the city, which is 3 km away. All rooms have hot and
cold running water. A fully equipped kitchen and laundry are
available for guests' use.
Berghof Deutsches Gaestehaus   Tel. (021) 23-7229
1 Faure Street, Gardens, 8001
This is a clean, homely and owner-run guest house. It is on a bus
route to the city centre, which is 2 km away. Seven rooms have
bathrooms and ten are without.
Palm Court Holiday Lodge   Tel. (021) 23-8721
11 Hof Street, Gardens, 8001
Swimming-pool, tennis
A home-from-home atmosphere is created in beautiful surroundings. It is on a bus route to the city centre, which is 2 km away.
All rooms have hot and cold running water. A fully-equipped
kitchen and laundry are available for guests' use. Cars can be
hired at exellent rates.
Unity House   Tel. (021) 24-7668
159 Longmarket Street, Cape Town, 8001
It is very close to the city centre and all the bus stops. This
comfortable guest house accommodates visitors in large, comfortable, air-conditioned rooms. Guests can make use of the kitchen
to prepare their own meals.
Chartfield Residential   Tel. (021) 88-5071
30 Gatesville Road, Kalk Bay, 7975
Fishing
Comfortable accommodation overlooking Kalk Bay fishing harbour, close to beaches and the railway station, is offered.
Ocean View Residential   Tel. (021) 88-4289
122 Beach Road, Muizenberg, 7945
Fishing
Ocean View is situated on the beach and offers a relaxed homely
atmosphere. It is five minutes' walk from the station.

Youth Hostels   **YMCA**   Tel (021) 24-1247
and YMCAs   60 Queen Victoria Street, Gardens, 8001
YWCA   Tel (021) 23-3711
20 Bellevue Street, Gardens, 8001
Both provide comfortable basic accommodation at a bed and
breakfast rate for people under 30. Accommodation is either in
dormitories, shared, or single rooms. Facilities include table
tennis, a TV room and a laundromat. Keys can be arranged. The

YMCA accommodates both male and female guests, while the YWCA caters only for women.

Stan's Halt Youth Hostel   Tel. (021) 48-9037
The Glen, Camps Bay, 8001
This youth hostel has a superb view of the sea, with Table Mountain behind it. Accommodation is basic, in dormitories. To get there from the city centre, take the Kloof Nek bus (no. 3) in lower Saint George's Street to the terminus. From there follow the signposts.

The Abe Bailey Youth Hostel   Tel. (021) 88-4283
2 Maynard Road, Muizenberg, 7945
Fishing
Situated within two minutes' walk of the beach and Muizenberg station. There is a kitchen containing the basics for the guests' use.

SELF-CATERING   **Diplomat Holiday Flats**   Tel. (021) 25-2037
Tulbagh Square, Cape Town, 8001
These flats in the city centre are fully equipped, including linen and TV. Flats vary in size between one, two and three rooms.

Garden City Holiday Flats   Tel. (021) 46-5827/8
Mill Street, Gardens, 8001
They are situated above the city, approximately 20 minutes' walk from the city centre and are fully serviced and equipped, including linen, TV, second channel video and telephone. The flats are above Gardens Shopping Centre, which houses a large supermarket, good restaurants and a laundromat. Parking is no problem. Each flat has one and a half rooms.

Portofino Apartments   Tel. (021) 44-9321
Beach Road, Sea Point, 8001
These luxury apartments have a beautiful view over the sea, and are 6 km from the city centre. All flats are fully equipped with linen, towels and kitchen utensils. They are serviced daily and offer a laundry service and TV with second channel. There is also a 24-hour telephone and porter service. Free covered parking is available within the building. Flats are spacious and have balconies overlooking the sea.

Serengeti Executive Suites   Tel. (021) 686-3457
Cnr. Kotzee Road and Long Street, Mowbray, 7700
They are 8 km from the city centre and are close to a bus stop and station. The University of Cape Town as well as the Baxter Theatre are close by. All suites are fully furnished, serviced and include TV with second channel and telephone. Lock-up parking is available. Suites have one or two rooms.

Applegarth Farm   Tel. (021) 790-2160
Main Road, Hout Bay, 7800
These cottages are beautifully situated 3 km below Constantia Nek on the oak-lined avenue heading towards Hout Bay. Each cottage is self contained, including fully equipped kitchens and linen.

Houtkapperspoort Cottages   Tel. (021) 74-1216
Constantia Nek Farm, Hout Bay Road,
Hout Bay, 7800
Swimming-pool, tennis, hiking, horse-riding
This luxurious village of fully equipped cottages, built from mountain stone and timber, is situated in the saddle between Constantiaberg and Table Mountain. Each cottage is supplied

with linen, is fully carpeted, serviced and has a TV and telephone. There is a choice of one-, two- and three-bedroomed units, all including kitchen, lounge/dining room and a verandah with barbecue facilities. Laundry facilities are also available.

Oatlands Holiday Village   Tel. (021) 86-1410
Froggy Pond, Simonstown, 7995   Club Caraville
Swimming-pool, games field, games room, wind surfing, fishing
The village is on False Bay, just across the road from the beach, where bathing is safe. It is close to Simonstown. Chalets are fully equipped and self-contained, including T.V. There are communal facilities for people in caravans and rondavels. Linen can be hired and there are laundry facilities.

CARAVAN AND   **Zandvlei Caravan Park**   Tel. (021) 210-2507
CAMPING   The Row, Muizenberg (Postal Address: Bathing Amenities, Cape Town Civic Centre, Cape Town, 8001)
Laundry, recreation hall, tennis, bowls, water sports, wind surfing, fishing
It is close to the beach and situated on a lagoon. There are both camping and caravan sites.

Oatlands Holiday Village   Tel. (021) 86-1410
Froggy Pond, Simonstown, 7995   Club Caraville
Electric plugs, laundry, gas, shop, recreational hall, swimming-pool, games field, wind surfing, fishing
Situated in the same complex as the chalets and rondavels (see above). Both camping and caravan sites are available.

Imhoff Park   Tel. (021) 83-1634
Wireless Road, Kommetjie, (P.O. Box 18, Kommetjie, 7976)
Electric plugs, laundry, recreational hall, fishing
It is close to the beach and village of Kommetjie. Camping and caravan sites are available.

Ou Skip Caravan Park   Tel. (02224) 2058
P.O. Box 13, Melkbosstrand, 7437
Electric plugs, laundry, gas, shop, recreational hall, restaurant, swimming-pool, wind surfing, fishing
It is situated north of Cape Town, close to the beach. This comfortable resort has all the facilities needed for a relaxing stay for both the camping and caravan visitor.

Restaurants

Cape Town has many fine restaurants, and superb estate wines which are not often found on the shelf of a bottle store are served in the restaurants. Cape Malay food — sweet spiced curries —have their roots here and are definitely worth trying. Cape Town has long been known as the Tavern of the Seas, and as such, is famous for its seafood. These include Cape lobster (known as crayfish), snoek, abelone (known as perlemoen), tuna, and yellowtail (a game fish). In the summer and autumn there is no finer way to end a meal than with the sweet abundant fresh fruits of the area.

DE LUXE   **Floris Smit Huijs**   Tel. 23-3414   Fully licenced
55 Church Street,
Central Cape Town   South African
This restaurant, located in a house in Church Street, offers

perfectly prepared and beautifully presented food in comfortable
surroundings. Tables set out to allow privacy during meals.

The Roundhouse Restaurant

Tel. 48-7193   Wine and malt licence

The Glen, Camps Bay   South African

This magnificent restaurant is set in the forests, high above
Camps Bay on the old site that served as Lord Charles Somerset's
hunting lodge. It has a superb view of the bay. The decor is
homely and the service is superb. Among the many specialities
is the tasty Karoo lamb, grilled whole on the spit over an open
fire. They also claim to have the most comprehensive cellar in
Cape Town.

Al Gambero   Tel. 44-8769   Fully licensed

Medical Centre, Kloof Road,

Sea Point   French and seafood

Al Gambero is well known for its traditional French cuisine and
good cellar. Pastries and sauces play an important role at Al
Gambero. Desserts are not to be missed.

Buitenverwachting

Tel. 74-3522   Wine and malt licence

Klein Constantia Road, Constantia   Belgian

Regarded as one of the finest restaurants in Cape Town, Buitenverwachting nestles in the midst of the vineyards of the Constantia Valley. The decor is elegant and food is a gourmet's delight.

MEDIUM-PRICED   **Dragon Inn** Tel. 25-3324   Not licensed

1st Floor, Broadway Centre, Heerengracht,

Central Cape Town   Chinese

Cantonese food is served in this elegantly furnished and authen-
tically draped room.

Harbour Café   Tel. 419-1913   Fully licensed

Pier Head, Cape Town Docks,

Central Cape Town   Portuguese/seafood

The Harbour Café overlooks the tug basin. The food and service
are not always up to scratch (prices also tend to be high) but this
establishment is well worth a visit for its location.

Hildebrand Restaurant   Tel. 25-3385   Fully licensed

1st Floor, Old Mutual Centre, St. Georges Street,

Central Cape Town   Italian/seafood

A relaxing atmosphere with attentive service and good food
makes Hildebrand one of the most enjoyable restaurants in
which to spend an evening. Their seafood specialities include
fresh crayfish cooked in different ways, and a giant seafood
platter with a wide variety of Cape fish and shellfish. They also
serve a good selection of fresh home-made pastas.

Kaapse Tafel   Tel. 23-1651   Not licensed

90 Queen Victoria Street,

Central Cape Town   Cape traditional

True traditional foods such as bobotie and waterblommetjie-
bredies are served at this establishment. Most of the recipes
used here have been handed down from generation to generation.

Le Pot Au Feu   Tel. 24-4740   Not licensed

4 Burnside Road, Tamboerskloof   French

Le Pot is one of the smallest restaurants around, creating an
overcrowded but cosy ambiance. Food is different to run-of-the-
mill French cooking, with some exciting combinations such as
smoked yellowtail and tripe in a Mexican chilli sauce.

Metropole Hotel Restaurant
Tel. 23-6363   Fully licensed
38 Long Street, Central Cape Town   Seafood
Prawns and fresh line-fish are both specialities here, and for the
meat eaters they serve roasts and seasonal game dishes. A good
value-for-money restaurant.

Old Colonial Homestead Tel. 45-4909   Wine and malt
29 Barnet Street, Gardens   Cape traditional
The old Cape homestead is comfortably homely. Food reflects
the true traditions of the Cape, blending the Eastern spices with
Western ingredients.

Oriental Restaurant   Tel. 46-5858   Fully licensed
Oriental Plaza, Sir Lowry Road,
Central Cape Town   Indian curries
You name it, they curry it, in degrees from mild to very hot.
These curries are very good.

Pagoda Inn   Tel. 25-2033   Not licensed
First floor, 29 Bree Street
Central Cape Town   Chinese
This establishment is unpretentious, noisy and full of the charac-
ter that a good simple Chinese restaurant should display. Por-
tions are large and cooked to the original Chinese recipes, not
Western substitutes.

Rozenhof   Tel. 24-1968   Fully licensed
18 Kloof Street, Gardens   South African
A casually relaxed and intimate atmosphere with attentive service makes dining in this converted house a memorable experience. Wines offered have been specially selected from some of
the smaller estates in the Cape and the limited (but more than
adequate) menu is changed periodically.

Black Angus   Tel. 44-6120   Not licensed
20a Norfolk Road, Sea Point   Steaks
Service is not always up to standard and only cash is accepted,
but the steaks, cooked to perfection, are the best in town.

Word of Mouth   Tel. 44-3344   Fully licensed
Arthur's Seat Hotel, Arthur's Road,
Sea Point   Carvery
This carvery is fantastic value-for-money, with two to three
roasts each day, plus a huge selection from the buffet and salad
bar.

Barristers Grill Room   Tel. 64-1792   Wine and malt
Corner of Kildare and Main Street,
Newlands   Steaks and seafood
Steaks are well hung, well cooked, and served plain or with a
choice of sauces. Service is attentive and the Tudor setting and
atmosphere relaxing.

Farthings Restaurant   Tel. 61-8235   Not licensed
1 Wessels Road, Kenilworth   Nouvelle cuisine
This delightfully renovated cottage is divided into four small
dining rooms, each with its own fireplace. The decor is elegant
and comfortable. Food is fresh and cooked in a truly French
manner: in rich sauces and well presented. Sunday brunches are
also served.

Mariner's Wharf   Tel. 790-1100   Fully licensed
Harbour Road, Hout Bay Harbour   Seafood
It is situated within the charming fishing harbour, with a fine
view of the bay and boats. Fish include grilled snoek and crayfish.

The Brass Bell   Tel. 88-5456   Wine and malt
Kalk Bay Station, Waterfront, Kalk Bay   Seafood
This restaurant has a happy informal atmosphere and a fine
view over the sea. Bouillabaise, fresh line fish and Sunday
evening fish barbecues are specialities.

BUDGET   **City Hall Hotel**   Tel. 46-5947   Fully licensed
50 Darling Street, Central Cape Town   Pub Meals
Best value-for-money four-course meals in Cape Town, but very
basic.
Good Hope Hotel   Tel. 23-3340   Fully licensed
87 Loop Street, Central Cape Town   Pub Lunches
Speciality is low-priced, tasty pub lunches.
Pleinpark Travel Lodge   Tel. 45-7563   Not licensed
Barrack Street, off Plein Street,
Central Cape Town   Cape traditional
Good home cooking is served here. Last orders are taken at
19h00.
St. Georges Cathedral   Not licensed
Wale Street   Breakfast, lunch and teas
By far the cheapest meals in Cape Town can be bought here. The
more than substantial meals are served by voluntary organisa-
tions in the basement of the church.
Granary Vegetarian Restaurant
Tel. 44-3841   Not licensed
72 Regent Road, Sea Point   Vegetarian
All food is made from natural ingredients and a high standard is
maintained.
The Aloe   Tel. 64-3000   Not licensed
1st floor, Garlicks, Cavendish Square,
Vineyard Road, Claremont   Light meals
Salads and carvery are their specialities. It has a friendly atmos-
phere.
Foresters Arms Bar   Tel. 69-5949   Wine and malt
Newlands Avenue, Newlands   Pub lunches
This pub has a convivial atmosphere and always fills up during
the lunch rush. The food is good. Outside seating is available.

Nightlife

Cape Town is a bustling centre for nightlife. Apart from the
many good restaurants, there are a host of good theatres, movie
houses, pubs with live music and discos.

THEATRE   There are eleven theatres in Cape Town which cater for a variety
of tastes. For a full list of what is on at the various theatres,
consult the daily papers in Cape Town.
   Bookings can be made through either Computicket Tel. (021)
21-4715, which has agencies throughout the Peninsula, or at the
theatre. It is always advisable to make reservations. The main
theatres are:
The Nico Malan Theatre Centre   Tel. 21-5470
D.F. Malan Street, Central Cape Town
This theatre features a 1 200-seat opera house, and 570-seat
theatre. There is a restaurant and undercover parking in the
complex.

The Little Theatre   Tel. 23-9843
Orange Street, Central Cape Town
Specialises in a wide variety of new and experimental plays, and ballet.

The Labia Theatre   Tel. 24-5927
68 Orange Street, Central Cape Town
Art and festival films are usually shown here. Prices are reasonable, and there are no commercials.

The Baxter Theatre Complex   Tel. 689-5991
Main Road, Rosebank
The complex features a 657-seat theatre, 640-seat concert hall and 100-seat studio, and restaurant.

Maynardville Open Air Theatre   Tel. 21-5470 (reserve through Nico Malan, corner Church and Wolfe Street, Wynberg)
This theatre usually has a Shakespeare season every year in January and a ballet season in March.

Three Arts Theatre   Tel. 77-2507
Main Road, Plumstead
This theatre often features visiting pop groups and entertainers.

The Masque Theatre   Tel. 88-1898
Main Road, Muizenberg
Amateur drama.

MUSIC AND CABERET   Many of the casual restaurants and ladies' bars in Cape Town offer some form of live entertainment at least three nights a week (usually Wednesday, Friday and Saturday). The type of live entertainment varies greatly, from hard-driving rock and roll, bluegrass, to folk, often with a bit of humour thrown in. For a full list of entertainment, check the daily press for details. Here are the addresses of a few places that offer some sort of entertainment.

Oasis Restaurant   Tel. 23-1000
Mount Nelson Hotel, 76 Orange Street, Central Cape Town

The Galley   Tel. 21-1150
Capetonian Hotel, Pier Place, Central Cape Town

Kings Hotel Grill   Tel. 49-6040
94 Regent Road, Sea Point

London Town Pub   Tel. 49-1181
Century Hotel, Main Road, Sea Point

Riempies Pub   Tel. 49-6101
Regency Hotel, 90 Regent Road, Sea Point

Bruegels Restaurant   Tel. 689-4805
Main Road, Mowbray

Hard Rock Café   Tel. 69-1160
Main Road, Rondebosch (open till very late)

Pig 'n Whistle   Tel. 69-9794
Main Road, Rondebosch

Speakeasy Restaurant   Tel. 686-3603
Cnr. Main and Dean Street, Newlands (open till late)

Coach House   Tel. 61-1105
Newlands Hotel, Main Road, Newlands

The Forester's Arms   Tel. 69-5949
Newlands Avenue, Newlands

Classical/Orchestral   Opera and other musical events occur periodically at the theatres mentioned below. Check the daily press for details.

City Hall   Tel. 21-2905
Corporation Street, Central Cape Town

The Cape Town Symphony Orchestra performs in the Grand Hall on Thursdays and Sundays, in the evening. Organ recitals are held on Tuesdays at lunch times.

The Hohenort Hotel Tel. 74-1027
Hohenort Avenue, Constantia
Classical music evenings are held on Sundays.

Jazz Jazz has a strong following in Cape Town and there are many venues where good jazz can be heard, especially on Saturday afternoons. Watch the press for details. One such venue is:

Hohenort Hotel Tel. 74-3201
Hohenort Ave, Constantia

DANCING **City Limits Nightclub** Tel. 21-1150
Capetonian Hotel, Pier Place, Central Cape Town
This club offers live music with a caberet show.

Grill Room Tel. 23-1000
Mount Nelson Hotel, 76 Orange Street, Central Cape Town
Elegant dinner/dance atmosphere with mainly continental music.

Villa Dei Cesari Tel. 23-8844
Cape Sun Hotel, Strand Street, Central Cape Town
Elegant dinner/dance atmosphere.

Charlie Parkers Tel. 44-5521
120 Main Road, Sea Point
A licensed disco with a dining area.

The Millionaire Tel. 49-1181
Century Hotel, Main Road, Sea Point
Disco dinner/dance with a caberet show.

Constantia Nek Restaurant Tel. 74-1132
Constantia Nek Road, Constantia
A thatched stone building in beautiful surroundings makes for a perfect night of dining and dancing with a live band. Food is excellent and atmosphere is intimate.

Useful addresses and telephone numbers

Cape Town area telephone code: **(021)**

TOURIST
INFORMATION **Captour** (Cape Tourism Authority) Tel. 25-3320, Strand Concourse, Cape Town Central (P.O. Box 863, Cape Town, 8000)
South African Tourism Board (Satour) Tel. 21-6274, Sanlam Centre, Golden Acre, Central Cape Town (Private Bag X9108, Cape Town, 8000)

TRANSPORT
Airlines SAA and British Airways have flights from London to Cape Town.
Air Cape, Tel. 934-0572, P.O. D.F. Malan Airport, 7525
British Airways, Tel. 25-2970, 2 St. Georges Street, Cape Town, 8001
Court Republic Helicopters, Tel. 25-2965, Back Beach, Granger Bay, Cape Town, 8001
Namaqualand Airways, Tel. 931-4183, P.O. D.F. Malan Airport, 7525
South African Airways, Tel. 25-4610 — after hours 93-6222, SAA Terminal, Adderley Street, Cape Town, 8001

City bus services	**Inter-Cape,** Tel. 934-4400, for transfers to and from the airport to central Cape Town.
	City Tramways, Tel. 45-5450, for details of local bus timetables
Inter-city bus services	**Citiliner,** Tel. 21-4205
	Greyhound, Tel. 419-2244
	Inter-Cape, Tel. 934-4400
	Translux, Tel. 218-3871
Coach tours	**Hilton Ross Tours,** Tel. 48-1500, 7 Central Parade, Camps Bay, 8001
	S.A.R. Travel, Tel. 218-2191, Travel Centre, Station Building, Cape Town, 8001
	Springbok Atlas Safaris, Tel. 45-5468, Shop 2, Sun Gallery, Street George's Street, Cape Town, 8001
Car, caravan and motor-bike hire	**Avis,** Tel. 21-6650, 84 Strand Street, Cape Town, 8001
	Beetle Drive, Tel. 46-7806, 62 Roeland Street, Cape Town, 8001
	Budget, Tel. 23-4290, 63 Strand Street, Cape Town, 8001
	Easy, Tel. 23-3834, 150 Buitengracht Street, Cape Town, 8001
	Imperial, Tel. 44-9921, 6 Three Anchor Bay Road, Three Anchor Bay, 8001
	Priclo Caravans, Tel. 51-4208, 299 Koeberg Road, Brooklyn, 7405
	Camperent, Tel. 25-1056, 20 Hudson Street, Cape Town, 8001
	Rent-a-Scooter, and Car Hire, Tel. 49-2400, 126A Main Road, Sea Point, 8001
Railways	**Enquiries,** Tel. 218-2991, main lines
	Tel. 218-2791, suburban
	Reservations Tel. 218-3871
	Blue Train Tel. 218-2672
Taxis	**Marine Taxis** Tel. 21-6160
	Owner Driver Taxis Tel. 25-1837
	Green's Tel. 41-0608
OTHER NUMBERS	**Ambulance** Tel. 51-5151 or 685-3931
	Automobile Association Tel. 21-1550
	Cableway Tel. 43-0866
	Hospital (Groote Schuur) Tel. 47-3311
	Main Post Office Tel. 96-5543 Cnr. of Parliament and Darling Streets
	Police Tel. 1-0111
	Sea Rescue Tel. 218-3500

Sightseeing

THE CITY CENTRE	The centre of Cape Town has many interesting sights relating to the city's past. The best way of viewing many of these is by foot. A two-hour "city on foot" tour is conducted every Saturday at 15h00, weather permitting from September to May. For further information contact Captour (see telephone number above).
A Walking tour of the historic city	(See map on page 68)
	The Golden Acre shopping complex has a main entrance from Adderley Street. Within are a wide variety of shops, from food to fashion, records, books, etc. Two points of historic interest are: *The high water mark* which indicates the approximate position of the shoreline of Table Bay in 1693. All the land between this point and the present-day harbour was reclaimed from the sea after 1935. The mark can be seen on the concourse level at

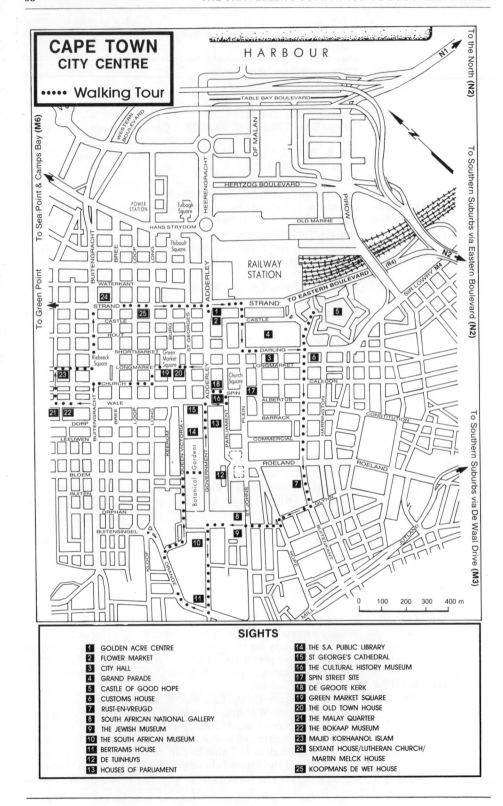

SIGHTS

1 GOLDEN ACRE CENTRE
2 FLOWER MARKET
3 CITY HALL
4 GRAND PARADE
5 CASTLE OF GOOD HOPE
6 CUSTOMS HOUSE
7 RUST-EN-VREUGD
8 SOUTH AFRICAN NATIONAL GALLERY
9 THE JEWISH MUSEUM
10 THE SOUTH AFRICAN MUSEUM
11 BERTRAMS HOUSE
12 DE TUINHUYS
13 HOUSES OF PARLIAMENT

14 THE S.A. PUBLIC LIBRARY
15 ST GEORGE'S CATHEDRAL
16 THE CULTURAL HISTORY MUSEUM
17 SPIN STREET SITE
18 DE GROOTE KERK
19 GREEN MARKET SQUARE
20 THE OLD TOWN HOUSE
21 THE MALAY QUARTER
22 THE BOKAAP MUSEUM
23 MAJID KORHAANOL ISLAM
24 SEXTANT HOUSE/LUTHERAN CHURCH/
   MARTIN MELCK HOUSE
25 KOOPMANS DE WET HOUSE

the exit leading to the station; and *The ruins* of part of a reservoir built in 1663 by Commander Zahorias Wagenaer were discovered when building began on the complex. They are preserved in their original position and can be found within the complex in the east wing. This is the oldest remaining Dutch structure in South Africa.

The Flower Market is just above the Golden Acre, in Adderley Street. It is a colourful, fragrant thoroughfare where flowers are on sale from Monday to Saturday.

The City Hall overlooks the Grand Parade. It is a Victorian structure built in the Italian Renaissance style, of sandstone, and was completed in 1905. The Cape Town Symphony Orchestra gives concerts there every Thursday and Sunday (see entertainment section on page 65).

The Grand Parade was used in the days of Jan van Riebeeck as a parade ground. Today a variety of stalls are found on its perimeter, and an interesting flea market is held on the site every Wednesday and Saturday morning.

The Castle of Good Hope was built in 1666. It is a pentagonal medieval fortress almost in the heart of present-day Cape Town. All the early governors of the Cape lived here. The state rooms house the William Fehr Collection of period furniture, paintings and china. A maritime and military museum, displaying interesting relics, is also situated within the Castle grounds. Guided tours are conducted from Monday to Friday at 10h00, 11h00, 12h00, 14h00 and 15h00. The Castle is closed to the public on public holidays and weekends.

Customs House on the corner of Buitenhout and Longmarket Streets was once a grocery store. The pediment carries the British Coat of Arms.

Rust-en-Vreugde (78 Buitenkant Street; Tel. 45-3628) is a restored double-storey town house built in about 1777. The teak front door was carved by the sculptor Anton Anreith. The property houses an extensive part of the William Fehr Collection of early South African paintings and prints. Open weekdays from 09h30 to 16h30. It is closed on public holidays.

South African National Gallery (84 Hatfield Street, Gardens; Tel. 021-451628) houses a permanent exhibition of local and international artists' works. The Gallery is open on Mondays from 13h00 to 17h00 and on Tuesdays to Sundays from 10h00 to 17h00.

The Jewish Museum (Tel. 45-1546) contains a collection of Jewish ceremonial art and items of Jewish history in South Africa. It is housed in the oldest synagogue in South Africa, adjacent to the Gardens Synagogue. It is open on Tuesdays and Thursdays from 10h00 to 12h30.

The Company's Gardens and Government Avenue is part of the site of Jan van Riebeeck's original vegetable garden, which was used to replenish the passing ships. Under the rule of Simon van der Stel they were converted to botanical gardens, as the government gardens had been moved to Newlands. Early South African botanists contributed indigenous as well as exotic species to the gardens. Today the gardens are bisected by Government Avenue, a paved walkway lined with beautiful oaks, which replaced the original lemon trees. Grey squirrels, introduced from America by Cecil Rhodes, are abundant and are so tame that they can be fed by hand. Within the gardens and on its perimeters the following buildings can be found:

The South African Museum (Tel. 24-3330), which was established as a natural history museum in 1825. Exhibits include fascinating reconstructions of the traditional life of various black tribes of southern Africa and rock engravings. Open daily from 10h00 to 17h00.

De Tuinhuys was built in 1751 by Willem van der Stel (son of Simon) as a pleasure lodge. It became the official residence of a number of later governors. The lodge is now the town house-cum-offices of the State President. It is not open to the public.

The Houses of Parliament (Tel. 45-8311) were completed in 1885. Parliament sits between January and June and gallery tickets are available from room 12. Entrance is from Parliament Street. During the recess (July to January) guided tours are offered from Mondays to Thursdays from 09h00 to 12h00, and 14h00 to 15h00, and morning tours are offered on Fridays. Jacket and tie is required during sessions.

The South African Public Library (Tel. 24-6321) was opened in 1822 and contains valuable first editions, including a manuscript dating back to 900 *(The Four Gospels)*, and a first folio of Shakespeare dated 1623. It is also a national reference and research library. It is open on weekdays from 09h00 to 19h00 and on Saturdays from 09h00 to 18h00. Entrance is from Queen Victoria Street.

St. George's Anglican Cathedral stands at the entrance to Government Avenue. It was built on the site of an older church which was built in 1834. The present Cathedral was designed by Sir Herbert Baker. The altar, western windows and hundred-year old cross in St. David's Chapel are from the original church.

The Cultural History Museum (Tel. 46-8280) was originally built in 1679 as the slave lodge of the Dutch East India Company. Structural alterations were completed in 1810, when the building was inaugurated as the Old Cape Supreme Court. Points of architectural interest include the pediment over the Parliament Street entrance, sculptured by Anton Anreith, and the yellow-wood floors and ceilings. The museum is open from Mondays to Saturdays from 10h00 to 16h45 and from 14h00 to 16h45 on Sundays.

The Dutch East India Company Hospital stood on the corner of Adderley and Wale Streets, where the Board of Executors building now stands.

The Spin Street Site marked by a plaque, is where slave auctions were held until 1834.

The Groote Kerk was built in 1841 on the site where two previous churches had stood. The first was built in 1678 and was the first Dutch Reformed Church to be built in South Africa. The clock tower of the present church was part of a second church, built in 1703. Of particular interest in the church is the wooden pulpit, carved by Anton Anreith in 1779. It is open to the public from Tuesday to Friday from 08h30 to 12h00 and 13h00 to 16h30, and on Saturdays from 08h30 to 11h30.

Greenmarket Square was the original central square of Cape Town and was the site of Cape Town's first market. Many interesting buildings surround the cobbled square, including the Old Town House and Metropolitan Methodist Church. Today a flea market is held here from Monday to Saturday from 07h30 to 15h30.

The Old Town House on the square (Tel. 24-6367) dates from 1755. It originally housed the town guard and later became the town hall. The Cape Town Coat of Arms was added in 1804. Today it houses the Michaelis Collection of seventeenth century Dutch and Flemish paintings. It is open on weekdays and Sundays from 10h00 to 17h30 and on Saturdays from 10h00 to 13h00.

St. Stephen's Church was built in 1800 as a theatre for the British garrison stationed at the Cape. In the 1830s it was converted into a school for free slave children and used as a Sunday school on Sundays. In 1857 it was incorporated into the Dutch Reformed Church and is the only Dutch Reformed Church in South Africa bearing the name of a saint.

The Malay Quarter is bordered by Wale, Waterkant, Rose and Chiappini Streets. In it are fine examples of early nineteenth century architecture. Inhabitants are descendants of Malays brought to the Cape as slaves and political refugees during the Dutch occupation.

Buildings of particular interest are: **The Bokaap Museum** (Tel. 24-3846; 71 Wale Street) furnished in the style of the nineteenth century and portrays the lifestyle of a typical Malay family. It is open from Tuesday to Thursday from 10h00 to 16h30 and on Saturday, Sunday and public holidays from 10h00 to 16h30. **Majid Korhaanol Islam** (Longmarket Street) is a Mosque that has remained unchanged since its construction in 1886. Visit this area in groups rather than on your own.

Strand Street was one of the first thoroughfares of Cape Town. It then ran along the beach front of Cape Town. During the seventeenth and eighteenth centuries, most well-to-do merchants had their houses along this street. The following are still standing today:

Sextant House, on the corner, now houses the Netherlands Legation. It was completed in 1783. **The Lutheran Church** was built in the guise of a warehouse in 1774 by Martin Melck as the Dutch East India Company tolerated only the Dutch Reformed Church up to 1779. Two main features of the church are the elaborate pulpit, carved by Anton Anreith, and the clock tower added on in 1818. **Martin Melck House** was built in 1781, as the parsonage, soon after Melck's death, and was named in his honour in 1932. The carved door, fanlight and plaster pediment are all works by Anreith. The house is now a shop. **Koopmans de Wet House** further down on the opposite side of the road, was built in 1701 and is the oldest house still standing in the street. The two hundred year old grape vine in the courtyard still bears fruit. A second storey was added on in the latter part of the eighteenth century. The house contains a fine collection of Dutch colonial furniture and antiques. Open Monday to Saturday 10h00 to 16h45.

Table Mountain by public transport

To reach the cable station from town, take the **Kloof Nek Bus** which leaves from the front of the OK Bazaars in Adderley Street. At the Kloof Nek terminus, change to the cable station bus which will take you to the lower cable station. (See map on page 72)

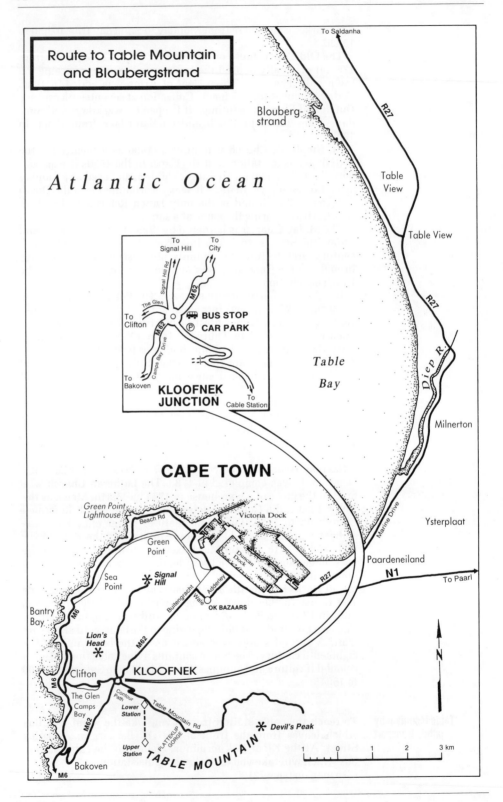

Route to Table Mountain and Bloubergstrand

CITY VIEWS AND THE HARBOUR (90 km)

Take the Buitengracht, New Church, Kloof Nek road towards the mountain. At the Kloof Nek traffic circle take the first exit left (Tafelberg Road), signposted to the Cable Station. Just over 1,5 km from the turn-off is the cable station.

Table Mountain offers one of the grand views that should not be missed by any visitor to Cape Town. The summit can be reached by various footpaths as well as by cableway (Tel. 24-5148). The cableway lifts passengers to the summit in five minutes (1067 m above sea level) from there one has a majestic view of the Cape Peninsula and Western Cape. There is also a restaurant and a souvenir shop on the mountain. The mountain is covered with a wide variety of wild flowers. Weather permitting, the cable car operates daily between 08h30 and 22h30 from December to April, and 08h30 to 18h00 between May and November.

From the lower cableway station the road takes you to a turning point 5 km further on. There are magnificent views of the city and Table Bay along the way. At Platteklip Gorge, 3 km from the Kloof Nek turnoff, one of the easiest hiking routes up Table Mountain, via The Saddle between Table Mountain and Devil's Peak can be found. (Remember to take water, something to eat and warm clothing with you if you plan to walk up the mountain, as the mist can come over very quickly.) The walk takes approximately three hours. (See also page 79 for mountain climbing.)

Another very pleasant walk can be taken on the contour path, beginning at the cableway station turn-off at Kloof Nek traffic island. The walk along the Twelve Apostles provides a superb view over Camps Bay.

The **Signal Hill** turn is the fourth exit from Kloof Nek Road at the traffic circle into Signal Hill Road. It is part of the "Lion's Rump" and "Lion's Head" can be seen on the left as you drive along. Signal Hill used to be a signal post between the city and ships in the Bay. At noon each day, except on Sundays, a shot is fired by the signal gun: most Capetonians still set their watches by it. Excellent views over greater Cape Town, the harbour and Sea Point are to be had from various vantage points along the way, especially at night when the city lights can be seen. One of the six **Kramats**, which make up the "sacred circle" of Cape Town can be found on Signal Hill. The Muslims who live within the circle believe it protects them from natural disasters. Signal Hill is also a popular launching site for hang-gliders.

The Glen turn off is the one before Signal Hill at the Kloof Nek circle. This picturesque descent to Clifton winds through a pine forest. Half-way along the road is the **Round House** turn-off. It was once used by Lord Charles Somerset, one of the Cape governors, as a shooting lodge, before it became a hotel in the nineteenth century. Today, it is the premises of a fine restaurant, which boasts a panoramic view of Camps Bay.

From here, continue down The Glen and at the bottom turn left into Lower Kloof Road. At the end, turn right into Victoria Road (M6), which is the main road running along the impressive coastline through **Clifton,** with its seaside cottages balancing on the cliffs and golden beaches far below.

To reach the beach, turn left at the fourth beach signpost which brings you within two minutes' walk from the beach. Just before the road reaches Sea Point, it turns left into Sea Cliff

Road. Go down the steep hill and then turn right into Beach Road, which runs along the coast.

Sea Point beachfront promenade, which is 3 km long, is used extensively by flat dwellers of this densely populated suburb for their recreational needs. Main Road, running parallel to Beach Road, is noted for its variety of restaurants. At Three Anchor Bay, Beach Road veers left at the traffic lights and passes the **Green Point Lighthouse**, which is the oldest lighthouse in South Africa and was built in 1824. On misty days, its foghorn can be heard throughout the area. Beach Road comes to an end at Portwood Road, with the **Somerset Hospital** on the right at the intersection. The hospital was built in 1862, and was used as the first hospital for training doctors in South Africa. Turn left to enter the docks through the west gates.

Once inside the **Docks** turn right along East Pier and follow the road to see the following sights:

The Penny Ferry, costing more than a penny these days, takes passengers from the Harbour Café to the Clock Tower, Monday to Friday (Tel. 218-2812).

The Harbour Café overlooks Victoria Basin, the oldest part of the harbour, which is now a tug and fishing fleet harbour. (See restaurants on page 62.) Permits are required for cars entering the docks on a Sunday.

The Fish Market at Victoria Dock is open every Monday to Friday. Boats return usually around noon and the best time to visit is between 12h00 and 14h30.

Close by is the **Clock Tower** which was built in 1883, the oldest building in the docks. It houses a small museum (open on Saturday afternoons) with a collection of photos and ship souvenirs from the past.

Leave the docks from the gates closest to Victoria Basin and take the N1 motorway towards Paarl. From here, take exit no. 2 (Paarden Eiland, Milnerton) onto Marine Drive (R27) and continue for about 12 km until you reach the **Blouberg** signpost (R303). Turn left. From this seaside road there are spectacular views of Table Mountain. The seaside village of Bloubergstrand is situated on the site of the battle between the Batavian Republic, allied to France, and British troops in 1806, at the start of the second occupation of the Cape by Great Britain. Drive to the end of the road past various villages to a T-junction where the road meets the R27 again and then turn right back to Cape Town.

SHORT TRIPS FROM CAPE TOWN

A number of breath-taking sights are within an easy day's drive from Cape Town. These include the awe-inspiring Table Mountain, Cape Point where many believe that the Indian and Atlantic oceans meet, gracious Cape Dutch homesteads, simple mosques, peaceful fishing villages, golden beaches and fertile winelands. For those who would rather just sit back and enjoy the scenery, there are a variety of guided half- and full-day tours of many of the sights mentioned below (see page 67 for tour companies).

Cape Point
Total distance:
170 km

The drive around Cape Point rates as one of the scenic wonders of the world. The contrasts of modern buildings and Cape Dutch architecture, seaside villages and dramatic seascapes all blend to give an overall image of constant change and beauty. There

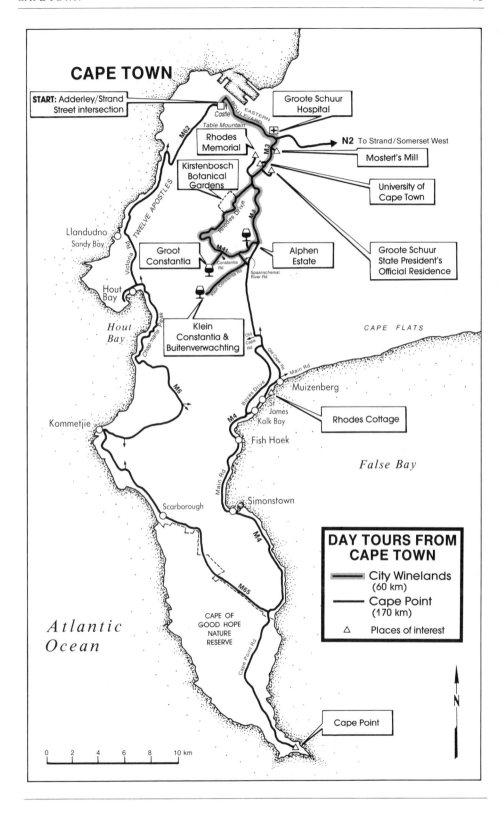

CAPE TOWN

START: Adderley/Strand Street intersection

Castle

Table Mountain

Groote Schuur Hospital

Rhodes Memorial

N2 To Strand/Somerset West

Mostert's Mill

Kirstenbosch Botanical Gardens

University of Cape Town

Llandudno

Sandy Bay

TWELVE APOSTLES

Victoria Rd

Rhodes Drive

Groot Constantia

Constantia Rd

Alphen Estate

Groote Schuur State President's Official Residence

Spaanschemat River Rd

Klein Constantia Rd

Hout Bay

Hout Bay

Chapman's Peak

Klein Constantia & Buitenverwachting

Old Cape Rd

CAPE FLATS

Old Cape Rd

Main Rd

Muizenberg

M6

Boyes Drive

St James

Kalk Bay

M4

Rhodes Cottage

Kommetjie

Fish Hoek

False Bay

Main Rd

Scarborough

Simonstown

M4

DAY TOURS FROM CAPE TOWN

━━━ City Winelands (60 km)

━━━ Cape Point (170 km)

△ Places of interest

M65

CAPE OF GOOD HOPE NATURE RESERVE

Cape Point Rd

Atlantic Ocean

Cape Point

N

0 2 4 6 8 10 km

are many ways of travelling around the Peninsula, but I find the most pleasing, photographically, along the route outlined below.

Using the Strand/Adderley Street intersection as a starting point, turn into Strand Street to travel in an easterly direction past the Castle. Just after the Castle take the left fork onto the N2 (Muizenberg/ Airport).

Groote Schuur Hospital on the left, is the first point of interest you will pass. It became internationally famous when Prof. Chris Barnard performed the first heart transplant operation here in 1967. Opened in 1938, the hospital is used by the University of Cape Town's medical school as a teaching hospital.

As you pass the hospital, stay in the right-hand lane (Muizenberg M3). Just after the fork, **Mostert's Mill** can be seen on the left. The mill was built in 1796 as a wind-operated grain mill and stall. In 1936 the Dutch Government helped restore it to working order. It is the only one in the Cape and is open daily between 09h00 and 17h00.

The University of Cape Town (UCT) follows, on the right hand side, on the slopes of Devil's Peak. UCT has 10 faculties and over 12 000 students. It was started in 1829 by the churches and citizens of Cape Town, and housed in premises in the city. In 1887 the first women students were admitted. In 1918 UCT gained University status, and in 1928 the faculties began moving to the present campus.

The western entrance to **Groote Schuur** (on the left), the official residence of the State President, and before independence, the Governor-Generals' residence, is passed next.

Take the following off-ramp **(Zoo/Rhodes Memorial),** turn right towards Rhodes Memorial and then keep left. After driving under the bridge, and after a pretty drive through parkland with occasional glimpses of fallow-deer, the parking area to Rhodes Memorial is reached. The memorial was built of Table Mountain granite as a tribute to Cecil John Rhodes, and portrays physical energy. It provides a fine view over the Cape Flats.

Return to the M3 highway and follow the signposts to Muizenberg. Turn left at the end of the highway, and then right (following the Muizenberg signposts) into Main Road. From here there is a choice of two routes to Kalk Bay:

- Via Boyes Drive, which offers the driver fine views of the False Bay shoreline from its elevated position on the mountainside. To reach this route, turn to the right (Kalk Bay via Boyes Drive) off Main Road, just after joining it from the highway.
- Via Main Road, which passes through the picturesque coastal villages. **Muizenberg**, with its long safe bathing beaches, became South Africa's premier bathing beach in the early 1900s and is still popular today. Just outside Muizenberg along Main Road towards St. James is **Rhodes' Cottage,** where Cecil Rhodes died in 1902. Today it houses his possessions and photographs of the era. (Open Tuesday to Sunday 10h00 to 13h00 and 14h00 to 17h00.) **St. James** is a charming seaside village with a sheltered beach and tidal pool and a distinctive row of Victorian bathing boxes. It was named afer the first church built here in 1874. A ceramic tile depicting the church can be seen on the post office wall.

Kalk Bay (where both routes meet again) has a busy fishing harbour and is the home of the False Bay fishing fleet. Fresh fish is sold at the harbour when the fleet returns, usually in the early afternoon.

Fish Hoek is known as the "dry town" of the Peninsula as no alcohol outlets are allowed to be established within the municipal limits. In the early days the Dutch East India Company had a fishing station here. In 1927 the remains of a Pleistocene or Holocene human, who lived about 15 000 years ago, were found in caves behind the town. (Follow signs to Simonstown/Cape Point.)

Simonstown is the headquarters of the South African Navy, and was developed by the British from 1814 as the base for the South Atlantic fleet, until 1957. The main street is known as Historical Mile, and contains 21 buildings which are all more than 150 years old. (Please note that this whole town is classified as a defence installation and therefore no photographs may be taken.) **Admiralty House,** on the left as you enter Simonstown, was built in 1740 in the Cape Dutch style. It is now the residence of the Chief of the South African Navy. **Martello Tower** on the left at the naval dockyard, is one of the oldest surviving British Corsican-pattern defence towers in the world. It now houses the South African Naval Museum. Open weekdays 10h00 to 16h00.

From Simonstown the road winds along the coastline towards Cape Point. Follow the Cape Point signs.

The Cape of Good Hope Nature Reserve, started in 1936, is a flora and fauna reserve for the protection of the indigenous species, including protea and heather, of the Peninsula. The 7 700-ha reserve has more plant varieties than the whole of Great Britain. For those with time on their hands, it is well worth taking a drive around the reserve. At the tip of the reserve is Cape Point, which can be reached by the principal road. Visitors can walk or take a bus from the parking area, up the steep slopes to the look-out point, with its breath-taking panoramas of False Bay and the mountains beyond. Down below, the Atlantic crashes onto the rocks, but is not the point where two oceans meet. To the west of Cape Point is the Cape of Good Hope. Halfway between the entrance to the reserve and Cape Point is a delightful little restaurant where reasonably priced teas and mouth-watering seafood lunches can be enjoyed. The reserve is open from 06h00 in summer and 08h00 in winter, to sunset.

Return to the main road from the reserve, turn left to Scarborough (M65), and drive on to Kommetjie through a few small holiday resorts.

Kommetjie is a picturesque seaside village. From here, follow the signposts to Cape Town via Chapman's Peak (M6).

Chapman's Peak is one of the world's most spectacular scenic drives, cutting into the cliffs high above the pounding surf. It was built between 1915 and 1922. Numerous look-out points are dotted along the way.

After about 10 km, the road begins to wind downwards towards **Hout Bay**, the centre of a large fishing industry and the headquarters of the crayfish fleet. It gets its name from the Dutch word "hout" meaning wood, as it was once heavily wooded. The harbour is very picturesque and definitely worth a visit. To get there, follow the "Harbour/Boat trips" signs. Boat trips to view the seal and bird life at Duiker Island (approximately one hour) and sunset cruises (approx. two hours) from Hout Bay to

Cape Town harbour run from the harbour. For departure time call (021) 790-1040 or 51-4336. World of Birds Sanctuary in Hout Bay has 5 000 indigenous and exotic birds. It is situated in Valley Road and is clearly signposted. Open daily from 09h00 to 18h00.

From Hout Bay take the road towards **Llandudno**, a seaside village at the foot of Little Lion's Head. From the main road, after the Llandudno turn off, a fine view of the village is to be had. The beach offers pleasant bathing. The tanker Romelia was stranded off the rocks in 1977, and its remains can still be seen. A twenty-minute walk south from the parking area below leads to **Sandy Bay**, the unofficial — and controversial — nude beach of Cape Town.

After Llandudno, the road leads on to the city, first via a marine drive along the coast, past the Twelve Apostles towering above and then through the suburbs.

Simonstown by train

There is a regular commuter service between the city centre and Simonstown. The train leaves from the central station in Cape Town and stops at a number of seaside villages on its way to Simonstown, where the service terminates. The line hugs the shoreline between Muizenberg and Simonstown, giving a splendid view of False Bay. It is also an easy way to get from the city to the beaches by public transport.

Cape Town Wine Route and Kirstenbosch
Total distance: 60 km
See map on page 75

Before Cape Town expanded into the major city it is today, many fine wine farms were situated in the beautiful valleys of the Peninsula. Today a few of these estates in the Constantia Valley are still producing superb wines.

From the city centre, follow the Eastern Boulevard (extention of Strand Street towards Muizenberg, the N2 and then M3). Take the Constantia turn-off (M41) and follow the hotel sign to the Alphen Hotel.

The **Alphen Estate** was once noted for its burgundy and claret. The land was first granted to Theunis van Schalkwyk in 1714. The farm was owned by a succession of people until it was bought in 1854 by Dirk Cloete. Today his descendants still own the property. Owing to urban development, vineyards gave way to houses. But the owners purchased land near Stellenbosch and turned the Alphen homestead into a fine hotel. Alphen wines (grown near Stellenbosch) are still produced and products are on sale at the hotel cellars.

From Alphen, drive along the M41 to the Ladies Mile turn-off and turn left. From there, turn right into Spaanschemat River Road and then bear right into Klein Constantia Road. This will bring you to Buitenverwachting.

Buitenverwachting (Tel. 74-1190) was sold to Cornelis Brink in 1793. The original buildings date from 1769 when the farm was still part of Klein Constantia. Today the whole estate has been beautifully renovated, and vineyards re-established. The first new wines were made in 1985. Wine-tasting is done here in the special wine-tasting room. The estate also has a superb restaurant (see page 62).

Klein Constantia, with a total of 85 ha of vineyards, is another of the fine old estates in the area that has been given a new lease of life.

Return to the Klein Constantia Road, turn left into Spaanschemat River Road, and left into Ladies Mile Road, and left again into Constantia Road. One kilometre further on, turn left into the road signposted "Groot Constantia".

Groot Constantia (Tel. 74-1128) is the centre of the original Constantia estate, given to Simon van der Stel in 1685 by the Dutch East India Company. The farm became famous for its sweet wines then in fashion in both Europe and England. In 1778 Hendrick Cloete bought the property and continued the tradition of fine wine-making. He also built a beautiful homestead. The sculptor Anton Anreith sculpted the pediment of the wine cellar which is regarded as one of the greatest works of art in South Africa. In 1885 the buildings were bought by the government. The homestead was destroyed by fire forty years later but fortunately it was faithfully restored to its original glory. Today the complex houses a museum, a restaurant (serving tasty, light lunches at reasonable prices), and a wine cellar, which still produces wonderful wines. The complex is open daily from 10h00 to 16h00.

Return to Constantia Road and turn left up to Constantia Nek. At the circle, take the second exit into Rhodes Drive and follow the Kirstenbosch sign.

Kirstenbosch Botanical Gardens have been the headquarters of the South African Botanical Gardens since 1913. They started off as the Dutch East India Company gardens, but were sold in 1811. In 1895 Cecil Rhodes bought them and bequeathed them to the nation. They cover 560 ha with four hundred indigenous Cape Peninsula species and are among the major botanical gardens in the world. The gardens are open daily from 08h00 to 18h00.

From here follow the city sign posts back to the city centre.

See page 82 for a tour of the Paarl/Stellenbosch Wine Routes.

Outdoor Activities

Cape Town is the perfect location for all outdoor activities.

Surf and rockfishing is good all along the Peninsula and a variety of fish can be caught. A particularly good place is off the rocks near Cape Point, where game fish are often caught.

Game fishing is also very popular, and a number of boats can be chartered to catch tuna, mainly in October, and snoek during autumn and winter. For further information telephone 64-2203, 94-1114, 83-1020 or 70-9177.

Freshwater trout fishing, Tel. (021) 903-2727, can be enjoyed at Rainbow Fish Farm in Stellenbosch.

Eight **golf** courses in Cape Town welcome visitors:
— *Clovelly Fish Hoek Club*   Tel. 82-1118
— *King David Club*   Tel. 934-0365
— *Metropolitan Club*   Tel. 44-7808
— *Mowbray Club*   Tel. 69-4176
— *Royal Cape Club*   Tel. 71-6551
— *Simonstown Club*   Tel. 86-1233
— *Milnerton Club*   Tel. 52-1047

Cape Town has no shortage of slopes for **hang-gliding**. (See Aeroclub p. 281.)

Table mountain is ideal for **hiking** and **mountaineering**. The

following groups specialise in **hiking tours** around the peninsula and further afield.
— *Bain's Kloof Wilderness Promotions,*   Tel. 53-8860 — 22 Stellenberg Road, Pinelands, 7405
— *Roaming Tours,*   Tel. 71-7489 — P.O. Box 295, Constantia, 7848
— *Wanderlust,*   Tel. 65-4380 — P.O. Box 154, Rondebosch, 7700
For climbing information contact the Mountain Club at Tel. 45-3412.

There are few things more exciting than **horse-riding** along the beach, with nobody else in sight. There are many stables dotted around the Cape Peninsula where horses can be hired for an hour or half a day.

Skin-diving is a very popular sport in this area with its extensive coastline. Equipment can be hired through *Underwaterworld*, Tel. 46-8290 — 12 Caledon Street, Cape Town

In addition to the numerous beaches, Cape Town's inland waterways make it a paradise for **wind-surfing**. (Phone 88-4697 to hire sailboards.)

Annual Events

Jan., 1 and 2:   The Minstrel Carnival is a colourful event when minstrels, dressed in brilliant costumes, compete at Hartleyvale in Observatory and the Goodwood Showgrounds.
Jan., 1st week: Fishhoek Mardi Gras.
Metropolitan Handicap, at Kenilworth race course, Cape Town's most important race meeting.
Jan., 3rd week: Shakespeare Festival at Maynardville open air theatre.
Easter Saturday: Two Oceans Marathon around the Peninsula.
April: Ballet season at Maynardville open air theatre; power boat race from Simonstown to Gordon's Bay and back.
Mid-July: Canoe marathon on the Berg River, starting from Paarl.
September: Cape Town Festival is a programme of fun for everyone: firework displays, special events in culture and art, and open air carnivals; spring Wild Flower Show at Kirstenbosch gardens.
October: Sea Harvest Festival at Hout Bay.
December: Rothman's Sailing week in Table Bay.

Shopping

The normal trading hours in Cape Town are between 09h00 and 17h00 on weekdays and from 09h00 to 12h30 on Saturdays. The most valuable item is without a doubt the excellent wine grown in the area. Most of the wine farms have a special arrangement to ship cases of wine back home for you at a nominal charge (see farms on page 85, 86 & 88).

For other shopping the following shops can be found in Cape Town:

ART, ANTIQUES, TAPESTRY   **Atlantic Art Gallery**   Tel. 23-5775 — 71 Burg Street: Oils, graphics and watercolours by South African artists
Cape Gallery African Crafts   Tel. 21-7881 — 108 Long Street:

Antique silver, porcelain, paintings and other collectors' items
Cape Gallery   Tel. 23-5309 — 60 Church Street: Paintings and watercolours by South African artists
Cape Tapestry Weavers   Tel. 24-7878 — 63 Loop Street: Original woven art
Master Weavers   Tel. 419-1663 — 6 Strand Concourse: Hand-woven rugs and mohair tapestries
Myra's Antique Jewellery   Tel. 23-6561 — 78 Church Street: Antique jewellery
Peter Visser Antiques   Tel. 23-7870 — 117 Long Street: General antiques, African rugs and prints

CLOTHING   **Grigsby's**   Tel. 23-1634 — Guarantee House, 37 Berg Street: Men's evening dress hire service
Hetha   Tel. 49-2524 — Designer T-shirts and casual wear
Louis et cie (Pty) Ltd.   Tel. 23-4354 — 566 Union Castle Building, St. Georges Street: Ladies' designer clothes
Over the Top Clothing   Tel. 24-0810 — New Zealand House, Berg Street: Avant-garde unisex designer clothing
Woolworths   Tel. 23-4200 — Adderley Street: The Marks and Spencers of South Africa specialising in quality family clothing

JEWELLERY, CURIOS, GIFTS   **Afrogem**   Tel. 24-8048 — Mercantile Centre, 198 Bree Street: Semi-precious jewellery and stone carvings
Diamond Factory Sales   Tel. 24-3818 — St. Georges Street: Diamonds, gold and silver jewellery
Kwazulu Curios (Pty) Ltd.   Tel. 24-3775 — Castle Street, Mall: African carving and South African jewellery
Golden Cape Gifts (Pty) Ltd.   Tel. 25-2290 — 1703 Golden Acre: Typical South African gifts

PHOTOGRAPHIC PROCESSING   **Procolor**   Tel. 21-2242 — 33 Bree Street

Tour of Western Cape Winelands

THE BERG RIVER VALLEY
Total distance: 190 km

Although the first vines were planted close to Cape Town, the potential of the fertile Berg River Valley was quickly realised. Today this historic valley with its old gabled homesteads is the headquarters of the South African wine industry, and produces 900 million litres of wine annually. Apart from cellar tours and wine-tasting, many of the estates have superb restaurants offering traditional meals. From Cape Town take the N1 highway to Paarl. Take exit 17 (marked Franschhoek/Paarl) and then turn left into Paarl. (See map on page 83.)

PAARL

The name is derived from the three enormous granite domes behind the town that glisten like pearls when wet. The first farmers settled there in 1687 and the town was established in 1690 as a major wagon-building centre. Today Paarl is an important town in the Western Cape. It is surrounded by vineyards and has many well-preserved buildings of different styles and beautiful oak-lined avenues. Paarl is also considered the headquarters of the Afrikaans language, because it was here that the first Afrikaans newspaper was published and the Bible was translated into Afrikaans.

Accommodation

HOTELS AND COUNTRY HOUSES

Mountain Shadows   Tel. (02211) 62-3192
It is 7 km north of Paarl, just off the N1. (P.O. Box 2501, Paarl, 7620)   Portfolio of Country Places
Swimming-pool, tennis, bowling, golf, horse-riding and hiking
This charming Cape Dutch homestead nestles in the vineyards of the Drakenstein Valley and recalls the graciousness of bygone days. The owners take pride in their old fashioned hospitality which offers excellent food and noble wines. They also offer the guests a number of interesting outings.
Picardie Hotel   *TYYY Tel. (02211) 2-3118/9
158 Main Street, Paarl, 7620 (P.O. Box 167)
Swimming-pool
Offers comfortable accommodation at medium prices.
Huguenot Station Hotel   *TYYY Tel. (02211) 2-2490/303
3 Keerom Street, Huguenot, 7621
Very clean hotel close to the station. Bar lunches are good here.

SELF-CATERING AND CAMPING

Campers Paradise Holiday Resort   Tel. (02211) 63-1650
Two kilometres from Paarl station on the Simondium/Franschhoek Road (P.O. Box 552, Suider-Paarl, 7624)

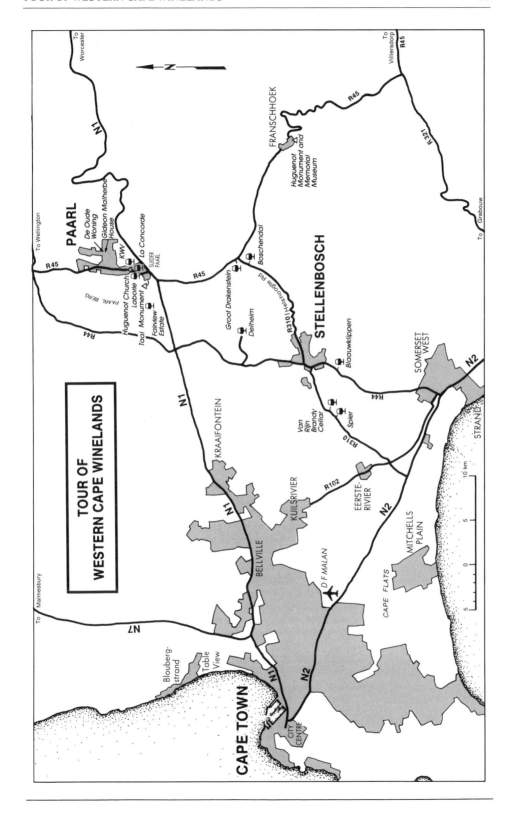

Laundry, gas, shop, recreation hall, swimming-pool, golf, horse-riding

Situated in pleasant surroundings outside Paarl, the resort offers cottages, camping and caravan sites.

Wateruintjiesvlei Municipal Camping Site
Tel. (02211) 63-1250

One kilometre from the N1 on the R303 Wemmershoek/Fransch-hoek road (P.O. Box 12, Paarl, 7620)

Electric plug, laundry, gas, shop, recreation hall, bowls and golf

The park is situated close to the Berg River.

Restaurants

Laborie Wine House   Tel. 63-2034   Wine only
Taillefer Street, Suider-Paarl   Cape traditional

The Wine House is one of four which belong to KWV. All feature period architecture and furnishings, as well as traditional food and wines of the region.

Schoongezicht   Tel. 62-3137   No licence
On the Wellington Road, 7 km from Paarl (Schoongezicht Farm, Dal Josaphat)   Cape traditional

The restaurant is the converted farmhouse of the original water-blommetjie farm established in 1694. It has a tranquil atmosphere. Apart from the excellent traditional dishes, teas are served in the mornings and afternoons.

Tourist information

Paarl area telephone code: **02211**

Paarl Valley Publicity Association   Tel. 2-4842
216 Main Street, Paarl, 7646

Sightseeing

As you come off the highway turn into Main Street. As you drive along, the following can be seen:

Laborie Homestead and Wine Cellar, Tel. 63-2034, off to the left as you enter the town (see restaurants). Visits to the Homestead can be arranged by phoning the above number.

La Concorde, Tel. 63-1001, on the right is the headquarters of KWV, the Co-operative Wine-Growers Association. Cellar tours take place every weekday (excluding public holidays) at 09h30, 11h00, 14h15, 15h45. To reach the cellars in Kohler Street, drive past La Concorde and turn right at the next road. Follow the signs from there.

The **Strooidak** or **Huguenot Church** was consecrated in 1805, and is the oldest church building in South Africa still used as a church. The pulpit is from a church which had been built on the same site in 1771. Keys to the church can be obtained from the church office in Klein-Reservoir Street.

De Oude Woning is a restored typical H-shaped house on Main Street and is furnished exactly as it was in 1825.

Afrikaans Language Museum, Tel. 2-3441, is housed in **Gideon Malherbe House** in Pastorie Avenue, which runs off to the right, parallel to Main Road. It is the house in which the Society of True Afrikaners was founded on 17 August 1875 by Gideon Malherbe. Open weekdays 09h00 to 13h00 and 14h00 to 17h00.

From here return to Main Street and drive back towards the highway, but do not rejoin the highway. Continue under the highway and turn right up to the **Taal or Language Monument.** (Pay careful attention to signposting as the signposts are not very clear.)

The monument was inaugurated in 1975 and formed part of the celebration of Language Year in 1976. It is located on the top of the Paarl rocks and therefore visible from far away. It symbolises the culture and languages of the West, Africa and of the Malays, all of whom had an influence on the birth and development of the Afrikaans language.

From the monument, return to the Main Road and turn right, following the road until you get to the Suid-Agter-Paarl road. Turn right into it. Just 2,3 km further, on the right, is the entrance to Fairview Estate.

Fairview Estate (Tel. 2-2367) is known for its award-winning wines and goats' milk cheese. What makes the estate unique is the opportunity to taste a variety of superb cheese at the same time as the wine. Both cheese and wine can be bought on the estate. Open Monday to Friday 08h30 to 12h30 and 13h30 to 18h00, Saturday 08h30 to 13h00. The goats are milked at 16h00.

From here there is a choice of two routes to **Stellenbosch:** Direct (35 km), which includes a visit to Delheim, or via Franschhoek.

To take the direct route, turn right out of the estate and then left, 4 km further on, turn into the R44 towards Stellenbosch, and follow the road. The Delheim turnoff is marked (WR3).

Delheim (Tel. 02232-394 or 424) is situated on the slopes of Simonsberg, and is one of the most beautifully situated farms in the area. Apart from the superb wines, including the famous Delheim Edelspatz (a noble late harvest in the noblest tradition), the estate offers superb brunches, either in the garden or in the cellars, between October and April from Monday to Friday from 11h00 to 14h00 and on Saturdays from 10h30 to 12h00; wine-tasting on Mondays to Fridays from 08h30 to 17h00 and Saturdays from 08h30 to 12h00; closed on Sundays and public holidays. From the estate, return to the main road and turn left towards Stellenbosch.

To take the route **via Franschhoek** (56 km), return to the Suid-Agter-Paarl turn-off and turn left, back towards Paarl, and then immediately right into the R45 towards Franschhoek. Follow the road for 15 km.

FRANSCHHOEK

The town was originally known as *Le Quartier Français* as over 200 French Huguenot refugees settled here between 1688 and 1690. Many had been wine-makers, and continued to apply their skills here. As you drive towards the town, you will notice that many of the farms still bear French names.

Accommodation

HOTELS **Protea Farm Excelsior**   **TYYY Tel. (02212) 2071/2
3 km out of town.
(P.O. Box 54, Franschhoek, 7690)   Protea Hotels and Inns

Snooker, sauna, jacuzzi, gym, tennis, squash, bowls, swimming-pool and hiking

The Swiss-looking hotel is superbly situated in the mountains just outside Franschhoek and has an elusive atmosphere. This is a wonderful place if you want to relax for a few days.

Restaurants

La Quartier Francais   Tel. (02212) 2248   Wine only
18 Main Road, Franschhoek   French
Food is typically French with a Cape touch.

The Huguenot Monument and Memorial Museum are situated in town at the foot of the Franschhoek Pass and are worth a visit. The museum covers the history of the Huguenots and is open from Monday to Saturday between 09h00 and 17h00.

Return toward Paarl on the R45, but at Groot Drakenstein, about 15 km from Franschhoek, turn left towards Stellenbosch along the Helshoogte Road (R310). You will pass the Boschendal Wine Estate on the left, about 1 km up the road.

The **Boschendal** farm (Tel. 02211-41034) dates back to 1865 and has a magnificent H-shaped homestead and extensive out-buildings on the property, which is open to visitors. The buildings include the "Taphuis", where wines can be tasted, the "Waen-huis", which is a quaint gift shop specialising in home-made items, and a superb restaurant (Tel. 02211-41252). The estate wines are also very well known, and for good reason. The gracious restaurant serves typical Cape cuisine, with a strong French influence. Between December and March, picnic lunches may be bought at the estate and enjoyed in the spacious grounds. The wine cellar is open between 08h00 and 17h00 during the week and between 08h30 and 12h30 on Saturday.

From Boschendal, continue up the pass, through the Rhodes Fruit Farms, which formed the nucleus of the deciduous fruit industry back in 1890, and are still one of the main suppliers of "Cape" fruit throughout the world. The road winds its way over the pass and down into Stellenbosch.

STELLENBOSCH

It is the second oldest European town in South Africa. It was established in 1685 and named after Simon van der Stel, then the Governor of the Cape. The town is renowned for its gracious Cape-Dutch buildings and oak trees, the first of which were planted by Van der Stel.

Accommodation

HOTELS AND GUEST HOUSES

D'Ouwe Werf
Tel. (02231) 7-4608   Portfolio of Country Places
30 Church Street, Stellenbosch
This is the oldest guest house in South Africa (built in 1803) and still offers the gentle traditions and hospitality of the past. D'Ouwe Werf is situated in the heart of Stellenbosch, within walking distance of all the main tourist attractions. Rooms are

graciously furnished and all the modern necessities are supplied. The coffee shop sells light lunches and teas.

Lanzerac Hotel   ***TYY   Tel. (02231) 7-1132
Jonkershoek Road (P.O. Box 4, Stellenbosch, 7600)
Swimming-pool
The 150-year old homestead, a splendid Cape Dutch building situated in spacious grounds, is now a hotel. It lies on the outskirts of Stellenbosch off the Jonkershoek Road and is sign-posted by a "Hotel" sign. The hotel is especially famous for its lunches. The cheese lunch is the most popular: for a fixed fee you can help yourself to a buffet of a variety of cheeses and salads.

SELF-CATERING AND CAMPING

Bergplaas Holiday Ranch   Tel. (02231) 7-5719
Helshoogte Road, outside Stellenbosch (P.O. Box 2172, Stellenbosch, 7600)
Electric plugs, laundry, gas, shop, recreational hall, swimming-pool, tennis, bowling and golf
This holiday resort has both cottages and caravan sites. It is situated in a picturesque setting outside town.

Restaurants

De Kelder   Tel. 3797   Fully licensed
63 Dorp Street, Stellenbosch   Continental
Set under oaks off Dorp Street, this elegant restaurant was originally built as a wine cellar in 1791.

Die Volkskombuis   Tel. 7-5239   Wine and malt licence
Old Strand Road, Stellenbosch   Cape traditional
The building was originally a farm labourer's cottage, but was converted into a restaurant in 1977 without losing its simple charm. The restaurant was set up "to preserve the culinary arts and traditions of old Cape cooking". The service often leaves a lot to be desired.

Doornbosch   Tel. 7-5079   Wine licence
Old Strand Road, Stellenbosch   Continental
Old world atmosphere, and good service blend to give a relaxed atmosphere.

Tourist information
Stellenbosch area telephone code: **(02231)**

Stellenbosch Visitor's Bureau   Tel. (02231) 3584
30 Plain Street, Stellenbosch, 7600

Sightseeing

The Braak is the old village green, still an open space in the middle of town. It was once used for parades and festivals, and is surrounded by a number of interesting buildings.

St. Mary's-on-the-Braak is the only building on the green itself and dates back to 1852.

The V.O.C. Arsenal was built in 1777 to store the arms for the garrison stationed here. It now houses a small military museum, open from Monday to Friday from 09h00 to 13h00 and from 13h30 to 17h00.

Burger House, next to the arsenal, was built in 1797, and has been restored and furnished in period style. It is open on weekdays from 09h00 to 12h45 and from 14h00 to 17h00, and on Saturday from 10h00 to 13h00 and from 14h00 to 17h00.

Dorp Street is an oaklined street with quaint small whitewashed houses dating back to Stellenbosch's early days. Starting from the lower end one finds:

The Oude Meester Brandy Museum (on the corner of Old Srand Road), which gives an insight into the development of brandy in the Cape. It is open from Monday to Saturday from 09h30 to 12h45 and from 14h00 to 17h00, and on Sundays from 14h30 to 17h30.

Libertas Parva where Gen. Jan Smuts married his wife. Today this beautifully restored gabled homestead houses the Rembrandt van Rijn Art Gallery. Open as above.

"Oom Samie se Winkel", which was one of the first trading stores in Stellenbosch, has recently been restored to its original form.

Stellenbosch Village Museum, which is a complex of houses dating from 1709 to 1923. The houses have been restored and furnished in period style. The entrance is in 18 Ryneveld Street and it is open from Monday to Saturday from 10h00 to 17h00 and on Sundays and public holidays between 14h00 and 17h00.

Wine cellars in and close to Stellenbosch of special interest are:

Bergkelder, Tel. (02231) 7-2440, is located in the Papengaaiberg, just behind the station in Stellenbosch. The cellars are known for their beautifully carved vats. Tours are conducted on Mondays at 15h00, Tuesdays at 10h00 and 15h00 and Fridays at 10h00.

Blaauwklippen, Tel. (02231) 7-1245, is 4 km out of town on the R44 towards Somerset West/Strand. The magnificent H-shaped homestead was completed in 1789. Cheese is also made here, and vineyard tours by horse-drawn vehicles are conducted between November and March. There is also a restaurant on the farm where lunch can be enjoyed. Wine can be tasted from Monday to Friday from 08h45 to 12h45 and 14h00 to 17h00, and on Saturdays from 09h00 to 12h45.

Van Ryn Brandy Cellar, Tel. (02234) 478, is out of town near Vlottenberg, on the Cape Town/Kuilsrivier Road (R310). Coopers can be seen at work, and cellar tours are conducted from Monday to Thursday at 10h30 and 14h30, and on Fridays at 10h30.

Spier, Tel. (02234) 725, is further out of town also along the R310. The farm produces both superb red and white wines. The farm buildings have been tastefully restored and two superb restaurants are housed in the buildings:

– **Spier**, Tel. (02234) 242, is housed in the old slave quarters. Traditional Cape dishes are served in an elegant atmosphere.

– **Jonkershuis**, Tel. (02234) 512, is housed in the old bachelor quarters and has a more relaxed atmosphere. Cape traditional dishes are also served here.

From Spier, follow the R310 to the N2 highway, and then take the road back to Cape Town.

Cape Town to Oudtshoorn via the Coast
(699 km)
See map on page 90

The road hugs the south coast, passes through quaint fishing villages and holiday resorts and brings you to the southernmost tip of Africa, before turning inland towards Swellendam and the Bontebok National Park, which is one of the great successes in nature conservation; from Swellendam to Mossel Bay the road winds through wheat fields, touches the coast and then passes over the Outeniqua Mountains to Oudtshoorn.

From Cape Town, take the N2 motorway, past the airport towards Somerset West and Strand. Take the Strand (R44) turn-off and head for the coast.

STRAND

Strand has been a holiday resort for the up-country farmers since the mid-1800s and is still very popular because of its long stretches of safe bathing beaches. Only 45 km from Cape Town and close to Stellenbosch, Strand is a perfect location for those who wish to have a quiet beach holiday. There is a regular train service between Strand and Cape Town.

Accommodation

Metropole **TYYY Tel. (024) 3-1501
99 Beach Road (P.O. Box 21, Strand, 7140)
It is on the beach front and is close to the town centre. Rooms are clean and comfortable.
Andersons Strand Guest House Tel. (024) 3-7265/6
106 Beach Road, Strand, 7140   Club Caraville
Both rooms and flats are available. Residents may also use Sea Breeze facilities (page 92) close by. Delicious Cape food is served in a traditional atmosphere in the restaurant.
Blakes Guest House Tel. (024) 3-4755
45 Beach Road, Strand, 7140
It is across the road from the beach and all rooms are comfortably furnished and clean. Meals are available — good home-cooking predominates.
Voortrekker Park Tel. (024) 3-2316
Hofmeyer Street (P.O. Box 3, Strand, 7140)
Laundry, gas, shop, restaurant, tennis, bowls and golf.
The resort has both serviced cottages and caravan sites.

Restaurants

Somerset West, close by, has two outstanding restaurants.
Die Ou Pastorie Tel. 2-2120   Wine and malt
41 Lourens Street, Somerset West   Nouvelle cuisine
Few restaurants in South Africa measure up to the standards set by this charming restaurant — a must for those with a few

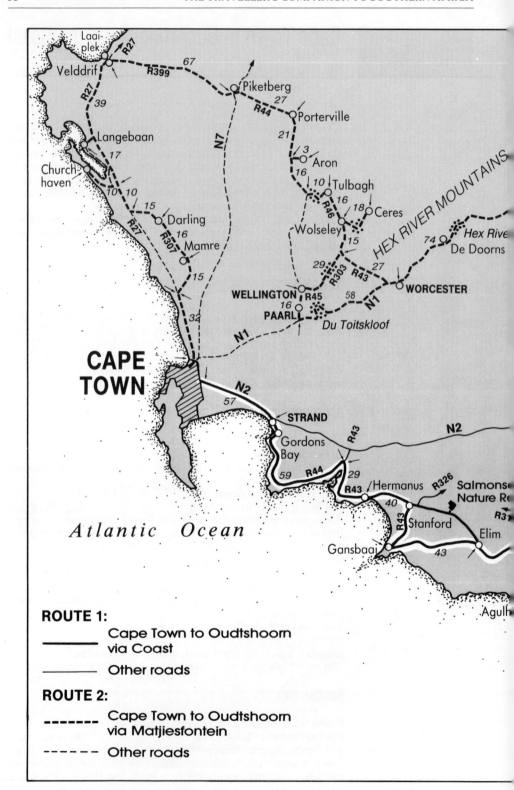

ROUTE 1:

———— Cape Town to Oudtshoorn
via Coast

———— Other roads

ROUTE 2:

‐‐‐‐‐‐ Cape Town to Oudtshoorn
via Matjiesfontein

‐ ‐ ‐ ‐ ‐ Other roads

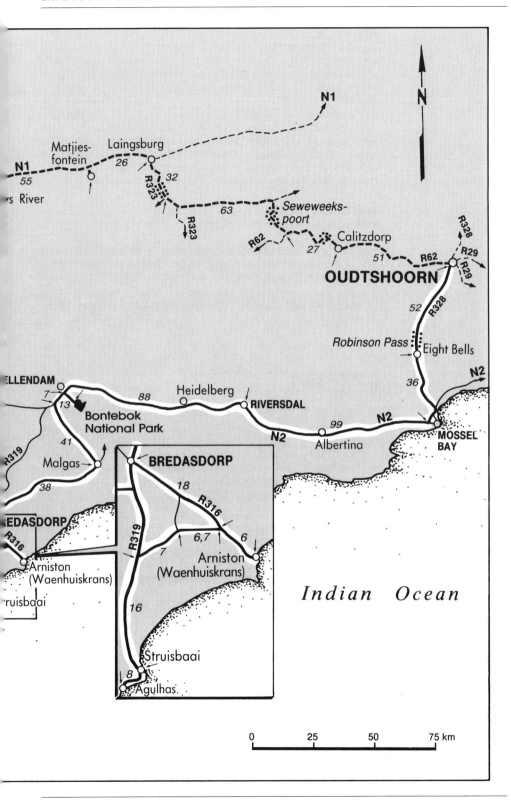

leisurely hours to enjoy a gourmet's delight. All cooking is personally supervised by the owners, who offer a small menu which changes periodically. They use only the freshest ingredients which complement each other to perfection. Although the atmosphere is relaxed, jacket and tie are required in the evenings.

Hobbits   Tel. 2-5810   Wine and malt
133 Irene Avenue, Somerset West   Continental
This restaurant, situated in the hills above the town, has a fine view over the bay and town. The food is wholesome, and a delicious dessert trolley complements the meals. The restaurant offers *table d'hôte* menus at reasonable prices during the week, a Sunday carvery, and dancing on Fridays and Saturdays.

Tourist Information
Strand area telephone code: **(024)**

Hottentots Holland Publicity Association   Tel. (024) 3-1333 ext. 215 — Municipal Building, Cnr Main Road and Fagan Street (P.O. Box 414, Strand, 7140)

From Strand, follow the R44 until you get to Gordon's Bay.

GORDON'S BAY

This quaint little town is a popular holiday and retirement resort. It was originally known as Fisch Hoek, but the name was changed at the end of the eighteenth century to Gordon's Bay in honour of the last Dutch East India Garrison Commander, Colonel Gordon. Safe bathing can be enjoyed along the beaches and a number of water-sport facilities are available.

Accommodation

Van Riebeeck Hotel   **TYYY   Tel. (024) 56-1441
Beach Road (P.O. Box 10, Gordon's Bay, 7150)
This hotel is rather pricey for this part of the world, but it is well situated and many rooms have views across False Bay. A dance band plays here on Saturday evenings.
Sleepy Shores Private Hotel   Tel. (024) 56-2041
83 Beach Road, Gordon's Bay, 7150
Tennis, bowls, golf and squash
It is situated across the road from the bathing area and has a verandah and lounge which have an unobstructed view of the coast and Table Mountain in the background. The rooms have handbasins but no bathrooms. Dinner is available.
Sea Breeze Holiday Resort   Tel. (024) 56-1400
Waterways Road, Gordon's Bay   Club Caraville
Electric plugs, laundry, gas, shop, recreation hall, restaurant, swimming-pool, tennis, bowls, golf, riding, fishing and wind-surfing
This well-run resort has caravan sites and self-catering chalets, which are fully equipped. It is one kilometre from the sea.

Restaurants

Neptune's Grill   Tel. 4-1511   Fully licenced
7 Bay Crescent, Gordon's Bay, 7150   Steak/seafood
The high standard of their steaks and the famous Neptune's
Platter (seafoods) are the two drawcards to this casual, but
enjoyable restaurant.

Outdoor Activities

Deep-sea fishing trips, which leave from the harbour, can be
organised. The beaches offer excellent opportunities for wind-
surfing and surf fishing, while the section of rocky coastline
offers perfect rock fishing and skin diving possibilities.

From Gordon's Bay follow the R44 along Clarence Drive. The
road winds along the east side of False Bay — offering a beautiful
view across the Cape Peninsula — and then further south towards Hermanus, passing a number of holiday resorts.
   Rooiels is a safe and attractive beach for leisurely sunbathing.
From here the tar road swings inland, but a dirt road can be
followed from Pringle Bay around Cape Hangklip.
   Cape Hangklip is the easterly cape of False Bay. In the past a
whaling station was situated here, but it has long gone and now
just a few holiday houses and a basic hotel remain.
   Betty's Bay is another retirement and holiday village. Stretch-
ing up the mountainside at Disa Kloof is the **Harold Porter
Botanic Garden**, which is renowned for its wild flowers, espe-
cially in mid-summer. It is open from sunrise to sunset.
   From Kleinmond, the road again swings inland past the Bot
River Marsh. At the end, take the Hermanus turn-off to the right
(R43).

HERMANUS

Hermanus is a popular resort with both holiday and retirement
folk because of its pleasant climate, safe beaches and good
fishing.

Accommodation

HOTELS   **Marine Hotel**   **TYYY   Tel. (02831) 2-1112
Main Road (P.O. Box 9, Hermanus, 7200)
Swimming-pool
The hotel is perched on top of the cliff, with a wonderful view of
the bay. It has recently had a face-lift and is now tastefully
furnished in old Cape Dutch furniture and fine prints, depicting
the past. The rooms are spacious and the food is a delight.
Astoria Hotel   **TYYY   Tel. (02831) 2-2039
Main Road (P.O. Box 1, Hermanus, 7200)
Swimming-pool
The hotel is centrally situated. Rooms are comfortable, service
good and friendly, and the food is above average. They also
serve superb bar lunches.

SELF-CATERING **Club Riviera**   Tel. (02831) 2-3272
AND CAMPING   11th Street, Voëlklip, 7203
This self-catering hotel is situated on the beach, 5 km from the town centre. All two- and three-roomed units are fully serviced and guests can make use of the large kitchen, which includes stoves, microwave ovens and utensils.
Lakeview Chalets   Tel. (02831) 2-1696
17th Avenue (P.O. Box 20, Hermanus, 7200)
Golf, tennis, squash, bowls and hiking
Pleasant cottages in a relaxing environment. All cottages are fully equipped.
De Mond Caravan Park   Tel. (02831) 2-1617
Voëlklip, Hermanus, 7200
Electric plugs, laundry, restaurant, tennis, bowls and golf
De Mond is on the lagoon to the east of Hermanus. The lagoon offers facilities for a variety of water sports and safe bathing.

Restaurants

Both hotels mentioned above have outstanding restaurants, and the Marine serves a superb buffet lunch.
Cypress Tavern   Tel. 2-2000   Wine licence
Harbour Road   Cape/seafood
The restaurant forms part of a cluster of old fishermen's cottages which have all been redecorated. Fresh fish cooked with home-grown herbs, is a speciality. Wine comes from the owner's estate.

Tourist Information
Hermanus area telephone code: **(02831)**

Tourism Bureau   Tel. (02831) 2-2629, Main Road, Hermanus, 7200

Sightseeing

The Old Harbour Museum has a collection of old fishing boats which have been restored. For more than a century the harbour was the heart of the fishing industry, despite its exposed position and tricky entrance. It has now been replaced by a new harbour out of town.
   The Fernkloof Nature Reserve is in the saddle between Lemoenskop and Olifantsberg. Over 25 km of footpaths wind up the mountain through wild flowers. It is open from sunrise to sunset.

Outdoor Activities

Hermanus has many sporting facilities, including an 18-hole **golf** course, **bowls, squash** and **tennis**. There are more than 45 km of laid-out **hiking trails** in the area and a very scenic walk from the old to the new harbour all along the cliffs. Whales can often be seen in the bay below. **Sailing and wind-surfing** can be enjoyed at Kleinrivier Lagoon and in the sea. There ar many **fishing** opportunities. **Surf and rock fishing** are very popular all along the coast, and **game fishing** boats can be chartered at the new harbour. **Skin diving** sites are plentiful: the best locations are near Onrus River. **Hang-gliding** from the mountain slopes behind Hermanus is popular.

From Hermanus take the R43 and drive inland towards Stanford. At Stanford turn left onto the R326 (or continue on to Gansbaai, and then on to Elim) towards Salmonsdam, and then turn right 4 km further onto the Salmonsdam/Elim road (which is gravel). After 7 km you will reach a road heading left, turn to Salmonsdam. Along this road is the nature reserve.

Salmonsdam Nature Reserve, in the valley of the Perdeberg River, is renowned for its variety (over 1 000 species) of fynbos. In spring the mountain slopes become alive with colour as the fynbos comes into flower.

On leaving the reserve return to the Elim road and turn left towards Elim.

Elim, a Moravian Mission Station, was founded in 1824. This quaint white-washed settlement with thatched cottages is slowly being restored. Wild flowers are dried here and exported. The church and watermill (dating from 1828 and still working) are worth seeing.

Continue along the dirt road towards Bredasdorp. When you reach the tarred road (R319) turn left towards Bredasdorp, and then turn right onto a dirt road towards Waenhuiskrans/Die Mond. Follow the Waenhuiskrans signpost until you reach the tarred road (R316) and turn right to reach Arniston.

ARNISTON (WAENHUISKRANS)

The name Waenhuiskrans comes from the large cavern in the nearby cliffs which could accommodate a few wagons. Arniston, the unofficial English name for the settlement, comes from the British troopship with the same name that was wrecked off the coast in 1815, with the loss of 372 lives. Arniston's quaint fishermen's cottages overlooking the sea have been painted by countless artists. It is also a photographers' paradise.

Accommodation

Arniston Hotel   **TYYY   Tel. (02847) 640
P.O. Box 126,
Bredasdorp, 7280   Portfolio of Country Places
Swimming-pool, fishing, skin diving, wind-surfing
The gracious hotel, with its authentic Cape country furniture and homely atmosphere is the ideal base from which to explore the surrounding countryside. Rooms are comfortable, service is friendly and the food is superb: a blend of French cuisine with a strong emphasis on fresh fish.

From Arniston a pleasant days' drive can be enjoyed to Struisbaai.

STRUISBAAI

Struisbaai is one of the many typical fishing villages along the coast. It is also a popular holiday resort and has a beautiful 16-km long beach which offers safe bathing and good fishing.

Accommodation

HOTELS **Struisbaai Motel** *TYYY Tel. (02846) 625
Minnetonba Street (P.O. Box 210, Struisbaai, 7280)
This is the most southerly hotel in Africa. It swings in season,
and chugs along during the rest of the year. All accommodation
is in rondavels.

SELF-CATERING AND **Struisbaai Caravan Park** Tel. (0284) 4-1126
CAMPING P.O. Box 35, Bredasdorp, 7280
Laundry, gas, restaurant and tennis
The park has rondavels and caravan sites.

Sightseeing

As you enter Struisbaai you pass a few typical fisherman's
cottages, with their white walls and straw roofs. The little
fishing harbour is also pretty and fresh fish can be bought there
when the boats return.

From Struisbaai the road winds along the coast to Agulhas.
   Aghulhas is the most southerly tip of Africa. The lighthouse,
built in 1848, is the second oldest in South Africa. Fishing along
the coast is very good.

From Arniston return along the R316 to Bredasdorp.
   Bredasdorp is the centre of the wheat and dairy farming of
this region. It was established in 1837 around the Dutch Reformed Church on the farm of Michael van Breda. The small museum
exhibits pieces of wreckage salvaged from wrecks along the
coast: open on weekdays from 09h00 to 13h00 and from 14h00 to
17h00; on Saturdays from 09h00 to 13h00 and on Sundays from
14h00 to 17h00.
   A few kilometres outside Bredasdorp (on the R319 towards
Swellendam), turn off to the right onto a dirt road towards
Wydgelee, Malgas and Infanta. Follow the road to **Malgas**, a
former port on the Breda River.
   In Swellendam's more prosperous days most freight between
the area and Cape Town was transported by coaster, which
came 50 km upstream to Malgas. Today only ghosts occupy this
former port. Motorists wishing to cross the river do so by pont,
the last still in use in South Africa.
   Return to the turn-off, 2 km back, and then turn right towards
Swellendam. Turn right again at the N2 intersection.

SWELLENDAM

This picturesque town nestles beneath the majestic Langeberg
mountain range. It is the third oldest town in South Africa —
established in 1747 — and has a chequered and exciting past. In
the early days the plains were teeming with game. In 1795 the
residents of the area, dissatisfied with Dutch rule, proclaimed
Swellendam a republic. The republic lasted for only four months
until the residents swore allegiance to the British crown at the
start of the first British occupation. From then on the town grew
in prominence as a sheep and cattle farming centre. The Barry

family set up a thriving "export" business, using Malgas as a port. Local produce was sent to Cape Town, and on return voyages, local necessities brought back. But disaster struck in 1865, when a spark from a baker's oven all but gutted the town, destroying forty homes. This, together with a prevailing drought, brought about the bankruptcy of the Barry empire, and with it the end of Swellendam's importance as a commercial centre.

Accommodation

Swellengrebel Hotel   **TYYY   Tel. (0291) 41144
91 Voortrek Street (P.O. Box 9, Swellendam, 6740)
Swimming-pool, sauna, jacuzzi
This modern, well-run hotel is situated in the centre of town, within easy walking distance of most amenities. Rooms are spacious, well furnished and spotlessly clean, and there are more than ample facilities. The two restaurants offer *table d'hôte* as well as à la carte menus.
Municipal Caravan Park   Tel. (0291) 4-1100
Glen Road (P.O. Box 20, Swellendam, 6740)
Golf, squash, hiking and bowls
Well situated, within walking distance of all amenities, the park has caravan sites as well as quaint self-contained cottages, built in the Cape Dutch style.

Restaurants

Die Kaapse Kombuis   Tel. 4-1600   No licence
110 Voortrek Street   Cape traditional/pastries
This restaurant offers good wholesome Cape cooking; and the adjoining bakery serves superb pastries and fresh bread.
Zanddrift   Tel. 4-2550   No licence
Drostdy Centre, Swellengrebel Street   Cape traditional
The restaurant, in the grounds of the Drostdy and Craft Centre, was reconstructed on its present site from the original materials of a typical 18th century farmhouse which stood near Bonnievale. Both lunch and dinner are served. The food is flavoursome and well presented.

Tourist Information
Swellendam area telephone code: **(0291)**

The Town Clerk   Tel. 4-1100
Voortrek Street, Swellendam, 6740

Sightseeing

The Drostdy and Craft Centre in Swellengrebel Street, as you leave town towards Riversdale, depicts the early history of the town. The craft centre houses a blacksmith's shop, shoemaker, charcoal burner, cooper and coppersmith. It is open from Monday to Saturday from 08h00 to 13h00 and from 14h00 to 17h00.
   The Bontebok National Park, 7 km south of the town on the Breede River, is one of the success stories in nature conservation in South Africa. By 1927 there were just over one hundred

bontebok left. The Bontebok Park was established south of Bredasdorp in 1930 with 18 of these animals, but poor grazing and disease resulted in the park being moved to its present location in 1961. Since the move, the herd has grown from 84 to over 400. The overflow has been used to stock other reserves in the area. Other animals to be seen include rhebok, steenbok and grysbok. The park is open between May and September, from 09h00 to 18h00, and between October to April from 08h00 to 19h00. There are also pleasant camping facilities in the park. For reservations contact the National Parks Board (see page 290).

Outdoor Activities

A six-day **hiking trail** along the Langeberg begins at Swellendam Forest Station. Shorter routes can also be followed. For more information contact the Department of Forestry, Hiking Trails, Pvt. Bag X9005, Cape Town, 8000 (Tel. (021) 45-1224).

Freshwater fishing is very popular along the banks of the Breede River. Carp have been introduced, and a variety of indigenous fish can also be caught, including eel. Licences are available from any magistrate's office in the Cape. You need a permit from the warden to fish inside the park.

From Swellendam the road winds east, through the wheatlands of Heidelberg, Riversdale and Albertinia, and on to Mossel Bay.

Both **Riversdale** and **Albertinia** have first class two-star hotels where hearty meals and comfortable accommodation can be found.

Royal Hotel   **TYYY   Tel. (02932) 184
Long Street (P.O. Box 5, Riversdale, 6770)
Swimming-pool and sauna
The running of the hotel is under the personal supervision of the owners who see to it that guests enjoy friendly, efficient service. Meals are typical country fare.

Albertinia Hotel   **TYYY   Tel. (02952) 30
Main Street (P.O. Box 85, Albertinia, 6795)
This is a real home-from-home country inn run by the owner, who has built up quite a reputation for atmosphere and *table d'hôte* dinner menus. A typical menu, at very reasonable rates will include a choice of three starters, soups, two entrées, seven meat dishes, at least two desserts, and cheese and biscuits.

About 14 km beyond Albertinia, the road crosses the spectacular gorge of the **Gourits River**. Until the first bridge was built, in 1892, this gorge presented a tricky obstacle for those travelling east from the Cape. The present bridge was opened in 1977. To get a good view of the gorge, stop at the view site just beyond the bridge and walk back to the view point.

The whole region comes ablaze with flowering aloes from June to August. The aloes are *farmed* for alain, which is extracted from the fleshy leaves and used for various forms of medication.

MOSSEL BAY

The town is on the site of the first landfall made by Bartholomew Dias in 1488. Because of a spring near the beach and availability of fresh produce from the local tribes, the site became a regular stopping point during the sixteenth century. Sailors also left messages and letters underneath stones for other passing ships here. In 1848 a town was established on the shores of the bay. Today, Mossel Bay is the fifth busiest port in South Africa, and growing centre for the natural gas and oil industry based on off-shore deposits. It is also a popular holiday resort.

Accommodation

HOTELS

Santos Protea Hotel **TYYY   Tel. (04441) 7103
Santos Road,
Mossel Bay, 6500   Protea Hotels and Inns
Swimming-pool, sailing, wind-surfing and fishing
The hotel has a fine view over the bay and is within walking distance of a pleasant beach. The rooms have been comfortably furnished and the restaurant serves a variety of meals, including a good choice of seafood.

SELF-CATERING AND CAMPING

Die Bakke Beach Chalets and Santos Caravan Park Tel. (04441) 4526
P.O. Box 25, Mossel Bay, 6500
Electric plug, laundry, gas, shop, swimming-pool, tennis, bowls, golf, horse-riding, wind-surfing and fishing.
The park is situated on the beach-front close to town. Chalets are all self-contained and serviced.

Restaurants

Plaka   Tel. 2270   Not licenced
85 Blond Street   Seafood/continental
This small restaurant, close to the old harbour, has a warm, relaxed atmosphere. Food is fresh and service attentive.
Camelot   Tel. 3003   Fully licenced
Marsh Street   Steakhouse/continental
The restaurant, approached through a mock Saxon keep, consists of a lounge/ladies bar and two dining rooms, all tastefully furnished and dimly lit, with an open fire in winter.

Tourist Information

Mossel Bay area telephone code: **(04441)**

The Town Clerk, Tel. (04441) 2043, Municipal Office, 101 Marsh Street (P.O. Box 25, Mossel Bay, 6500)
For Inter-City bus service from Mossel Bay to Johannesburg, see George (page 118).

Sightseeing

The **Post Office Tree** is a large milkwood tree, near the harbour, where early sailors once left letters hanging from the tree in a boot. Today tourists can post their letters in a shoe-shaped letterbox underneath the tree. The whole site was re-developed for the 500-year celebration in 1988, to commemorate Bartholomew Dias' landing on the shores of Mossel Bay. The completed complex comprises: **The Spring;** the **Post Office Tree; The Shirley**

Building, which was erected in the late nineteenth century and has been converted into a museum depicting the history of the tree, and local flora and fauna; the **Old Mill,** which has been turned into a maritime museum depicting the Portuguese voyages of discovery and has a life-size replica of Dias' ship on display; and the **Customs Officials' Cottages,** erected in 1786, which have been converted into a cosy restaurant.

Seal Island, within the bay, has a population of over two thousand seals. Trips can be made to the island. For further information telephone (04441) 3101.

Outdoor Activities

The bay offers many opportunities for water sports. **Wind-surfing** and **surfing** are very popular. The town also boasts a good 18-hole **golf** course, **bowls** and **tennis** facilities. Fishing is also very popular. **Rock and surf fishing** spots are to be found all along the bay; while boats can be chartered for **deep-sea fishing** (Tel. (04441) 3101).

From Mossel Bay, follow the road out of town (R328) towards Oudtshoorn (the end of this tour) via the **Robinson Pass.** The pass — 860 m at the summit —winds its way over the Outeniqua Mountains. In the past, this mountain range was a formidable barrier between the Little Karoo and the harbour at Mossel Bay. The first passes were a great distance away, and so in 1867 Thomas Bain, one of the great road builders of the time began work on the pass, which was completed in 1869. It was widened and tarred in the 1950s. At the foot of the pass (35 km from Mossel Bay), is the delightful holiday retreat of Eight Bells Mountain Inn.

Eight Bells Mountain Inn   **TYYY   Tel. (04441) 5-84800
P.O. Box 436,
Mossel Bay, 6500   Portfolio of Country Places
Swimming-pool, tennis, table tennis, billiards, riding, bowls, squash, fishing and hiking
This superb resort offers accommodation in either quaint Swiss-type chalets, all tastefully furnished, or in rooms in the main blocks. Proprietors are caring about their guests' well-being, and service is attentive. Food is typically South African, very tasty and good value for money.

(See page 110 for Oudtshoorn.)

Cape Town to Oudtshoorn via Matjiesfontein

(753 km)
See map on page 102

The route first winds up the West Coast to the charming holiday resort of Langebaan, before swinging east through the winelands of the Swartland. From here it climbs over the Hex River Mountains to the Great Karoo and then over the Witteberge and Swartberg into the Little Karoo and on to Oudtshoorn. In all, seven spectacular passes are traversed.

From Cape Town, take the N1 towards Paarl. At exit 2 turn onto the R27 towards Velddrift. About 32 km out of Cape Town, take the R307 towards Atlantis, and follow it towards Darling, turning off to Mamre.

Mamre is a Moravian Mission Station established in 1808. The most interesting buildings nestle among the pine and oak trees at the end of the road. Many of the original picturesque white-washed, thatched cottages still stand, as does the original church, parsonage and watermill. The restored watermill is open to the public on weekdays between 09h00 and 17h00, and Sundays from 14h00 to 17h00.

Return to the R307 and head towards Darling. During early spring (August/September) the countryside is covered with wild flowers and many farms are open to visitors who want to wander into these fields.

Darling is the centre of a rich sheep and dairy farming area. The **Tinie Versfeld Flora Reserve** (for information call (021) 77-1166) 10 km out of the town on the R315 is renowned for its wild flower display in spring.

Turn right towards Velddrift at the E27 intersection, and then left onto a dirt road towards Churchhaven and Langebaan. When the road forks, turn left again towards Churchhaven.

Churchhaven is a restful little fishing village on the shores of the Langebaan Lagoon. Headstones in the graveyard bear the names of many foreign sailors who either jumped ship or were stranded there. Further on from Churchhaven there are a number of sheltered, attractive beaches on the lagoon, which are ideal and very safe for bathing and wind-surfing. The **Postberg Nature Reserve**, also along this road, is open to the public during August and September when it is transformed by the delicate colours of the wild flowers.

Return along the road to the Langebaan signpost and turn left to Langebaan.

LANGEBAAN

This holiday village is the ideal setting for a few days' rest at the seaside. The beaches offer calm, safe bathing and are ideal for sailing and wind-surfing.

Accommodation

The **Langebaan Lodge**
Main Road, Langebaan

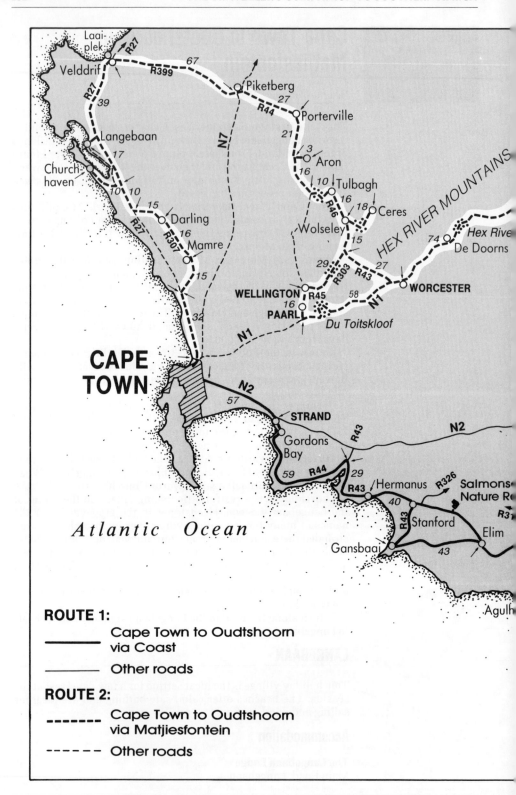

ROUTE 1:

──────── Cape Town to Oudtshoorn
via Coast

──────── Other roads

ROUTE 2:

▬ ▬ ▬ ▬ ▬ Cape Town to Oudtshoorn
via Matjiesfontein

─ ─ ─ ─ ─ Other roads

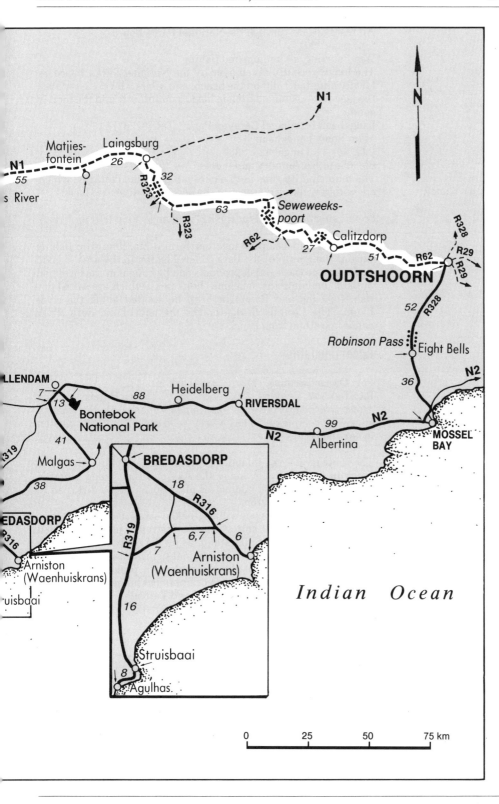

All reservations through the National Parks Board
(See page 290)
Wind-surfing, swimming and fishing
The lodge, recently taken over by the National Parks Board, is
ideally situated, right on the beach, and offers a lovely view over
the lagoon. Accommodation is basic, comfortable and the food is
good.
Langebaan Municipal Caravan Park   Tel. (02287) 615
Main Road, Langebaan
P.O. Box 11, Langebaan, 7357
Electric plugs, laundry and tennis
The municipality runs both a caravan park and cottages, which
are within walking distance of the beach. Facilities are basic.

From Langebaan, head for the R27 and on to Velddrift and Laaiplek.
   Velddrif and **Laaiplek** together form a bustling little fishing
port at the mouth of the Berg River. Fishing in the area is good
and many processed fish products can be bought at the local fish
outlets, including the delicious "bokkoms", which are salted dry
fish. Pelicans and flamingoes can be spotted along the river
banks. The Carinus Bridge marks the end of the Berg River
canoe marathon from Paarl.

Accommodation

Port Owen Cabanas   Tel. (022882) ask for 653
P.O. Box 117, Velddrif, 7365   Protea Hotels and Inns
These are comfortable self-contained cabanas on the water's
edge. The complex also has a very good restaurant, specialising
in sea-foods.

The route now turns inland, east along the R399 towards Piket-
berg, on to Porterville, along the R44 and then along towards
Tulbagh. Twenty-one kilometres after Porterville a dirt road to
the left leads off to Saron.
Saron is a typical mission village tucked away in the mountains.
Many of the original cottages were destroyed during the 1969
earthquake, but a few still stand, as do the church, dating from
1852, and the parsonage. The original homestead dates back to
the late 1700s. Some of the residents still practise the art of
making velskoens (shoes made of untanned hide). Return to the
main road and head for Nuwekloof and Tulbagh.

TULBAGH

On 29 September 1969 a devastating earthquake (measuring 6,5
on the Richter scale) shook this quaint town into the news.
Many of the houses which had stood for over two hundred years
were badly damaged. Out of this disaster a huge restoration
programme was set up to restore Church Street to its former
eighteenth-century image. Thirty-two buildings have been restored to form the largest concentration of national monuments
in the country. The area has an excellent climate for fruit-growing.

Accommodation

Tulbagh Hotel   *TYYY   Tel. (02362) 71
22 Van der Stel Street, Tulbagh, 6820
This simple hotel offers comfortable accommodation and good country cooking.
    The closest self-catering and camping facilities are in Ceres, 35 km away.
Pine Forest Holiday Resort   Tel. (0233) 2-2060
The Town Clerk, P.O. Box 44, Ceres, 6835
Electric plugs, laundry, gas, shop, recreation hall, swimming-pool, tennis, bowls and golf
This resort offers both cottages and camping facilities. The park is near the river, and is ideally situated for touring the area.

Restaurants

Paddagang Wine House   Tel. 242   Wine licence
23 Church Street, Tulbagh   Cape traditional
This is one of the oldest of KWV's four wine houses that promote wine and Cape cooking. The restaurant also has a taproom where a few of the excellent wines of the area can be tasted. Genuine Cape favourites such as bobotie and waterblommetjie-bredie can be enjoyed here. Booking is always recommended.

Tourist Information
Tulbagh area telephone code: **(02362)**

Old Church Museum.   Tel. (02362) 41, 14 Church Street, Tulbagh, 6820

Sightseeing

The main buildings of interest in Tulbagh are all along Church Street. It is a good idea to park at one end of the street and to walk down the road. Many are private homes and may not be entered, but the following are open to the public:
    The **Old Church Museum,** which was beautifully restored after the earthquake. The gable is richly decorated with various motifs. It is open from Monday to Saturday 09h00 to 13h00 and 14h00 to 17h00.
    The **Victorian House,** built in 1892, is decorated with period furniture and is open during the same times as the Church Museum.

The route turns south from Tulbagh, towards Wellington along the R46, to Wolseley and then onto the R43. About 31 km out of Tulbagh the road forks and here you have a choice of two routes:
● direct to Worcester (37 km) via the R43; or
● via the magnificent passes of Bain's Kloof and Du Toit's Kloof (105 km).
If you do not wish to go straight to Worcester, branch right onto the R303 and head towards Wellington. **Bain's Kloof Pass** was built by Andrew Geddes Bain and completed in 1853. It is regarded by many as a masterpiece of engineering, and provides panoramic views over Wellington and Paarl from its 595 m sum-

mit. From Wellington, continue along the R303 towards Paarl, and then to the N1 motorway. Turn left towards Worcester (take the old road, not the new toll road and tunnel). **Du Toit's Kloof Pass** connects the Berg River Valley to the Breë River Valley via 48 km of road that winds to a height of 820 m and then drops to the Molenaars River with its towering rock buttresses on both sides. The surrounding cliffs are a favourite haunt of mountain climbers. At the end of the pass, the road opens up into the beautiful Hex River Valley.

WORCESTER

The town, named after the Marquis of Worcester, Lord Charles Somerset's older brother, is surrounded by the imposing ranges of the Du Toit's, Stangehoek, Waaihoek and Hex River Mountains. Grapes are produced here in abundance, and processed as table grapes, or for wine and brandy. A very good school for the deaf and blind has been established here.

Accommodation

Cumberland Hotel   ***TYYY   Tel. (0231) 7-2641
2 Stockenström Street (P.O. Box, Worcester, 6850)
Sauna, swimming-pool and squash
This well-run hotel offers all the comforts and personal touches that will make your stay a pleasant one. It is situated in the town centre.
Hotel Brandwacht   *TYYY   Tel. (0231) 2-0150
Cor. High and Napier Streets (P.O. Box 192, Worcester, 6850)
Sauna and swimming-pool
This simple, clean family-run hotel has become well-known for its food. Continental and British dishes are served in pleasant surroundings.

Restaurants

Good Hope   Tel. 2-0373   No licence
75 High Street   Tea room/steakhouse
If a tasty giant-size steak is what you feel like, then this is the place for you. The menu is short, but the meat is very good.
Kleinplasie   Tel. 2-0430   Wine licence
Worcester showgrounds,
off Robertson Road   Cape traditional
This is another KWV wine house featuring the wines of the area and serving hearty traditional dishes. It is simply furnished with old Cape antiques and South African artists' works are displayed on the walls.

Tourist Information
Worcester area telephone code: **(0231)**

Information Bureau, Tel. (0231) 4408, 23 Baring Street, Worcester, 6850

The Hex River Valley in autumn

The Lord Milner Hotel, Matjiesfontein

A familiar Oudtshoorn scene

Ostrich chicks

Sightseeing

In town there are three houses facing Church Square which together form the **Worcester Museum. Beck House** is furnished as a late nineteenth century home. The **Afrikaner Museum** depicts a dentist's and doctor's room, and lawyer's office from the early 1900s; and **Stofberg House** has a collection of paintings and documents tracing the town's history. It is open from Monday to Saturday from 09h00 to 17h00, and on Sundays from 14h00 to 16h30.

The **Hugo Naudé House,** 113 Russel Street, houses a permanent exhibition of the works of Hugo Naudé and his fellow artist, Jean Welz. Open from Monday to Saturday from 09h00 to 13h00, and from 14h00 to 17h00.

The **Karoo Botanic Garden,** in Roux Road off the N1, 3 km north of the town, has a large collection of plants from all parts of South Africa and is open from sunrise to sunset.

The **Boland Farm Museum,** Tel. (0231) 2-2225 depicts the farming history of South Africa. Well re-constructed replicas of old farm houses and traditional implements can be viewed. Demonstrations on various farming methods and cooking practices are given. Give yourself at least three hours to visit this extremely interesting museum which is open from Monday to Saturday between 09h00 and 16h30.

On leaving Worcester, return to the N1 highway and head for Touws River. The road winds through vineyards and orchards — a beautiful sight in autumn —and then climbs steadily up the Hex River Pass and into the barrenness of the Great Karoo.

Touws River, just off the N1, is a railway junction and storage yard for old steam locomotives — a steam enthusiast's dream. A locomotive museum is also located here. Continue along the N1 to the Matjiesfontein turn-off and turn right.

MATJIESFONTEIN

This village monument is a relic of colonialism at its grandest. In 1883 an enterprising young Scot by the name of Jimmy Logan opened a refreshment room on the platform of Matjiesfontein station. From then on, he developed the village into a charming Victorian health and holiday resort. The resort attracted many of the rich and famous from the colony, as well as the aristocracy from Britain who came to rest and breathe the clean fresh air. By 1920, the year of Logan's death, the fortunes of the resort had begun to decline and continued to do so until 1968. In that year David Rawdon bought the village, and two years later, in 1970 the **Lord Milner Hotel** (**TYYY) opened its doors.

Today the complex comprises the hotel with its beautifully furnished bedrooms, a very elegant dining room (tie and jacket required for evening meals) and public areas; the **Laird Arms** Victorian country pub; post office; museum; bank (only open on Thursdays between 09h30 and 12h00); the **Coffee House** where light meals can be bought; **Die Losieshuis**, providing cheaper comfortable family accommodation; **The Chop House**, a Victorian steakhouse; and an assortment of other buildings and cottages also used for accommodation.

Reservations: Tel. (0020) and ask for Matjiesfontein 3 or 4
Lord Milner Hotel, P.O. Matjiesfontein, 6910

From Matjiesfontein continue along the N1 to Laingsburg and
turn right at the Standard Bank (no signpost) onto the R323
towards **Seven Weeks Poort**. The road winds through the foothills of the Elandsberg, over the Rooinek Pass. At Wit Nekke the
road becomes gravel. Still following the Seven Weeks Poort sign,
turn right into the Seven Weeks Poort just after the Koueveld
Pass. The road winds back and forth over the stream (which can
flood in heavy rains) following it through the gap in the Swartberg Mountains, between towering red cliffs — often barely
wide enough for a car to pass through. At the end of this magnificent pass, the road meets the R62 leading to Calitzdorp in the
Little Karoo.

CALITZDORP

Calitzdorp is the centre of a farming community known for its
dried fruit and wine industry. Many products can be bought at
roadside stalls in and around the town. Calitzdorp's **wine route**
boasts a range of more than 14 wines from two estates and a
co-operative (see map on page 109). As you enter Calitzdorp you
will come across a sign on the right indicating a turn into Van
Riebeeck Street (the start of the wine route).
    Follow the signs to **Boplaas Estate,** Tel. (04437) 326, P.O. Box
156, Calitzdorp, 6660. Both wine and brandy have been made at
this estate since 1860. Today a variety of cultivars are planted
on the farm, but it has become especially well-known for its
port, which has won a number of gold medals locally. The farm
also sells dried fruit and is open to the public, Monday to Friday
from 08h00 to 13h00 and from 14h00 to 17h00, and on Saturdays
from 09h00 to 12h00.
    Die Krans Estate Tel. (04437) 314, P.O. Box 28, Calitzdorp,
6660. The estate has ten lables, of which the sweeter wines are
most popular. Dried fruit is also available on the estate. Open as
above.
    Calitzdorp Fruit and Wine Cellars are also worth a visit for
their wine and dried fruit. Open as above.

Continue from here along the R62 to Oudtshoorn.

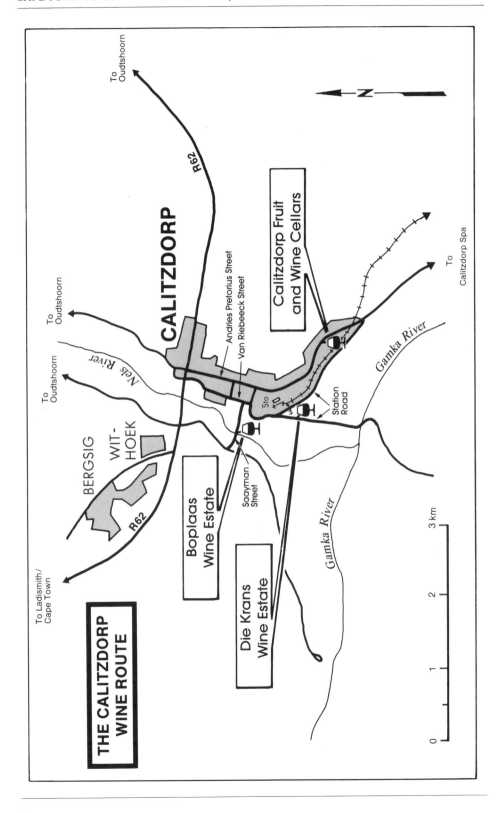

Oudtshoorn

Apart from being the major town of the Little Karoo, Oudtshoorn is also the ostrich-feather capital of the world. Ostriches are farmed like cattle and sheep, and can be seen in large flocks throughout the district. The fertile valley produces many agricultural products, including dried fruit, honey, dairy products, wheat, mohair, tobacco, lucerne and onion seed.

The town, founded in 1847, was named after Baron Pieter van Rheede van Oudtshoorn. When, in the 1880s, ladies' fashions throughout the world relied on ostrich feathers, Oudtshoorn was ready to supply this demand. By 1882 there were over 100 000 birds in domestic flocks; this number grew rapidly until the start of World War I, when there were over 750 000 birds in the region, supplying half a million kilograms of plumes, and fetching close to three million pounds per year. Millions were made overnight and breeding pairs fetched unprecedented prices. With the advent of the war, fashions changed, and with change came bankruptcies as the market slumped. Only after World War II did the market begin to pick up again, and today it is once more a thriving business, although nowhere near what it was in the golden years.

Today very little of the bird is wasted. The feathers are marketed throughout the world, the skin is used for quality leather goods, and the meat is processed and exported worldwide as a delicacy.

The Little Karoo is a semi-desert area with low rainfall and humidity. Water is obtained from storage dams fed by the Swartberg Mountains, which receive a fair amount of rain and occasional snow in winter. Nights are cool, often becoming very cold during winter when snow falls on the mountains. During the day, temperatures rise fast, and in summer occasionally top 45 °C.

Accommodation

HOTELS   **Holiday Inn**   ***TYYY   Tel. (04431) 2201
Baron van Rheede Street
(P.O. Box 52, Oudtshoorn, 6620)   Holiday Inns
Swimming-pool
This comfortable hotel, with its typical Holiday Inn layout, is fairly centrally situated. All the rooms are spacious, clean and well serviced. Apart from the dining room, where buffet meals, including a superb breakfast, are served, the hotel also has an action bar with live music and an elegant restaurant serving, amongst other delicacies, ostrich steak.
Kango Protea Inn   **TYYY   Tel. (04431) 6161
Baron van Rheede Street (P.O. Box 370,
Oudtshoorn 6620)   Protea Hotels and Inns
Swimming-pool
The hotel is located just outside Oudtshoorn on the Cango Caves

road. Guests are accommodated in well-furnished thatched chalets with individually controlled air-conditioning — a must at the height of summer when temperatures reach 45 °C. The restaurant serves buffet/carvery meals as well as one of the best á la Carte menus in town.

Queens Hotel **TYYY   Tel. (04431) 2101/4
Baron van Rheede Street (P.O. Box 19, Oudtshoorn, 6620)
Swimming-pool and tennis
This, the most centrally situated hotel in Oudtshoorn, is an old world comfortable hotel. The restaurant serves good wholesome food.

SELF-CATERING AND CAMPING

Kleinplaas Holiday Resort   Tel. (04431) 5811
171 Baron van Rheede Street, (P.O. Box 24, Oudtshoorn, 6620)
Electric plugs, laundry, swimming-pool, restaurant and shop
A beautifully laid out, lawned resort providing both chalets and camping facilities. All chalets are fully equipped and completely self-contained, including a car port and private braai area.

N.A. Smit Municipal Tourist Camp   Tel. (04431) 2221
Park Road (P.O. Box 255, Oudtshoorn, 6620)
Electric plugs, laundry, swimming-pool and tennis
Cottages, rondavels and camping sites are available. Rondavels are more basic, but a lot cheaper than cottages.

Restaurants

See the three hotels above.

Useful addresses and telephone numbers

Oudtshoorn area telephone code: **(04431)**

TOURIST INFORMATION

Oudtshoorn Publicity Association,   Tel. (04431) 2221, P.O. Box 255, Oudtshoorn, 6620

AIRLINES

Air Cape   Tel. 3660

CAR HIRE

Avis   Tel. 7505
Budget   Tel. 3660
For Inter-City bus services from Mossel Bay to Johannesburg, see George (page 118).

Sightseeing

The two most important and unique sights in the Oudtshoorn district are the ostrich show farms and the Cango Caves, but the town itself also has a few interesting places.

The **C.P. Nel Museum** (146 High Street) is a superb example of the stone masonry of the period. During the ostrich boom, a number of stone masons from Ireland came to the area and were involved in the building of the fine mansions in the area. The museum was originally built to house the Boys High School. Today it has an interesting collection of local antiques which together depict the history of the town and ostrich boom. It is open from Monday to Saturday from 09h30 to 13h00 and from 14h00 to 17h00 and on Sundays from 14h30 to 17h00.

Arbeidsgenot, in Jan van Riebeeck Road, was the home of the writer, poet, politician, C.J. Langenhoven, the man who penned,

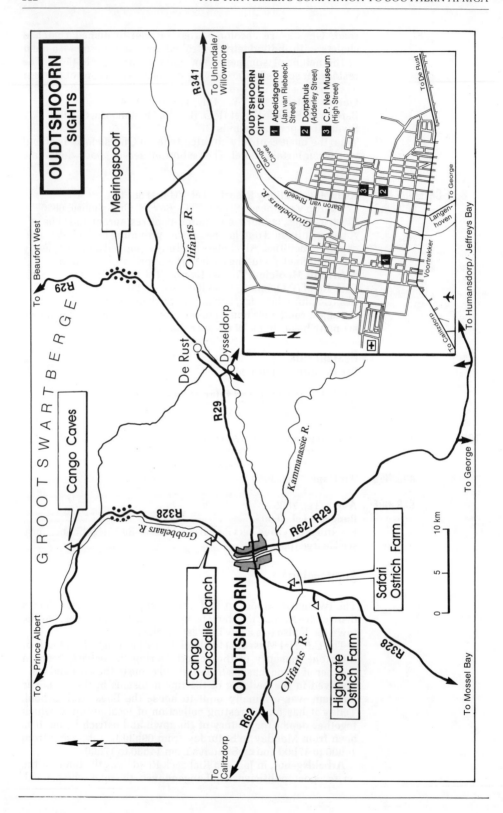

among other well-loved works, the South African National Anthem, *Die Stem*. It now contains a collection of his personal belongings. It is open on weekdays from 09h00 to 12h30 and 14h00 to 17h30 and on Saturdays from 09h00 to 12h00.

Dorpshuis, in Adderley Street, is a fine example of an old "ostrich palace", built during the ostrich boom — open on weekdays from 09h00 to 13h00 and 14h00 to 17h00.

Highgate and Safari Ostrich Show Farms are situated outside the town, on the Mossel Bay road (R328). A fascinating two-hour guided tour of the farms allows one to see the ostrich at close quarters and to learn about ostrich farming techniques. No tour of the Garden Route is complete without a visit to one of these farms. The farms also have a large curio shop where a variety of ostrich goods such as feather boas, ostrich leather shoes and handbags, and egg shells can be bought. Open from 07h30 to 17h00 daily, throughout the year.

The Cango Crocodile Ranch, Tel. 6014, is 3 km from Oudtshoorn on the Cango Caves road. Although the ranch is a commercial concern, they do conduct very informative tours during which the visitor is shown over 200 crocodiles varying from 30 cm to 4 m in length. One-hour tours leave every half an hour from 09h00 to 17h00.

The Cango Caves are 26 km from Oudtshoorn. A guided two-hour tour takes the visitor through calcite caves, revealing fascinating shapes and forms enhanced by strategic lighting. They also have a crèche for small children. The caves are open from 08h00 to 17h00 from December to February and in April (tours leave every hour) and during the rest of the year from 09h00 to 15h00 (tours leave every two-hours).

From Oudtshoorn the route once again branches into two: *route 1* (page 114) follows the coast; while *route 2* (page 147) turns inland over the Swartberg Mountains and into the Karoo, before winding back and forth across the mountains.

Oudtshoorn to Umtata via the Coast
(1029 km)
See map on page 116

The route follows the coast to East London before branching inland, through the Transkei to Umtata. Along the route one passes through beautiful coastal forests and bustling holiday resorts with long golden beaches. This is an ideal area to spend a few days relaxing on the beach, exploring the forests and villages, taking a ride on a steam train, or enjoying a champagne and oyster breakfast on the shores of the Knysna Lagoon.

From Oudtshoorn drive southwards, along Langenhoven Road towards George (R29). The road winds slowly to the summit of the **Outeniqua Pass**. About 35 km out of Oudtshoorn the road forks. Take the right fork to George. Just at the fork, farm stalls sell juicy fresh peaches as well as dried peaches grown in the valley. If you are fond of these, it is well worth a stop. From the summit of the Outeniqua Pass, 800 m above sea-level, the road descends to George, situated on the narrow coastal plain 200 m above sea level. The road was started in 1943 with the help of Italian prisoners of war, and completed in 1951. At the view site, 50 km from Oudtshoorn, one has a fine view of George as well as the three other passes crossing the mountains. The three other passes are:

- The **original Voortrekker route,** which is marked by white stones and was the gateway for many early farmers.
- The **Montagu Pass**, winding its way through the gorge below, which was used as a link between Oudtshoorn and the coast before the present road was built. On the George side of the pass, the old Toll House can still be seen.
- The **Railway line** which winds up the mountain on the opposite side of the valley.

GEORGE

The Garden Route has a variety of sights to offer the tourist: long deserted golden beaches, walks through indigenous forests, steam train rides on the Outeniqua Choo-Tjoe, spectacular walks through national parks and good food. George is the gateway to the Garden Route, served by a modern domestic airport, a choice of car-hire companies and a modern coach tour company to whisk the traveller away to explore the exciting area.

This picturesque town lies on the coastal plateau below the Outeniqua Mountains, and is the principal town of the Garden Route. Today it is a bustling business and educational centre as well as a thriving farming community, producing vegetables, which are frozen and distributed throughout the country, hops for the brewing industry, and dairy products. In 1811 the town was declared a separate magisterial district, and named George-town, after King George III of England. At the time forestry, based on the extensive indigenous forest around George, was the principal industry; but exploitation became so rife that in 1936 the government was obliged to declare a 200-year ban on the felling of indigenous trees. Today large plantations of exotic species exist and forestry is still the backbone of the area's economy. Fortunately large tracts of indigenous forest have also been saved.

Accommodation

HOTELS

Far Hills Protea Hotel　**TYYY　Tel. (0441) 4941
On the N2 road between George and Wilderness (P.O. Box 10, George, 6530)　　　　　　　　　Protea Hotels and Inns
Swimming-pool
Set in 13 ha of land, Far Hills has a superb view of the Outeniqua Mountains. Apart from luxury bedrooms, there are also five self-contained fully equipped chalets. The hotel is about halfway between George and Wilderness, and 1 km from Victoria Bay.
Outeniqua Hotel　*TYYY　Tel. (0441) 71428
123 York Street, George, 6530
The hotel is built on the site of the old Dutch East India Company's "poshuis", where travellers used to rest on their journeys up the coast. Today it is a simple, but comfortable family-run hotel, perfect for an overnight stop.

SELF-CATERING AND CAMPING

Pine Lodge Holiday Cottages　Tel. (00441) 72775
P.O. Box 296, George, 6530
Swimming-pool
Situated on the outskirts of George, just off the N2 to Wilderness, the lodge has a number of self-contained chalets of different sizes which are all comfortably furnished. The Hunter's Grill restaurant on the property serves good food.
Sea Glimpse　Tel. (0441) 4660
P.O. Box 307, George, 6530
Electric plugs, laundry and swimming-pool
It is situated off the N2, 8 km from George and 4 km from Wilderness, on the Victoria Bay road. The caravan park is well laid out and secluded. Each cottage is self-contained.
Victoria Bay Lodge　Tel. (0441) 4496
P.O. Box 229, George, 6530
Close to Victoria Bay, off the N2. All chalets are self-contained and overlook the Outeniqua Mountains.

Restaurants

Copper Pot　Tel. 6518　　　　　　　Wine and malt licence
Multi Centre, Meade Street　　　　　　Cape Dutch/seafood
This is most definitely the top restaurant on the Garden Route, and possibly one of the best in the country. The proprietors understand the fine art of service, and meals are prepared to perfection, and served in a relaxed atmosphere.
Geronimo Spur　Tel. 4279　　　　　Wine and malt licence
126 York Street, George　　　　　　　　　　　Steakhouse
Simple steakhouse where value-for-money meals are served with efficient service: the perfect place for a quick lunch when in a hurry.
Hunter's Grill　Tel. 74-4350　　　　Wine and malt licence
Pine Lodge, just out of town on the N2 to
Wilderness　　　　　　　　　　　　　Seafood/steakhouse

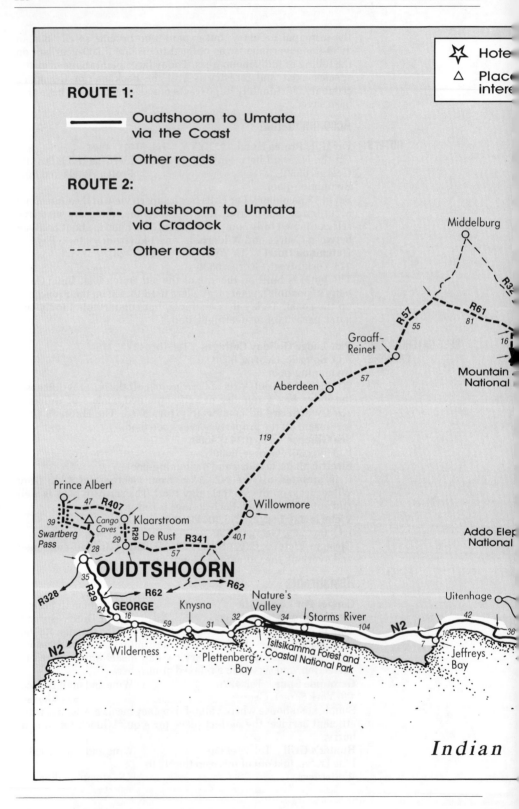

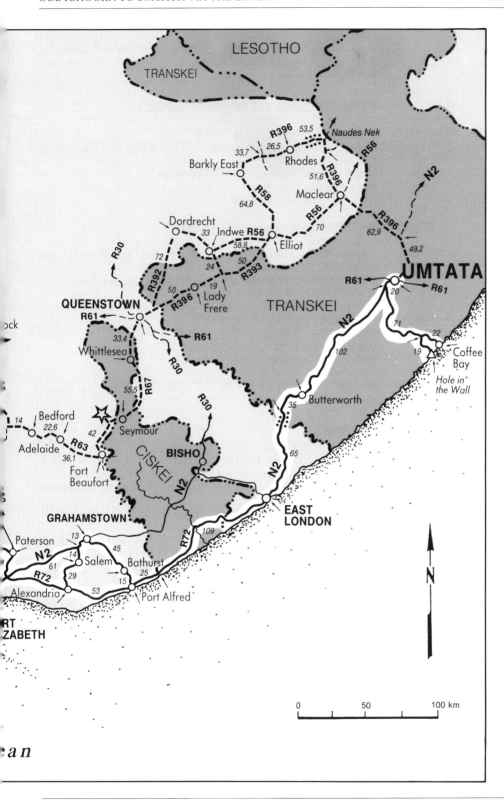

A relaxed friendly atmosphere makes this pleasant restaurant a joy to eat in. Steaks are large, but tender, and seafood, including Knysna oysters and Mossel Bay sole, is always fresh. The venison dishes are also very good.

Useful addresses and telephone numbers

TOURIST INFORMATION   George area telephone code: **(0441)**
George Publicity Association, Tel. 74-4000, P.O. Box 1109, George, 6530
South African Tourism Board (SATOUR)
Tel. 5228, 124 York Street
(P.O. Box 312, George, 6530)

AIRLINES   **South African Airways,** Tel. 74-3344

COACH TOURS   **Garden Route Tours,** Tel. 70-7993/4, P.O. Box 4179, George East, 6539
Inter-City bus services Mossel Bay to Johannesburg, Tel. 74-2823/4, P.O. Box 2004, George, 6530

CAR HIRE   **Avis** Tel. 74-5082
Budget Tel. 76-9216
Imperial Tel. 6724
Outeniqua Motor Hire Tel. 74-4140

RAILWAYS   **Station** Tel. 6-8202 (also for the Outeniqua Choo-Tjoe enquiries)

Sightseeing

The **Dutch Reformed Church** in Courtenay Street is the oldest church in town. The pillars and the dome are of yellowwood, while the pulpit is carved out of stinkwood. Both woods are indigenous to the area.

St. Mark's Cathedral in York Street is reputed to be the smallest cathedral in the southern hemisphere.

The **George Museum,** in the old Drostdy building at the top of York Street, houses an interesting collection of phonographs and old musical instruments. Open on Monday to Friday from 09h00 to 16h30, and Saturday from 09h00 to 12h30.

The **Slave Tree** in York Street, in front of the SATOUR offices, is an oak tree planted when the town was first laid out. A length of chain embedded in its trunk is believed to have been used to fasten slaves to it before they were sold under the shade of the tree.

The **Outeniqua Choo-Tjoe** is a steam train running daily, except on Sundays, between George and Knysna. The rail link, completed in 1928, was built to carry freight between the two centres — general merchandise to Knysna, and oysters, boats and timber to George. The route weaves through some of the most scenic parts of the area: it starts off along the coastline, above the pounding waves, winds its way between the lakes of Wilderness and finally crosses the two-kilometre bridge at Knysna. At the time of writing, the train departs from George at 08h10 and reaches Knysna at 11h00, departing again at 12h50.

For reservations and tickets, contact the stationmaster at George or Knysna.

Outdoor Activities

A variety of outdoor activities can be enjoyed along the Garden Route, including surfing, hiking, sailing, fishing, riding and golf.

The **George Golf Course,** Tel. 2411, in Langenhoven Road, is renowned as one of the top courses in the country and is situated in beautiful surroundings.

The **Riding Club,** Tel. 2672, in Glenwood Avenue, offers exciting outrides to experienced horse-riders.

The **Outeniqua Hiking Trail** (reservations through: The Regional Director, Southern Cape Forest Region, Private Box X12 Knysna, 6570; Tel. (0445) 2-3037) has its starting point in George. The trail covers 148 km, ending at Diepwalle, and normally takes eight days to complete. There are overnight huts along the way.

Fishing: rock and surf, river, deep-sea, and lake fishing can be enjoyed in the area. Garden Route Tours (see address above) offers exciting seven-day packages which include a combination of these activities.

From George take the N2 towards Wilderness. The first turn-off takes you to Victoria Bay, a small holiday village 3 km from the main road. The tiny bay has a safe bathing beach and is very popular with surfers.

Continuing along the N2, the road winds down the gorge and over the Kaaimans River. The bridge crossing the river is the first curved bridge to have been constructed in South Africa. As you meander down the gorge, you can catch glimpses of the steam-train bridge at the Kaaimans River mouth. After crossing the bridge the road runs next to the river, before curving to follow the coastline. As you round the corner there are splendid views of Wilderness and the beaches; whales can sometimes be seen in the sea below.

WILDERNESS

A popular holiday resort with beautiful beaches (bathing is not all that safe owing to dangerous backwashes) and a lagoon which is popular for swimming, skiing and wind-surfing. The **Wilderness Lakes** area is a proclaimed national park covering 50 km of lakes, lagoons, ferns and river. Vegetation ranges from rain forest to dune grass. A variety of small mammals and birds, including the clawless otter and Knysna loerie, populate the area.

Accommodation

HOTELS **The Holiday Inn** ***TYYY Tel. (0441) 9104
P.O. Box 26, Wilderness, 6560   Holiday Inns
Swimming-pool
It is situated on the N2 past the Wilderness settlement. This is a regular Holiday Inn, with large comfortable rooms, many overlooking the sea. The hotel is very popular with groups.

SELF-CATERING AND | **Lakes Holiday Resort**   Tel. (0441) 91101
CAMPING | P.O. Box 38, Wilderness, 6560   Club Caraville
Electric plugs, laundry, gas, shop, recreation hall, swimming-pool, tennis, bowls, wind-surfing, canoeing, fishing and water-skiing
The resort, which offers cosy chalets, caravan and camping facilities, is located on the banks of the Touws River, 200 m from the beach. A host of outdoor activities are offered inclusive of free wind-surfing and canoeing. All chalets are fully equipped and have radio and TV.

Wilderness Rest Camp   Tel. (0441) 74-6924
National Parks Board, P.O. Box 787, Pretoria, 0001
Fishing, wind-surfing and swimming
The park is well signposted from the Wilderness intersection on the N2. Accommodation consists of two-bedroomed chalets, caravans and camping facilities. All chalets and caravans are fully equipped and serviced. The park is spaciously laid out and a perfect base from which to explore the area. Paddle and row-ing-boats are available for hire.

Restaurants

Wilderness Hotel Carvery
Tel. 9-1110   Fully licensed
Karos Wilderness Hotel   Carvery
The buffet carvery offers a wide variety of food, including three or four roasts, fresh fish, oysters and a variety of desserts. Good value-for-money with enough food to satisfy the largest of appetites. Situated in the centre of the village.

A choice of two roads can be taken from Wilderness to Sedgefield:
• the N2, which follows the coast, but has no view of the sea;
• the dirt road which winds between the lakes. (To reach this road, follow the signpost into Wilderness, and then drive along the banks of the lagoon, following the Sedgefield sign via the lakes. The road follows the lakes, from Lower Langvlei to Rondevlei and meets the N2 road again just before Swartvlei.)

SWARTVLEI

Swartvlei is the largest of the lakes and is popular for yachting, waterskiing, wind-surfing and fishing. Two holiday resorts are situated on its banks:

Montmere Holiday Resort   Tel. (04455) 304
P.O. Box 248, Sedgefield, 6573
Swimming-pool, sailing, wind-surfing and fishing
All chalets are fully equipped including TV. The resort is well laid out to offer privacy and tranquility to all its guests.

Pine Lake Marina   Tel. (04455) 742
P.O. Box 8, Sedgefield, 6573
Gas, shop, recreation hall, restaurant, laundry, swimming-pool, fishing, wind-surfing and skiing
The resort has chalets, caravan and camping facilities. All chalets are self-contained and fully equipped.

SEDGEFIELD

This is a popular holiday resort at the mouth of the Swartvlei estuary.

Forest Inn   Tel. (04455) 637
P.O. Box 29, Sedgefield, 6573
The Inn is situated on the N2 and perfect as a stop-over point. All rooms are fully serviced and have baths. There is also a licensed (wine and malt) restaurant in the complex.

Continuing along the N2 the next point of interest to be passed is Groenvlei.

GROENVLEI

This is the only freshwater lake in the Wilderness lakes chain. Groenvlei was once also connected to the sea, but many thousands of years ago was cut off by the high sand dune ridge. Through the years the water became less saline and the marine life slowly adapted to fresh-water conditions. Today a fragile and unique eco-system exists within the lake. A hotel, chalets and camping facilities are to be found on the lake shores.

Lake Pleasant Hotel **TYYY   Tel. (04455) 313
P.O. Box 2, Sedgefield, 6573 (Signposted from the N2)
Swimming-pool, tennis, black bass fishing, wind-surfing and hiking
If you are looking for a quiet hotel away from it all, then this is the place. All rooms are comfortably furnished and face the lake. The hearty English food is very good. Guests can hire boats.

Lake Pleasant Caravan Park Tel. (04455) 985
P.O. Box 16, Sedgefield, 6573 (Signposted from the N2)
Electric plug, laundry, gas, shop, recreation hall, swimming-pool, black bass fishing, wind-surfing and hiking
This well-run resort has comfortable chalets and well-appointed camping and caravan facilities. All chalets are self-contained and serviced, and have a fine view of the lake.

At the end of the Groenvlei Valley the road passes over a saddle, and into the beautiful Goukamma Valley, once a densely wooded valley where woodcutters were plagued by the local elephants. Today this fertile valley is given over to dairy farming. At the end of the valley, turn right towards Buffelsbaai, or continue on to Knysna.

BUFFELSBAAI

At the coast you will come to the entrance of the **Goukamma Nature Reserve** Tel. (04455) 50. (For information contact: The Senior Nature Conservation Officer, P.O. Sedgefield, 6573.) The reserve stretches from the Sedgefield area to Buffelsbaai, and includes part of Groenvlei's southern shore. It was established to protect the coastal dunes and abundance of bird life in the area. A picnic site and hiking trails have been established in the reserve. A permit to visit the reserve is obtainable from the ranger's office, through the gate marked "No admittance". The reserve is open from sunrise to sunset. Buffelsbaai is another of the many holiday resorts established along the coastline. The beach on the bay offers safe, pleasant bathing, wind-surfing and fishing from the rocks.

Return to the N2 and continue towards Knysna. Just before you reach the bridge crossing the Knysna lagoon, turn left and then immediately right, under the bridge, following the Brenton/ Belvidere signpost.

Turn off to **Belvidere,** which is a quaint little village on the banks of the Knysna lagoon. The **Holy Trinity Church** was built in the eleventh-century Norman style with timberwork of local stinkwood and yellowwood. The stained glass windows in the west wall come from the bombed ruins of Coventry Cathedral in Britain. For those wishing to stay over, the historic inn, Ferry House, is a perfect choice.

Ferry House   Tel. (0445) 2-4490
St Andrews Road (P.O. Box 1195, Knysna, 6570)
Situated on the water edge, Ferry House offers exclusive accommodation and superb home cooking, all supervised by the owners. This country house was well known as a pub and inn between 1850 and 1930.

From Belvidere return to the Brenton road and turn left towards Brenton. Along the road there are magnificent views of the lagoon. Five kilometres along the road is the turn-off for Lake Brenton Holiday Resort.

Lake Brenton Holiday Resort   Tel. (0445) 2-1501
P.O. Box 235, Knysna, 6570
Electric plug, gas, laundry, recreation hall, shop, swimmingpool, fishing, wind-surfing, snooker and table tennis
Apart from caravan and camping facilities, the resort offers accommodation in log cabins, chalets and rondavels. The resort is well laid out to give everybody privacy; and it blends in with the surroundings, making it a perfect site for a few days' rest.

After returning to the N2 follow the road along the lagoon into Knysna.

KNYSNA

This very popular holiday resort is situated between the indigenous forests and shores of the lagoon. It is a centre for furniture-making and boat-building, and has a few sawmills in the vicinity. The Knysna oysters are also becoming well-known as large oyster hatcheries have been established in the lagoon.

Knysna was founded by George Rex, a man with a legendary past. Many people believed him to be the eldest of three of King George III's illegitimate sons, but this has not been confirmed by modern research. He arrived at the Cape in 1797, during the first British occupation and was appointed marshal of the Vice-Admiralty court, notary public to the governor and advocate to the crown. When the Cape was handed back to the Dutch in 1802 he settled on a farm at Knysna. It was he who persuaded the government to build a harbour, but it was dangerous and caused many ships to be wrecked and ceased to be used for trading purposes after the railway was built.

In 1876 gold was discovered in the forests near Knysna. This sparked off a goldrush to a nearby town known as Milwood. By 1889, the mining camps had close to one thousand residents, three newspapers and six hotels. As most of the gold was alluvial, findings became fewer as time passed and so, with the discovery of gold on the Witwatersrand, miners moved on. By 1924 the field was deproclaimed and all that is now left are a few overgrown shafts and rusty machinery.

Accommodation

HOTELS

The Knysna Protea ***TYYY   Tel. (0445) 22127
51 Main Street
(P.O. Box 33, Knysna, 6570)   Protea Hotels and Inns
Situated in the town centre, this hotel is well appointed with comfortable rooms. The hotel restaurant is also worth a visit.
Leisure Isle **TYYY   Tel. (0445) 2-3143
Links Drive, Leisure Isle (P.O. Box 19, Knysna, 6570)
Swimming-pool, fishing, wind-surfing, sailing, diving and golf
This bungalow-style hotel is located in wooded surroundings on Leisure Island, between Knysna centre and The Heads. It is close to the lagoon, on which many water sports can be enjoyed. All bungalows are comfortably furnished.

OTHER ACCOMMODATION

Fair Acres   Tel. (0445) 22442
Thesens Hill (P.O. Box 201, Knysna, 6570)
Swimming-pool
It is located in tranquil surroundings and offers a magnificent view of the lagoon and Knysna Heads. All rooms have bathrooms, are comfortably furnished and are fully serviced. There is also a fully equipped communal kitchen on the property.
Bed and Breakfast   Tel. (0445) 2-2758
P.O. Box 530, Knysna, 6570
This organisation can find accommodation, at reasonable rates, in private homes throughout the Garden Route.

SELF-CATERING AND CAMPING

Knysna Heads Holiday Flats   Tel. (0445) 2-2759
36 George Rex Drive (P.O. Box 137, Knysna, 6570)
Fishing, skin diving, wind-surfing and hiking
The flats are situated at The Heads and have a superb view of the lagoon. All flats are self-contained, fully equipped and serviced daily. A restaurant and take-away shop are on site.
Ashmead Resort   Tel. (0445) 2-2985
George Rex Drive, Knysna, 6570
Golf, squash, tennis, table-tennis, fishing and wind-surfing
It is situated on the road to The Heads, and has its own beach on the lagoon. Accommodation includes chalets, cottages and flats, all fully equipped, as well as caravan and camping sites. Boats can be hired at the resort.
Lagoonside Holiday and Caravan Park   Tel. (0445) 2-1751
Main Street, East End (P.O. Box 116, Knysna, 6570)
Electric plugs, laundry, gas, swimming-pool, games room, fishing and wind-surfing
The park looks out over the lagoon, towards The Heads. All flats and cabins are self-contained, but cabins don't have baths. Camping and caravan sites are all grassed.

FLOATING HOLIDAYS Two companies in Knysna have cabin cruisers for hire for those who would enjoy a holiday with a difference. The boats are easy to operate.
Lightleys Holiday Cruises   Tel. (0445) 2-3071
P.O. Box 863, Knysna, 6570
The marina at which this company moors its cruisers is situated at the Brenton turn-off, on the George side of Knysna. All cruisers are fully equipped, including chemical toilets.
Southern Seas Charter Company   Tel. (0445) 2-1693
P.O. Box 753, Knysna, 6570
This marina is situated close to the town centre, just behind the railway station. All cruisers are fully equipped, and wind surf-boards can be hired.

Restaurants

The Heads   Tel. 2-2581   Wine and malt licence
The Heads, Knysna   Seafood
This popular restaurant is situated on the rocks, and has a superb view of the lagoon. Seafood featured includes locally caught fish and oysters.
Joan's Coffee Place   Tel. 2-2961   Not licensed
Memorial Square, Main Street.   Teas and light snacks
Joan's Coffee Place is situated in the centre of town. It is a delightful little restaurant that gives clients a choice of sitting outside in the sun or inside. They serve excellent freshly ground coffee, and a variety of home-baked cakes and sandwiches are served.
Seahorse Inn   Tel. 2-2431   Wine and malt licence
Main Street   Seafood/steaks
As one leaves Knysna on the road to Plettenberg Bay, Seahorse Inn is on the right, just behind a service garage. The restaurant has a fine view of the lagoon and The Heads. Local line fish and oysters dominate the menu, but steaks are also good.

Useful addresses and telephone numbers
Knysna area telephone code: **(0445)**

TOURIST INFORMATION   **Knysna Publicity Association**   Tel. 2-1610, P.O. Box 87, Knysna, 6501

RAILWAY INFORMATION   **The Stationmaster**   Tel. 2-1361

BOAT AND   **Knysna Hire Centre**   Tel. 2-1342, 62a Main Street, Knysna
WINDSURFER HIRE   **Lagoon Charters**   Tel. 2-1693, P.O. Box 753, Knysna

Sightseeing

The Heads are the two sandstone cliffs at the mouth of the lagoon. Spectacular views over the lagoon and Knysna can be had from the summit of the eastern head.
   Milwood Museum in Queen Street is located in Milwood House, an original building from Milwood gold town. The

museum is filled with artefacts related to the history of the town. It is open from Monday to Friday from 10h00 to 12h00.

Furniture stores located along Main Street in the centre of town offer a variety of wood articles and fine furniture, made out of local woods.

Featherbed Nature Reserve is situated on the western head and should be on every tourist's list of places to visit in the area. The reserve offers a day-trip, which includes a ride on the lagoon, a late champagne and oyster breakfast, a walk through the reserve and a braai (barbecue) lunch, and a return trip to town via the lagoon again. The walk takes the tourist through some superb coastal scenery. For reservations contact **Featherbed Nature Reserve** Tel. 2-1233.

Outdoor Activities

The Knysna lagoon offers a variety of watersports, including fishing, wind-surfing, scuba diving and sailing. Boats, diving equipment and windsurfers can be hired from **Knysna Hire Centre** Tel. 2-1342. In addition to hiring out boats and windsurfers, **Lagoon Charters** Tel. 2-1693 also organise deep-sea fishing trips.

Horse-riding is also very popular in the Knysna area. Horses can be hired from Misty Morn Riding School   Tel. 7661.

From Knysna, the road to Plettenberg Bay winds up to the plateau, through forests and small woodcutters' hamlets. At the top of the plateau, about 4 km from Knysna, you will find a turn-off to Noetzie, onto a dirt road.

Noetzie is about 5 km from the main road. This is a holiday village with a difference: all the houses are constructed in the shape of small castles. The beach is a steep 2 km from the parking area above the resort.

Return to the N2 and continue toward Plettenberg Bay. **The Garden of Eden,** on the main road, is a pleasant picnic site in the midst of beautiful indigenous trees (all named). This is also the section of forest where the **Knysna elephants** are to be found. Once a great number of elephants roamed these forests, living off the abundant vegetation; but the destruction of the forests and man's love of fine ivory, have forced the few remaining elephants to retreat to the depths of the forest. Today one would be lucky to catch a fleeting glimpse of one.

Continue along the N2 until you reach the Harberville turn-off, and turn right onto the dirt road. At the fork turn left and then immediately right; keep left until you reach the **Kransbos** picnic spot. The road runs up to the parking area at the edge of the cliff, high above the coast. From here one has a spectacular view of the sea pounding on the rocks 200 metres below. Return to the N2 for the final run into Plettenberg Bay; take the Pisang River turn-off into the resort.

PLETTENBERG BAY

With more than 10 km of safe bathing beaches, a magnificent setting and facilities for all water sports, it is not surprising that Plettenberg Bay has become known as the Riviera of South

Africa. It was originally named Bahia Formosa (Beautiful Bay) by the first Portuguese who sailed into it early in the fifteenth century.

The first church was erected in the bay in 1630 by a group of a hundred survivors off the wrecked Sáo Gonçalo. After eight months they had built two ships from local timber. They set sail again from the bay: one group headed for India and the other for Portugal. The present name was given by Governor Joachim von Plettenberg in 1778 when he erected a slate beacon on the island in the bay. During the 1780s the Dutch began to exploit the surrounding forests, and established a permanent settlement here. In 1912 a Norwegian whaling station was established in the bay, on Beacon Island. Fortunately it operated only until 1920, when the area started being developed for tourism. Today the only industry is tourism and the whales come back to the bay every year in spring to give birth to their young.

Robberg peninsula, on the southern end of Plettenberg Bay, is a nature reserve rich in bird and intertidal life. Spectacular scenery and excellent fishing can also be enjoyed along the peninsula.

Accommodation

HOTELS **Beacon Island** ***TYYY Tel. (04457) 3-1120
Private Box 1001,
Plettenberg Bay, 6600   Southern Sun
Swimming-pool, golf, squash, tennis, bowls, wind-surfing, skin-diving, fishing and sailing
Resting on the rocks of Beacon Island, this resort hotel has one of the best locations in South Africa, with magnificent views of the ocean and bay, and endless beaches stretching off on both sides of the hotel. Rooms in the hotel are all comfortably furnished and the majority have seaviews. There are two ladies' bars in the hotel, and a number of dining venues. Breakfast and lunch are served on the lawns in season.
Formosa Inn **TYYY Tel. (04457) 3-2060
National Road just outside of Plettenberg Bay (P.O. Box 121, Plettenberg Bay, 6600)
Swimming-pool
The inn is situated just outside Plettenberg Bay, and is one of the old inns of the Garden Route. The building has stinkwood and yellowwood beams dating back to 1820. Accommodation is offered in chalet-type rooms, each with its own car-port. In the main building you will find a cosy ladies bar, well insulated discoteque and very good restaurant.

OTHER **Bobby's Holiday Farm** Tel. (04457) 8657
ACCOMMODATION P.O. Box 37, The Crags, 6602
The Crags is about 15 minutes' drive from Plettenberg Bay. Guests are accommodated in cottages or rooms in the main house. All the rooms are comfortable and have pleasant views.
Forest Hall Tel. (04457) 8869
P.O. Box 38, The Crags, 6602   Portfolio of country places
A limited number of beds are offered at this charming old country estate. The house is furnished with period pieces which make the rooms elegant and very comfortable. The kitchen is famous in the area.

SELF-CATERING AND CAMPING

Heideveld Chalets   Tel. (04457) 7820
P.O. Box 572, Plettenberg Bay, 6600
Swimming-pool, riding and hiking
These chalets are set in the country, 7 km from town on the Knysna road. All chalets have superb views onto the mountains and are fully equipped. They have two bedrooms and a lounge that opens onto a verandah with braai (barbecue) area.

Keurbooms River Public Resort   Tel. (04457) 9309
Private Bag, Plettenberg Bay, 6600
Wind-surfing, fishing and hiking
This resort is 5 km east of the town, on the Keurbooms River. It is a secluded, well laid-out resort with both rondavel and camping sites. All rondavels are fully equipped.

Piesang River Holiday Resort   Tel. (04457) 3-1640
Beacon Island Drive (P.O. Box 185, Plettenberg Bay, 6600)
Electric plugs, gas, shop, swimming-pool, games room, snooker room, sauna, laundromat, fishing and wind-surfing
This five-star resort is situated in the village itself, within walking distance of the best beaches. All chalets and rondavels are fully equipped, excluding bedding, which can be hired. Camping areas are well laid out. The resort is very secure.

Robberg Holiday Resort   Tel. (04457) 3-2571
P.O. Box 81, Plettenberg Bay, 6600
Electric plugs, gas, shop, laundry, fishing, wind-surfing, skin-diving and hiking
Situated on the far end of Robberg Beach, the resort is the only one in Plettenberg Bay which can claim a beach frontage. One has a choice of fully equipped wooden chalets, and well laid out camp sites.

Restaurants

Formosa Inn   Tel. (04457) 3-2060   Fully licensed
On the national road just outside
Plettenberg Bay   Steakhouse/seafoods
Whether its a good steak or fresh fish that you are looking for, you will find it here. And the dessert trolley is well worth a try. Service is efficient and attentive, while the atmosphere is pleasant.

Useful addresses and telephone numbers

Plettenberg Bay area telephone code: **(04457)**

TOURIST INFORMATION

Plettenburg Bay Publicity Association   Tel. 3-2050. P.O. Box 26, Plettenberg Bay, 6600

AIRLINES

Air Cape   Tel. 3-1630, Lookout Centre, Main Street, Plettenberg Bay, 6600

CAR HIRE

Avis   Tel. 3-1315
Budget   Tel. 3-3570

Outdoor Activities

The most pleasant way to spend a day in the area is, of course, just relaxing on the beach. If, however, you need more vigorous exercise, Plettenberg Bay is the perfect place.

The **golf course** in the Piesang River Valley welcomes visitors and has a very pleasant course. The beaches offer kilometres of pleasant **walks**; and the more adventurous could spend a pleasant day walking around the Robberg peninsula's well-marked paths.

There are a number of fishing opportunities in the area: **river fishing** can be enjoyed along the banks of the Keurbooms River; **surf** and **rock fishing** are good all along the coast, but especially from Robberg Peninsula; **deep-sea fishing** is also good in the area, and trips can be arranged. For further information contact the Publicity Association or Angling Club (from December to mid-January) Tel. 3-1325. The bay offers excellent possibilities for both **wind-surfing** and **Hobi-cat sailing. Skin diving** is also very popular. The best sites are off Beacon Island and Robberg Peninsula. Equipment can be hired from Tel. 3-1120.

Leaving Plettenberg Bay, the road crosses the Keurbooms River before winding its way back up to the plateau, past The Crags. From here the road splits, and one can choose between going via the new toll road or via two spectacular passes. A good compromise is to go via the **Groot River Pass** and then over the **Bloukrans Bridge.** The turn-off for this road is marked **Port Elizabeth via Nature's Valley** (R102). Keep an eye open for the beautiful yellowwood trees as you meander down the pass. At the base of the pass is **Nature's Valley**, a quaint village that forms part of a nature reserve. The lagoon offers safe bathing as well as good wind-surfing opportunities. One can enjoy pleasant walks and good fishing along the beach as well as on the buttlands on either side. An especially pleasant walk is south, along the beach. Park at the tearoom in the village, and walk along the rocks until you come to a secluded little bay, where good fishing and pleasant bathing can be enjoyed.

From Nature's Valley the road crosses the Groot River, before climbing up to the plateau. There is a parking area at the top of the pass where one can look back over Nature's Valley. Further along, the road rejoins the N2 toll road, and one passes through the tollgates before crossing the magnificent Bloukrans River Bridge. About a kilometre after crossing the bridge, a turn-off to the left leads to the Bloukrans rest area, where one can find clean toilets, a restaurant, picnic spots and enjoy a fine view of the bridge and valley below.

Continuing along this road, the next point of interest is the village of Storms River. To reach it, turn off onto a dirt road at the signpost. Here you will find the Tsitsikamma Forest Inn.
Tsitsikamma Forest Inn   *TYYY   Tel. (004237) 711
Dornell Street
(P.O. Storms River, 6308)   Portfolio of Country Places
Swimming-pool, tennis, hiking and sauna
The inn was originally built in 1850, as a shooting base. Today, much of the old character remains: magnificent yellowwood ceilings, antiques and the **Hunters' Inn Pub,** where the old muzzel loaders and trophies still hang. Guests are accommodated in chalets in the garden: a few have open fires for the cold winter

nights. Home-cooked meals can be enjoyed in the dining room, and teas on the lawns.

Just further down the N2, to the right, you will find the turn-off to **Storms River Mouth** and **Tsitsikamma Coastal National Park Rest Camp**. The entrance to the park is 6 km down the road. The restaurant and car park another 4 km along the road.

TSITSIKAMMA COASTAL PARK

The **Rest Camp**   Tel. (012) 44-1191 or Tel. (021) 24-3124
Bookings: National Parks Board, P.O. Box 787, Pretoria, 0001
Accommodation is offered in wooden chalets, flats or in a caravan park. The flats and chalets are completely self-contained. They all have a superb view of the sea. The restaurant offers a wide variety of simple, but substantial meals as well as teas. Evening meal orders have to be put in early in the afternoon, and the meal is served promptly at the specified times. There is also a provision store in the park.

One can take a number of walks of varying distance within the park. The most enjoyable and well-known walk is the five-day **Otter Trail**, from Storms River westwards to Nature's Valley — a distance of 48 km. There are four overnight huts along the trail. All provisions and sleeping equipment need to be carried by the hikers. Reservations for the trail (which is usually fully booked well in advance) can be made through the address above.

From Nature's Valley a second trail — the five-day **Tsitsikamma Hiking Trail** — extends inland for 72 km, back to Storms River. Reservations: The Regional Director, Tsitsikamma Region, Private Bag X537, Humansdorp, 6300; Tel. (042312) 656.

A pleasant morning or afternoon walk brings one to the river mouth, and further details can be obtained from the rest camp office. Angling and skin diving can also be enjoyed. A special **diving trail** has been laid out in the area, but divers must bring their own equipment.

From Storms River Mouth, return to the N2 and continue along towards Humansdorp. The turn-off to the **Big Tree** is on the left, 9 km along the road. The dirt road is in rather poor condition, but well worth the drive (or walk) of about one kilometre. The giant Outeniqua yellowwood is 37 m tall, with a crown spread of 34 m, and is estimated to be over 800 years old. While walking through the peaceful surroundings, you might try to identify other species, such as the stinkwood, ironwood, white pear, wild olive and Cape ash.

Three kilometres further along the N2 is the spectacular **Paul Sauer Bridge** over the Storms River. At the bridge you will find a shop, restaurant and service station, as well as camping facilities.

Continue from Storms River Bridge east along the N2, to Humansdorp and then on towards Port Elizabeth, through forest which gradually opens to farmland. Eleven kilometres after the Humansdorp turn-off you will find the turn-off for Jeffrey's Bay, which is yet another 7 km from the N2.

JEFFREY'S BAY

The resort gets its name from a retired whaleman, J.A. Jeffrey, who in the mid-nineteenth century set up shop here to supply Port Elizabeth with fresh produce. The produce was shipped to Port Elizabeth by coaster, but this activity ceased after a narrow-gauge railway line was constructed into the fertile Langkloof. Jeffrey's Bay survives as a fishing village and holiday resort. It boasts a temperate climate, golden beaches and perfect surfing conditions. It became popular with members of the alternative culture in the 1960s. Today, surfers from all over the world still flock there to ride the perfect waves. A variety of handcraft and leatherwork can be bought from local residents. The resort is also famous for its beautiful seashells.

Accommodation

Savoy **TYYY   Tel. (04231) 3-1106
Da Gama Street (P.O. Box 36, Jeffrey's Bay, 6330)
Swimming-pool, golf, fishing, tennis, surfing and wind-surfing
It is situated in the main street, close to the shops and beach. The rooms are comfortable and always clean. Food is basic country fare.
Kabeljous Holiday Resort   Tel. (04231) 3-1775
Da Gama Street (P.O. Box 21, Jeffrey's Bay, 6330)
Fishing, wind-surfing and surfing
The resort, situated opposite the beach, offers rondavel accommodation and caravan and camping facilities.
Municipal Caravan Park   Tel. (04231) 3-1111
Da Gama Street (P.O. Box 21, Jeffrey's Bay, 6330)
Electric plugs, laundry, recreation hall, swimming-pool, fishing and wind-surfing
This is a well-planned caravan park close to the beach.

Tourist Information
Jeffrey's Bay area telephone code: **(04231)**

Jeffrey's Bay Publicity Association   Tel. 3-1111
21 Da Gama Street, (P.O. Box 21, Jeffrey's Bay, 6630)

Sightseeing

The **Kritzinger Sea Shell Collection**, housed in the local library, on the seafront road, is well worth a visit. It is also well worth watching the surfers' manoeuvres on the waves.

On departing from Jeffrey's Bay, take the Kabeljousbos road, then right onto the R102 towards Port Elizabeth. This road takes you back to the N2, and on to Port Elizabeth.
    If you have time on your hands, take the route via the scenic coastal resorts just outside the city. This can be done by taking the Van Staden's Mouth/St. Albans exit and following the "Beach Views" signs.
    The first resort one reaches is **Maitland River Mouth:** a popular resort with both surf anglers and bathers. It has golden beaches,

The Beacon Island Hotel, Plettenberg Bay

A herd of elephants in the Addo Elephant National Park

The Belvidere Church, Knysna

The Storms River mouth

flanked by towering sand dunes stretching for miles on either side of the mouth.

The next resort is Beach View Holiday Resort.

Beach View Holiday Resort   Tel. (041) 7-4884
P.O. Box 318, Port Elizabeth, 6000
Laundry, gas, shop, swimming-pool, tennis and fishing
This pleasant resort offers the visitor both cottages, which are fully equipped, and comfortable camping sites, all overlooking the sea.

From Beach View continue to **Sea View.**

Minhetti Hotel   **TYYY   Tel. (041) 7-4611
P.O. Box 237, Port Elizabeth, 6000
This well-run hotel on the shoreline is situated on the site of the Royal Naval Officers' training base in South Africa during World War II. Rooms are clean and well appointed, while fresh fish dominates the restaurant menu, which is always good.

The road curves inland from Sea View through farmlands and Port Jackson scrub. After 19 km, turn right at the T-junction, towards Skoenmakerskop. From here the road again follows the coast (on Marine Drive) to Port Elizabeth, passing The Willows along the way.

The Willows Holiday Resort   Tel. (041) 36-1717
P.O. Box 318, Port Elizabeth, 6000
Electric plugs, laundry, shop, swimming-pool, fishing, tennis and hiking
This resort, with its well laid out camping facilities, rondavels and self-contained cottages, is ideal for those who want a beach holiday, but also wish to be close to the city, which is only 16 km away.

PORT ELIZABETH

The centre of the motor industry in South Africa, Port Elizabeth is South Africa's fifth largest city and a popular holiday resort. The first European to visit Algoa Bay was Bartholomeu Dias in 1488, when he named it *"Bahia de Lagoa"*. For the next three hundred-odd years very little happened in the bay as far as European settlement is concerned; but in 1799 Fort Frederick —named after the Duke of York — was built by the British to guard the landing place and water supply in the bay. By 1819, 35 settlers were living on the shores of the bay. The next year, 1820, over four thousand British Settlers landed on the shores. They were to become farmers in the area, and were intended to form a buffer between the black tribes, who were moving south, and the ever-expanding new Colony. The acting governor at the time, Sir Rufane Donkin, named the city after his late wife, Elizabeth, who had died two years previously in India. With the arrival of the 1820 Settlers in the area, trade began to flourish, and the town began to grow as a port and commercial centre. In 1869 the first diamond auction in the Colony took place here; and the first gold was shipped from the harbour in 1874. With the strong English influence, rugby and cricket were both popular. The first cricket test in South Africa was played here in 1889 with Sir Aubrey Smith as the British team captain; and the first rugby test against Britain was played in 1891. As the farming community grew, so did the port, and industry around the port.

But the anchorage was not always safe, as was shown on 31 August 1902. Overnight a strong south-west gale picked up, and 19 ships in the bay broke anchorage and were driven onto the rocks. Today Port Elizabeth has a secure deep-water harbour.

Accommodation

HOTELS

Elizabeth Sun *****TYYY   Tel. (041) 52-3720
La Roche Drive (P.O. Box 13100,
Port Elizabeth, 6000)   Southern Sun
Swimming-pool and sauna
This hotel is located across the road from the beach, near the amusement park and oceanarium complex, and a short drive from town. The only drawback is that the well-appointed rooms are small. The Oyster Box serves fresh oysters every lunch and dinner time: either as a full meal or as a starter before moving onto a restaurant.

Algoa Protea Inn   ***TYYY   Tel. (041) 2-1558
7 Lutman Street,
Port Elizabeth, 6001   Protea Hotels and Inns
Sauna
Close to town and within driving distance of all the beaches and the airport, this small hotel (only 10 suites) is well run, and offers all the comforts one would expect from such an establishment.

Beach Hotel   ***TYYY   Tel. (041) 53-2161
Marine Drive, Humewood, Port Elizabeth, 6001
On the beachfront, with an open verandah overlooking the sea, this is an ideal spot in which to relax. Rooms are large and comfortable, and the food is well up to standard. Tennis, golf, bowls facilities and a swimming-pool are all located close by.

Holiday Inn   ***TYYY   Tel. (041) 53-3131
Marine Drive, Summerstrand
(P.O. Box 204, Port Elizabeth, 6000)   Holiday Inns
Swimming-pool and tennis
It is situated at the end of Marine Drive, a fair way from the city, and across the road from pleasant bathing beaches. All the rooms in this large hotel more than measure up to the standard that Holiday Inns have set throughout the country. There are a variety of bars and restaurants in the hotel — the best is the Piazza Restaurant, which serves French and Italian dishes.

Edward   **TYYY   Tel. (041) 56-2056
Belmont Terrace (P.O. Box 319, Port Elizabeth, 6000)
Located above the city, this fine old hotel still echoes the grace and elegance of the past when stage-coaches and horsemen used to come riding into the courtyard and stable up for the night. The atmosphere is this hotel's strongest point. It is the ideal stop for the more budget-conscious.

OTHER ACCOMMODATION

Richly House   Tel. (041) 33-7995
76 Cape Road, Port Elizabeth, 6001
Swimming-pool
Richly House is situated in the suburbs close to the city and has a bus-stop outside the door providing transport to the city, the various tourist attractions and the beaches. Accommodation is comfortable and wholesome home-cooked meals are provided.

YMCA   Tel. (041) 2-9792
31 Havelock Street (P.O. Box 12007, Centrahil, Port Elizabeth, 6006)
This is ideal for the very budget-conscious. Meals are good and also available to non-residents.

**SELF-CATERING
AND CAMPING**

Bliss Holiday Apartments   Tel. (041) 53-2171
Marine Drive, Summerstrand, Port Elizabeth, 6001
These apartments are ideally located opposite the beach. All flats are self-contained.
Langerry Holiday Flats   Tel. (041) 2-2654
31 Beach Road (P.O. Box 46, Port Elizabeth, 6000)
These flats are located opposite the beach and close to many amenities. All flats are self-contained. (See also page 131.)

Restaurants

Homestead   Tel. 52-3720   Fully licensed
Elizabeth Sun, La Roche Drive   Carvery/buffet
This restaurant has a fine view over the Bay and is perfect for an informal meal. Big appetites are definitely satisfied here.
Lychee Gardens   Tel. 52-2471   Wine and malt licence
10 Parliament Street   Chinese
As Port Elizabeth has the largest Chinese community in South Africa, it is to be expected that at least one good Chinese restaurant would be found here. The décor is splendid, and the presentation of the food is excellent. However, special requests need to be made for the genuine dishes, as many are spiced down for South African tastes.
Sir Rufane Donkin Rooms
Tel. 2-5534   Wine and malt licence
5 George Street, Upper Hill   Home cooking
This is the ideal place for a romantic meal, complete with candle-light and classical music. The menu changes every two weeks and complements the atmosphere perfectly.
Up the Khyber
Tel. 52-2200   Wine and malt licence
Cnr. Western Road and Belmont Terrace   Indian
With a typical Indian atmosphere, including staff in traditional Indian dress, and burning incense, this restaurant is a must for those who enjoy this type of food. A wide variety of Indian dishes, not only curries, are served.

Useful addresses and telephone numbers
Port Elizabeth area telephone code: **(041)**

TOURIST INFORMATION

Port Elizabeth Publicity Association Tel. 52-1315, Library Building, Market Square (P.O. Box 357, Port Elizabeth, 6000)
South African Tourism Board   Tel. 2-7761, 310 Mutual Building, 64 Main Street (P.O. Box 1161, Port Elizabeth, 6000)

TRANSPORT

Airlines   **Airline reservations**   Tel. 34-4444
Airport enquiries   Tel. 51-3601
SAA   Tel. 520-2500

Bus departures

P.E. Tramways Ltd. Market Square Bus Station Tel. 2-8751
Copper Rose (between Port Elizabeth and East London) Tel. 2-8555
Leopard Express (between Port Elizabeth and Grahamstown) Tel. 54-1057
Translax (between Port Elizabeth, Cape Town and Durban) Tel. 520-2074
Trans City (between Port Elizabeth and Cape Town) Tel. 53-3184
Greyhound (between Port Elizabeth and Johannesburg) Tel. 34-4550

Coach Tours

Algoa Tours Tel. 2-7410
Tour and Trail Tel. 52-2814

Car Hire

Avis Tel. 51-4291
Budget Tel. 51-4242
Imperial Tel. 51-2709

Railway reservations

Mainline reservations and enquiries Tel. 520-2975, Station Street
Apple Express Tel. 520-2360

Taxis

Ranks at: Fleming Street Tel. 2-3296; station Tel. 2-6280; Russel Road Tel. 2-1814; and airport
Radio cabs Tel. 2-1756

Sightseeing

Port Elizabeth has many reminders of the 1820 Settler arrival and the subsequent growth of the city. Owing to the layout of the city on the coastal cliff, walking to various points can be strenuous. If you walk, it is best to park in Belmont Street above Donkin Reserve and then walk to:

Donkin Reserve, proclaimed an open space in 1820 by Sir Rufane Donkin. On the reserve is a lighthouse, dating from 1861, now housing a military museum; and a stone pyramid, erected by Donkin in memory of his wife, Elizabeth, who died in India in 1818.

From here walk down **Donkin Street** with its row of brightly painted terrace houses dating from the early Victorian era. In Main Street (the main street of Port Elizabeth), turn right and walk along until you get to . . .

The Market Square, which is the original **Outspan,** from a time when ox-wagons still visited the city. On the square stands the City Hall, built in 1858. It was restored in 1977 after having been gutted by fire. In front of it stands a replica of Dias Cross, which was originally erected at Kwaaihoek by Bartholomeu Dias in 1488. From here, walk under the freeway towards the harbour.

The Camponile was built in 1923 to commemorate the landing of the 1820 Settlers. From its top, reached by a 204-step spiral stairway, one has an excellent view of the city and harbour. It is open on Mondays, Tuesdays and Fridays from 09h00 to 13h00 and from 14h00 to 16h00, and on Wednesdays and Saturdays from 08h30 to 12h30. From here, return to the Market Square, and then up Castle Hill, stopping at . . .

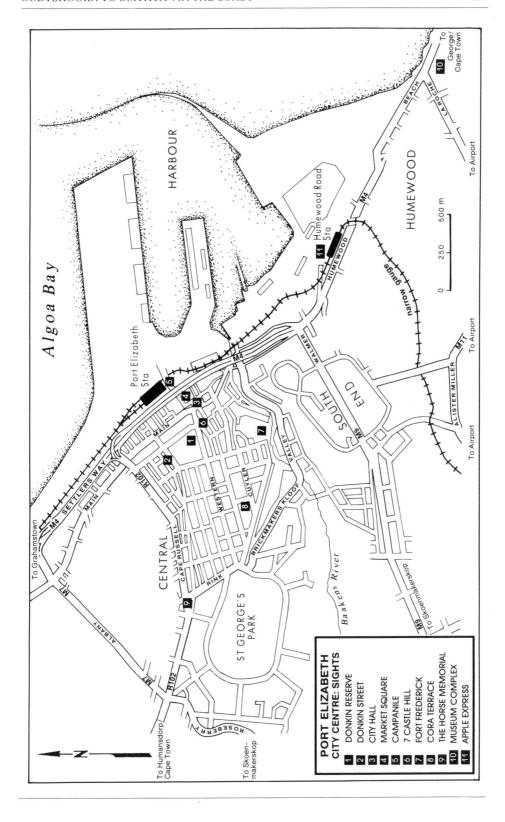

PORT ELIZABETH
CITY CENTRE: SIGHTS

1. DONKIN RESERVE
2. DONKIN STREET
3. CITY HALL
4. MARKET SQUARE
5. CAMPANILE
6. 7 CASTLE HILL
7. FORT FREDERICK
8. CORA TERRACE
9. THE HORSE MEMORIAL
10. MUSEUM COMPLEX
11. APPLE EXPRESS

7 Castle Hill, built in 1827 by the Rev. McClelland. It is the oldest surviving private dwelling in Port Elizabeth and is furnished with period furniture. It is open from Tuesday to Saturday from 10h00 to 13h00 and 14h00 to 17h00, and on Sunday and Monday from 14h00 to 17h00. From here return to your car.

Other places of interest to visit Port Elizabeth are the following:

Fort Frederick, built in 1799, overlooks the old landing place and water-hole. It was built for the defence of the bay, but was never used as such.

Cora Terrace, off Cuyler Street, is a row of Regency-styled houses built between 1831 and 1834 as officers' residences.

The Horse Memorial, at the junction of Cape and Russel Roads, which was erected by public subscription in 1905. It is dedicated to the horses killed in action during the Anglo-Boer War of 1899–1902.

The **Museum Complex** on Beach Road in Humewood comprises:

— **The Oceanarium,** which has dolphins, seals and penguins that perform a variety of manoeuvres for spectators daily at 11h00 and 15h00. Seals and fish are fed after each performance.

— **The Snake Park,** which is renowned for its many indigenous and exotic reptiles.

— **The Tropical House,** which can be entered through the snake park. It is a large enclosure beautifully laid-out with paths through dense tropical vegetation and has a number of tropical birds flying around.

— **The Museum** includes a costume gallery of early twentieth-century clothing, a marine hall depicting the marine life of the bay, and a bird hall.

— **The Children's Museum** has a variety of exhibits especially intended to be touched by children. The complex is open daily from 09h00 to 13h00, and 14h00 to 17h00 except on Christmas day.

The Apple Express is one of the few narrow-guage railway lines (a 61 cm-wide line) left in the world. It has been running from Port Elizabeth through the fertile fruit-growing Langkloof Valley to Avontuur since 1906. The train travels through some of the most scenic parts of the eastern Cape, including a spectacular crossing of the Van Staden's River Gorge over a steel girder bridge 77 m above the river — the highest bridge of its kind in the world. Excursions can be made every Saturday between June and January from Port Elizabeth to Loerie. Reservations can be made at the main line ticket office in Port Elizabeth (Tel. (041) 520-2360).

Outdoor Activities

The most predominent outdoor pursuits in the area are water-related. **Fishing** is the most popular: **Surf, rock and river fishing** can be enjoyed along the coast as well as in the various estuaries all year round. **Deep-sea fishing** trips can be arranged through *Hasties Sports Shop,* Tel. 52-4238 or 52-4138, in Main Street.

Wind-surfing is also very popular —there is no shortage of wind in this part of the world. Algoa Bay **Diving School**, Tel. 2-3367, will be glad to assist all those wishing to dive in the area.

Visitors are welcome at the following **golf courses:**
— *Humewood Golf Course,*   Tel. 53-2137
— *Port Elizabeth Golf Course,*   Tel. 34-3140
— *Wedgewood Country Club,*   Tel. 72-1212
— *Walmer Country Club,*   Tel. 51-4211

Leave Port Elizabeth on the M4 motorway which becomes Settlers Way, and then joins the N2 for Grahamstown. About 12 km from town, take the St. George's Strand exit and then follow the Addo signs along the R335. Turn right off the tarred road to the Addo Elephant National Park at **Coerney Station,** 52 km further along the road.

ADDO ELEPHANT NATIONAL PARK

Major P.J. Pretorius in his book *Jungle Man*, published in 1947, described the park as follows: "... if ever there was a hunter's hell here it was — a hundred square miles or so of all you would think bad in central Africa, lifted up as by some Titan and plonked down in the Cape Province". He was describing the area from bitter experience.

At the turn of the century, more and more farmers settled along the fertile banks of the Sunday River to practise irrigation farming. One of the two remaining pockets of elephant in the Cape Province was also settled here. During the dry season herds of elephant would move across to the river to drink, while enjoying the cultivated produce on the way. By the end of the World War I, there was total uproar in the area and Major Pretorius, a war hero and renowned big game hunter, was hired to eradicate the group. Battling through the bush he managed to shoot 110 of the estimated 135 animals before public indignation called a halt to the slaughter.

In 1931 the government proclaimed a 9 712 ha section of bush as a park for the remaining herd.

Harold Trollope, a game ranger of tremendous foresight and patience, was given the task of herding the elephants into the area and keeping them there. Keeping them in the area was a major task that took over twenty years to complete. After having tried fires, trap guns, trenches and electrified fences without success, a team of workers with Graham Armstrong, Trollope's successor, came up with a solution. The result was the construction of the Armstrong Fence out of old lift cable and tramlines in 1954. Boreholes were sunk and dams constructed within the park and for the first time the herd began to increase in size. But there was another problem. To keep the animals in the area, they were fed oranges near the rest camp. This meant that a very small area was supporting most of the herd. By 1976 thirty tonnes of oranges a month were used, and the elephants were showing signs of stress and increased aggression due to competition for food. Drastic steps needed to be taken, and in 1978 the practice was stopped. Today, visitors may not take fruit into the park.

Now there are over 135 elephants in the park and a new danger has surfaced: the elephants are outgrowing the park. In the future the herd will be used to stock new conservation areas in the Cape. Other animals in the park include buffalo, eland, red hartebeest, black rhino, as well as smaller buck and over 170 species of birdlife.

Facilities within the park include self-contained huts (no cutlery or crockery), camping facilities, petrol station, a restaurant, and a shop where basic commodities can be bought. For reservations contact the National Parks Board (address on page 290).

If you wish to miss the park, continue along the N2 towards Grahamstown, and then either branch off towards Alexandria (R72) at the Ncanaha interchange, or continue on to Grahamstown.

From the park exit take the road towards the Zuurberg and then turn right onto the road to Paterson. On reaching the R32, turn right towards Ncanaha and at the N2 interchange take the R72 to Alexandria. Just before you reach Alexandria, there is a dirt road to the right which leads to the **Kaba Forest** — a beautiful place for a picnic. Continue into Alexandria and follow the left turn to Salem. The road passes through some interesting farmland scenery originally opened up by the 1820 Settlers.

Salem. The name was taken from Psalm 76 and means "peace". It was peace that Hesekiah Sephton and his party of 345 London settlers were seeking when they came to settle here in 1820. The village is a well-preserved relic of the period, with its stoutly constructed double-storey houses, church (which also served as a fort during the numerous Xhosa raids that the Settlers had to weather) and village green, which is still used for cricket matches.

From Salem continue on towards Grahamstown.

GRAHAMSTOWN

The city was originally established as an army garrison in 1812, when Colonel John Graham was sent to the area to drive the Xhosas from the buffer zone east of the Fish River. The white trekkers, who were moving eastwards, and the Xhosas, who were moving further south-west in search of new grazing, met in this region, and a series of wars ensued. Graham set up a military post on the abandoned farm of De Rietfontein. In 1819 the area was again attacked by nine thousand warriors. The garrison of 301 men managed to repulse the attack, leaving over one thousand Xhosas dead. The following year saw the arrival of the 1820 Settlers, who at first settled in the area as farmers. Many of the farms granted were totally unviable, and many Settlers were unsuited to farming. This led to a number of them abandoning their farms and settling in the town, practising their original trades. By 1931, Grahamstown had become the second largest town in the Colony, after Cape Town. Each time a war broke out with the Xhosas, more Settlers moved into town. In 1853 a cathedral was built and the post of the Bishop of Grahamstown was created, thus turning Grahamstown into a city. In 1864 a full parliamentary session was held in Grahamstown because of its central position. The town grew in importance as a market place: ivory, skins, beads, blankets and produce were traded and up to two thousand wagons visited the town on market days. To handle this traffic all the streets in and out of the town were made wide enough to allow a wagon and full team of oxen to turn. Today the many schools and Rhodes University make it a centre for education. It also has over 40 churches and is sometimes called the City of Saints.

Accommodation

HOTELS

Cathcart Arms Hotel **TYYY   Tel. (0461) 2-7111
5 West Street (P.O. Box 143, Grahamstown, 6140)
Swimming-pool
This, the oldest hotel in the city, was established in 1831 and has been run continuously as a hotel since then. This charming hotel has an interesting history attached and is worth staying in if you are passing through Grahamstown. The hotel is well-run and all rooms are decorated in cottage décor. The food served in St. George's Restaurant comprises simple grills and seafood, but is served precisely to the diner's specifications.

Settlers Protea Inn **TYYY   Tel. (0461) 2-7313
Port Elizabeth Road (P.O. Box 219, Grahamstown,
6140)   Protea Hotels and Inns
Swimming-pool and hiking
The inn is located just outside Grahamstown on the N2 towards Port Elizabeth. It is professionally run and the rooms, which are in the form of chalets, are all very spacious and comfortable, offering fine views over the valley below. Good bar lunches are also served.

SELF-CATERING
AND CAMPING

Grahamstown Caravan Park   Tel. (0461) 2-2043/ 2-4366
Mountain Drive (P.O. Box 176, Grahamstown, 6140)
Electric plugs and laundry
The park offers camping facilities as well as accommodation in cottages and rondavels. All accommodation is fully equipped and all camping sites are well grassed.

Restaurants

See two hotels above.

Tourist Information

Grahamstown area telephone code: **(0461)**

Grahamstown Publicity Association   Tel. 2-3241, Church Square, Grahamstown, 6140

Sightseeing

On the town square, around the Anglican Cathedral of St. Michael and St. George and along High Street, the many fine facades of the original Grahamstown shops are well worth seeing.

The **Observatory Museum** in Bathurst Street houses — along with other articles of historical interest — the only Camera Obscura in South Africa. It is a wonderful way of enjoying a static tour of Grahamstown on sunny days! Open Monday to Friday 09h30 to 13h00 and from 14h00 to 17h00. Saturday from 09h30 to 13h00.

At the top of High Street the gateway to the **Old Drostdy** now serves as the entrance to Rhodes University.

The **Albany Museum complex** has exhibits on the Settler history of the region as well as the history of the Xhosa. It is open from Tuesday to Friday from 09h30 to 13h00 and from 14h00 to 17h00 and on Saturdays and Sundays from 14h00 to 17h00.

In the park behind the museum the Provost is located. It was built in 1836 as a military prison. On **Gunfire Hill** behind the town, on the N2 to Port Elizabeth the following are located:

— **Fort Selwyn** was built in 1836 for the defence of the town. It still contains a battery of guns. It is open from Tuesday to Saturday from 09h00 to 16h00 and on Sundays from 12h00 to 16h00.

— The **1820 Settlers' Monument** was opened in 1974 to commemorate the valuable contribution made by these gallant people towards the growth of South Africa. It is also one of the most practical monuments in the country, comprising two conference halls, a theatre and restaurant. The abstract sculptures of the interior, created out of local wood, represent the merging of cultures of Great Britain and South Africa. It is open daily from 08h00 to 17h00.

Annual Event

Each year in June/July the Grahamstown festival takes place. This festival encompasses a variety of cultural events including musical recitals, the launching of new plays and art exhibitions. For further information contact the Grahamstown Publicity Association.

Shopping

Makana Handicrafts at 8 Bathurst Street creates, amongst other things, beautifully handwoven wall-hangings and carpets. They are even able to export to most destinations.

From Grahamstown take the R67 towards Bathurst and Port Alfred. The road passes through some fine farming country, including vast pineapple fields totalling some seventy million plants.

BATHURST

The village was founded in 1820 and was intended to be the administrative capital of the district. But with Grahamstown's quick expansion, it remained only the religious and community centre for the surrounding settlers. The village is named after the Earl of Bathurst, who was the British Colonial Secretary at the time. The two churches built by the settlers, St. John's Anglican Church and the Wesleyan Church served as shelters during the Xhosa wars and are now national monuments.

HOTEL   **Pig 'n Whistle**   *TYYY   Tel. (0464) 3673
Kowie Road, Bathurst, 6166

Built in 1821, this is one of the oldest licensed hotels in the country and retains much of the character of a typical old English pub, where the locals mingle with the visitors. Standards are very high. Food is also very good in the style of typical hearty South Arican home-cooking.

Sightseeing

Bailies Beacon, also known as the Toposcope, 2 km from the village (follow the signposts), identifies various points of interest in the countryside as well as places where 1820 Settler parties were allocated land.

Bradshaw's Mill is sited 1,1 km south of Bathurst. The mill was set up by Samuel Bradshaw soon after his arrival, in 1822, and provided the settlers with blankets and jersey material for clothing.

From Bathurst, the road winds its way down to the coast.

PORT ALFRED

Throughout the nineteenth century the settlers in the area tried in vain to turn the river mouth of the Kowie into a port. In 1821 a small brig, the Locust, was dispatched from Cape Town to sound the river entrance, resulting in a pilot and a harbour-master being appointed. Unfortunately, due to the shallow mouth, the changing winds and tidal currents, the mouth became a death-trap to many ships and in 1831, the harbour-master was with-drawn. Thereafter it was left to the residents to try to develop the harbour. In 1857 the government again launched a scheme to develop the port by building piers and stationing a steam tug and dredger here. During this period the harbour became a hive of activity: 101 ships landed 13 000 tons of cargo in 1876. In 1881 a railway line was built between Grahamstown and the port. During the 1890s the harbour finally fell into disuse and from then on has been used only by fishing and pleasure craft. The town, originally named Port Frances, after Lord Charles Somer-set's daughter-in-law, was renamed Port Alfred in 1860 to mark the visit of Prince Alfred. Today the town is renowned as a pleasant holiday resort, with fine beaches and good fishing.

Accommodation

HOTELS   **Kowie Grand Hotel** *TYYY Tel. (0464) 4-1150
Grand Street (P.O. Box 1, Kowie West, 6171)
It is located high on the hill and affords a fine view of the river and sea. This well-run hotel is ideal for an overnight stop, or a relaxing few days. The food is recommended.
Langdon Hotel *TYYY Tel. (0464) 4-1122
Beach Road (P.O. Box 177, Port Alfred, 6170)
It is located the closest to the beach of all the hotels, and across the road from the river. Accommodation is basic, but as comfort-able as one would expect from a one-star hotel.

SELF-CATERING
AND CAMPING

Bretton Beach Crest   Tel. (0464) 4-1606
Bretton Beach (P.O. Box 117, Port Alfred, 6170)
Fishing, golf, tennis, bowls and wind-surfing
Fully equipped beach cottages, for those who are looking for
relaxing accommodation at the beach.
Kowie Beach Cabanas   Tel. (0464) 4-2404
West Beach Drive (P.O. Box 88, Port Alfred, 6170)
Fishing, golf, tennis, bowls and wind-surfing
The cabanas are located on the beach, close to the river mouth.
All are well-furnished and self-contained.
Medolina Caravan Park   Tel. (0464) 4-1651
23 Steward Road (P.O. Box 20,
Port Alfred, 6171)   Club Caraville
Electric plugs, laundry, gas, tennis, bowls, golf, wind-surfing
and fishing
Fully equipped chalets and caravans can be hired on the site.
This is a very well laid out camping area in a garden environ-
ment. The park is close to the beach and sports facilities.

Tourist Information

Port Alfred area telephone code: **(0464)**

Port Alfred Publicity Association   Tel. 4-1235

Outdoor Activities

The **Royal Port Alfred Golf Club** (Tel. 4-2500) welcomes visitors
and has one of the best coastal courses in the country.

Tennis and bowls clubs also welcome visitors and more information can be obtained from the Publicity Association or the
hotels.

Wind-surfing can be enjoyed from the beach, and in the elbow
of the river behind the town.

Fishing is also very good in the area. **Rock** and **surf** fishing are
good all along the coastline, while the river offers ample opportunity to enjoy estuary fishing. **Deep-sea fishing** can be arranged
through the Publicity Association.

From Port Alfred continue along the coast past various holiday
resorts before entering Ciskei at the Great Fish River (make sure
you have a passport or book of life when entering the Ciskei).
The first resort reached in Ciskei is Mpekweni Marine Resort.
Fish River Sun   Tel. (0403) 61-2101
(P.O. Box 232, Port Alfred, 6170)   Sun International
Swimming-pool, tennis, squash, golf, bowling, wind-surfing,
fishing
Mpekweni Sun Marine Resort   Tel. (0403) 61-3126
(P.O. Box 2060, Port Alfred, 6170)   Sun International
Swimming-pool, tennis, squash, bowls, snooker, wind-surfing
and fishing
Both the abovementioned resorts are part of the Sun International
group and are located on the beach front. The Fish River Sun is
the more upmarket of the two hotels and boasts casino facilities.
The resort is perfect for those who wish to have a few days
away from it all.

The R72 swings inland and then back to the coast, winding

through the beautiful Keiskamma River Valley, and then climbs up through the Cayenne Hills towards Kidd's Beach and then on to East London.

EAST LONDON

Many shipwrecked Dutch and British sailors were stranded on the shores near East London at one time or another. But it was given its first name — Port Rex — only in 1836, when the brig *Knysna*, owned by George Rex of Knysna, sailed into the mouth of the Buffalo River to trade with the local tribes. In 1847, at the outbreak of the War of the Axe between the Xhosa and British Settlers, the HMS Beagle (the same ship used by Darwin on his journey around the world) was dispatched to survey the area. The mouth of the Buffalo River was found to be a suitable port, and troops and supplies were landed. The interior, between the Keiskamma and the Kei River mouths, was annexed and proclaimed a separate colony — the Province of British Kaffraria. Port Rex was renamed East London. Fort Glamorgan was then built on the west bank of the river to protect the settlement. In 1857, 2 362 veterans of the German legion who fought for Britain during the Crimean War, together with 361 women and 195 children were brought out to settle in British Kaffraria.

In 1859 a further 2 315 settlers arrived, giving the region a strong German character. Their influence is still present today: many towns in the area bear the names of towns left behind in Germany, including Berlin, Frankfurt, Hamburg and Hanover. In 1886 the dredging of the river mouth was begun in earnest, and the harbour built. Now East London is the only river mouth harbour in operation in South Africa.

Accommodation

HOTELS **Holiday Inn** ***TYYY Tel. (0431) 2-7260
John Baillie Road (P.O. Box 1255,
East London, 5200)   Holiday Inns
Swimming-pool and tennis
This is not top of the list as far as Holiday Inns go, but all rooms comply with the high standard expected from this chain's hotels.
Kennaway Protea Hotel ***TYYY
Tel. (0431) 2-5531
Beachfront (Box 583, East London, 5200)   Protea Hotels and Inns
This comfortable hotel caters for both business and holiday visitors in spacious, well-appointed rooms. Service is good, and the standard of the food is high. The beach is a short walk away, and many of the rooms have a fine sea view.
Kings Hotel ***TYYY Tel. (0431) 2-2561
Esplanade (P.O. Box 587, East London, 5200)
Swimming-pool (bowls, golf and mini golf within walking distance)
All of the rooms in this comfortable hotel are sea-facing. (The hotel is also within easy walking distance of the sea.) All the rooms are well-furnished and service is discreet, but attentive. Their food is above average.
Dolphin Hotel **TYYY Tel. (0431) 5-3314/5
85 Harewood Drive, Nahoon Mouth (Box 8010, Nahoon, 5210)

This is a gracious hotel, reminiscent of an old English country house, with elegantly furnished rooms and fine service. It is close to the best beaches in the area. Children are especially catered for.

Esplanade Hotel **TYYY   Tel. (0431) 2-2518
6 Clifford Street, Beach Front, East London
This is the ideal hotel for the budget-conscious looking for a comfortable hotel within walking distance of the beach.

Hotel Osner **TYYY   Tel. (0431) 43-3433
Beach Front (Box 334, East London, 5200)
Swimming-pool and sauna
All the rooms in this well-appointed hotel have their own lounge. The hotel is close to the beach front and amenities.

Dorchester Hotel *TYYY   Tel. (0431) 2-4253
Rees Street, East London, 5201
(Tennis and bowls nearby)
It is a small family-run hotel close to the beach and amenities. The two restaurants in the hotel also serve above-average meals.

OTHER ACCOMMODATION

Craighall Guest House   Tel. (0431) 2-5247
Inverleith Terrace (P.O. Box 912, East London, 5200)
The Guest House is located within easy reach of both the beaches and the city. Rooms are clean and comfortably furnished, and evening meals and breakfast are available to guests.

SELF-CATERING AND CAMPING

Mimosa Holiday Flats   Tel. (0431) 2-1903
Marine Terrace, Quigney, East London (P.O. Box 334, East London, 5200)
Ideal for a group, or family, travelling together. These flats are clean and fully equipped.

Protea Holiday Flats   Tel. (0431) 2-1903
Marine Terrace (P.O. Box 334, East London, 5200)
The flats are located close to the sea and are fully equipped and comfortable; perfect for a family or a group of friends.

Marina Glen Caravan Park   Tel. (0431) 2-8753
John Bailie Road (Box 7247, East London, 5200)
Electric plugs, laundry, recreation hall, fishing, swimming-pool and wind-surfing
The park is only 3 km from the city centre, yet it is set in the tranquil surroundings of East Beach. Most sites are shady and all are well-grassed.

Pirates' Creek Holiday Resort   Tel. (0431) 47-1160
South Bank, Quinera Lagoon (Box 2065, Beacon Bay, 5205)
Electric plugs, laundry, gas, shop, swimming-pool, tennis, bowls, fishing and wind-surfing
Accommodation is offered in either fully equipped cottages, or well laid-out camping sites on the banks of the lagoon.

Cintsa West   Tel. (0431) 95-1176
South of Cintsa River Mouth (Box 2059,
Beacon Bay, 5205)   Club-Caraville
Laundry, gas, shop, recreation hall, swimming-pool, tennis, fishing, wind-surfing, hiking, horse-riding, squash and sauna
This superb resort is 37 km from the city and boasts 11 km of unspoilt beach with safe bathing and excellent fishing. All rondavels are fully equipped and grassed camping sites are well treed. It also has a lounge, sun deck and dry pub. A variety of activities are available.

Restaurants

Kelly's Tel. 2-5585   Wine and malt licence
40 Terminus Street   Continental
Kelly's is an elegant restaurant, situated in the city centre, with
an attractive ladies' bar and separate dining area. Cuisine is
typically continental with sauces predominating in many dishes.

Le Petit Tel. 5-8085/6   Wine and malt licence
54 Beach Road, Nahoon   French
This is one of the more up-market restaurants in the city, with
decor and service to match the superb cuisine. The restaurant
offers an excellent selection of desserts.

Mike's Tavern Tel. 43-5171   Wine and malt licence
Marine Glen, Beach Front   Steakhouse/seafoods
Quality meat and fresh seafood, done to perfection, is served in
this well-located restaurant.

Monarch Tel. 2-2561   Fully licensed
Kings Hotel, Beachfront   Continental
This is the ideal restaurant for an elegant night out, with fine
food and band to dance to.

Mövenpick Tel. 2-1840   Fully licensed
Esplanade, Orient Beach   Continental
The restaurant boasts a splendid view of the beach and harbour
mouth. It is a little hard to find, but worth looking for. It is an
elegant, yet informal restaurant, which serves a variety of continental dishes, but leans towards French and Swiss. A band
provides music for dancing.

Mussel-Inn Tel. 2-4767   Fully licensed
Oceanic Hotel, Westbank   Seafood
Situated in the dockland area, this popular restaurant offers a
variety of perfectly prepared fresh local fish. Although it is not
located in the best part of town, the restaurant is neat and well
run.

Royal Hotel Tel. 2-4248   Fully licensed
23 Buxton Street   Bar lunches
This is a small commercial hotel in the city centre offering
excellent bar lunches.

Useful addresses and telephone numbers

East London area telephone code: **(0431)**

TOURIST INFORMATION **Greater East London Publicity Association** Tel. 2-6015, City
Hall, Oxford Street (P.O. Box 533, East London, 5200)
South African Tourism Board Tel. 2-6410, NBS Building, Ter-
minus Street (P.O. Box 1794, East London, 5200)

Transport

AIRLINES **Airport enquiries** Tel. 46-1400
SAA reservations Tel. 44-2535

RAIL **Enquiries** Tel. 44-2020

INTER-CITY COACHES **Copper Rose** (between Port Elizabeth and East London) Tel.
47-1559

Translux (between Port Elizabeth, East London and Durban) Tel. 44-2718/9

CAR HIRE **Avis** Tel. 46-2252
Budget Tel. 46-2364
Imperial Tel. 46-1533

Sightseeing

The **East London Museum** is worth a visit. Amongst other things, the first known coelacanth to be identified is preserved and on permanent display here. In 1938 this unique fish was landed by an East London-based fishing boat, and identified by the famous ichthyologist, Prof. J.L.B. Smith. Also on display is the only known dodo egg as well as an interesting collecton of Xhosa dress.

Outdoor Activities

Golf: visitors are welcome at the *East London Golf Club*, Tel. 5-3350.

For **deap-sea fishing** and **wind-surfing** contact the Publicity Association.

On your departure from East London, follow the N2 to Umtata. The road winds its way through farmland, and then down through the Kei cuttings to the border post at the Kei River. From the border post the road winds through vast grasslands and numerous small settlements until it reaches Umtata, which is the end of this part of the tour (see page 20 for Transkei entry requirements).

Young entrepreneurs vend their wares in Cradock

The bright side of Bedford

<table>
<tr><td>2</td></tr>
</table>

Oudtshoorn to Umtata via Cradock

(1 345 km)
See map on page 148

The route takes the traveller over some of the most spectacular mountain passes in South Africa as it winds its way into the Great Karoo, on to the Mountain Zebra National Park, through Ciskei, and over the Drakensberg, into Transkei.

From Oudtshoorn, head towards the Cango Caves on the R328, and follow the road towards the Swartberg Pass and on to Prince Albert, calling in at the Cango Caves along the way (see Oudtshoorn, page 113). The tar road ends as you begin to ascend the **Swartberg Pass**, and becomes a dirt road. This spectacular pass was built by Thomas Bain. It was completed in 1888, seven years after construction commenced. As you crawl slowly up the mountain, spectacular views over the Little Karoo present themselves. From the summit, 1 585 m above sea level, the road drops slightly along the summit, before snaking its way down a spectacular series of U-turns and zig-zags onto the valley floor below; and then twists through the gorge, with towering rock faces on either side. Plant life, especially a wide variety of protea and heathers, are found in abundance on the mountain. This is certainly one of the most spectacular passes in the world and should not be missed. Rain, snow and ice, do, however, occasionally make the pass inaccessible during the winter months. At the base of the pass lies Prince Albert.

PRINCE ALBERT

This is a charming little Karoo town in a rural setting: a mixture of farming-related activities and businesses. A variety of architectural styles are reflected in the buildings, including Cape Dutch, Georgian, Karoo and Victorian.

Accommodation

Swartberg Protea Hotel *TYYY Tel. (04436) 332
77 Church Street, Prince Albert, 6930   Protea Hotels and Inns
Swimming-pool, golf and tennis
This charming well-run hotel still has all the graces of a country hotel, in addition to the modern amenities one has come to expect. Guests are accommodated in rondavels or rooms within the hotel. The simple country cooking is of a very high standard.
Hanet Caravan Park Tel. (04436) 128
Adderley Street (P.O. Box 20, Prince Albert, 6930)
Electric plugs, laundry, tennis and hiking
This is a small park offering both camping facilities and limited basic accommodation in rooms.

Tourist Information

Prince Albert area telephone code: **(04436)**

The Town Clerk Tel. 320, P.O. Box 25, Prince Albert, 6930

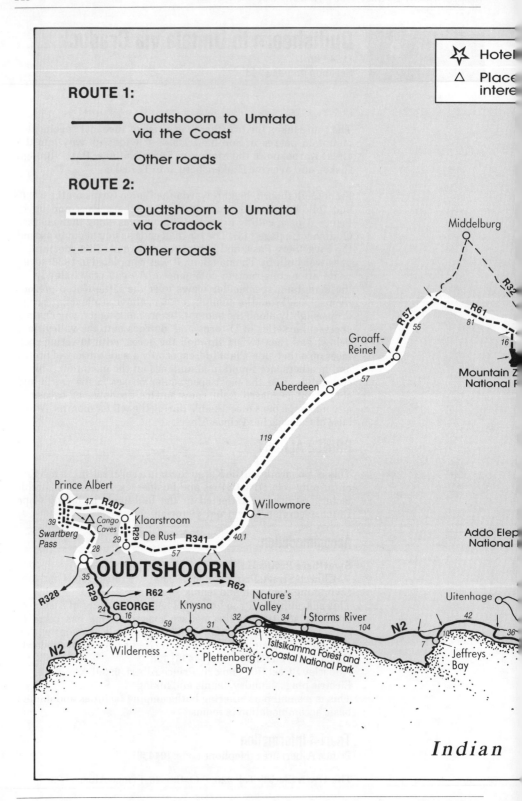

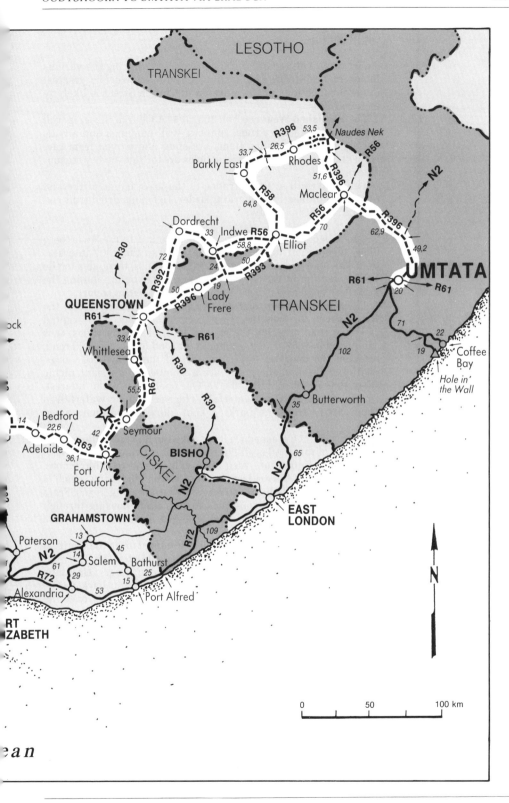

Sightseeing

Apart from walking around the town and admiring the various forms of architecture, a visit to one of the world's greatest mineral collections at the **museum** in Church Street is likely to be rewarding.

The Woolshed Weavery Tel. 363, at 11A Church Street is well worth a visit. Quality rugs, runners, wall-hangings and a wide variety of other woollen items are spun and woven from raw wool at the weavery. Finished articles are for sale at very reasonable prices.

The Watermill at the entrance to the town is one of the last remaining mills still in working order. Delicious dried fruit can also be bought in the town.

On your departure from Prince Albert return to the Swartberg Pass, turning left towards Meiringspoort at the R407 intersection. The road passes along the Kredouws Pass, through a fertile valley nestling in the Swartberg Mountains, before joining the R29. Turn right towards De Rust, going via Meiringspoort.

The **Meiringspoort** road follows the spectacular gorge of the Groot River through the Swartberg Mountains. The original 17 km of road crossing the river a total of twenty times, was completed in 1857. Today a smooth tar road follows the old road, between the majestic towering cliffs of the Swartberg Gorge. Scattered through the gorge are a number of pleasant picnic spots, many with ablution blocks. One spot of particular interest, on the left, is marked **waterfall**. The spectacular waterfall is about 500 m from the parking spot along a well-maintained path.

Once you have reached De Rust, take the R341 to Willowmore. A section of this road is still untarred, but is being tarred slowly. At the R57 T-junction, turn once more towards Willowmore, passing through the arid semi-desert Karoo landscape which is famous for its stud-sheep and Angora goat-breeding farms. From Willowmore, the road continues to Aberdeen, passing through an area of rugged beauty, where jagged mountain ridges rise from the flat Karoo floor.

Aberdeen was founded in 1855, and named after the Scottish birthplace of the famous Dutch Reformed minister, the Reverend Andrew Murray. It is a typical Karoo town: large verandahs surround the tin-roofed houses with windmills in back yards. From Aberdeen continue on the R57 to Graaff-Reinet over the Plains of the Camdeboo.

GRAAFF-REINET

During the 1770s the early *trekboers* (wandering farmers) reached the banks of the Sundays River in the Karoo, and settled in the area. In 1786 two farms belonging to Dirk Coetzee were bought for the site of a new town, named Graaff-Reinet, after Governor van der Graaff and his wife, Cornelia Reynet.

Life in the early days was full of turmoil, and not without dissatisfactions. In 1796, after the first British occupation of the Cape, a group of burghers declared the area an independent republic. Independence was short-lived, however, and necessity soon forced the burghers in the area to accept British rule. After the return of the British in 1806 relations between the Cape and Graaff-Reinet deteriorated even further, and by 1834 a large exodus of trekboers started. This marked the start of the Great Trek under the leadership of Andries Pretorius (after whom Pretoria was named), and Gerrit Maritz (after whom Pieter-maritzburg was named). British and German settlers were quick to take their place as Merino sheep and Angora goat farmers.

The town slowly grew in economic importance to become the second largest agricultural and commercial centre in the Cape during the late nineteenth century. Many fine buildings from the past still stand today, providing a glimpse of the splendour of that era. Graaff-Reinet is uniquely located in the centre of the Karoo Nature Reserve, which has many wilderness trails and birdwatching hides, as well as an abundance of indigenous wildlife.

Accommodation

Drostdy Hotel   **TYYY   Tel. (0491) 2-2161
28 Church Street (P.O. Box 400, Graaff-Reinet, 6280)
Swimming-pool
This magnificently restored hotel comprises the original Drostdy (Magistrate's Court) and the Drostdyhof. The Drostdy now houses the reception and public rooms of the hotel, all furnished in period antiques and paintings. The Drostdyhof is a cluster of small houses along a cobbled street, which once housed emancipated slaves. Today the houses are the hotel's accommodation: each suite is elegantly furnished in the style of a bygone age, but also supplies all the modern conveniences.

Panorama Protea Hotel   **TYYY   Tel. (0491) 2-2233
Magazine Hill (P.O. Box 314,
Graaff-Reinet, 6280)   Protea Hotels and Inns
Swimming-pool
This is a very popular family/budget hotel with a view of the town. All rooms and chalets are clean and comfortable. Traditional country food is served.

Graaff-Reinet Chalets and Caravan Park   Tel. (0491) 2-2121
The Municipality, P.O. Box 71, Graaff-Reinet, 6280
Electric plugs, laundry, swimming-pool, tennis, golf, bowls, hiking and wind-surfing
The park is situated just outside town. Each chalet is fully equipped and completely private. The camping sites are all well grassed and the ablution blocks are clean.

Tourist Information
Graaff-Reinet area telephone code: **(0491)**

Graaff-Reinet Publicity Association   Tel. 2-2479, P.O. Box 153, Graaff-Reinet, 6280

Sightseeing

A WALKING TOUR
(Map page 153)

Start at the **Drostdy Hotel** (see above). From the hotel, walk down Parsonage Street. On the right side, the first building of interest is the **John Rupert Little Theatre,** originally built as a church for the London Missionary Society. It served as their church for more than a century, until 1920. In 1969 it was restored and after serving first as an Art Gallery, was converted into a theatre in 1980. Further down the street you will pass a number of privately owned typical Karoo-style houses.

20 Parsonage Street, on the corner of Cross Street, is a typical example of a Karoo house, with its decorative woodwork known locally as "broekies lace", which was added later during the Victorian period. Further along, on the right hand side of Parsonage Street is a well-restored house, where South African antiques are sold — a perfect haunt for the collector.

The last house on the right is now part of the **Graaff-Reinet Museum** and houses, among other collections, the Jan Felix Lategan Gun Collection. It is a well-preserved model of an early nineteenth century H-shaped house. The museum is open on weekdays from 09h00 to 12h00 and from 15h00 to 17h00, and on week-ends from 10h00 to 12h00.

At the head of the street is **Reinet House,** the former Dutch Reformed Church parsonage built in 1812. In 1822 the Rev. Andrew Murray became resident minister. From then the parsonage was occupied by Murrays until 1904 when his son, the Rev. Charles Murray, died. Today the house contains an interesting collection of period furniture. In the grounds you will find a reconstructed waterwheel and a grape-vine, which is reputed to be the largest grape-vine in the world: it has a circumference of 2,38 m. The house is open at the same time as the museum.

Return along Parsonage Street to Cross Street and then turn into Somerset Street. Along the way you will pass a number of well-preserved examples of decorative woodwork.

Reinet Museum, in Somerset Street, houses the Lex Bremner Fossil Collection, Rykie Pretorius Costume Collection, and Townley Johnson reproductions of Bushman Art. It is open at the same time as the Graaff-Reinet Museum. Opposite is **The Water House**, with its decorative wooden verandah. It houses **Graaff-Reinet craft**, where handspun and woven articles are made from local wool. Turn right into Church Street, passing the home of the **Graaff-Reinet Advertiser**, which has been printed continuously for over 130 years. At the top of the street is the **Dutch Reformed Church**, built in 1886, along similar lines to Salisbury Cathedral in the United Kingdom. Inside the church is a priceless collection of Cape silver which can be viewed by the public on weekdays from 09h00 to 12h00 and from 14h00 to 16h00, and on Saturdays from 09h00 to 11h00.

From here, turn right into Caledon Street and proceed to **Reinet Pharmacy,** which is an excellent example of a Victorian pharmacy dating from the 1870s. It is open during business hours. Across the street is **Kingray's,** which has a splendid wrought iron facade.

Return to **Church Square**, which originally served as the outspan for the farming community who came to town every four months for *nagmaal* (communion) in their ox-wagons.

Continue up Queen Street, turn left into North, right into Bourke, left into Park and then left into Cradock Street. This route takes you past a number of well-preserved houses from different periods in the history of Graaff-Reinet. Cradock Street is the second-oldest street in Graaff-Reinet, with many houses dating back to the early nineteenth century. Walk down Cradock

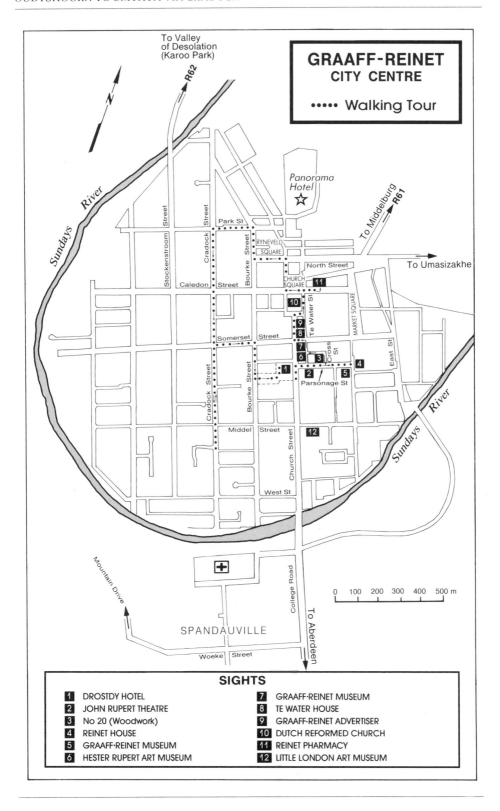

GRAAFF-REINET
CITY CENTRE

····· Walking Tour

To Valley
of Desolation
(Karoo Park)

R62

Sundays River

Stockenstroom Street

Cradock Street

Bourke Street

Park St

Panorama
Hotel

To Middelburg R61

RYNEVELD
SQUARE

North Street

To Umasizakhe

CHURCH
SQUARE

Caledon Street

11

10

Te Water St

MARKET SQUARE

Somerset Street

9

8

7

6 3

Cross St

East St

4

Cradock Street

Bourke Street

1

2 5

Parsonage St

Middel Street

Church Street

12

West St

To Aberdeen

Sundays River

Mountain Drive

College Road

0 100 200 300 400 500 m

SPANDAUVILLE

Woeke Street

SIGHTS

1	DROSTDY HOTEL	**7**	GRAAFF-REINET MUSEUM
2	JOHN RUPERT THEATRE	**8**	TE WATER HOUSE
3	No 20 (Woodwork)	**9**	GRAAFF-REINET ADVERTISER
4	REINET HOUSE	**10**	DUTCH REFORMED CHURCH
5	GRAAFF-REINET MUSEUM	**11**	REINET PHARMACY
6	HESTER RUPERT ART MUSEUM	**12**	LITTLE LONDON ART MUSEUM

Street as far as you wish and then return to the Drostdy via Somerset Street.

VALLEY OF DESOLATION From town take the R62 for Richmond/Murraysburg, and branch off left, about 5 km out of town, following the "Valley of Desolation" sign. Nine kilometres further on the summit is reached, 120 m above the valley floor. From here you will have a magnificent view of the town and surrounding countryside.

Return to town and take the R57/61 for Middelburg and Cradock. The road passes through the grass hills of the Karoo, past numerous sheep farms. The mountains are often snow-capped in winter. Fifty-five kilometres along the road, turn right on the R61 towards Cradock, and 81 km further on turn right again onto a dirt road marked "The Mountain Zebra National Park".

THE MOUNTAIN ZEBRA NATIONAL PARK

The park landscape combines grass-covered mountains with a high-lying plateau that is 1 900 m above sea level; deep ravines and low valleys which are lightly wooded and about 1 200 m above sea level. Seventy per cent of the rain falls in the summer months, often accompanied by dramatic thunder storms. Temperatures sometimes soar to 42 °C (108 °F). In winter frost and occasional snowfalls are experienced. Temperatures have been known to drop to -10 °C (14 °F). The first farm was purchased for the conservation of the endangered Mountain Zebra in 1937. At the time there were only six Zebra in the park, none of which survived beyond 1950. A new start was made with the donation of five stallions and six mares from a nearby farm and by 1964 the herd had grown to 25. Six more farms were purchased in 1964 to give the park a total area of 6 536 hectares, and an additional population of thirty zebra. By 1978 the 200-mark was reached and 23 of the animals were transferred to the Karoo National Park. Today the population is kept between 150 and 200 animals. The excess population is translocated to other parks in the area. Other antelope in the park include springbok, blesbok, black wildebeest, red hartebeest, eland and kudu, as well as a number of smaller buck, mammals and birds.

Accommodation

All reservations for the park can be made through the National Parks Board (see page 290).

The guest house at Doornhoek Dam has been beautifully refurnished with original antiques from the area. The house has three bedrooms, with bathrooms *en suite*, a fully equipped modern kitchen, dining room and lounge. It can be rented as a unit or as separate rooms.

The rest camp offers twenty fully equipped two-bedroom chalets, a spotless campsite, and restaurant, with a small shop. There is also a swimming-pool on site.

Hiking trails

There is a two-night/three-day/25 km hiking trail in the park, with rustic huts along the way for overnight accommodation. There is also a half-day hiking trail and a half-day riding trail.

For reservations contact the National Parks Board (see page 290).

Return to the R61 and then to **Cradock**, a rural farming community and important centre for mohair, wool and cattle-farming. Outside Cradock on the R32 going towards Cookhouse and Port Elizabeth, you will come across young children selling decorative wire windmills. The R63 turn-off going towards Bedford and Fort Beaufort is 63 km further down the R32. The road winds its way through Bedford and Adelaide, two charming farming towns, before reaching Fort Beaufort, which was an important outpost during the frontier wars.

In 1822 **Fort Beaufort** was established on the Kat River to keep a check on marauding Xhosa tribes. The military post was named after the Duke of Beaufort, Lord Charles Somerset's father. The remnants of the garrison stationed here are of particular interest. The former officers' quarters house an interesting museum, containing weapons and other memorabilia from the frontier wars.

From Fort Beaufort take the R67 towards Seymour and Whittlesea. About 29 km out of Fort Beaufort, you will come across the turn-off, left, onto a dirt road going to Balfour and then on to Katberg.

Katberg Protea Hotel   Tel. (0020) and ask for Katberg 3.
P.O. Box 3, Balfour, 5740   Protea Hotels and Inns
Swimming-pool, tennis, squash, golf, bowls, croquet, riding and hiking

This picturesque resort nestling in the Katberg Mountains at an altitude of 1 000 m is surrounded by forests, in which beautiful walks can be enjoyed. It is the ideal mountain hideaway for those who are looking for a relaxed atmosphere away from it all. Accommodation varies from garden suites to standard rooms. Meals are simple and wholesome. Children have their own dining room. (The hotel is fully licensed.)

Return to the R67 and continue towards Seymour. From Seymour a gravel road takes the traveller across to Hogsback, where another fine hotel can be found:

The Hogsback Arminel Mountain Lodge   Tel. (0020) and ask for Hogsback 6.
P.O. Box 67, Hogsback, 5312   Portfolio of Country Places
Swimming-pool, tennis, hiking and fishing

J.J. Tolkien's *Hobbit* stories were inspired by the mystical atmosphere of Hogsback. The lodge is set high in the mountains in a magnificent garden surrounded by indigenous forests. On wet days and winter evenings guests can relax in front of roaring log fires. Each of the comfortable rooms has an individual character. Hearty appetites are more than catered for by excellent home-cooked food.

Continue along the R67, up the spectacular Nico Malan Pass, towards Whittlesea and from there up to **Queenstown**.

One of the main features of this frontier town is the unique hexagonal open square at its centre. The hexagon, with six streets radiating from it, was constructed as a defence measure to allow fast access from the command post at the centre to any point on the periphery. Today the town is the educational and commercial centre of the north-eastern Cape.

From Queenstown, take the R392 to Dordrecht, and then the R56 to Elliot. This enclave, flanked by Lesotho and the Transkei, in the foothills of the Drakensberg, is a very prosperous sheep- and cattle-farming area. It has spectacular scenery and some of the best trout-fishing in South Africa. It is also one of the coldest areas in South Africa, where snow is not uncommon and temperatures often drop below freezing point.

Accommodation

Mountain Shadows *TYYY Tel. (0020) and ask for Barkly Pass 3.
P.O. Box 130, Elliot, 5460
Trout-fishing and hiking
This is a good, clean, comfortable hotel in the country, between Elliot and Barkly East (17 kilometres from Elliot). Good food is prepared mostly from local produce.
Stanford Hotel *TYYY   Tel. (045312) 90
Voortrekker Street, Elliot (Box 23, Elliot, 5460)
Trout-fishing and hiking
These clean, comfortable rooms are perfect for an overnight stop. Wholesome home cooking and good pub meals are served.
Royal Hotel *TYYY   Tel. (034322) 176
Royal Road (Box 244, Maclear, 5480)
Trout-fishing and hiking
A clean, but basic, country hotel.
Elliot Municipal Caravan Park   Tel. (045312) 11
Maclear Road (P.O. Box 21, Elliot, 5460)
Laundry, gas, swimming-pool, fishing and hiking
This is a basic campsite ideal for an overnight stop.
Ben MacDhui Caravan Park   Tel. (04542) 123
Brownlee Street, Barkly East (Private Bag X15, Barkly East, 5580)
Electric plugs, laundry, swimming-pool, trout fishing and hiking
A basic campsite — ideal for an overnight stay.

There are two routes from Elliot to Maclear.

Via **Ugie:** (70 km of tar) along the R56. This road passes some of the finest and best-cared for dairy farms in South Africa and has the majestic Drakensberg Range as a backdrop. Ugie itself started out in 1863 as a mission station and gradually expanded as the centre of the farming community. Today it is also the home of the Smit Children's Haven, which cares for destitute children from all over South Africa.

Via **Barkly East:** (65 km of tar and 165 km of gravel road). This is an awe-inspiring route, which passes over two of the highest passes in South Africa, and is not meant for the faint-hearted or those not used to driving on gravel roads. Furthermore, it should not be attempted in wet weather or in the snow. From Elliot take the R58 to Barkly East, via the scenic Barkly Pass and Langkloof-spruit, twisting through picturesque sheep farms and between gigantic sandstone rock formations. The gravel begins at Barkly East. Take the R396 to Rhodes.

Rhodes was founded in 1893 and named after Cecil Rhodes. In its heyday it was the closest South Africa ever got to the American Wild West. Regular race meetings were held here, and it was a haven for gamblers. Liquor was brought in by the wagon load from the coast. It is said that often "cowboys" rode their horses right into the local hotel bar. Today the village is fast fading into the past, with only a few earth-walled and corrugated iron cottages left, which are used by local farmers when they come to the village for "Nagmaal" or to escape the snow in winter.

From Rhodes, the road twists and turns its way up **Naudes Nek Pass**, towards Maclear. For 19 km the road zig-zags up the mountain to the summit at 2 920 m. The road is rough and narrow, but the view is very picturesque: often a shepherd and his flock of sheep can be seen as they wander up the pass in search of new grazing. From the summit the road slowly descends to Maclear.

Take the R396 from Maclear to Tsolo, crossing into Transkei, 18 km from Maclear. Five kilometres from Tsolo, the R296 crosses the N2. Turn right for Umtata, which is 37 km from the junction.

Umtata

Founded during the 1860s, Umtata is the capital of Transkei. The settlement was developed on land ceded to white settlers on the banks of the Mtata River by the Tembu and Pondo tribes. These two warring tribes thought that the settlers would form a buffer zone between them. By 1900 the village had become a thriving business community, with shops, churches, schools, a newspaper, hospital and industry. In 1903 the Transkeian Territories' General Council, the Bunga, declared the town the capital. Transkei gained self-government in 1963 and independence in 1976. In 1981 the town was proclaimed a city. Today the city is a business and educational centre and the seat of the Transkeian government. It boasts a university.

Accommodation

HOTELS **Holiday Inn**   Tel. (0471) 2-2181
National Road (P.O. Box 334,
Umtata, Transkei)   Holiday Inns
Swimming-pool
It is located on the outskirts of Umtata (East London side, on the N2). This comfortable Holiday Inn is well run, and by far the best hotel in town. Rooms comply with the high standard set by Holiday Inn, and the restaurant gives a choice of à la carte and buffet.

CAMPING **Umtata Municipal Caravan Site**   Tel. (0471) 3204
(P.O. Box 45, Umtata)
Electric connections
This is a basic site which is ideal for overnight camping. It is located close to the Holiday Inn on the N2 towards East London.

Tourist Information

Tourist Bureau,   Private Bag X5029, Umtata, 5100
Department of Agriculture and Forestry,   Private Bag X5002, Umtata, 5100
Visas: The Secretary for the Interior,   Private Bag X5006, Umtata, 5100
(See Embassies on pp. 289)

Sightseeing

One of the most enjoyable drives from Umtata is to **Coffee Bay** and **Hole in the Wall**. From Umtata, take the N2 back towards East London for 20 km. Turn left at the Coffee Bay/Mqanduli sign post. Coffee Bay is 93 km along the tarred road. Driving down this scenic road one passes large numbers of traditional huts and rural landscapes. Although the road is tarred, it is advisable to drive with extreme care. Apart from the large

amount of traffic on this road, it is not uncommon to have to stop
for animals crossing the road.

COFFEE BAY

Coffee Bay got its name from the coffee trees which once grew
along the coast. It is believed that the coffee beans were washed
ashore from some wrecked ships. This delightful bay offers a
pleasant beach and some of the finest fishing along the southern
African coast.

Accommodation

HOTELS **Lagoon Hotel**   Tel. (0020) and ask for Coffee Bay 6.
P.O. Coffee Bay
Tennis, bowls, golf, riding, swimming-pool, fishing and hiking
This is a simple, but well run, comfortable hotel on the coast,
ideal for an informal relaxed holiday. Seafood dominates the
menu.
Ocean View Hotel   Tel. (0020) and ask for Coffee Bay 7.
P.O. Coffee Bay
Tennis, golf, riding, swimming-pool, fishing and hiking
A perfect hotel for those not looking for the frills of a city hotel:
comfortable rooms and friendly, relaxed atmosphere.

CAMPING **Coffee Bay Caravan Park**   Tel. (0471) 9309
Close to Lagoon Hotel. (Book through Secretary of Agriculture
and Forestry, Umtata.)
This is one of the most basic campsites in southern Africa,
providing an ablution block and shaded sites.

From Coffee Bay drive 22 km towards the N2 and then take a
sharp left turn to Hole in the Wall, which is 19 km away. The
road is gravel and badly corrugated, especially after rains, but
well worth the trip for those who are adventurous enough.
   Hole in the wall was named by Captain Vidal of the Barra-
couta, in 1823, during an expedition to survey the coast. The
name is derived from a huge rock with a tunnel through it,
standing a short distance out to sea. The Xhosa refer to it as
esiKhaleni meaning "the place of the sound". Stories about the
treacherous coast and the shipwrecks are reflected by the claim
of many tribes in the area to European and Asian ancestry.
   From here return to Umtata.

Local handicraft

Izandla Pottery and **Transkei Hilmond Weavers**, situated about
2 km out of town on the R61 towards Engcobo, offer locally
produced handicraft. The pottery, boasting some top potters,
produces work of a very high standard; from complete dinner
services to ornamental containers and hangings. The weavers
produce mohair products such as table cloths, wall hangings,
cushions and curtaining in gay African styles. Both factories are
well worth a visit.

Umtata to Kruger National Park via Durban
(1138.5 km)

This route takes you along most of the subtropical Natal Coast, pausing in the holiday city of Durban, before visiting the famous Zululand Game Parks, where the rhino was saved from near extinction. From here the route crosses into Swaziland, travelling through the entire kingdom, before crossing into the Kruger National Park.

Take the N2 towards Kokstad from Umtata. After leaving Transkei, follow the N2 towards Port Shepstone. Turn to the left 103 km after the Kokstad turnoff; travel through the **Oribi Gorge Pass and Nature Reserve**. The road winds through lush vegetation, at times almost forming a tunnel around the road. At the end of the pass, at the T-junction, turn right and 7 km further on, turn right again at the **Fair Acres Viewing Sites.** There is an entrance fee entitling the visitor to drive to the top of the gorge. From the top one has a spectacular view of the rugged landscape 366 m below. The gorge is 24 km long and 5 km wide at its widest.

From here return to the tar road and turn right, following the road back onto the N2, and on to Port Shepstone, 12 km away. Here the road reaches a T-junction: the right, along the R61, goes towards the lower South Coast resorts, while the left continues on the N2 to Durban.

THE LOWER SOUTH COAST

The area stretching from Port Shepstone in the north, to the Wild Coast Casino, just inside Transkei in the south, offers the visitor a choice of accommodation, as well as long golden beaches which are well protected by shark nets for safe bathing. Although it is hot and often very humid during the summer months, the sea is very pleasant during winter.

Tourist Information

Natal South Coast Publicity Association, Panorama Drive, Margate   Tel. (03931) 2-2322, (P.O. Box 25, Margate, 4275)

PORT SHEPSTONE

Port Shepstone is the administrative, commercial and educational centre of the lower South Coast. The first involuntary settlers to set foot on this stretch of coast were three hundred Portuguese, in 1635, when their ship, the *Nossa Senhora de Belem* was wrecked here. As they had no plans of remaining here, they built boats from the wreckage and set sail for Angola the following year. Settlement of the area began only in the mid-nineteenth century with the establishment of the village,

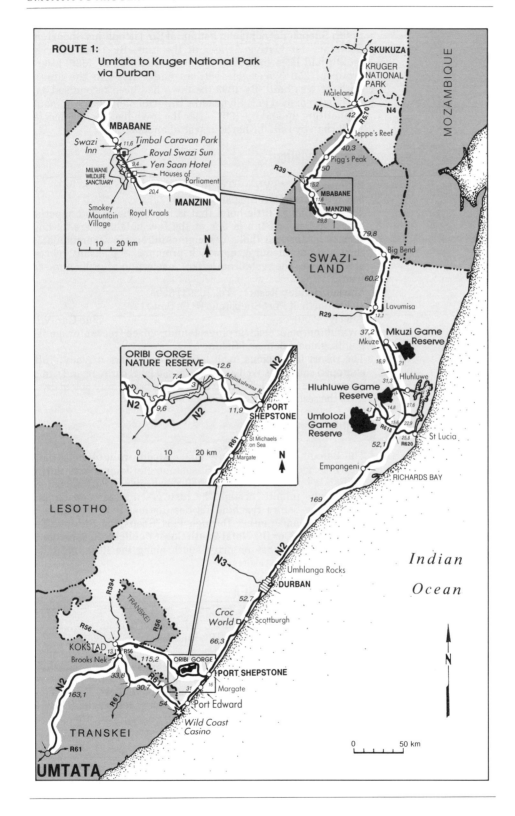

South Shepstone, named in honour of Sir Theophilus Shepstone, Secretary for Native Affairs at the time. By 1880, the river mouth had been improved for navigation and in 1886, after a group of 250 Norwegian settlers had arrived in the area, a harbour was built. By 1893 the town had been recognised as a port and renamed Port Shepstone. Unfortunately the river mouth kept silting up and by 1901, after the town had been connected to Durban by rail, the harbour was abandoned.

Accommodation

Bedford Inn   **TYYY   Tel. (0391) 2-1085
64 Colle Street, Port Shepstone, 4240
This is a quaint little hotel that is full of charm and superbly run. The Bedford Inn is one of the few hotels where 24-hour service means just that. Although children are accommodated, they are not encouraged, which promotes a pleasant relaxed atmosphere. The restaurant offers a selection of grills and sea-foods.

Marlon Holiday Resort   Tel. (0391) 3596
10 km north of Port Shepstone (P.O. Box 112,
Anerly, 4230)   Club Caraville
Swimming-pool, electric plugs, laundry, deep freeze storage, TV points, games room and fishing
The resort is spacious, well laid-out and offers privacy. Fully equipped chalets as well as well-grassed level caravan and camping sites are offered. There is a sheltered beach only 500 m away from the resort.

Sightseeing

The **Banana Express** narrow guage steam train offers a daily return service between Port Shepstone and Izingolweni during the holiday periods. The scenic journey begins in Port Shepstone and climbs inland through the lush green sugar and banana plantations before reaching its destination. It is advisable to book in advance, either through Port Shepstone Station, Tel. (03931) 7-6443, or the **Natal South Coast Publicity Association.**

From Port Shepstone drive south along the R61, through a number of seaside resorts:

ST. MICHAELS-ON-SEA

St Michaels Sands   **TYYY   Tel. (03931) 5-1230
1 Marine Drive (P.O. Box 45, St. Michaels-on-Sea, 4265)
Bowls and nine-hole golf course
This is a pleasant hotel located in very spacious grounds, which include the golf course and bowling greens. All the rooms are large and comfortably furnished; and kept spotless. Bar lunches are good and the intimate restaurant offers good steaks. There is a pleasant beach close by.

UVONGO

Close to the beach the Ivungu River tumbles 23 m into the lagoon

A farmhouse on the Naude's Nek Pass near Rhodes

A church in the Transkei

Rural Transkei

below. Along the upper reaches of the river pleasant walks can be enjoyed.

Hotel la Crête   **TYYY   Tel. (03931) 5-1301
Signposted from the R61
P.O. Box 1, Uvongo, 4270
Swimming-pool, tennis, squash, bowls and fishing
This large elegant hotel is one of the best in the area. It is perched right on the rocks overlooking the beach. Service, though discreet, is attentive and rooms are large. Food is wholesome and includes fresh, well-prepared fish.

Costacabana   Tel. (03931) 5-1203
73 Collins Street (P.O. Box 3, Uvongo, 4270)
Swimming-pool
A private hotel with the cheerful atmosphere one needs for a family holiday. Rooms are clean and cosy, meals are wholesome (and included in the price) and the dining room has a pleasant view of the sea, which is close by.

MARGATE

Margate is the largest resort along the coast and has much to offer the holiday crowd, including a number of discos as well as live caberet during the holiday season. A number of beach activities are also organised.

Faerie Glen Lake Hotel   **TYYY Tel. (03931) 2-1280
250 Quarry Road (P.O. Box 60, Margate, 4275)
Swimming-pool, golf, tennis, bowls, squash and wind-surfing
Guests are accommodated in comfortable, well-appointed chalets and rondavels on the banks of the lake. Meals are satisfying and cheap. There is hotel transport to the beach and to Port Shepstone.

Margate Hotel   **TYYY   Tel. (03931) 2-1410
Marine Drive (P.O. Box 4, Margate, 4275)
Swimming-pool
This pleasant hotel is as close to the beach as possible and offers comfortable rooms and lots of entertainment. Bar lunches are popular and a variety of night entertainment is offered at the **Palm Grove** nearby.

Palm Beach Hotel   *TYYY   Tel. (03931) 2-1612
Duke Road (P.O. Box 39, Margate, 4275)
Swimming-pool, tennis and bowls
The lawns of the hotel run right down to the beach, making it an ideal location for an inexpensive beach holiday. Good food and fresh fish are served in the dining room.

Marine Palms Holiday Apartments   Tel. (03931) 2-0990
Marine Drive (P.O. Box 27, Margate, 4275)
Swimming-pool, sauna, squash and fishing
The apartments are situated on Margate Beach. All rooms have a pleasant view. All apartments are serviced and fully equipped.

Villa Del Sol   Tel. (03931) 2-1438
Cnr. Marina Drive and Finnis Road (P.O. Box 577, Margate, 4275)
Swimming-pool, golf, tennis, squash, bowls and fishing
All the chalets, set in beautiful gardens, are fully equipped. Each has its own patio and braai area. They are within walking distance of the beach and shops.

RAMSGATE

This is a pleasant resort with good bathing beaches and safe lagoon where boats can be hired.
Crayfish Inn   **TYYY   Tel. (03931) 4410/1
Marine Drive (P.O. Box 7, Ramsgate, 4285)
Squash, tidal pool, tennis, bowls and fishing
Cluttered with maritime memorabilia, both inside and outside (even the bar has a boat acting as the counter), this well-known hotel has many points of interest to keep a browser interested for hours. It is close to the beach. All rooms are comfortably furnished. The hotel restaurant also offers a number of pleasant surprises and seafoods.
Inn on the Sea   *TYYY   Tel. (03931) 4521
Marine Drive (P.O. Box 284, Ramsgate, 4285)
Looking directly over Ramsgate's lagoon and beach, this pleasant hotel is ideal for the casual holiday visitor.
Teahouse of the Blue Lagoon
Tel. (03931) 4149   Not licensed
Main Road, Ramsgate   General
This restaurant offers a fine view over the lagoon and a wide variety of delights: from excellent waffles with various toppings, to seafoods, steaks and even good Chinese dishes.

SOUTHBROOM

With its large, safe bathing beach, tidal pools and calm lagoon, this is an ideal base for wind-surfing and bathing. There are also several good fishing points and a pleasant 18-hole golf course in the area.
Paradise Holiday Resort   Tel. (03931) 30655
P.O. Box 55, Southbroom, 4277   Club Caraville
Electric plugs, gas, laundry, recreation hall, shop, swimming-pool, bowls, tennis, golf, wind-surfing and fishing
Although this resort is not on the coast, the beaches are only a few minutes' drive away. The resort itself is located in beautiful subtropical surroundings and offers fully equipped chalets and well-grassed shaded caravan sites.

MARINA BEACH

The beach is one of the finest along the coast. It has over 5 km of golden sands and is protected by shark nets.
San Lameer   Tel. (03931) 3-0011
P.O. Box 78, Southbroom, 4277   Protea Hotels and Inns
Swimming-pool, tennis, squash, 9-hole golf, bowls, fishing, horse-riding, wind-surfing, canoeing and gym
The resort, built around the lagoon, offers comfortable accommodation in rooms in the main complex, as well as in one- to four-bedroomed villas set in lush parkland. The restaurants in the resort serve a variety of meals, from international fare to light buffets.

From here, one carries on through the subtropical forests and banana plantations on to Port Edward, the most southerly resort on the coast, situated on the banks of the Mtamvuna River. Just across the river in Transkei is the Wild Coast Sun.

Wild Coast Sun   Tel. (0471) 511/2

P.O. Box 23, Port Edward, 4295   Sun International

Swimming-pool, tennis, bowls, squash, golf, fishing, hiking, riding, wind-surfing and casino

All international and South African visitors are free to visit this resort without applying for a visa. This glittering resort, with its superb golf course and other sporting attractions, as well as luxurious rooms, is ideal for those who want a leisurely beach holiday mixed with the spice of a pulsating nightlife. The resort also boasts many restaurants: from simple (though expensive) take-aways and poolside snacks to lavish international cuisine.

Returning to Port Shepstone, continue north along the coastal road (not the N2 highway) towards Durban. The road runs parallel to the coast and passes a number of holiday resorts along the way. Sixty-six kilometres from Port Shepstone a turn to the left (just before Scottburgh), takes the traveller to **Croc World**, Tel. (03231) 2-1210. The park gives the visitor an insight into the breeding habits and conservation of crocodiles. A further 9 km along the road, just after Umkomaas, a large **Zulu Handicraft Market** is found. Pottery, weaving and leather goods are sold at the market. The weaving is especially good; as are the vast array of mats and baskets. Durban is 43 km away.

DURBAN

Durban is a subtropical winter playground. It is South Africa's third largest city and has the busiest port in southern Africa. Holiday-makers can sun themselves on miles of safe golden beaches, or visit one of the many beachfront attractions, including the superb oceanarium, and enjoy the pulsating nightspots or dine out at lavish restaurants.

The site that Durban now occupies was first charted in 1497 when the Portuguese navigator, Vasco da Gama, anchored off the lagoon. As it was Christmas Day he named the section of coastline *Terra de Natal,* and gave the lagoon the name *Rio de Natal.* The first Europeans to occupy the area for any length of time were a group of survivors from the British ship, *The Good Hope,* wrecked in 1685. They later joined a group of survivors from the Dutch East Indian *Stavenisse,* and together built a boat and sailed to Cape Town. In 1823 the *Salisbury* sailed into Rio de Natal and anchored off the central island (given the name of Salisbury Island), with the mission of trading with the local inhabitants. Owing to the success of this mission, eighteen Britons returned the following year and settled on a tract of land around the bay, granted to them by Shaka, the Zulu king. Among these settlers was Dick King, who later became a national hero and Francis Farewell, who's wife joined him a year later, making her the first female European settler on the coast.

In 1835 the settlement was proclaimed a town, and named after Sir Benjamin D'Urban, Governor of the Cape at the time. The area also had its problems: after Shaka's death, his successor, Dingane, raided the settlement, forcing the settlers to flee to Salisbury Island. From 1839 more Voortrekkers arrived from the other side of the Drakensberg and Natal was proclaimed a (Boer) Republic. A new settlement was laid out.

In May 1842 the British Government, who up to now had given the settlement little recognition, decided to dispatch a garrison to occupy Durban and build what came to be known as the Old Fort. This angered the Voortrekkers, who besieged the fort for 34 days. It was during this siege that Dick King, in the dead of the night, crossed the bay and rode to Grahamstown for help to relieve the fort. He completed the distance of 960 km in ten days. A relieving force was dispatched and the Boers were repulsed. More British settlers arrived and soon the Voortrekkers returned to the Transvaal.

The lagoon was developed into a deep-water harbour and from then on Durban grew. The farming district expanded rapidly with successful sugarfarms. More labour was needed, and shiploads of Indian immigrants from the poorest centres in India were brought to the area. This Indian community has grown steadily, contributing greatly to Durban's well being. Today they occupy an important part in the city's cultural and business affairs.

Accommodation

The Durban Publicity Association offers an Accommodation Booking Service through their offices: Tel. (031) 32-6421, Church House, Church Square (P.O. Box 1044, Durban, 4000).
(See also Umhlanga Rocks on page 180.)

HOTELS
De Luxe   **Maharani Hotel**   *****TYYY   Tel. (031) 32-7361
83-91 Snell Parade
(P.O. Box 10592, Marine Parade, 4056)   Southern Sun
Swimming-pool, sauna, golf, tennis, bowls, squash (and fishing can be arranged)
It is the only five-star hotel on Durban's beachfront: all rooms command a superb view over the sea and beachfront promenade. On arrival guests are met by an Indian doorman, dressed in traditional Indian clothing, and effortlessly whisked off to one of the spacious and superbly furnished rooms. The suites are luxurious, with all the trimmings of a comfortable apartment, including dressing rooms, very large bathrooms and bedrooms. There are several restaurants in the hotel including an informal Indian restaurant on the ground floor, where delicious curries can be enjoyed. The discoteque on the 31st floor can be reached by an exterior lift which gives guests a panoramic view of the bay as it ascends.
The Royal Hotel   *****TYYY   Tel. (031) 304-0331
267 Smith Street (P.O. Box 1041, Durban, 4000)
Swimming-pool, squash and sauna
One of the finest, if not **the** finest hotel in South Africa is located in downtown Durban. Guests have a choice of rooms overlooking either the city or the bay. All rooms have traditional Cape furnishings plus all the modern gadgets expected of a hotel of this calibre. Service is the key-word here, and the friendly staff make it their business to see that each guest is well cared for.

The hotel boasts six restaurants, from a buffet-style **carvery** and informal pool deck restaurant, through the elegant **Royal Grill** with its French classical cuisine, to **Top o' the Royal,** which offers seafood and dancing.

Elangeni Hotel   ****TYYY   Tel. (031) 37-1321
63 Snell Parade
(P.O. Box 4094, Durban, 4000)   Southern Sun
Swimming-pool, gymnasium, sauna, golf, bowls, tennis (and fishing can be arranged)
Although not in the same class (or price bracket) as the Maharani, this is still an excellent beachfront hotel, ideal for holiday visitors. Rooms are all sea-facing and offer the comfortable facilities expected of a hotel in this class. Another big plus factor is the huge pool deck, with two pools. The hotel also offers a variety of restaurants and bars.

Marine Parade Holiday Inn   ***TYYY   Tel. (031) 37-3341
167 Marine Parade
(P.O. Box 10809, Marine Parade, 4056).   Holiday Inns
Swimming-pool
From the outside this de luxe hotel does not look like the average Holiday Inn; but once inside you will find the usual comfortable fittings and large rooms. All rooms have a superb view of the bay and the hotel is across the road from the best beaches in Durban. There is ample parking within the hotel, as well as the usual assortment of restaurants.

Medium-priced   **Tropicana**   ****TYYY   Tel (031) 37-6261
85 Marine Parade
(P.O. Box 10305, Marine Parade, 4056).   Kondotel Inns
This long-established hotel has been refurnished and upgraded (which included a change of name). It still, however, caters very well for family holiday visitors. It is centrally situated along Marine Parade and all the rooms have a splendid view of the bay.

Albany   ***TYYY   Tel. (031) 304-4381
225 Smith Street, Durban, 4001.   Protea Hotels and Inns
Located in the centre of town, this is an ideal site for the business visitor or holiday-maker who does not need to be close to the beachfront. The two restaurants in the hotel both have good menus.

Malibu   ***TYYY   Tel. (031) 37-2231
73 Marine Parade
(P.O. Box 10199, Marine Parade, 4056)   Southern Sun
Swimming-pool and sauna
If you are looking for a relaxed family hotel that swings, then look no further. This seems to be the favourite meeting place in Durban for all the holidaymakers in the city. During the day a host of programmes keep the kids amused, while at night you have a choice of restaurants, the Father's Moustache Beer Garden and discos.

New Beach   ***TYYY   Tel. (031) 37-5511
107 Marine Parade
(P.O. Box 10305, Marine Parade, 4056)   Kondotel Inns
This is a reasonably priced, well-run, family beach hotel close to all amenities. Rooms, although large and comfortable, are not to everyone's taste. There are a number of lively pubs and restaurants in the hotel.

Westville Hotel   ***TYYY   Tel. (031) 86-6326
124 Jan Hofmeyer Road (P.O. Box 145, Westville, 3630)
Squash
Located between Pinetown and Durban. The entire hotel has
been charmingly done out in yellowwood and stinkwood and
everything is kept shining and clean. The public rooms offer
elegant dining and live entertainment.

Belgica Hotel   **TYYY   Tel. (031) 31-1064
74 St. George's Street, Durban, 4001
This is a small well-run downtown hotel with neat rooms and
pleasant low priced meals. The Rubenshof Restaurant (see
restaurants) is well worth a visit.

Parkview   **TYYY   Tel. (031) 37-4311
16 Boscombe Place
(P.O. Box 10203, Marine Parade, 4056)   Trusthouse Forte
Swimming-pool
The Parkview is an elegantly furnished, well-run, modern hotel,
close to the beaches. Here the visitors are left to their own
devices to enjoy their holiday as they see fit. The hotel has a
number of restaurants.

Budget   **Berea Inn**   **TYYY Tel. (031) 21-1241
337 Berea Road, Durban, 4001
This pleasant mock-Tudor style hotel is a little way from the
beaches, but, nonetheless, centrally situated. Although catering
mainly for residents, it also offers the visitor pleasant surroundings.

Lonsdale   **TYYY   Tel. (031) 37-3361
52 West Street (P.O. Box 10444, Marine Parade, 4056)
Swimming-pool
The Lonsdale is a large, well-run hotel, with modern, clean,
comfortable rooms. During the season a variety of activities are
organised for the guests. There are also a number of action bars
where night-time entertainment can be enjoyed. It is situated
close to all the beaches.

Baldwin   *RYYY   Tel. (031) 37-3987
144 West Street, Durban, 4001
One will find this pleasant well-run hotel located between the
shopping areas and the beachfront. The rooms are spotless, and
enjoyable food is served.

Balmoral   *TYYY   Tel. (031) 37-4392
125 Marine Parade (P.O. Box 10935, Marine Parade, 4056)
This is an old beachfront hotel which still supports traditions
such as a silver dinner service in the dining room. Many of the
rooms have a fine sea view.

Empress   *TYYY   Tel. (031) 37-2783
211 Marine Parade (P.O. Box 10771, Marine Parade, 4056)
This small informal hotel right on the beachfront is ideal for
families with limited budgets. Bar lunches and dining-room meals
are real value for money.

Parade Hotel   *TYYY   Tel. (031) 37-4565
191 Marine Parade (P.O. Box 10693, Marine Parade, 4056)
The Parade Hotel is unpretentious, low-priced, well-run and
close to the beaches. Rooms are more than adequate, and the
hotel serves wholesome, reasonably priced meals.

Pavilion Hotel   *T   Tel. (031) 37-7366
1066 Marine Parade, North Beach, 4056

A quiet hotel offering cheap, clean, simple accommodation and food for budget-minded guests.

YMCA and YWCA   **YMCA** Tel. (031) 304-4441
Cnr Beach Walk and Esplanade (P.O. Box 2181, Durban, 4000)
They offer clean, cheap rooms, good meals and are central.
YWCA Tel. (031) 21-5121
311 Musgrove Road, Berea, 4001
They have clean and cheap rooms; but are often fully booked.

SELF-CATERING   **Golden Sands Holiday Flats** Tel. (031) 37-4995
95 Snell Parade, Durban, 4001
They are over the road from the beaches and close to beachfront amusement centres. All flats are self-contained and have air-conditioning. There is covered parking for residents.
Marine Sands Holiday Flats Tel. (031) 32-3232
237 Marine Parade (P.O. Box 10777, Marine Parade, 4056)
These flats offer a fine view of the beach just across the road. The self-contained flats all have TVs and telephones, and fully equipped kitchens. Covered parking is available to residents and two restaurants do business in the complex.
Seaboard Holiday Apartments Tel. (031) 37-2601
Cnr. West Street and Point Road (P.O. Box 10555, Marine Parade, 4056)
They are ideally located within walking distance of the beach, as well as most of the nightlife and amusement centres. The well-appointed apartments all have telephones, TVs and air-conditioning. There are two restaurants and a swimming-pool on the premises.

Restaurants

De Luxe   **Fozzi's** Tel. 22-4059   Not licensed
36 Ritson Road, Berea   French
This very pleasant restaurant can be found near the Botanical Gardens. It has its own little tropical courtyard and serves dishes from provincial France, always with the freshest of vegetables, steamed to perfection. The atmosphere is relaxing, and the service pleasant.
La Popote Tel. 32-7887   Fully licensed
21 Gillespie Street   French
Possibly one of the finest French restaurants in the city, this elegant restaurant serves mainly French provincial cuisine, complemented by a well-stocked cellar offering some of the top South African and French wines. Service is friendly and attentive, and booking is essential.
Roma Tel. 37-3872   Fully licensed
193 Smith Street   Italian
Roma is ideal for an elegant night out on the town. The restaurant offers a wide selection of Italian delicacies and attentive service. To top it all, diners can take a twirl on the dance floor to the sounds of a band that plays everything but ear-shattering pop music.
Rubenshof Tel. 31-1064   Fully licensed
Belgica Hotel, 74 St. George's Street   Belgian

True to Belgian tradition, this restaurant offers many delights —
especially those flavoursome sauces that have made Belgian
cooking famous. The restaurant has been in operation for over
thirty years and has never lowered its standard. Diners can
dance on Wednesdays, Fridays and Saturdays.

Saltori's   Tel. 305-3361   Fully licensed
320 West Street (2nd Floor)   French/Italian
An elegant yet relaxed atmosphere greets diners at this establishment. Food is generally prepared and presented as delicious
works of art. At Saltori's all the elements of fine dining fall
comfortably into place.

Le St. Geran   Tel. 304-7509   Fully licensed
31 Aliwal Street   Mauritian
This is regarded as one of the top Mauritian restaurants in the
country: the staff has managed more than admirably to merge
French provincial and Creole cooking, presenting dishes that are
a gastronomic delight. Add to this a well-stocked cellar and
attentive service and you have a perfect night of dining out.

Medium-priced   **Aldo's**   Tel. 37-0990   No licence
137 West Street   Italian
Aldo's is a casual trattoria in downtown Durban, where a
pleasant atmosphere and reasonable prices make for a fun night
out. A speciality here is the variety of homemade pastas.

Atoca   Tel. 32-4829   Wine and malt licence
1st Floor, Chisnor Building,
574 Point Road   Portuguese
This restaurant serves mainly seafoods with a strong Portuguese
flavour. Service and presentation are as good as the food —
which means that it is advisable to book in advance.

British Middle East Indian Sporting and Dining Club
Tel. 31-2717   Wine and malt licence
16 Stanford Hill Road   Eastern
Both the name and the decor remind one of the early colonial
days. The restaurant is set in a charming old building now
declared a national monument. They serve a variety of dishes,
from Middle Eastern to Oriental, all accompanied by the appropriate garnishes.

Jean's Place   Tel. 37-6037   No licence
40 Mona Road   Seafood
Located in a small cottage in a tiny street, this cosy old-world
restaurant offers many delights from the sea. The fish is always
fresh and well-presented.

Khyber   Tel. 306-1575   No licence
180 Grey Street   Indian
Here you have the authentic restaurant with decor and music to
match. A rich choice in Indian delicacies await the diner, with an
interesting array of desserts to round off the meal. As it is
Muslim, no liquor may be consumed on the premises.

La Mafia   Tel. 32-0519   Wine and malt licence
Cnr. West Street and Kearsney Road   Italian
Split into two rooms — one for fast pizzas and the other for more
intimate dining — this excellent establishment offers good inexpensive food. The fresh pasta, made daily, is delicious.

Leipoldts of Port Natal   Tel. 304-6644   Fully licensed
Cnr. Commercial and
Aliwal Streets   South African buffet
There is no better place to sample the widest array of South

African culinary delights at one sitting. And despite the variety, the food is well-presented, freshly prepared and continuously replenished.

Lobster Pot   Tel. 37-8258   Wine and malt licence
20 Belmont Arcade, West Street   Seafood
Friendly service and good value are the hallmarks of this restaurant, which offers some of the best seafood found along the Durban coastline.

Budget

Curry Den   Tel. 32-6410   No licence
66 Broad Street   Curries
Simple decor and a variety of good Natal curries from mild to very hot, with all the trimmings, are the features of this restaurant.

Mike's Kitchen   Tel. 304-1104   Wine and malt licence
58 Albany Grove   Steakhouse
They offer good steakhouse food and a wide variety of salads.

One Rander Steakhouse   Tel. 32-4950   No licence
Nedbank Centre, cnr West and Point Streets   Steakhouse
Although very little can be bought these days for one rand, you will still find exceptional value for money here from breakfast till late.

Cockney Pride   Tel. 37-5511   Fully licensed
New Beach Hotel, Marine Parade   Pub food
Typical pub lunches and bar-counter meals are offered.

Greenwich Village Wine Bar
Tel. 37-3451   Fully licensed
Palm Beach Hotel, 106 Gillespie Street   Pub food
A wide variety of typical English pub food is served here.

London Town Pub   Tel. 37-3451   Fully licensed
Palm Beach Hotel, 106 Gillespie Street   Pub food
Budget-priced English pub food and lots of music and humour to wash it down with can be found at this pub.

Nightlife

THEATRE

Reservations for all shows in and around Durban can be made through **Computicket:** Tel. 304-2753 or **C.O.D. Bookings:** Tel. 32-2611

The Natal Playhouse,   Tel. 304-3631, in Smith Street, opposite the City Hall, offers the visitor a choice of 5 venues which host diverse performing arts, from opera to ballet, drama, musicals and caberet. The complex also houses a number of restaurants, from the elegant **L'Artiste Legends** (Tel. 304-3297) which serves French cuisine, to a number of snack bars.

LIVE ENTERTAINMENT
Classical music

The City Hall hosts a variety of concerts on its premises, including Sunday afternoon concerts beginning at 15h00; lunchtime concerts; and organ recitals on its fine pipe organ. Programmes can be obtained from the Durban Publicity Association.

Jazz

A few venues have regular jazz sessions over weekends. They are:
Albany Hotel,   Tel. 35-4381, Cnr. Albany Grove and Smith Street: Saturdays from noon.
Maître Per's,   Tel. 32-8866, 6 Mona Road: Sundays from 18h30.

Ports O'Call,   Tel. 37-2231, Malibu Hotel, Marine Parade: Sunday from 18h30.

Action Bars   **The Barn,**   Tel. 84-1251, Athlone Hotel, 10 Northway, Durban North: Sing-along.

Cockney Pride,   Tel. 37-5511, New Beach Hotel, Marine Parade: English pub/honky-tonk piano.

Father's Moutache,   Tel. 32-7361, Malibu Hotel, Marine Parade: show band and comedy.

London Town Pub,   Tel. 37-3451, Palm Beach Hotel, Gillespie Street: English pub, sing-along.

Pig 'n Whistle,   Tel. 37-4281, Killarney Hotel, Brickhill road: English pub, folk music.

Ports O'Call,   Tel. 32-7361, Malibu Hotel, Marine Parade: latest rock bands.

Robert E. Lee,   Tel. 21-1351, Los Angeles Hotel, St. Thomas Road: rock bands, student haunt.

San Antone Rose,   Tel. 37-3361, Picardi Lonsdale Hotel, West Street: country and western music.

The Durban Folk Club   meets every Monday at 19h30 in the Blue Waters Hotel. Guests are welcome. For further information contact Tel. 46-3738.

Disco and cabaret   **Club Med,**   Tel. 37-4281, Killarney Hotel, Brickhill Street: live band.

Millionaire,   Tel. 37-3451, Palm Beach Hotel, Gillespie Street: cabaret/disco.

Nello's,   Tel. 37-0060, 185 Smith Street: disco/cabaret and resident band.

Red Garter,   Tel. 37-3361, Lonsdale Hotel, West Street: live band, disco and cabaret.

Raffles,   Tel. 32-7361, Maharani Hotel, Marine Parade: top disco with fine views over the city and the beachfront.

Speakeasy,   Tel. 97-1355, Executive Hotel, Umlazi: top bands and disco.

DINNER-DANCING   **Causerie,**   Tel. 37-3681, Edward Hotel, Marine Parade: sophisticated dance band on Fridays and Saturdays.

Fingers,   Tel. 33-3781, Blue Waters Hotel, Snell Parade: disco on Mondays and Tuesdays, live pop groups the rest of the week.

Lara's,   Tel. 37-1321, Elangeni Hotel, Marine Parade: French cuisine and elegant atmosphere, open late.

Roma Restaurant,   Tel. 37-3873, 193 Smith Street: elegant, Italian food and enjoyable live dance music.

Ruby Tuesday,   Tel. 37-5511, New Beach Hotel, Marine Parade: plush club, lively cabaret and dancing.

Top O'the Royal,   Tel. 32-0331, Royal Hotel, Smith Street: resident band, fine view of the harbour.

Useful addresses and telephone numbers

Durban area telephone code: **(031)**

TOURIST INFORMATION   **Durban Publicity Association,**   Tel. 304-4981, Church Square (or beachfront office close to oceanarium — Tel. 32-2595) (P.O. Box 1044, Durban, 4000).

South African Tourism Board,   Tel. 304-7144, Anglo American Life Centre, 320 West Street (P.O. Box 2516, Durban, 4000).

TRANSPORT **Airlines**	South African Airways has weekly departures from Durban to London and to Mauritius, as well as flights from Durban to Swaziland and Zimbabwe. Internal flights connect Durban to all major centres. The following airlines fly out of Durban: **Air Mauritius** to Mauritius **Air Zimbabwe** to Harare **British Airways** to London **Citi Air** to Ladysmith, Newcastle, Richards Bay and Vryheid **Magnum Airways** to Nelspruit **Royal Swazi National Airways** to Manzini **SAA** **UTA** to Reunion **Flight information** Tel. 42-6145 **Reservations** Tel. 310-2133 **Air charters** — **Natal flight centre** Tel. 84-4720/84-9908 — **Helicopter services** Tel. 42-6101
Bus Services	**City services:** **Durban Transport Management Board,** Tel. 37-7766 or 37-3920, located on the corner of West and Gardiner Streets, and on the south beach opposite the Claridges Hotel. Special money-saving coupons can be bought for 10 journeys between various points. **Regional services to:** Umhlanga Rocks Tel. 51-1226 Pietermaritzburg Tel. 310-2325 Margate Tel. 3-1766 Richards Bay Tel. 32-1155 **Inter-city:** **Greyhound,** Tel. 37-6478: To Johannesburg via Pietermaritzburg, Mooi River, Estcourt, Ladysmith, Newcastle, Villiers and Heidelberg. **Citiliner,** Tel. 304-2753; Book through Computicket, one stop to Johannesburg. **Translux,** Tel. 37-7766: To Johannesburg, Port Elizabeth and East London, with stops along the way.
Coach tours	The Durban Publicity Association co-ordinates a number of tours to various attractions in and around Durban. For information and bookings telephone 304-4934 or 304-4981. The following companies also offer full day and half-day tours: **Durban Transport Management Board** Tel. 37-7766 **Springbok Atlas Safaris** Tel. 304-7938/9 **Umhlanga Tours and Safaris** Tel. 561-3777/561 **Venture Tours and Safaris** Tel. 42-4541
Car Hire	**Avis** Tel. 42-6333 **Budget** Tel. 304-9023 **Forest Drive Rent-a-Car** Tel. 52-5866 **Windermere** Tel. 23-0339 **Kempster Ford** Tel. 23-5373 **Imperial** Tel. 31-7161
Bicycle hire	**Ride A While** Tel. 32-5294/5, Cnr. Tyzack and Gillespie Streets.
Motorcycle Hire	**Hire Bike** Tel. 32-9932, 72 Prince Alfred Street.
Taxis	**Eagle** Tel. 37-8333, 37-0706 **Aussies** Tel. 304-2345
Rail	The station is in Umgeni Road. A regional service runs down the South Coast. Trains to Johannesburg run regularly, with a choice between the Trans-Natal departing in the evenings and arriving

the following morning, and the transit train offering low tariff daylight journeys.

Reservations   Tel. 310-2931
Enquiries   Tel. 310-2792

EMERGENCY NUMBERS

Ambulance   Tel. 48-5252
Hospital   Tel. 37-3333
Pharmacies   Beachfront, Tel. 32-2458
— City centre Tel. 301-2345
— Berea Road Tel. 31-8922
A.A. Breakdown Services   Tel. 31-1568
Fire Brigade   Tel. 31-3434
Police   Tel. 1-0111
Sea Rescue   Tel. 37-2011

Sightseeing

Durban's main attractions are the beaches. The most popular ones are along the Parade, from Addington in the south to Battery Beach in the north. It is therefore not surprising that a wide variety of entertainment is to be found along the beachfront. However, the city also has a number of sights of historical and cultural interest.

THE BEACHFRONT

Starting at South Beach and moving north.

The Little Top, which looks like a giant golfball, is used as an entertainment centre on the beachfront during the holiday season. Various activities, such as beauty contests, music and theatre can be enjoyed here.

The **Rickshas** are a reminder of the past, when this type of transport was common. Today a few of these men with their highly decorative carts are still to be found near the Malibu Hotel. If you want a ride, check the rate card displayed first, as tariffs are fixed. Photos also need to be paid for, so before pointing your camera, negotiate a fee.

Zulu beadsellers are mainly found under thatched shelters close to the Dolphinarium. They sell hand-made wares, from necklaces to mats and baskets; and they enjoy bargaining.

The Dolphinarium and Aquarium, Tel. 37-4079. The aquarium has local and exotic marine life in both small and large tanks. Feeding times are at 11h00 and 15h00 daily. The dolphinarium has a well-choreographed show five times a day featuring dolphins, Cape seals and penguins. Shows are at 10h00, 11h30, 14h00, 15h30 and 17h00.

The Amusement Area stretches from the dolphinarium to North Beach and offers a number of activities from cableway rides to paddling pools, larger pools, a water slide, dodgem cars, miniature railways, restaurants, etc.

The Amphitheatre in sunken gardens in front of the Maharani Hotel, between Snell Parade and the beach, is the venue of a twice-monthly fleamarket (every second and last Sunday of the month).

Minitown, Tel. 37-7892, is a miniature city built to a scale of 1:24. Many of Durban's well-known landmarks are depicted here as is a scale model of a harbour, airport and railway line. Open from Tuesday to Saturday and public holidays from 09h00 to 20h30 and on Sundays from 09h30 to 17h30.

Fitzsimons Snake Park, Tel. 37-6456. Although not the best in the country, it is well worth a visit. Exhibits include an interesting collection of both indigenous and exotic snakes, as well as crocodiles, iguanas, and terrapins. Demonstrations are held at 10h00, 11h30, 14h30 and 15h30 during weekends, school holidays and on public holidays. Open daily between 09h00 and 16h30.

THE HARBOUR AND EMBANKMENT

This tour is best done during the morning, as parking restrictions are in force during the late afternoon along Victoria Embankment. Durban harbour is the busiest in Africa and therefore fascinating to anyone interested in maritime affairs.

From the city, take Point Road and drive south. Take the last road to the left just before the harbour gates are reached and then follow it, keeping to the right. This will bring you to the **North Pier.** Before the pier was constructed and the entrance dredged, Durban Bay was notorious for the number of ships that sank there. Between 1845 and 1885 more than sixty large ships were wrecked on the beaches. From the pier one can enjoy an imposing view of the Durban skyline. Fishing from this point is also very good. Return to Point Road, stopping for a while at Signal, Escombe and Browers Roads to view the Chelsea-type **Point Row Houses,** which were built in the 1890s for harbour staff. Continue along Point Road and turn left into Bay Road and left again onto Victoria Embankment.

The first point of interest you will pass is **Da Gama Clock** on the left. The clock was presented to the city in 1897 by the Portuguese government. It commemorates the naming of Natal by Da Gama more than 500 years ago.

From here, cross the railway line to the **Small Crafts Harbour** by means of the pedestrian subway. The ferry can be caught here for a round-the-bay cruise of about one hour. Tickets are bought on board.

The **Maritime Museum** is also located here. Visitors can go on board an old tug and view its interior. Return to the clock and along the embankment to **Dick King's statue.** The statue commemorates Dick King's 960-km, ten-day ride to Grahamstown in 1842 to obtain help for the British garrison who were besieged by the Boers.

From here either walk through the subway, or drive and take the first street left into the **yacht basin,** which affords a lovely view of the city centre. On the eastern side of the basin (towards the coast) is the jetty where the **Sarie Marais Pleasure Cruises** (Tel. 31-6091) start their trips. One-hour out-of-season trips leave at 11h00 from Monday to Saturday and also at 15h00 on Sundays. In-season trips leave at 10h00, 11h30, 14h30 and 16h00 daily.

Leaving the yacht basin, continue along Victoria Embankment and then turn left into Maydon Wharf. Turn left again into Parker Street to reach the quayside in the harbour. From here a leisurely drive can be taken through the harbour enjoying the various activities. Keep an eye open though for shunting and loading activities.

CITY CENTRE

Start at the Durban Publicity Association Offices, opposite the City Hall, in Pine Street.

The **City Hall,** inaugurated in 1910 and modelled on the Belfast City Hall in Ireland, houses the public library, museum and art gallery, and various council rooms. At the back of the city hall is the **Local History Museum.**

From here walk north across Church Square (with the post office on your left) and under the subway to the **Workshop Complex**. This fascinating shopping centre with 120 speciality stores, restaurants and cinemas has been constructed within the walls of the old Durban railway station workshop. It is well worth a visit.

Continue up Pine Street and turn right into Field, and then left into Queen Street. On the corner of Queen and Grey Streets is the **Juma Mosque**, the largest Muslim place of worship in the southern hemisphere. It is worth a visit and just remember to remove your shoes before entering the building.

Just behind the mosque between Grey Street and Cathedral Road are two arcades, Madressa and Ajmeri, known collectively as the **Oriental Arcades.** They are crammed with small traders whose wares spill onto the passageways, giving a fascinating insight into the eastern cultures. Pickpockets are common here, though, so be on the look-out.

Follow Grey Street and turn right into Smith and right again at Warwick Avenue to reach the **Indian Market.** This fascinating market is filled with fragrances and curios of the East. Spices and herbs of every description can be bought here. The fish and meat sections are worth visiting if you are not too squeamish.

GARDENS AND NATURE RESERVE From the city take the Northern Freeway (M4). Just after crossing the Umgeni River, take the first exit into Riverside and follow the signposts to the Japanese Gardens (in Tinsley Road). These pleasant Japanese gardens are full of tropical flora.

From the gardens, return to Riverside and turn right to reach the **Umgeni Bird Park** (Tel. 84-1733). This fascinating park, rated as one of the best in the world, has indigenous as well as exotic birds. There are two large well-constructed aviaries through which guests can stroll at leisure and observe the various birds in their natural surroundings. Open daily.

Continue from the birdpark onto Umgeni Road (R102) and then back towards town. Turn right into Innes Road (6th on the right) and follow it to Rosetta Road, from where a beautiful view of the city can be seen. Continue along Innes Road to **Jameson Park,** which boasts over 200 rose varieties and is alive with colour during the rose season.

From the park turn south into Musgrove Road, then left into Springfield Street, which becomes Argyle (M17), then right into Cowey Road (M8) and then into Sydenham Street, which will bring you to the entrance of the **Botanical Gardens.** The gardens comprise 20 ha of lawns, beautiful trees and colourful beds of flowers. Also within the grounds is a herbarium and orchid house. The **Orchid House** has a beautiful display of orchids from around the world. The Orchid House is open from 09h30 to 12h30 and 14h00 to 17h00 daily. The Botanic Gardens are open daily between 07h00 and 17h30. From here, return to town.

TEMPLE OF UNDERSTANDING This fascinating temple is 30 minutes' drive from the city centre and was built by the International Society for Krishna Consciousness. It is a unique architectural masterpiece and a sign of the contemporary renaissance of ancient Vedic culture and philosophy in South Africa. It is open daily from 04h30 to 21h00. There is a vegetarian snack bar (open from 11h00 to 18h00 — except Saturdays) and a vegetarian buffet restaurant (open from 18h00 to 21h00) in the building. To reach the temple take the N3 towards Pietermaritzburg and branch off on the N2 south. Take the Chatsworth turn-off and turn right onto the highway (R629). Exit at the Chatsworth Centre sign. (Tel. 43-5815)

ANTI-SHARK MEASURES BOARD A fascinating insight into this organisation is offered to all those who are interested. The visit will involve an excellent audio-visual presentation on shark control, by the world's forerunners in the field, followed by a discussion and dissection of a shark caught in the nets. To reach the board's offices, take the M4 northern freeway and branch off at Umhlanga Rocks. Drive inland at the intersection towards Mt. Edgecombe. The board is located amidst canefields on the right, about 3 km up the road. (Tel. 561-1001)

Annual events

January: **Duzi Canoe Marathon** – canoe and portage marathon starting in Pietermaritzburg and ending 150 km downstream at the Umgeni River mouth 3 days later.

March: **Lifesaving National Championships** – for all top life-savers in the country.

April: **Toyota National Rugby Tournament** at King's Park Stadium (usually over Easter week-end).

May: **Comrades Marathon** (31 May) is a world-renowned road race of 90 km between Durban and Pietermaritzburg.

July: **Rothman's July Handicap** – most popular race meeting in South Africa, held on 1st Saturday of July since 1897.

Military Tattoo – rated as one of the best in the world, with all the pomp and ceremony. Many of the acts are international.

Gunston 500 – the premier surfing event attracting the world's top surfers to compete in Durban's "Bay of Plenty".

Durban Triathlon – comprising of 6 km swimming, 100 km cycling and 42 km running.

Shopping

Although Durban cannot compete with either Johannesburg or Cape Town, there are a few places worth visiting.

ART **African Art Centre**, Tel. 304-7915, Guildhall Arcade, 36 Gardiner Street: mainly black artists.
Graham Gallery, Tel. 304-4705, 16 Fenton Road: mainly Natal artists.

CLOTHING **Bilbo Boutique,** Tel. 304-6642, Ashley House, Smith Street: comtemporary clothes by Durban designers.
Box 3, Musgrove Centre, Berea: expensive clothes from top South African designers.
Go East, Tel. 328-757, West Street (near beach) and West Walk: Indian cottons and silks.
Teazero, Salisbury Arcade, West Street: "alternative" clothes and latest fashions.

CURIOS   The best place is the **Indian Market** where one should shop around and bargain for best prices.

SPORTS   **Kings Sports**,   Tel. 304-9551, 343 West Street: Durban's largest sports shop with knowledgeable staff. See also Outdoor Activities for specialists.

Outdoor Activities

With Durban being a seaside resort, watersports dominate the leisure activities of most visitors.

Cricket: *Old Kingsmead Cricket Ground* in N.M.R. Avenue is the venue for most big games (Tel. 32-9703).

Fishing: Natal's coastline is said to have the largest number of angling oportunities in South Africa. One of the most popular fishing events is the **Sardine Run**, which takes place usually towards the end of June each year when large shoals of sardines come up the coast to breed. They tend to move to shallower waters at the South Coast and as they travel up the coast, large numbers are beached — at times up to knee-deep. This is when every able-bodied person is on the beach with a scoop to get his share. The consequence of this run is that many game fish and shark follow the sardines, resulting in very good **game-fishing**. Conservation measures have been established in Natal which limit the size, season and number of any one type of fish that may be caught. For the amateur fisherman these are not restrictive, as all quotas are more than reasonable. It is, however, advisable to take note of these rules, which are obtainable from the Natal Parks Board (Tel. 39-2305, Private Bag 4316, Durban, 4000). Fishing gear can be hired from *Ride-a-while*, Tel. 32-5294/5, corner of Tyzack and Gillespie Streets.

Rock and surf angling is the most popular form of fishing along the coast and is administered by the Natal Coast Angling Union, Tel. 28-1617 and the Association of Natal and North Coast Anglers, Tel. 51-1333. Fish commonly caught include cob (winter to spring), shad (protected from September to November), stumpnose, kingfish (especially during the sardine run), spotted grunter, rock cod, blacktail, pompano and a variety of shark. The best weather conditions for fishing are an inshore Northeaster with a falling barometer. Best times of day are early morning and late afternoon. Piers where fishing is permitted include North Pier, at the harbour entrance, and those north of the Snake Park. Fishing off the two piers on either side of North Beach is prohibited. The section of beach between Umgeni River Mouth and Umhlanga Rocks lighthouse is very popular. To reach it take the M4 out of town and then branch off at the Broadway off-ramp. Cross a bridge and turn right, back towards the city. Access to the beach is through a gate on the left, where a catch-card (for research purposes) may need to be filled in. Further along the coast a number of good fishing spots can be found.

Deep-sea fishing is also very rewarding with catches of marlin, tunny and shark — even tiger and great white. A variety of bottom fish are also often caught, including cob, garrick and mussel-cracker. A number of companies offer fishing trips. For further information call 37-7751, 31-8152 or the *Durban Publicity Association*.

The Durban yacht basin

Above left: Orchids are part of
Durban's tropical splendour
(Orchid House, Durban Botanical
Gardens)

Centre left: Catching a wave off North
Beach, Durban

Below left: Pavement vendors,
Margate Beach

Below right: Inside the Temple of
Understanding, Durban

Golf: two courses which welcome visitors are the *Windsor Park Course*, Tel. 32-5294/5, in Athlone Drive, which also has equipment hiring facilities and the *Royal Durban Golf Club*, Tel. 33-5927, inside the Greyville Racecourse.

Hang-gliding is a popular sport in Natal, especially inland where there are some magnificent launch sites. For information and regulations contact *Wings Sky School*, Tel. 304-5069, or *Durban Hang-gliding Club*, Tel. 21-0786.

Rugby fixtures are planned by the *Durban Rugby Union*, Tel. 33-2073.

Sailing in Durban Bay is very popular. The *Ocean Appletiser Sailing Academy*, Tel. 301-5726 or 301-5766, offers a number of courses on ocean-sailing. Students are accommodated on board for the duration of the course (usually four and a half days) with meals included. Dingy sailors are also catered for by the *Point Yacht Club*, Tel. 32-4787.

Scuba-diving and spear-fishing can be enjoyed along much of the coast. A licence is needed for spear-fishing or catching crayfish. (Apply to *Natal Fisheries Licensing Department*, Tel. 39-2305, Maple Road, Greyville.) The best spots for spear-fishing are south of the Bluff and north of Umhlanga, but not near bathing areas. *Trident Dive Shop* (see address below) also offers boat-diving at reasonable prices. Crayfish-diving can be enjoyed along most of the coastline where rocky outcrops are found. There are also many places amongst the coral reefs or in the harbour where scuba-diving can be enjoyed. Equipment can be hired (a recognised diving certificate needs to be produced) from *Trident Dive Shop*, Tel. 31-1742, 18 Boatman's Road, or from *Underwater World*, Tel. 32-5820, 44 Farewell Street. The *Durban Undersea Club*, Tel. 85-7079 after hours or 32-0654 during weekends, welcomes qualified visitors who may need advice or wish to join club dives.

Surfing is one of the most popular part-time activities amongst the youth of Durban. The beachfront itself is known as the *Bay of Plenty* because of the large number of locations and regular waves. The best spots are along the beachfront, from Addington in the south to Battery Beach in the north. Boards can be hired from *Safari Surf Shop*, Tel. 37-2176, 26 Somtseu Road, and *Surfmaster*, Tel. 37-4038, 6 Winder Street. Paddle-skis can be hired from *Surfmaster*.

Squash courts can be hired at a number of places, including *Disc Squash*, Tel. 37-4431, Brickhill Road; *Central Courts*, Tel. 31-4707, 320 West Street; and the *Royal Health and Squash Centre*, Tel. 32-0331, Royal Hotel.

Tennis court hire can be done through *Westridge Park Tennis Stadium*, Tel. 81-3901.

Tenpin bowling is popular and can be enjoyed at either *The Disc Tenpin Bowling Centre*, Tel. 32-4447, 100 Brickhill Road or *Berea Bowl*, Tel. 21-4297, Berea Centre, lower Berea Road.

Wind-surfing information can be obtained from the *Natal Boardsailing Association*, Tel. 37-1583. The two favourite sea-sailing sites are close to the North Pier and below the Snake Park. Boards can be hired either through *Sailteck*, Tel. 37-1583, or *Sail 'n Surf*, Tel. 32-6644.

Departing from Durban on the Northern Freeway (M4), the first resort reached is Umhlanga Rocks.

UMHLANGA ROCKS

This pleasant coastal resort, 18 km from Durban, is often preferred to Durban by holiday-makers. Most of the hotels lead directly onto the beach.

HOTELS **Beverly Hills** *****TYYY Tel. (031) 561-2211
Lagoon Drive (P.O. Box 71,
Umhlanga Rocks, 4320)   Southern Sun
Sauna, swimming-pool
One of the top hotels on the coastline, where service is of paramount importance. All rooms are sea-facing and have their own balconies. The hotel grounds lead directly onto the beach.
Cabana Beach ***TYYY Tel. (031) 561-2371
10 Lagoon Drive (P.O. Box 10,
Umhlanga Rocks, 4320)   Southern Sun
Swimming-pool, tennis, squash and fishing
Although this is a very large hotel, it is ideal for a family holiday as rooms are large (mostly suites) with kitchenettes. There are two pool areas and many activities for children during the season. The grounds lead onto the beach.
Oyster Box ***TYYY Tel. (031) 561-2233
2 Lighthouse Road (P.O. Box 22,
Umhlanga Rocks, 4320)   Portfolio of Country Places
Swimming-pool, tennis and fishing
This is a charming family-run hotel, set on the beachfront in five acres of tropical gardens. The rooms are all large, sea-facing and tastefully furnished. It is the ideal place for a relaxing holiday.
Breakers Resort **TYYY Tel. (031) 561-2271
88 Lagoon Drive (P.O. Box 75, Umhlanga Rocks, 4320)
Swimming-pool, tennis and fishing
The resort has two-bedroom apartments sleeping up to six guests and studio apartments sleeping up to four. All have fully equipped kitchens and balconies. The grounds are large and lead directly to the beach.

Continuing along the M4, which joins up with the N2, the road passes one or two more seaside villages before swinging inland. You will drive through subtropical forests and cane-fields as well as the occasional Zulu village until you reach the St. Lucia Estuary turn-off (R620), 221 km from Durban. If you have time on your hands, it is well worth spending a few days exploring the various Zululand game parks. All the parks offer the same facilities: huts sleeping between two and three people. Every hut has a fridge and is supplied with bedding. Communal ablution blocks are kept clean and tidy. Most have communal kitchens, where cooks prepare food for the guests. Food and utensils must be supplied by the guests. There are also usually braaiing facilities. Continue along the N2 towards Pongola and Swaziland if your time is limited.
The parks worth visiting are:

ST. LUCIA ESTUARY
(26 km from the N2 turn-off)

The estuary is the entrance to one of the most ecologically

important lagoon systems in southern Africa. The lagoon or lake covers an area of 36 000 hectares, shaped roughly in the form of an H, and is over 40 km long and an average of 10 km wide. The average depth of the water system is less than 2 m. The lake, together with a one-kilometre belt around it, which adds an extra 14 000 hectares, has been declared a game reserve. The coastal belt between the lake and sea has also been a declared reserve and is known as the **Eastern Shores Nature Reserve**. Buck such as the reedbuck, duiker and suni are to be found in the area, together with cheetah (which have been re-introduced to control the reedbuck population), crocodile and hippo, as well as a wide variety of birdlife (including both pelican and flamingo). Fishing is very popular: even the occasional game fish or shark have been caught. Because of the danger of shark and crocodile attacks, swimming or even wading in the waters is strictly prohibited.

Boating is allowed, if the boat meets the requirements of the Natal Parks Board. St. Lucia is a malaria risk area and it is advisable to take the necessary precautions.

Accommodation

HOTELS   **Lake View**   **TYYY Tel. (03592) 6/48
McKenzie Road (P.O. Box 6, St. Lucia, 3936)
Swimming-pool, fishing and hiking
A pleasant well-run hotel close to the lake, ideal for the fisherman and his family. Food in the à la carte restaurant is substantial if not adventurous: mainly steaks and fresh fish.
Estuary   *TYYY Tel. (03592) 9
McKenzie Road (P.O. Box 9, St. Lucia, 3936)
Swimming-pool, fishing and hiking
This simple waterfront hotel is ideal for the budget-conscious family. All the rooms have bathrooms and are comfortable. The country fare caters for hearty appetites and fish features strongly.

SELF-CATERING   **St. Lucia Travel Lodge and Caravan Park**
AND CAMPING   Tel. (03592) 36
McKenzie Street (P.O. Box 4, St. Lucia, 3936)
Electric plugs, laundry, gas, swimming-pool, fishing and hiking
This is a pleasant resort offering visitors accommodation in self-contained flats or rooms. Camping and caravan sites are well grassed.
St. Lucia Estuary Resort   Tel. (03592) 20/47
McKenzie Street (Warden-in-charge, Private Bag St. Lucia, 3936)
Shop, swimming-pool and fishing
This basic caravan and camping resort has been well laid-out by the National Parks Board.

Sightseeing

The **Crocodile Research Station,** which is run by the Natal Parks Board, is well worth a visit. It comprises a research centre and an interpretive display of the layout of the lagoon and surrounding areas. To get there drive 2 km along the Cape Videl Road. Crocodiles are fed every Saturday afternoon at 15h00.

From St. Lucia return to the N2. Follow it for 3,5 kilometres before turning left onto the R618 towards Umfolozi.

UMFOLOZI
(22,5 km from the N2)

This 47 753 ha reserve was proclaimed in 1897. The reserve is widely associated with the white (or square-lipped) rhino, which was saved from near extinction in Africa. The reserve supports over nine hundred of these magnificent creatures and has also re-located many to other reserves in Africa. The Umfolozi also supports black rhino, a large number of small antelope as well as nyala, kudu, zebra, buffalo, giraffe, lion, leopard, cheetah, spotted hyena and black-backed jackal. Over 300 species of birds are also found here. The park receives most of its rain (about 650 mm per year) between October and March. A simple reed-walled hide at the water-hole offers the patient visitor a host of surprises.

Accommodation

Reservations can be made through the Natal Parks Board (see page 290).
Mpila offers accommodation in twelve three-bedded rest huts, while **Masinda** has six three-bedded huts. Both camps have clean communal bathrooms and kitchens.

Wilderness Trails

Reservations can be made through the Natal Parks Board (see page 290).
  Trails, led by a ranger and a game guard, can be undertaken between March and November, for three days. Groups are limited to between three and six people, all of whom must be over 16 years of age. Hikers must supply their own food and bedding, but these are carried by pack-mules between huts.
  The Wilderness Leadership School also offers a five-day white rhino trail in the area (see page 293 for details).

From Umfolozi drive along the R618, either back to the N2, or to Hluhluwe. To reach Hluhluwe turn left after two and a half kilometres from the R618 turn-off and travel another 15 km.

HLUHLUWE GAME RESERVE

Umfolozi, St. Lucia and Hluhluwe were the first reserves to be proclaimed on the African continent. The climate in this 23 000 ha reserve is similar to Umfolozi's, but the vegetation differs in that it varies from forest to woodland, savannah and grasslands. Although it is less than 6 per cent of the size of the Kruger National Park, Hluhluwe contains more than 68 per cent of the plant species found in the Kruger Park. Game is similar to that found in Umfolozi, in addition to hippo, crocodile and elephant, which have been re-introduced.

Accommodation

Reservations can be made through the Natal Parks Board (see page 290). The hutted camp has two-bedded huts as well as four six-bedded self-contained cottages.

The N2 can be reached 14 km from the reserve. Along the way you will pass the Zululand Safari Lodge.
Zululand Safari Lodge   ***TYYY Tel. (03562) 63
P.O. Box 116, Hluhluwe, 3960   Southern Sun
Swimming-pool
This friendly, well-appointed hotel in the heart of Zululand is an ideal base for those who want a bit of pampering while enjoying the game parks in the vicinity. Guests are accommodated in air-conditioned rondavels, dotted around the main building. A variety of game wonders around the grounds as the hotel is located within the **Ulizane Game Ranch.** Also close by is the **Umsasaneni Kraal and Museum**, which is worth a visit.

The village of Hluhluwe, on the other side of the N2, has shops where provisions can be bought. Continue from the village to False Bay Park.

FALSE BAY PARK

The park offers open campsites along the north-western shores of the lake. A wide variety of birdlife can be observed while driving along the shore of the lake. Fishing is also good. The park has a number of well laid out camp sites as well as a rustic camp where basic accommodation is offered. Reservations can be made through the Natal Parks Board (see page 290).

Return to the N2 and continue north. The next turn-off will be for Mkuzi Game Reserve.

MKUZI GAME RESERVE
(21 km from N2 on dirt)

The Mkuzi was established in 1912 on 25 091 ha of land dotted with fever trees and massive sycamore figs. Game includes impala, giraffe, rhino (both white and black), nyala, kudu, leopard, hippo and crocodile. A large number of birds, including wild geese, inhabit the park and pan. Three hides offer rewarding viewing for those with patience, especially during the dry season. There are six huts with kitchens and separate bathrooms, five four-bedded bungalows and two two- to three-bedded bungalows located within the park, as well as a camping site. Half-and one-day trails can be undertaken through the park in the company of a guide, and can be booked through the reception on arrival at the camp.

Continue north on the N2 until you reach the turn-off to the right for Lavumisa/Big Bend (37 km from the town of Mkuze). The Swaziland border (part of Golela/Lavumisa) is reached 12 km further on and is open daily between 07h00 and 22h00.

SWAZILAND

Covering an area of only 17 000 km², Swaziland is one of the smallest sovereign states in the world. The country's western borders with South Africa are defined by the Khahlambra (the barrier) range of mountains, which reach their highest point at 1 862 m above sea level. Along this range the rainfall is high (1 000 mm per year), making Swaziland one of the best watered countries in the subcontinent. From here the land falls away slowly to a broad band of undulating hills before dropping to the lowveld, which links the savannah bushveld of the eastern Transvaal with Zululand. The country is sheltered in the east from Mocambique by the low-lying Lubombo range, and is a distance of only 145 km wide from west to east.

The original people who populated the area arrived in about 1750. They spoke a Nguni language. During the mid-1800s the first white traders and hunters began to penetrate the area and gave the people the name of Swazi, after their chief at the time, Umswati. Gold was soon discovered in the mountains, and a flood of fortune-hunters arrived, beginning Swaziland's famous *concession rush*, where immigrants were granted exclusive rights for establishing a range of enterprises. When it was found that the gold was limited, the flood of activity stopped and fortune-seekers left for other fields.

The South African Republic (Transvaal) took over the administration of Swaziland in 1895 and after the Anglo-Boer War, the British took over administration of the country and tried to sort out the confusion which arose from the aftermath of the concession rush. Most of the Swazi people had become squatters in their own country. Although they claimed that the concessions were only issued for a limited time, the British Commission appointed to look into the matter found otherwise. In 1907, a third of all land concessions were expropriated to provide homes for the Swazis, while the other two-thirds remained in the hands of the title holders. King Sobhuza II, installed as Paramount Chief in 1921, set about winning back the land for his people by negotiation, and today over 60 per cent of the land is in possession of the Swazi people.

On 6 September 1968 Swaziland became fully sovereign with King Sobhuza II as its king. In 1972 the king repealed the colonial constitution and replaced it with a form of tribal democracy, ratified in 1978 through a general election. In August 1982 King Sobhuza II died, and for the next few years the kingdom was run by a regent. In 1987 King Mswati II was crowned as the new king of Swaziland.

After completing all the necessary border procedures (see page 20), which includes the payment of road tax, continue on to **Big Bend**. Beware of the road, especially the first 30 km which has not yet been tarred, and can be very slippery, both during the wet and dry season. This is sugar cane area, and vast fields are passed on the way to Big Bend, where a sugar mill is located.

Accommodation

The Bend Inn   Tel. (0194) 3-6111
P.O. Box 37, Big Bend

Tennis, bowls and golf
This pleasant little motel is ideal for an overnight stop, especially for the more budget-conscious traveller. All rooms are air-conditioned and have bathrooms.

From Big Bend the road on to **Manzini** winds its way through cattle country and thorn trees for 80 km.

Manzini is Swaziland's principal industrial town and site of the country's only international airport. The first permanent white traders in the area arrived during the 1880s when business began to flourish because of the concession rush. Albert Bremer built a hotel and store, and the site became known as Bremersdorp among the European settlers. However, the Swazis always referred to it as Manzini, after the Chieftain Manzini Motha, whose kraal was located nearby. In 1960 Manzini became the town's official name.

Leave Manzini and head for Mbabane, the capital of Swaziland. The road slowly climbs up the **Ezulweni Valley**. Twenty kilometres out of Manzini on the left are the **Royal kraals of Lositha and Labamba**, the spiritual capital of the nation, and then on the right the **Houses of Parliament**. From here the following accommodation establishments are passed (see map on page 161):

Accommodation

Mlilwane Wildlife Sanctuary   Tel. (0194) 61037
P.O. Box 33, Mbabane
This beautiful little reserve was established on the site of an old tin mine, which scarred the landscape and killed off most of the surrounding vegetation. Through careful management and support from the king, the area was rejuvenated and moulded into a very pleasing nature reserve. A wide variety of wildlife has been re-introduced into the area and it also boasts a rich and interesting birdlife. The **Gilbert Reynolds Memorial Gardens** of aloes in the park is also worth a visit.

Accommodation is in the form of rustic two-bedded chalets, and well laid out campsites. There is also a restaurant and shop on the premises. One of the most pleasant ways of exploring the reserve is on horseback: horses can be hired in the reserve.

Smoky Mountain Village   Tel. (0194) 6-1291
P.O. Box 21, Ezulweni
Swimming-pool
This beautifully laid out well-grassed resort has a number of "A-frame" chalets positioned in a semi-circle. It also offers a recreational centre and a swimming-pool. The chalets are built of pine, and consist of a verandah, leading to a sitting room, kitchenette (which is fully equipped) bathroom and two bedrooms. Each chalet sleeps up to six people and is fully furnished and is serviced daily. The restaurant has the reputation of serving the best pizzas and pasta in the valley.

Yen Saan Hotel   Tel. (0194) 6-1051
P.O. Box 771, Mbabane
Swimming-pool and tennis
A fine hotel, which blends the best Chinese traditions and culture with Western standards. All the rooms are comfortably fur-

nished. The restaurant offers a wide variety of Chinese dishes, as well as European and Indian alternatives.

Royal Swazi Sun   Tel. (0194) 6-1001
Ezulweni Sun Cabanas   Tel. (0194) 6-1201
Legogo Sun Cabanas   Tel. (0194) 6-1101
Private Bag Ezulweni, Swaziland   Sun International
Swimming-pool, tennis, bowls, squash, sauna, golf, hiking and horse-riding

The resort complex comprises three hotels: the Royal Swazi Sun is the central hotel. The other two are converted Holiday Inns. Within the complex are a number of restaurants and a casino. Service is not always up to the standard expected of such a complex, but, with a bit of patience, an enjoyable holiday can still be had by the guest.

Timbali Caravan Park   Tel. (0194) 6-1156
P.O. Box 1, Ezulweni
Laundry, games room and swimming-pool

This is a pleasant park, with panoramic views of the Ezulweni Valley below. All sites are well-grassed and flat, with a number of shady trees scattered around. There are also ample braai and tap sites and the neat ablution blocks are centrally located. The central block contains a shop and licensed restaurant. Rondavels and rooms are also provided for two to four people. All the rooms have linen, fridges and stoves, and are serviced.

Swazi Inn   Tel. (0194) 4-2235
P.O. Box 121, Mbabane
Swimming-pool

This quaint, homely hotel is set in terraced, secluded gardens and has a splendid view of the valley below. Guests are accommodated in cosy rooms in the main building or cottages in the garden. The restaurant is renowned for its variety of well-prepared à la carte meals.

A further 4 km up the road lies the town of Mbabane.

MBABANE

The picturesque administrative capital of the country houses the ministeries, civil service and judiciary, as well as most of the foreign diplomatic missions. The town is situated in a bowl formed by the Dlangeni Hills. Climate is temperate and fairly wet. The town is located on the site where the British built their administrative headquarters in 1902.

Tourist information

Swaziland Government Tourism Office   Tel. (0194) 4-2531, P.O. Box 451, Mbabane

Shopping

Allister Miller Street is the main thoroughfare in Mbabane. Most of the shops, banks and diplomatic missions are located here. The most interesting place to shop though is at the **Swazi Market**. This is located near the entrance to the town, opposite the Swazi Plaza complex. This fascinating market offers many

The Drakensberg amphitheatre

Flamingos on Lake St Lucia

A rhino in the Hluhluwe Game Reserve

A view from the Oliviershoek Pass

interesting handicrafts, including wood and stone carvings, beadwork and weaving. Fruit and vegetables are also on sale here. Behind the market you will find what can best be described as "local restaurants".

From Mbabane follow the road towards Ermelo, for just over 15 km, and then turn right towards Pigg's Peak. Eighteen kilometres further on is the entrance to Malolotja.

Malolotja Nature Reserve   Tel. (0194) 4-3731
P.O. Box 1979, Mbabane
Hiking
Located in one of the most beautiful parts of Swaziland, this impressive reserve supports a large variety of antelope and bird species. There are a number of waterfalls in the reserve: the highest, with the same name as the reserve, is 90 m high. Also located in the reserve is the Ngwenya Iron Mine, dating from 4100 BC and believed to be the oldest known mine in the world. Accommodation in the reserve is provided in log cabins sleeping up to six people. They are fully furnished and equipped with all the necessary kitchen utensils. The road system in the reserve is not that good, but hiking routes through the park are well laid-out.

Continue from here on to **Pigg's Peak**.

Pigg's Peak was named after William Pigg, who discovered gold here in 1884. The town was a gold-mining centre, but after the gold had been exhausted, it became a centre for forestry.

Protea Pigg's Peak Hotel   Tel. (0194) 7-1162
P.O. Box 385, Pigg's Peak   Protea Hotels & Inns
Swimming-pool, tennis, bowls and squash
This is a new and modern hotel, which is well-located. Each room provides a fine view over the valley. The rooms are spacious and comfortably furnished. The hotel also has a casino.

The road from Pigg's Peak to the border post of Matsuma/Jeppe's Reef descends into the wide plains where sugar-cane and bananas are grown in abundance. From the border (open daily between 08h00 and 16h00) continue for a further 42 km on the R570 until you reach the N4 and Malelane. Turn right at the junction for the Malelane gate into the Kruger National Park (see page 198).

2   Umtata to Johannesburg via the Drakensberg
(924 km)

The route from Umtata to Port St. Johns should be attempted only by those who have time on their hands and are willing to drive on poor dirt roads. Extreme caution should be taken: you will often find animals crossing the road and oncoming traffic on the wrong side of the road. If you have the time, and wish to take the risk, the scenic rewards are spectacular.

The alternative route is via the N2 to Kokstad. From Kokstad the road winds its way through the foothills of the Natal Drakensberg, giving the visitor a chance to turn off and explore the various Drakensberg resorts along the way. These resorts all have a relaxed atmosphere and are ideal for those who wish to spend some time close to nature or doing a spot of trout-fishing.

In summer the weather is pleasantly warm during the day, and cool at night; but in winter snow often turns the area into a white wonderland. From Golden Gate, which is the last point of interest on this route, the road will take you through the Orange Free State up to Johannesburg.

If you wish to go to Port St. Johns from Umtata, turn right onto the R61. The tar ends after 40 km but the road passes through some spectacular scenery. The road slowly descends to the coast through the **Mlengana Pass**, which is one of the most scenic in Transkei. You will reach a fork in the road 88 km after leaving Umtata. The right fork leads to Umngazi Mouth, 11 km away; and the left fork continues to Port St. Johns, 12 km away.

UMNGAZI MOUTH

The road winds along the left bank of the Mngazi River (the scene of many tribal battles in the past) to a splendid beach and large lagoon. The area is rich in birdlife and a haven for fishermen.

Umngazi Bungalows Hotel   Tel. (0020) and ask for Umngazi Mouth 1
P.O. Box 75, Port St. Johns
Tennis, fishing, wind-surfing (free boards available), canoes and rowing boats, and hiking
This is definitely one of the best resorts on the Transkei coast. It offers a wide variety of activities to keep the whole family happy. Guests are accommodated in bungalows, each comfortably fitted out and close to the water's edge. The resort is also famous for its seafood, including crayfish and oysters throughout the season. Arrangements can be made for nursemaids.

PORT ST. JOHNS

Port St. Johns, a sleepy resort nestling in the subtropical forest, is certainly one of the most picturesque coastal towns of southern Africa. The town is entered through the Gates of Port St. Johns,

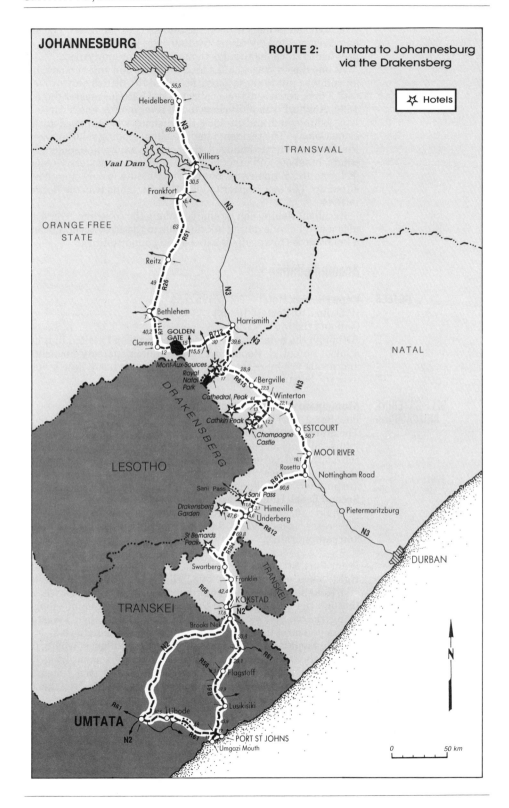

JOHANNESBURG

ROUTE 2: Umtata to Johannesburg via the Drakensberg

✫ Hotels

55,5
Heidelberg
60,3
N3
TRANSVAAL

Vaal Dam
Villiers
30,5
Frankfort
6,4
ORANGE FREE
STATE
63
R57
N3
Reitz
49
R26
N3
7 Bethlehem
40,2 R711
GOLDEN
GATE
15
Clarens 12
15,5
Harrismith
R712
30
39,6
N3
NATAL

Mont-Aux-Sources
Royal
Natal
Park
17
R615
28,9
Bergville
22,3
Winterton
22,1
DRAKENSBERG
Cathedral Peak 44
13 11
Cathkin Peak 12,2
8,8
Champagne
Castle
ESTCOURT
50,7

LESOTHO
16,1
Rosetta
MOOI RIVER
R617
Nottingham Road
90,6
Sani Pass
Sani Pass
Drakensberg
Garden
11,9 3,1
47,6 Himeville
4,6 Underberg
R612
Pietermaritzburg
St Bernards
Peak
69,8
R39
N3
Swartberg
Franklin
R56
42,4
DURBAN
TRANSKEI
KOKSTAD
17,6 N2
Brooks Nek
33,8
R61
R56
28,1
Flagstaff
R61
17,3
R61
Lusikisiki
Libode
UMTATA
48
R61
43,9
N2
PORT ST JOHNS
Umgazi Mouth

N

0   50 km

two high sandstone cliffs on the outskirts of the town. The site has been visited by ships trading wares and stocking up on provisions since the first Portuguese sailed around Africa.

At one time it was a haven for smugglers and gun-runners, but an end was put to these activities when the British Government sent a magistrate, customs collector and harbour master there in 1878. A wharf was built close to the river mouth, and a garrison was established and in 1884 the district was annexed to the Cape Colony. The residents had excellent trading relations with the Pondo, who exchanged their skins, ivory and maize for beads, blankets and other goods. At one stage coasters voyaged as far as 16 km upstream, but the river mouth is now completely silted up. The last coaster to visit Port St. Johns was the *Border*, in 1944.

Excellent fishing can be enjoyed along the coastline. There are also a number of exciting hiking trails in the area. Second Beach, 4 km from the town, offers safe bathing opportunities.

Accommodation

HOTELS

Cape Hermes Hotel   Tel. (04752) 35
(P.O. Box 10, Port St. Johns)
Golf and fishing
Although the hotel was rather run down when I visited it, it has a lot of potential. Rooms are large, though sparsely furnished, and meals are more than adequate. One also has a lovely view over the bay from the bedrooms.

SELF-CATERING
AND CAMPING

Municipality   Tel. (04752) 31/75
P.O. Box 2, Port St. Johns.
The municipality runs two resorts: one at First Beach, in Port St. Johns, and one at Second Beach, 4 km from the town. Both offer self-contained cottages and unequipped rondavels, as well as camping facilities. All sites are well grassed and secure. They are both within walking distance of the beach.
Second Beach Holiday Resort   Tel. (04752) 61
(P.O. Box 18, Port St. Johns)
This resort is located close to the beach and offers both cottages and camping sites.

From Port St. Johns go back along the Umtata road, but turn right 3 km out of town, over the bridge towards Lusiki-siki/Kokstad on the R61. The road twists and climbs slowly up through the hills of eastern Pondoland, passing quaint villages along the way. You will reach Lusikisiki and then Flagstaff before you meet the tarred road which leads back to the N2.

Both **Lusikisiki** and **Flagstaff** are rural villages where the locals buy their provisions. (Flagstaff gets its name from the time when two old traders used to signify closing times by flying a white flag from the flagpole.) After leaving Transkei on the N2, take the R56 for Kokstad.

KOKSTAD

The town was named after Adam Kok III, paramount chief of the Griquas. His great grandfather, Adam Kok I, was freed from slavery in the early 1800s and became leader of a large group of Hottentots who settled in the Philippolis area. After a quarrel with the Cape Government, the group settled in the Kokstad area, which became known as Griqualand East. This agricultural town at the base of the Drakensberg is a popular trout-fishing centre.

Mount Currie Motel   *TYYY Tel. (0372) 2178
Hope Street (P.O. Box 27, Kokstad, 4700)
This is a pleasant little motel, which is perfectly suited for an overnight stop. All rooms are clean and comfortable, and the restaurant offers continental cuisine.

Take the R394 from Kokstad to Franklin, and then on to Underberg, along the picturesque foothills of the Drakensberg. After Franklin you will pass the small village of Swartberg and then the turn-off on the left to St. Bernards Peak.

St. Bernards Peak   Tel. (0374) 241
P.O. Box 93, Swartberg, 4710   Club Caraville
Electric points, swimming-pool, tennis, bowls, putt-putt, horse-riding, hiking, fishing, hang-gliding, wind-surfing and a motor-cross track
This homely resort on the lower reaches of the Drakensberg offers visitors a number of activities. All the cottages are comfortable and well equipped, and many have fireplaces for cold winter evenings. Camping sites are well grassed and shaded. The central area has a good restaurant, library, TV room and games room.

THE DRAKENSBERG RANGE

The Drakensberg is the highest range of mountains in southern Africa, reaching 3 482 m at its highest peak, *Thabana Ntlenyana* (Sotho for "nice little mountain"), in Lesotho. The range forms an awe-inspiring wall of basalt from *Xalanga* (place of the vultures) in the south, around Lesotho, to *The Sentinel* in the north: a total distance of 450 km. From the Sentinel, the escarpment, (also named the *Drakensberg*), runs another 600 km into northern Transvaal, dividing the Transvaal plateau from the lowveld bush.

The Drakensberg (also known as "The Berg" among the locals) gets its name from the black folklore which held that dragons once lived in the mountains. And they were not far wrong. However, the last dinosaurs lived in the mountains millions of years ago.

Snowfalls are not uncommon, and in the summer spectacular thunderstorms occur. They usually start building up just before midday and by 14h00 a tremendous show of lightning and thunder is accompanied by driving rain: then it ends suddenly and by sunset the sky is clear and the air is cool. All along the base of the range you will find holiday resorts with fully-contained cottages and a wide variety of outdoor and indoor activities.

UNDERBERG

Underberg is the junction from which a number of Drakensberg resorts can be reached. Trout anglers can enjoy some good fishing in the vicinity.

Accommodation

HOTELS

Underberg Hotel   *TYYY Tel (033712) 22
Main Road (P.O. Box 28, Underberg, 4590)
Tennis, bowls, trout-fishing, golf and horse-riding
This quaint little hotel is an ideal base from which to explore the area and enjoy the fishing. (The hotel is the headquarters of the local trout-fishing club.) The à la carte restaurant offers substantial country food including some delicious trout dishes.
Drakensberg Garden Hotel   **TYYY Tel (0020) and ask for Drakensberg Garden 1
47 km from Underberg
(P.O. Underberg, 4590)   Kondotel Inns
Swimming-pool, golf (9-hole), tennis, bowls, horse-riding, fishing, archery, sauna and hiking
This comfortable resort hotel offers a wide variety of activities to keep even the most energetic of guests occupied. Good country-style food satisfies the hearty appetites that all the activities can build up.

SELF-CATERING
AND CAMPING

Naverone Estates   Tel. (033712) 1640
Drakensberg Gardens (Private Box 307, Underberg, 4590)
Swimming-pool, golf (9-hole), tennis, bowls, horse-riding, fishing, and hiking
Comfortable self-contained cottages and a well laid-out caravan site make this a pleasant resort where one can relax and enjoy the surroundings.

Take the R617 from Underberg to **Himeville**, another pleasant little village at the foot of the Drakensberg.
Himeville Arms   *TYYY Tel (033722) 5
P.O. Himeville, 4585
Swimming-pool, golf, tennis, squash, bowls, horse-riding, fishing, and hiking
This old country inn oozes charm and hospitality. Guests are accommodated in cosy, well-furnished cottages. In the main building you will find the old pub and Trout House, where one can enjoy the delights of good country cooking in an intimate atmosphere.

From here continue for 3 km, until you reach the turn-off to Sani Pass on the left, onto a gravel road. **Sani Pass** is regarded as the highest mountain pass in Africa and is the only eastern road into Lesotho. The Lesotho pass has been used since 1912 as a bridle-path for pack animals taking trading goods in and out of Lesotho. It was widened in 1949 to accommodate motor vehicles as well. Just under 12 km from the turn-off lies the hotel, and 3 km further is the **Mzimkulwana Nature Reserve**. The reserve is the home of a variety of unique flora, antelope and birds, including a number of raptors. It is, however, not advisable to travel further than the park entrance in anything other than a four-wheel drive.

Sani Pass Hotel   **TYYY Tel (033722) 29
P.O. Himeville, 4585
Swimming-pool, tennis, golf (9-hole), bowls, squash, horse-riding, fishing, hiking and sauna
This is the ideal resort for those who need to relax but also need to be active. Rooms are spacious and well-furnished. Daily excursions are organised up the pass in four-wheel drives. A number of bushmen paintings can be found in the vicinity.

Continue along the R617. The road becomes gravel (and rather poor in places) and crosses the various rivers originating in these mountains, winds up and down numerous passes until it reaches Nottingham Road. Drive with care, as the road is not very well signposted. From Nottingham Road, follow the R103 via Rosetta towards Mooi River, where you can join the N3. Follow the N3 via Estcourt and then branch off onto the R615 to **Winterton**, another junction for a number of resort hotels. The turn-off to the left, in Winterton, leads to both **Champagne Castle** and **Cathedral Peak**.

Accommodation

The Nest   *TYYY Tel. (03642) and ask for Nest 2
21 km from Winterton (Private Bag X14, Winterton, 3340)
Swimming-pool, tennis, bowls, horse-riding, fishing and hiking
Famous for its three championship bowling greens, this resort hotel also offers a wide variety of other outdoor activities. Rooms are more than adequate, and wholesome country food is served.

El Mirador   **T Tel. (03642) and ask for Ela 1
24 km from Winterton (P.O. Winterton, 3340)
Swimming-pool, tennis, bowls, squash, riding, fishing and hiking
The El Mirador is not licensed, so bring your own drinks. Another unique feature of this Spanish-styled hotel is its chapel, which is ideal for a wedding with a difference. A number of activities are organised for guests staying at the hotel, including tours of the area.

Cathkin Park Hotel   *TYYY Tel. (03642) and ask for Cathkin 1
29 km from Winterton (Private Bag X12 Winterton, 3340)
Swimming-pool, tennis, bowls, squash, badminton, riding, hiking, trout-fishing, wind-surfing and a 9-hole golf course (close by)
This little hotel has a superb view of the various peaks in the Drakensberg from its setting in the mountains. A lake close by provides for various water sports and a well-kept path leads to a beautiful fern forest.

Champagne Castle Hotel   **TYYY Tel. (03642) and ask for Champagne Castle 3
32 km from Winterton (Private Bag X8, Winterton, 3340)
Swimming-pool, tennis, bowls, riding, trout-fishing, hiking and mountaineering
Guests are housed in thatched cottages in an area which offers spectacular scenery. The hotel is very popular with mountaineers.

Cathedral Peak Hotel   **TYYY Tel. (03642) and ask for Cathedral Peak
P.O. Winterton, 3340 (44 km from
Winterton)   Portfolio of Country Places
Swimming-pool, tennis, bowls, squash, croquet, riding, fishing, and hiking
Many of the delightful cottages have splendid views of the various mountain peaks in the area, or of the river. One speciality of the hotel is fresh trout, caught in the streams nearby.

Dragon Peaks Holiday Resort   Tel. (03642) and ask for Dragon Peaks 1
28 km from Winterton (P.O. Winterton,
3340)   Club Caraville
Electric plugs, laundry, gas, shop, recreation hall, swimming-pool, tennis, bowls, wind-surfing, horse-riding, hiking and trout-fishing
This superb resort is close to the famous Drakensberg Boys Choir School and guests can attend performances on Wednesday afternoons. Visitors have a choice between fully-equipped cottages and camp sites which are well grassed. Bushman rock art can be seen at the end of a 3 km hike from the park.

From Winterton the R615 leads onto Bergville.

Sandford Park Lodge   Tel (03642) and ask for 61
P.O. Box 7, Bergville, 3350   Club Caraville
Swimming-pool, tennis, bowls, riding, wind-surfing, fishing and hiking
This charming old lodge, which once served as a coach house is located just outside Bergville in one hundred acres of woodland. Guests are accommodated (suites and standard) in quaint thatched cottages, each with its own charm. The restaurant specialises in old-fashioned home cooking. As the Lodge is not licensed, guests are encouraged to bring their own drinks.

Continue for another 29 km where a left turn takes one to Mont-aux-Sources and the Royal Natal National Park.

THE ROYAL NATAL NATIONAL PARK

This is one of the most spectacular areas of the northern Drakensberg. The 8 000 ha park has at one end the huge 8 km-long Amphitheatre, situated between the Sentinel (3 165 m) in the west and the Eastern Buttress (3 047 m). Also in the area is Mont-aux-Sources, which is 3 282 m high, and the source of the Tugela River, which cascades 853 m over the edge, forming the magnificent Tugela Falls. The reserve is also the Natal Parks Board's largest trout hatchery, supplying all rivers in the area from its abundent stock of fish.

Accommodation

Royal Natal National Park Hotel   **TYYY
Tel. (03642) and ask for Mont-aux-Sources 1
Private Bag 4, Mont-aux-Sources, 3353
Swimming-pool, tennis, bowls, riding, trout-fishing, hiking and sauna

Situated in the grounds of the park, this gracious hotel offers a number of amenities. All accommodation is in well-appointed chalets or rondavels. Food is hearty and satisfying, especially after a long day's walk. An added bonus is that often the parks board rangers give talks on the flora and fauna of the area.

Mont-aux-Sources Hotel   *TYYY Tel. (03642) and ask for Mont-aux-Sources 7

Private Bag 1,

Mont-aux-Sources, 3353   Protea Hotels and Inns

Swimming-pool, tennis, bowls, putt-putt, trout-fishing, hiking and riding

This hotel (just outside the gates of the Royal Natal National Park) is most beautifully situated and most of the rooms have a superb view of the Amphitheatre. Rooms are large, and well appointed, each having a secluded balcony. Food is very good.

Tendele Hutted Camp and Mahai Camp Site   Tel. (0331) 5-1514

In the Royal Natal National Park (P.O. Box 662, Pietermaritzburg, 3200)

Fishing, hiking and riding

The two camps offer the ideal setting for those who prefer to relax at a well laid-out camp site or in a fully equipped bungalow.

Outdoor Activities in the Drakensberg

Apart from the large variety of activities offered by the various resorts within the area, the Drakensberg is most famous for hiking, climbing and trout-fishing. When climbing or hiking in the area, remember the following:

- Never go alone. Always try and go with someone who knows the area.
- Complete the mountain register (found at most resorts or entrance gates) in full detail and leave a note on your car windscreen stating destination and approximate return time.
- Make sure you have the right equipment as well as an adequate supply of food and warm clothing, in case of a sudden change in weather conditions.
- Seek shelter in bad weather and avoid prominent spaces during storms
- Do not litter.

Booklets on fishing, hiking and mountaineering in the Drakensberg are available from the Natal Parks Board, P.O. Box 662, Pietermaritzburg, 3200; Tel. (0331) 5-1514 (reservations) 5-1221 (information).

HIKING   There are a number of one-day trails in the area and information about them can be obtained from most of the resorts. Many resorts will also be able to supply a guide for the day. The five-day Drakensberg Hiking Trail leads from Bushmans Nek Hotel to Sani Pass. For information and reservations write to: The Regional Director, Natal Forest Region, Private Bag 9029, Pietermaritzburg, 3200; or telephone (0331) 28101.

There is also a day-long trail leading hikers to the summit of Cathedral Peak. The Royal Natal National Park offers a variety of trails, the most exciting of which is to the top of Mont-aux-Sources, offering a panoramic view of the surrounding countryside. This hike should ideally include two nights in the cave at the top of the mountain. Bookings to stay in the cave can be made at the information centre. The hike is demanding and culminates in one having to climb two chain ladders up a sheer rock face.

MOUNTAIN-CLIMBING   There are a number of exhilarating climbing faces, varying in length and difficulty, in the area. In the south, Drakensberg Gardens is dominated by Garden Castle (1 400 m) and Rhino Horn (2 997 m). Between Cathkin Peak and Champagne Castle is the notorious Monk's Cowl (3 261 m), regarded as one of the most difficult peaks in the Drakensberg. In the vicinity of Cathedral Peak are a number of popular climbs, including (from south to north), Ndumeni Dome (3 285 m), Cleft Peak (3 281 m), the Pyramid (E grade, 2 914 m), the Column (F grade, 2 926 m), the Inner Horn (C grade, 3 005 m), Outer Horn (D grade, 3 006 m) and the Bell (E grade, 2 930 m). There are also a number of climbs in the Amphi-theatre. Full information on hikes and climbs can be obtained from the visitors' centre inside the Royal Natal National Park.

TROUT-FISHING   Most of the mountain streams in the area are well-stocked with trout and information on where to fish can be obtained from all resorts. To fish in the area one requires a trout licence, obtainable from the various resorts, Receiver of Revenue Offices and many sports shops in the area. The season is open from 1 September to 1 June. Fixed spool reels are prohibited.

On leaving the area, return to the R615 and turn left up **Oliviers-hoek Pass** towards Harrismith. This spectacular pass winds its way up the Drakensberg to a height of 2 095 m, giving a superb view back over the plains below, as well as the mountains. After passing the Sterkfontein Dam on the left, turn left onto the R712, towards Qua Qua/Bethlehem. From here follow the Golden Gate sign-boards. You will get to another corrugated dirt road (not recommended for caravans) with spectacular scenery, which will take you to Golden Gate.

GOLDEN GATE HIGHLANDS NATIONAL PARK

This national park is better known for its spectacular scenery than wildlife. It is located in the Maluti Mountains, on one of the highest plateaux in South Africa. The park covers an area of 6 241 ha varying in altitude between 1 892 and 2 770 m. It is ringed by massive golden sandstone cliffs which continuously change colour with changes in the weather. The weather can change very rapidly, from blazing sunshine to dramatic thunder-storms and snowfalls. Days are usually pleasantly warm, with nights cool in summer and cold in winter. Various antelope, including black wildebeest, eland, and blesbok have been re-introduced into the park. A large variety of bird species also live here. The most exciting are the black eagle and the lammergeyer (bearded vulture).

Accommodation

Bookings can be made through the National Parks Board (see page 290).

Brandwag, the main camp, offers accommodation in the main building in single and double rooms, all with radio, telephone and TV. Chalets, also fully equipped, have barbecue facilities. Within the main building is a restaurant, coffee-house, bar, library, curio shop, information centre and gymnasium. Outdoor activities include tennis, bowls, nine-hole golf course, riding and hiking.

Glen Reenen Rest Camp, located higher up the gorge, is meant for those who prefer self-catering accommodation. Guests are accommodated in rustic, fully-equipped huts and a well-laid-out caravan park.

HIKING A number of trails of varying length have been laid out in the park. The two-day **Rhebuck Hiking Trail** crosses the most scenic parts of the park.

In the vicinity of **Clarens**, 12 km from Golden Gate, there is a hotel, guest farm and caravan park.

Accommodation

Maluti Lodge Motel   **TYYY Tel. (0143262) 35
Steyl Street (P.O. Box 21, Clarens, 9707)
Swimming-pool, tennis, golf and sailing nearby
This charming motel reminds one of the genuine old English pubs of the past, with roaring log fires in winter and comfortable well-furnished rooms. Food is superb, and atmosphere warm and homely.
Sunnyside Guest Farm Tel. (0143262) 132
8 km east of Clarens (P.O. Box 24, Clarens, 9707)
Swimming-pool, hiking and horse-riding
Sunnyside is ideal for those who need to relax in tranquil farm surroundings away from it all. The hosts look after their guests' every need, and keep appetites satisfied with good country food.
Greenland Holiday Resort   Tel. (0143262) 340
15 km before Clarens
(P.O. Box 42, Clarens, 9707)   Club Caraville
Swimming-pool, restaurant, shop, laundry, gas and hiking
In the mountains just outside Golden Gate there are well laid-out camp sites and fully equipped self-contained bungalows. There are plenty of trails in the area for those who enjoy walking.

From Golden Gate the road leads through the farmlands of the Orange Free State, across the Vaal River, into the Transvaal, and on to Johannesburg. Take the R711 at Clarens and just before Bethlehem take the R49.

In **Bethlehem** a restaurant worth visiting is Athlone Castle.
Athlone Castle   (01431) 4681   Wine and Malt Licence
Loch Athlone   International
The restaurant is situated on the lake edge and was built to look like a Union Castle liner. The cluttered interior is filled with maritime memorabilia collected by the owner over many years. Food and service are good.

From Bethlehem continue on the R26 to Reitz; then take the R51 to Frankfort and Villiers, where the road meets the N3, which will take you to Johannesburg via Heidelberg (see page 225).

The Kruger National Park

This magnificent park covers an area of just under 2 million ha of the eastern Transvaal, making it the largest park in South Africa. It stretches from the Limpopo River in the north to the Crocodile River in the south, a distance of over 350 km; and has an average width of 60 km, with Mozambique on its eastern border.

The original park, situated between the Crocodile and Sabie Rivers, was known as the Sabi Game Reserve and was proclaimed by President Kruger in 1895. In 1902 Col. James Stevenson-Hamilton was appointed as the first park warden, and it was as a result of his foresight and persistence that the park grew to its present size and was renamed and proclaimed a national park in 1926.

The conservation area is still expanding with the establishment of privately owned parks on the western perimeter of the park.

The park has summer rainfall: the south receives about 700 mm and the north 400 mm of rain. Summer temperatures can rise above 40 °C during the day, while in winter the temperature hardly ever drops below 8 °C at night. Vegetation in the park north of the Olifants River comprises mopani and other taller trees, including the mighty baobab. In the southern section vast grasslands are interspersed with thorn trees of different varieties.

More species of wildlife are found in the Kruger Park than in any other African sanctuary. There are thirty species of mammal, 114 species of reptile, 468 species of birds and a wide variety of fish. Among the mammals there are over 7 500 elephants, 28 000 buffalo, 120 000 impala, 4 300 giraffe, 1 500 lion, 900 leopard, 250 cheetah, 300 wild dogs and a number of both black and white rhino.

Accommodation

Sixteen rest camps in the park offer a wide range of comfortable accommodation. All huts and bungalows are serviced, and linen, towels and soap are provided. A number of camps also have pleasant caravan and camping sites.

The following types of cottages are available:
- Family cottage with kitchenette. Two double bedrooms, bathroom, toilet, kitchenette (with gas stove, fridge, utensils) and screened verandah.
- Family cottage without kitchenette. As above, with fridge, but no kitchen.
- Self-contained thatched hut. One room with two to three beds, shower, toilet and fridge.
- Ordinary thatched hut. Two to five-bedded huts and hand basin. Ablution blocks nearby.
- Guest cottages. These are situated in the larger camps and accommodate parties from three to nine guests. All are fully equipped and can be reserved three months in advance.

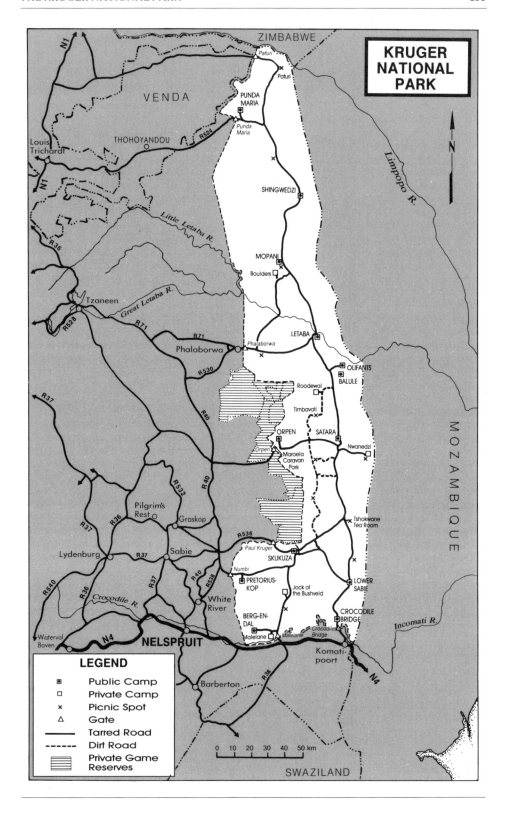

- Private camps. These camps, accommodating between fifteen and nineteen guests in cottages with showers and toilets, can be hired only as complete units. Each has its own fully equipped kitchen, but guests need to provide their own food.

All accommodation can be reserved through the National Parks Board offices (see page 290).

FOOD

Most of the rest camps have shops where groceries, perishables (including meat and fish) and liquor can be purchased. (See individual camps for details.) Shops are open between 08h00 and 13h00, and 16h00 and 18h00 (evening times are extended during summer) from Monday to Saturday, and between 08h30 to 11h30 and 16h00 to 18h00 on Sundays and public holidays. Many of the camps also have their own licensed restaurants offering very good, reasonable *table d'hôte* menus. They also offer a comprehensive snack take-away service. In Skukuza the **Selati Restaurant** offers an à la carte menu. The restaurant is situated in an old train which stands on the old siding above the Sabi River, affording a beautiful view over the river. Restaurant hours are:

Breakfast   07h00 to 09h00
Lunch   12h00 to 14h00
Dinner   18h00 to 19h30 (1 April to 30 August)
              18h30 to 20h00 (1 September to 31 March)

CAMPS WITHIN THE PARK

Driving from south to north the following camps can be found.

Malelane Private Camp
Electricity
Sleeps a maximum of nineteen guests in luxury huts. Large game in the area include lion, kudu, wild dog, cheetah and rhino.

Berg-en-Dal
Restaurant, shop, filling station, electricity, first-aid post, laundry, swimming-pool
Accommodation is offered in eighteen family cottages with kitchenettes, 69 three-bed, self-contained thatched huts, seven guest cottages and seventy sites for tents and caravans. The camp is well laid-out in spacious grounds, giving each visitor maximum privacy. It also commands a fine view of several dams where animals periodically come to drink.

Crocodile Bridge
Electricity
The camp offers twenty two- and three-bed thatched huts and twelve camping sites. Game in the area is similar to that in Malelane.

Jock of the Bushveld Private Camp
A maximum of twelve people can be accommodated in its three self-contained luxury cottages. It is a pretty camp situated at the confluence of the Mgyamiti and Mitomeni Rivers. There are many lions in this area and they are frequently heard at night.

Pretoriuskop
Restaurant, shop, filling station, electricity, first aid post, swimming-pool
Three hundred people in total can be accommodated in a variety of huts, including family cottages with or without kitchenettes, self-contained thatched huts and two- to six-bedded thatched huts. There are also fifty caravan and camp sites in the rest camp. During the summer months visitors often see new-born

animals in the area. The many roads criss-crossing the area make it easy to see the wide variety of game, including the white rhino, which were re-introduced to the area from the Umfolozi Game Reserve in 1961.

Lower Sabie

Restaurant, shop, filling station, electricity, first aid post, post office

There are 96 huts ranging from guest cottages, self-contained thatched huts, and two- to five-bedded thatched huts; and there are also 27 camping or caravan sites. This pleasant shady camp is on the banks of the Sabi River and the area affords fine game viewing.

Skukuza

Two restaurants, shop, garage, filling station, electricity, doctor, post office, police, bank, airport and car hire

This is the largest camp in the park and has accommodation for five hundred guests in two hundred huts ranging between guest cottages, family cottages with kitchenettes, self-contained thatched huts and two- to four-bedded huts. There is also space for fifty campers or caravanners.

The camp was named after Colonel Stevenson-Hamilton, who was called *uSikhukhuza,* meaning "the one who sweeps clean", by the local Shangaan population. He was the park's first warden and was based here between 1902 and 1946.

Today the busy camp is still the headquarters of the park. The restaurants offer a fine view of the Sabi River and the variety of game that drinks there. The drive from the camp, along the Sabie River to Lower Sabi, is very rewarding as hippo and crocodile can often be spotted.

Orpen

Shop, filling station, first aid post

This is a small camp with only a few two- and three-bedded thatched huts, located at the Orpen entrance gate. There is no restaurant; and no perishables are sold in the shop.

Maroela Caravan and Camping Park

This delightful park offers no amenities other than the neat ablution blocks. It is situated a few kilometres north of Orpen and overlooks the Timbavati River.

Nwanedzi Private Camp

This camp on the banks of the Sweni River has accommodation for up to fifteen people in a self-contained bungalow and two huts. The main kitchen is well equipped and provisions can be purchased at Satara, 23 km away. The picnic site on top of a cliff nearby offers a superb view of the river below. There are large herds of zebra and wildebeest in the vicinity as well as giraffe and elephant.

Satara

Restaurant, shop, garage, filling station, electricity, first aid post and laundry

This camp has 158 huts, ranging from guest cottages, family cottages with kitchenettes and self-contained thatched huts, and thirty camping and caravan sites. Although it is the second largest camp, it is well laid-out, and favoured by many visitors. The camp is located on the grass plains and large herds of up to three hundred zebra and buffalo as well as a wide variety of predators can be seen in the area. A number of birds can be seen in the camp.

Roodewal Private Camp

A family cottage and three huts which can accommodate up to twelve people. The camp is on the banks of the Timbavati River, which is seasonal, and offers fine game viewing.

Balule

This is a small rustic camp with five 3-bedded thatched huts and ten camping or caravan sites, ideal for those who do not like the larger camps.

Olifants

Restaurant, shop, filling station, electricity, first aid post

Situated on the cliffs, 100 m above the Olifants River, this majestic camp offers accommodation for 300-odd guests in guest cottages, family cottages with kitchenettes, self-contained thatched huts, and two-to four-bedded thatched huts, and also has a pleasant camping area. A reed-roofed lookout built on a rock promontory next to the main building offers superb views of game activities on the river banks below. The drive from Olifants camp along the Letaba River banks, where a variety of game can usually be spotted, is always very pleasant.

Letaba

Restaurant, shop, garage, filling station, electricity, first aid post and laundry

This camp is positioned on the bank of the Letaba River and the 91 huts vary from guest cottages to self-contained thatched huts. The camp also offers 20 caravan and camping sites. A wide variety of game can be spotted around the camp, including elephant, buffalo, waterbuck, cheetah, and roan and sable antelope.

Bolders Private Camp

The main building, and five huts, are on stilts and are all connected by covered catwalks. The camp is unfenced and accommodates a maximum of sixteen people. A waterhole 100 m from the main building draws a wide variety of game.

Shingwedzi

Restaurant, shop, garage, filling station, electricity, first aid post, swimming-pool

This is a medium-sized camp with self-contained thatched huts, two- to five-bedded thatched huts, and camping and caravan sites. The reception area is modern, and well laid-out, with the dining area overlooking the river. This northern section of the park is well known for its elephants, and leopards are often spotted in the riverine forest areas.

Punda Maria

Restaurant, shop, filling station, electricity, first aid post

This is the most northern camp, and offers accommodation in family cottages with kitchenettes, and in self-contained thatched huts, as well as a caravan and camping area. The camp started out as a ranger post in 1919 to counter the poaching of ivory. The region itself is extremely interesting because the northern section is the "crossroads" of nine of Africa's major ecosystems. Wildlife is abundant and a wide variety of trees and birds is also found in the area.

Picnic Spots

Throughout the park there are a number of picnic sites where visitors are allowed to leave their vehicles. Most of these have ablution blocks and facilities for braaiing. A number also have a small shop where a limited range of drinks and pre-packed snacks can be bought.

Wilderness Trails

Four trails are conducted twice a week (throughout the year) by experienced game rangers. These trails are not a test of endurance, but rather a wilderness experience involving natural beauty. All four trails commence on Mondays and Fridays and each accommodates a maximum of eight persons. They last for four days and three nights, ending on the morning of the fourth day. All food, light refreshments, and accommodation are included in the tariff.

The Bushman Trail in the south of the park has its base in a secluded valley surrounded by hills. Apart from game, many well-preserved examples of rock art are found in the area.

The Wolhuter Trail between Pretoriuskop and Malelane is well positioned for viewing a wide variety of game, including white rhino and mountain reedbuck.

The Olifants Trail has a camp on the southern bank of the Olifants River and close to the confluence with the Letaba River. Hippopotomus and crocodile are often seen along the banks.

The Nyalaland Trail, north of Punda Maria, is unparalleled in natural beauty and many of the rarer bird and plant species are found in this area.

Rules of the Park

The Kruger National Park is a wilderness area, where wild animals are free to roam and visitors are expected to keep to their *cages*, whether those cages be cars or rest camps. This is solely for the protection of the visitor. It is illegal, and very dangerous, to have any part of your body protruding from a vehicle. Animals may not be fed as this leads to them becoming aggressive in their demand for food, and having to be put down as a result.

Tourists are expected to remain on open public roads at all times. These roads are frequently patrolled, which means that help is usually close at hand, should a breakdown occur. Closed roads and fire breaks are not signposted and it is easy to get lost on them. The park and adjacent bushveld are in areas where malaria is still a threat. It is thus advisable to take precautions (see page 23).

Transport

The majority of visitors to the park drive there. It is, however, possible to fly in, either to Skukuza or Phalaborwa by Comair (Tel. (011) 973-2911, P.O. Box 7015, Bonaero Park, 1622) and hire a car. Avis is represented. Comair offers a number of exciting fly-in packages with trained guides on coaches.

CAR HIRE **Skukuza**
— *Avis* Tel. (0131252) 141
Phalaborwa
— *Avis* Tel. (01524) 5169

Kruger National Park to Johannesburg via the Eastern Transvaal
(453 km)

After the Kruger National Park a number of exciting private game parks can be visited. Here the accent is on creature comforts. The route takes you up the Transvaal Drakensberg, through a number of beautiful and historic resorts and towns. Once the highveld has been reached a straight three-hour trip takes the visitor on to Johannesburg.

PRIVATE GAME PARKS

Adjoining the western boundry of the Kruger National Park, running more or less from Phalaborwa in the north to the Paul Kruger Gate in the south, are a number of privately owned game parks which serve a multitude of needs, from hunting to nature conservation.

The most southern of these private reserves, collectively known as **The Sabi Sands Private Nature Reserve** has been expertly developed by the various landowners into a group of superbly run game lodges dedicated to the conservation of wildlife. The total area of the sanctuary is over 60 000 ha. The lodges all offer comfortable to luxurious accommodation and a full programme of daily activities. Activities begin at dawn, when guests are served tea or coffee and rusks before leaving for an early morning game drive in an open landrover, driven by an armed guide, accompanied by a tracker. Guests return for a leisurely breakfast and then are free to relax at the pool or catch up on lost sleep. Light lunches are served. During mid-afternoon a second game drive is undertaken, stopping at sunset for drinks in the bush. This is followed by spotting game in the dark, with the help of a spotlight. Dinner is served on the guests' return in an open-air *boma* – a circular meeting place surrounded by reeds, with a blazing log fire in the middle. Meals at all the lodges are a gourmets' delight, with venison usually featuring strongly.

To reach these private game parks, leave the Kruger National Park via the Paul Kruger Gate. The turn-off is 4,7 km along the road, to the right onto a dirt road. From the entrance follow the signposts to one of the following lodges. Drive with caution as the signs are not always visible, and animals often cross the road.

Sabi Sabi   Tel. (011) 833-7481
P.O. Box 1170,
Johannesburg, 2000   Portfolio of Country Places
Within its boundries are two lodges, **Bush Lodge** and **River Lodge**. Both can accommodate a maximum of 46 guests. The rooms are equally luxurious, well fitted, with their own bathrooms. Food is outstanding and the service and professionalism of the staff cannot be faulted. The park has a great deal of game, and is especially noted for its cats. In the evenings after dinner, rangers often give talks or slide shows on the bush. The lodge

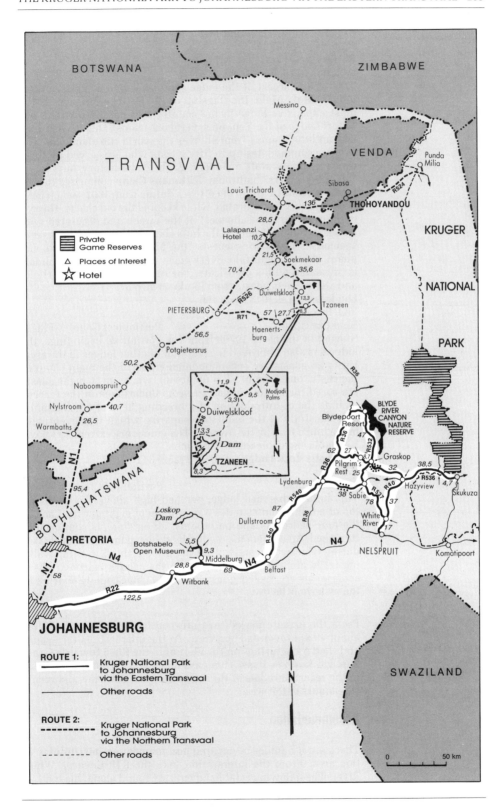

has its own airstrip and also collects guests off the scheduled
flight from Skukuza.

Rattray Reserves   Tel. (011) 789-2677
P.O. Box 2575, Randburg, 2125
This is the largest of the lodge complexes and comprises three
lodges. **Mala Mala**, the flagship of the Rattray Reserves is the
most expensive lodge in the country and has been voted *Top
Safari Lodge of the Year* on several occasions. This is where the
rich and the famous from all over the world rub shoulders. The
camp accommodates up to fifty guests who are served by three
times as many staff members. Each of the luxury huts has a
"his" and a "hers" bathroom. **Kirkmans Camp** comprises the old
farmhouse and a group of cottages dating from 1902, which have
been stylishly re-decorated, while keeping the old charm. **Harry's**
is informal (and the cheapest of the three), and decorated with
Ndebele designs. Many of the huts share bathrooms. The reserve
specialises in showing guests "the big five": lion, leopard, elephant, rhino and buffalo. Every guest who views all five animals
is presented with a certificate. The reserve has its own airfield,
and also collects guests from Skukuza airport.

Londolozi   Tel. (0131252) 166
P.O. Box 6,
Skukuza, 1350   Portfolio of Country Places
Started in the early 1970s from very primitive beginnings, the
lodge has also improved to rival that of other lodges in the area.
Up to 24 guests are accommodated either in the main camp or
the rustic bush camp, 1 km upstream, where up to eight guests
are cared for by the ranger. Projects undertaken in the reserve
include the re-introduction of a breeding herd of 34 elephants;
and the study of the habits of leopards, which was eventually
made into a film by the owners. The guides are extremely knowledgeable and dedicated to their jobs.

UluShaba Rock Lodge   Tel. (0131252) 611
P.O. Box 9,
Skukuza, 1350   Portfolio of Country Places
This luxury thatched lodge, perched high above the plains on
top of a hill, accommodates a maximum of eight guests. Each of
the four bedrooms and bathrooms, all *en suite*, is comfortably
furnished. Apart from the regular landrover game-viewing drives,
during which rhino and buffalo are often sighted, exciting walking trails are also conducted. From the camp's balcony, where
some meals are served, guests can view game coming to drink at
the waterhole below.

From the private parks' turn off, continue along the R536 for
about 40 km towards Hazyview. At the intersection, turn right,
and then 4 km further on turn left onto the R535 towards Graskop, via **Kowyns Pass**. This pass takes you up the Drakensberg
to the resort paradise at the top, where one can view the scenic
splendours of the area.

Accommodation

There are a number of exciting accommodation possibilities in
this area. From the intersection take the R40 towards White
River. The following establishments are found along this road:

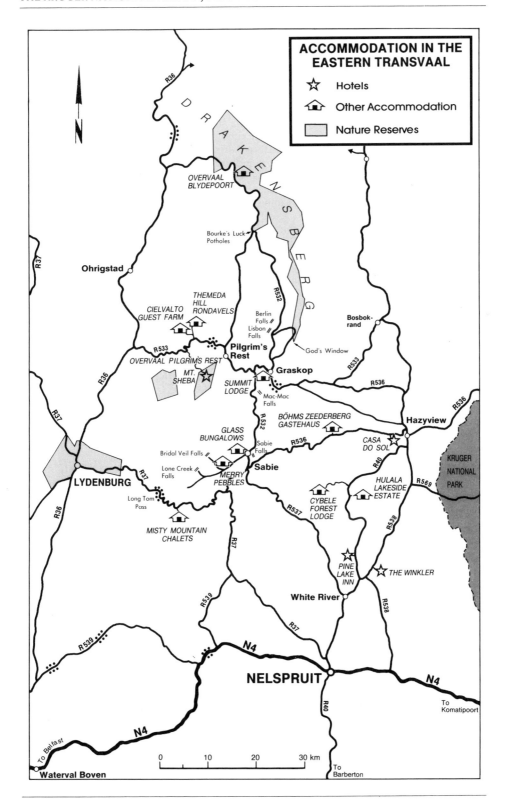

ACCOMMODATION IN THE
EASTERN TRANSVAAL

☆ Hotels

🏠 Other Accommodation

▢ Nature Reserves

Cybele Forest Lodge   Tel. (01311) 3-2791
P.O. Box 346,
White River, 1240   Portfolio of Country Places
Swimming-pool, golf, fishing, tennis, hiking and riding
Turn right onto the Hendriksdal road, 18 km from Hazyview.
Follow the gravel road for 5,4 km to reach the lodge, which is
located in the heart of the forest. This old hunting lodge has been
tastefully converted to serve as the lounge, dining room and
reception area. A maximum of twenty guests are accommodated
in cottages scattered around the rambling farmhouse. Each
spacious cottage is individually furnished with antiques. Some
have private patios, while others have separate sitting rooms.
All have fireplaces to warm cool winter evenings. Over and
above the charming surroundings, the lodge is usually best remem-
bered for its excellent food. Bread is always freshly baked and
vegetables come straight from the garden, while the imaginative
starters, main courses and desserts all linger in your thoughts
long after the meal has been completed.

Hulala Lakeside Estate   Tel. (0134) 3-1240
P.O. Box 1382,
White River, 1240   Portfolio of Country Places
Swimming-pool, golf, fishing, hiking, horse-riding, wind-surfing
and sailing
Four kilometres past Cybele, to the left, is the turn-off for Hulala.
The estate is located on a spire flanked on two sides by a lake. A
maximum of twenty guests are accommodated in either luxury
suites or bedsitters, each with its own private terrace and magnificent view of the pine-fringed lake. Traditional country fare
satisfies any hearty appetite.

Pine Lake Inn   ***TYYY Tel. (01311) 3-1186/7
P.O. Box 94, White River, 1240   Southern Sun
Swimming-pool, golf, bowls, tennis, squash, fishing, hiking, wind-
surfing and water-skiing
Travel for a further 17 km to the turn-off, on the right, for the
Pine Lake Inn. It may seem a bit out of place in the tranquil
surroundings but the Inn caters for those who wish to be enter-
tained all day long as well as those who want to relax in the sun.
Rooms are spacious and meals satisfying.

The Winkler   ***TYYY Tel. (01311) 3-2317/8
P.O. Box 12,
White River, 1240   Portfolio of Country Places
Swimming-pool, bowls, tennis, hiking and fishing
To reach the hotel continue to the intersection with the R538,
and turn left. A few kilometres further on you will find the hotel
signpost. The hotel building combines African and Japanese
architecture. Rooms are all well appointed and all have fine
views over the well laid-out gardens, and have their own verandas. *Table d'Hôte* and à la carte menus are both of an excellent
standard. Fresh vegetables are grown in the hotel's own gardens.
Service is superb.

Beyond Hazyview along the R536, towards Sabie, you will en-
counter the following establishments:

Casa Do Sol   ***TYYY Tel. (0131242) 22
P.O. Box 57,
Hazyview, 1242   Portfolio of Country Places
Swimming-pool, tennis, golf, fishing, hiking, horse-riding

The Casa portrays a small mediterranean village with arches and cobbled courtyards set in floral gardens and rolling lawns. Rooms range from standard to luxury suites, all of which are air-conditioned and spacious. The luxury suite has its own jacuzzi, sauna and swimming-pool and is really the ultimate in luxury. Meals are prepared by a Cordon Bleu chef who favours local ingredients, including venison. Service is discreet and attentive.

Böhm's Zeederberg Gastehaus   Tel. (0131242) 1111
P.O. Box 111,
Hazyview, 1242   Portfolio of Country Places
Swimming-pool, golf, tennis and hiking
Accommodation is in the form of chalets and rondavels all set in well-tended gardens leading down to the pool area. The guest house is run by the owners, who provide genuine German hospitality in an informal and relaxed atmosphere. Wholesome country food is served. The whole area can be explored in comfortable day drives from this base.

GRASKOP

Established during the 1880s as a gold-mining town, the town is now a major forestry centre, perched high on the Drakensberg escarpment.

Accommodation

Summit Lodge   Tel. (0131522) and ask for 58
P.O. Box 82, Graskop, 1270   Club Caraville
Electric points, swimming-pool and hiking
This is a well-run resort offering accommodation in either cosy thatched rondavels or chalets, some of which have fully equipped kitchens. All accommodation is fully serviced. There is a good braai area and pleasant restaurant where take-aways can also be ordered.

From Graskop follow the R534 towards God's Window and Wonder View.
    God's Window provides an unforgettable panoramic view of the Lowveld one thousand metres below. For the best vantage point, follow the signs to the north of the car park.
    Wonder View presents similar views. During the winter months the aloes along the roadside are ablaze with colour.

Continue along the R534 until the R532 is reached. From this point two of the most spectacular waterfalls in the area can be viewed. The **Blyderivierspoort Hiking** trail also starts from here (see page 214).
    The **Lisbon Falls**, 2 km back towards Graskop and then 2 km on tar road, cascade over a sheer semi-circular drop from a chain of pools.
    The **Berlin Falls**, 2 km north of the R532, on the left of the main road, plunge 48 m down into a deep pool. A footpath leads to an observation area above the falls.

Follow the R532 further towards Bourke's Luck, and turn right
to Bourke's Luck Potholes.

Bourke's Luck Potholes. Tom Bourke came to the area during
the gold-rush of the 1880s and predicted that gold would be
found here. He had no luck, but a small profitable mine was
worked for quite a while in the vicinity. The potholes, found at
the confluence of the Treur and Blyde Rivers, are deep cylindrical
cavities formed over thousands of years from the swirling action
of flood waters. A network of neat paths and bridges have been
built around the potholes. There is also a very interesting information centre and tearoom, open from 08h00 to 16h00. Both the
Eerste Liefde and **Op-de-Berg** hiking trails start from here (see
page 215).

Continue along the R532 for 14 km to the World's End turn-off,
turn to the right and continue for 3 km to the parking area.

Blyde River Canyon. This 26-km ravine lies more or less parallel
to the escarpment and is one of the most scenic splendours of
South Africa. Above the canyon are towering buttresses in all
shapes and sizes. The slopes to the river, 700 m below, are
covered with dense vegetation. From the car-park, walk to the
edge of the canyon and then around it for a breathtaking view.
The parking area falls within **Blyderivierspoort Nature Reserve**,
which shelters a wide variety of plants. It is also home for a
number of small antelope, baboon, leopard and bush pig.
    A few kilometres further on lies the public resort, F.H. Oden-
daal Camp.
F.H. Odendaal Camp   Tel. (013231) 881/891
Overvaal Blydepoort Public Resort, Private Bag 368, Ohrigstad,
1122,   Overvaal Resorts
Laundry, shop, gas, recreation hall, swimming-pool, nine-hole
golf, tennis, hiking and horse-riding
Situated on the lip of the canyon, the resort offers several vantage
points with superb views. Guests are accommodated in self-
contained fully equipped air-conditioned chalets and cottages.
The caravan and camping facilities are well laid-out, with
grassed sites and clean ablution blocks. The resort also has a
fully licensed à la carte restaurant, where substantial meals can
be enjoyed; a cafeteria; supermarket; and bottle store.

Continuing with the R532, veer away from the canyon, until the
R36 is reached. Turn left towards Ohrigstad. The road passes
through rich farmland, citrus orchards, and wheat and tobacco
fields. Continue along the R36 to the Pilgrim's Rest turn-off
(R533); 15 km from the junction, along the R533, is the turn-off
to Mount Sheba Hotel.
Mount Sheba Hotel   ***TYYY Tel. (0131532) 17
P.O. Box 100,
Pilgrim's Rest, 1290   Portfolio of Country Places
Swimming-pool, golf, tennis, squash, fishing, hiking, and horse-
riding
The hotel is in a nature reserve on the summit of the escarpment.
Accommodation varies from spacious double bedrooms with an
adjacent lounge and balcony, to duplex suites. All rooms have
fireplaces. The cosy dining room offers wholesome country food,
while the restaurant offers many local delicacies. A number of

De Berg Pass near Pilgrim's Rest

The Pilgrims Rest golf course

Viewing buffalo from an open
landrover in Mala Mala

Picking tea on an estate near
Magoebaskloof

interesting walks can be enjoyed through the forests and the hotel will arrange picnic lunches on request.

Thirty-one and a half kilometres on, to the left, is the turn-off to two self-catering resorts.

Cieloalto Guest Farm   Tel. (0131532) 97
P.O. Box 15, Pilgrim's Rest, 1290
Fishing and hiking
The fully-equipped chalets, each with its own carport and braai unit, are situated on a large farm. The chalets each have two bedrooms, a bathroom, complete kitchen and spacious well-appointed lounge. There is a small supermarket where groceries can be bought. The restaurant serves superb Italian meals, including some of the best pizzas and ice-cream in the country.

Themeda Hill Rondavels   Tel. (0131532) 1204
P.O. Box 32, Pilgrim's Rest, 1290
Rustic rondavels in spectacular surroundings make this location ideal for those who really want to get away. Each of the thatched rondavels can accommodate a maximum of six guests in two bedrooms. They also have a living room, bathroom and fully-equipped kitchen. They are serviced daily. From the rondavels, numerous walks can be enjoyed.

From these turn-offs the R533 passes down Robber's Pass to Pilgrim's Rest. **Robber's Pass** was so named because of the first hold-up that occurred on the pass. In the late 1800s two masked men held up the biweekly Lydenburg/Pilgrim's Rest coach and made off with £10 000 in gold, never to be seen again. The only other robbery happened in 1912 when a resident of the town instigated a robbery and then returned to town to spend his cash. He was arrested and spent five years in jail before returning to town again to open the Highwayman's Garage.

PILGRIM'S REST

This charming village was founded in 1873 as a gold prospecting town. The first known prospector in the area was a loner, Alec Patterson, known to his friends as *Wheelbarrow Alec* because he carried his possessions around in a wheelbarrow. He had left the crowded MacMac fields for this isolated area. His solitude was shortlived, however. Other diggers began arriving in the area, and soon the whole river was swarming with prospectors. The stream was a rich one, and many of the prospectors found large nuggets. The biggest was found in July 1875 and weighed 6 038 grams. During 1875 gold to the value of £200 000 was recovered from the stream, but being alluvial gold, deposits were quickly depleted.

As gold had been found elsewhere, the prospectors moved on. A few companies were formed to mine the mountainside and eventually joined forces to form the Transvaal Gold Exploration Company, (TGEC). The TGEC operated these mines until 1971, and processed over £20 million's worth of gold. During Pilgrim's Rest's heyday, the village grew, with traders, bankers, hoteliers and even a newspaperman flocking in. Fortunately the town has not become another ghost town, but was proclaimed a national monument and restored to its former glory.

Accommodation

Overvaal Pilgrim's Rest   Tel. (0131532) and ask for 4
P.O. box 59, Pilgrim's Rest, 1290   Overvaal Resorts
Swimming-pool, golf, tennis, bowls, hiking and fishing
Accommodation is offered at either the Royal Hotel, one of the
annexes, a number of restored miners' cottages or at the caravan
park on the banks of the Blyde River. The **Royal Hotel** was built
in 1888 and has been restored and refurbished in period style.
The hotel bar was once a chapel, which had been transported
from Maputo in 1893. The miners' cottages have been converted
to self-contained units with period furniture. There are also a
number of restaurants in the resort.

Tourist Information

The information centre is located opposite the Royal Hotel off
the main street and is open from 09h00 to 12h45 and 13h45 to
17h00 daily.

Sightseeing

Most of the town is open as a living museum and it is well worth
wandering around for a couple of hours. Guided tours of the
town are offered from the information centre twice daily during
the week (10h30 and 14h00) and on Saturdays (10h30). Some of
the shops offer interesting art work, herbal preparations and
local weaving.

From Pilgrim's Rest the road winds up the valley, meeting the
R532 to Sabie. Approximately 12 km along this road, on the left,
is the parking area for **Mac Mac Falls**. Follow the steps down to
the viewing site. The falls plunge 56 m into a deep chasm below.
The rocks at the rim to the falls were dynamited by prospectors
when they were found to contain gold, which resulted in a twin
stream.
    Two kilometres further is the turn-off for **Mac Mac Pools**, a
series of crystal clear pools, ideal for swimming in. There are
picnic facilities and change rooms on the site. The river was once
a hive of activity when more than a thousand prospectors dug
for gold along its banks. In these numbers were many Scots,
hence the name. Drive the last 10 km into Sabie.

SABIE

The sight on which Sabie is now built was long favoured by
transport riders as a campsite because of its well-watered position. A permanent settlement was established here when gold
was discovered in the area in 1869. The town is dominated by
Mt. Anderson and the Mauchsberg, and waterfalls and huge
tracts of plantations surround the town. Today it is a major
forestry centre. Large-scale planting of eucalyptus and wattle
(both exotics) was undertaken to supply the needs of the mines
and slowly the forest grew to become the largest man-made
forest in South Africa, supplying half the country's timber needs.

Accommodation

SELF-CATERING AND CAMPING

Glass' Bungalows Tel. (0131512) and ask for 110
Main Road (P.O. Box 59, Sabie, 1260)
Swimming-pool, golf, tennis, squash, hiking, bowls and trout-fishing
The resort is located on the banks of the Sabie River. Guests have a choice of bungalows or chalets, all of which are fully furnished, have bathrooms, a braai unit, carport and are serviced daily. Chalets each have a kitchenette, while bungalows have a kitchen recess on their verandas. The **Loggerhead Restaurant**, specialising in trout dishes, is located in the grounds of the resort and has a wine and malt licence.

Merry Pebbles Holiday Resort Tel. (0131512) and ask for 323/326
P.O. Box 131, Sabie, 1260   Club Caraville
Electric plugs, laundry, gas, shop, recreation hall, two swimming pools (one heated), tennis, hiking and trout-fishing
This ideally located resort on the banks of the Sabie River, offers the visitor many activities and is the perfect base from which to explore the eastern Transvaal. All chalets and cottages, accommodating from four to eight people, have a full bathroom, a braai area with free wood, are fully equipped, and are serviced daily. The caravan and camping sites are all well grassed and ablution blocks are clean. The **Restaurant** on site has a wine and malt licence.

Misty Mountain Chalets   Tel. (0131512) and ask for 1403
Long Tom Pass (on R37 approx. 24 km from Sabie) (P.O. Box 116, Sabie, 1260)
Swimming-pool, hiking and trout-fishing
This peaceful retreat in the mountains overlooks the Lowveld. Each chalet is fully serviced and self-contained, has two or four beds and a jetmaster fireplace. A number of walks can be enjoyed in the area.

Tourist Information

Publicity Department, Forestry Museum, Tel. (0131512) and ask for 244; P.O. Box 61, Sabie, 1260

Sightseeing

The Cultural Historical Forestry Museum, in Ford Street, houses a wide variety of exhibits on various aspects of South Africa's forestry industry. It is a unique museum and well worth a visit (open Monday to Friday 09h00 to 13h00 and 14h00 to 16h00; Saturdays from 09h00 to 11h30).

There are also three waterfalls worth visiting. To reach all three, leave town by Main Street along the Lone Creek Falls Road (2220). The first turn-off is to the right for Bridal Veil Falls, 3 km from town. Continue for 4 km along the dirt road to reach the carpark below the falls, and walk the remaining distance to the view site through indigenous forest. Continuing along the tarred road, the next turn-off is about 4 km further on to the left, to **Horsehoe Falls**. The falls are about half a kilometre from the main road. The last falls along this road are the **Lone Creek Falls**,

10 km from town. The road leads to a parking area near the base of the falls, and from there a well-maintained five minute walk through the forest takes the visitor to the falls. Close by is a pleasant picnic area.

Outdoor Activities

TROUT-FISHING   Twelve kilometres of the Sabie River has been reserved for trout-fishing. The local angling club keeps the river well stocked with mainly rainbow trout, although brown trout can be found in the upper reaches. For more information and licences contact: The Secretary, Sabie Rainbow Trout Angling Club, P.O. Box 139, Sabie, 1260; Tel. (0131512) and ask for 87.

HIKING TRAILS ON THE ESCARPMENT   There are a number of hiking trails in the area, varying from 1 km to 78 km. All are recognised and are well marked and controlled.

Day Hikes   There are no facilities on any of these trails.

Loerie   (14 km)
Report to the State Forester, Ceylon State Forest, Sabie. This circular route starts and finishes at the Ceylon forest station near Sabie.

Forest Falls   (4 km)
Report to the State Forester at Mac Mac State Forest (on the road between Sabie and Graskop), to follow the circular route between Sabie and Graskop which starts and finishes at Mac Mac Forest Station.

Information for the following six trails can be obtained from the officer-in-charge, Blyderivierspoort Nature Reserve.

Bushman Nature Trail — 5 km (four hours) starts at Bourke's Luck

Kadishi — 5 km (four hours)

Leopard Nature Trail — 5 km (four hours)

Lourie Nature Trail — 3 km (two hours)

Tarentaal Nature Trail — 4 km (three hours)

Tufa Nature Trail — 2 km (one hour)

The above 5 trails start at the F.H. Odendaal Resort.

Longer Trails   Reservations must be made for the following three trails. Contact the Regional Director, Eastern Transvaal Forest Region, Private Bag X503, Sabie, 1260; Tel. (0131512) and ask for 307.

Fanie Botha Trail (79 km — five days; or two circular routes of three days each.) A maximum of thirty hikers may use the trail at one time. The trail leads from the Ceylon State Forest to God's Window. Huts with bunks and mattresses are provided, but hikers need to bring all provisions, utensils, cooking equipment and sleeping bags.

Blyderivierspoort Trail (65 km — five days; or 32 km — two days). A maximum of thirty hikers may use the trail at one time. The trail is from God's Window to Swadini in the Sybrand van Niekerk Public Resort. Huts are equipped with bunks and mattresses, but hikers must provide everything else.

Prospector's Trail (69 km or 55 km — both five days). A maximum of thirty hikers can be accommodated at one time. This trail starts at Mac Mac and goes via Pilgrim's Rest to Bourke's Luck, or forms a circle, starting and finishing at Mac Mac, via Pilgrims Rest. It has the same facilities as the previous two trails.

The remaining two trails must be reserved through: Information Section, Blyderivierspoort Nature Reserve, P.O. Bourke's Luck, 1272; Tel. (0020) and ask for Bourke's Luck 15.

Eerste Liefde Trail (24 km — two days). A maximum of twenty hikers may use the trail at any one time. The trail winds from Bourke's Luck Potholes past Eerste Liefde and back. At Bourke's Luck four stone huts can be found, equipped with bunks and mattresses. Firewood is provided and there are toilet and open-air shower facilities. The camp at Eerste Liefde provides bunks and mattresses. Hikers must provide all necessities.

Op-de-Berg Trail (40 km — four days). A maximum of 10 hikers can be accommodated at one time. The trail starts from Bourke's Luck Potholes, goes via Muchhuis and Op-de-Berg near Devil's Window, and ends back at the Potholes. The first camp at Bourke's Luck is similar to the one on the Eerste Liefde Trail. The other two camps are basic, with huts and mattresses. Hikers need to bring everything else.

From Sabie take the R37 towards Lydenburg via the **Long Tom Pass**. The pass follows the route taken by the pioneer wagons transporting goods to the goldfields in the 1870s. It was named after the type of cannon used by the Boers during the Anglo-Boer War. A replica of the cannon stands at Devil's Knuckles. The pass is 2 150 m high – the highest tarred road in the Transvaal.

LYDENBURG

In 1849 the Voortrekkers moved from Ohrigstad in the Lowveld, which was rife with malaria and other tropical diseases, to this site, which they named *town of suffering* as a reminder of their past hard times. The town is the centre of a wealthy agricultural community and boasts a large hatchery where various indigenous and exotic fish are bred to stock rivers in the area.

Restaurants

Protea Restaurant (01323) 2521
Cnr. Barrack and   Wine and malt licence
Greyling Streets   Grills
More extensive than it appears from the outside, this relaxing establishment at the base of the Long Tom Pass has a simple menu which will satisfy most people. Although not fancy, it offers good wholesome food. Ideal for a lunch.

Tourist Information
Lydenburg area telephone code: **(01323)**

Town Clerk's Office, Sentraal Street, Tel. 2121 (P.O. Box 61, Lydenburg, 1120)

Sightseeing

Most of the old buildings related to the voortrekkers are concentrated around the corner of Church and Kantoor Streets. The

Voortrekker Mother Church was built shortly after the Voortrekkers arrived in Lydenburg. In 1894 it was replaced by a new church. The **Voortrekker School,** built in 1851, is the oldest school in the Transvaal. A ZAR Post Box erected at the end of last century also stands on the corner. None of the buildings are open to the public but can be viewed from the outside.

From Lydenburg continue along the R540 to Dullstroom.

DULLSTROOM

This peaceful village is located in the hills of the escarpment, 2 380 m above sea level, with the towering sentinel of De Berg, the highest point in the Transvaal, as its backdrop. The area has many streams and dams — all well stocked with trout. There are also a few hunting farms in the area.

Accommodation

The Critchley Hackle Lodge   ***TYYY Tel. (0132522) and ask for 52
P.O. Box 141, Dullstroom, 1110
Swimming-pool, hiking and trout-fishing
This delightful old-fashioned trout lodge is located on the Lydenburg side of Dullstroom, just off the R540. Guests are accommodated in luxurious suites, each with its own lounge, fireplace and bathroom. The Lodge's restaurant serves delicious food with the emphasis on trout (which can be caught in the Lodge's own dams by the guests). The menu is changed daily and is dependent on availability of produce.
Dullstroom Inn   *TYYY Tel. (0132522) and ask for 11
P.O. Box 44, Dullstroom, 1110
Swimming-pool, hiking, fishing and hunting
This ramshackle old inn is ideal for those who wish to do some fishing and hunting. Home cooking is very good as is the service and the pleasant welcome.

Outdoor Activities

FISHING   For more information on fishing in the area contact Mr. Yousuf Vaid, Tel. (0132522) and ask for 29.

Continue on the R540 — through scenic farming country — to Belfast, where you join the N4; then drive on to **Middelburg** where you can visit the interesting **Botshabelo Open Air Museum**, Tel. (01321) 3897, P.O. Box 14, Middelburg, 1050; open daily from 08h00 to 17h00. To reach the museum take the R35 towards Loskop Dam for just over 9 km and then turn left onto a dirt road towards the museum and nature reserve. The museum consists of a living south Ndebele village and old mission station. The village gives rich insights into the traditions and art forms of the Ndebele women; and their gaily coloured huts and clothing can be viewed. The mission was built in 1865 by the Rev. Alexander Merensky (father of the famous South African geologist, Dr.

Hans Merensky) in the Klein Olifants River Valley. The church, fort (built to protect the mission against its enemies) and various period houses can be viewed.

From Middelburg continue along the N4 (which now becomes a dual carriage highway) on to Witbank. Here the R22 branches off to Johannesburg (page 225), while the N4 continues on to Pretoria (page 251).

Kruger National Park to Johannesburg via the Northern Transvaal
(631 km)

From the north-west exit of the Kruger National Park the road passes through the independent homeland of Venda and then on to Louis Trichardt. From here one swings south to Tzaneen, home of the Rain Queen, before climbing up the Magoebaskloof Pass to the Highveld. From Pietersburg, the road winds through the bushveld via the hot springs at Warmbaths and on to Johannesburg.

Leave the Kruger National Park at Punda Maria and take the R524 towards Louis Trichardt. When driving through **Venda,** care should be taken of people and animals crossing the road as there are no fences on the side of the road.

LOUIS TRICHARDT

The area in which the town of Louis Trichardt is situated has a typical frontier town history. In about 1820 an adventurer by the name of Coenraad de Buys settled in the area and founded a community of part Venda ancestry. In 1836 a group of Voortrekkers under the leadership of Johannes van Rensburg passed through the area, hoping to reach a Portuguese trading post. They were confronted by the Venda and massacred. The next Voortrekker party to reach the area was a group under the leadership of Louis Trichardt. They camped in the area from May 1836 to August 1837, waiting for another group of Voortrekkers, under the leadership of Hendrik Potgieter, to join them. Tired of waiting, they decided to make a trip to the port of Delagoa Bay (now Maputo). During the trip more than half of the party, including Trichardt, lost their lives through disease.

In 1847 Hendrik Potgieter arrived in the area, and laid out a town which became known as Zoutpansbergdorp. As the most northern town in the Transvaal Republic, it became a centre for ivory hunters and traders. After Potgieter's death in 1852, Stephanus Schoeman took control and renamed the town, Schoemansdal. Tension ran high between the ivory traders and the local Venda population, and on 15 July 1867 the town was totally destroyed by the Venda. In 1898, the Transvaal Government regained control of the area and in 1899 the town of Louis Trichardt was proclaimed.

During the Anglo Boer War the women and children of the town were moved by the British to Pietersburg and the town was once again destroyed, but rebuilt after the war.

Today the town, 45 km north of the Tropic of Capricorn, is a prosperous agricultural centre.

Accommodation

HOTELS   **Clouds End**   **TYYY (01551) 9621
Three kilometres north of town on N1 (Private Bag X2409, Louis Trichardt, 0920)

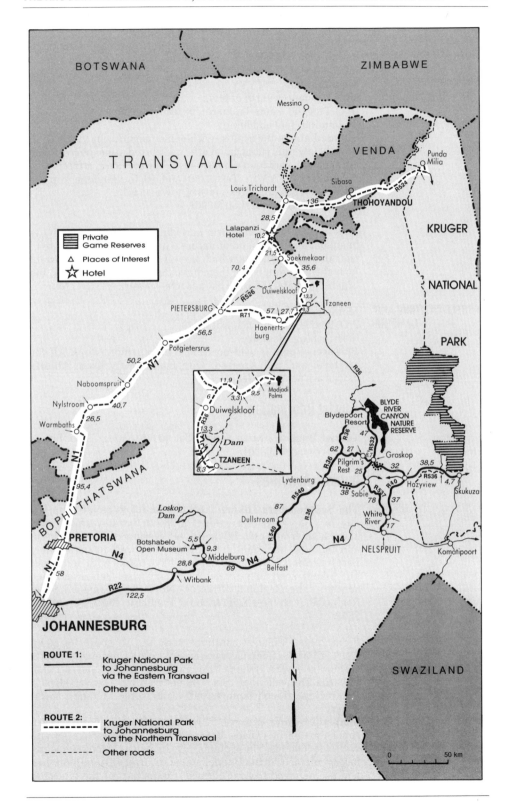

Swimming-pool, tennis, bowls and hiking
Situated just out of town, this retreat offers pleasant accommodation and restful surroundings, ideal for those who wish to relax. Food is plentiful and homely.
Mountain Inn **TYYY (01551) 9631
Nine kilometres north of town
(P.O. Box 146, Louis Trichardt, 0920)
Swimming-pool and hiking
Situated above the plains, with some magnificent views of the town below, this rustic hotel offers a relaxed atmosphere. Rooms are spacious, and food wholesome, while service is attentive.
Lalapanzi **TYYY   Tel. (0200) and ask for Bandolierkop 13
Twenty-eight kilometres south of town on N1
(P.O. Box 5, Bandolierkop, 0800)
Swimming-pool
This is a hotel full of charm and character, surrounded by the bushveld and the sound of nature. Guests are accommodated in neat thatched cottages which are all spacious and comfortably furnished. (A number of them have their own lounges.) The food is delightful and the wine list has a few surprises.

SELF-CATERING AND CAMPING

Municipal Caravan Park   Tel. (01551) 2212
P.O. Box 96, Louis Trichardt, 0920
Electric plugs, laundry
This secure park is well-positioned for overnight stops. All sites are level and well grassed, with many shady trees. Ablution blocks are neat and clean.

Tourist Information

Tourist Bureau,   Main Street, Tel. (01551) 2212; (P.O. Box 96, Louis Trichardt, 0920)

Outdoor Activities

HIKING

The Soutpansberg Hiking Trail can be taken as a 91-km five-day, or 21-km circular two-day, or 36-km two-day trail. It starts about 3 km from Louis Trichardt, at the Hangklip Forest Station, and follows the mountains through the forest to the Entabeni Forest Station. Huts along the way have bunks with mattresses, but hikers need to provide everything else. For reservations contact: The Regional Director, Northern Transvaal Forest Region, Private Bag X2413, Louis Trichardt, 0920, Tel. (01551) 2202.

From Louis Trichardt continue along the N1 south for 39 km. Turn left at the Soekmekaar turn-off (R36). Continue along this scenic route, which winds through forest reserves and farmland, towards Duiwelskloof. Six kilometres from Duiwelskloof an interesting, though bumpy road leads to the Modjadji Nature Reserve.
Modjadji Nature Reserve. The reserve has the world's largest concentration of cycads *Encephalartos transvenosus* growing within its bounds. These plants, also known as "Modjadji palms", have remained virtually unchanged for over fifty million years and are believed to have formed a large part of the dinosaur's

diet. The forest, through which pathways have been carefully constructed, are awe-inspiring. The area directly around the reserve is part of the Labedu tribe's homeland. They are a North Sotho tribe, unique in Southern Africa in that they are led by a chieftainess, Magoma Modjadji, the only female ruler in the subcontinent. She is the legendary *Rain Queen*, feared and respected throughout the region, and it is believed that she has the power to make rain. To reach the reserve, turn left onto the side road marked Modjadji, and follow the signs; turn left again after 15 km and fork right after 4,5 km. The last section of the road is very bad and not recommended for vehicles which are towing.

From Duiwelskloof continue along the R36 to Tzaneen.

TZANEEN

There are a number of tea and coffee plantations, and citrus and subtropical fruit farms in the Tzaneen district. The town was established in 1919 but grew slowly because of the prevalence of malaria in the area. However, in 1931 a pioneer in tropical diseases, Dr. Siegfried Annecke, established a malaria research station here, and managed to bring the disease under control.

Accommodation

HOTELS

Coach House   ****TYYY   Tel. (015236) 2-0100
P.O. Box 544, Tzaneen, 0850   Portfolio of Country Places
Swimming-pool and hiking
This delightful hotel, 16 km from town, is reached by following the Agatha signposts for 11 km. At the T-junction follow the Letsitele Valley road for 4 km and then take the left fork to reach the hotel, which is a further 1,5 km away. The present hotel was built in 1983 on the site of the original hotel which was built in 1892 and was used as a staging post for the Great North Road. It has sweeping views over the Drakensberg range. All the rooms are large and well-appointed, each with its own fireplace. The food is superb — only the freshest ingredients from the owner's farms are used.

Karos Tzaneen   **TYYY   Tel. (015236) 2-1056
Danie Joubert Street
(P.O. Box 1, Tzaneen, 0850)   Karos Hotels
Swimming-pool
This well-run hotel in central Tzaneen is ideal for overnight stops. Rooms are large and comfortable, service is attentive and the buffet is real value for money.

**SELF-CATERING
AND CAMPING**

Duiwelskloof Holiday Resort   Tel. (015236) 3651
Boltman Street
P.O. Box 36, Duiwelskloof, 0835
Electric plugs, laundry, recreation hall, swimming-pool, bowls, tennis and golf
Located in Duiwelskloof, this picturesque park is laid out in a well-treed and grassed surrounding. The thatched rondavels are divided into two types. The larger have a lounge, a separate bedroom with a fully fitted kitchen and a bathroom. The smaller rondavels only have beds and basins. They are furnished and

serviced daily. Caravan and camping sites are laid out on level grassed sites.

Restaurants

The Coach House and Karos Hotel both offer fine food in their restaurants. Also try:

Postilion Tel. (015236) 2-1308   Wine and malt licence
Danie Joubert Street   German/Swiss
This restaurant offers a few delightful surprises such as Eisbein, and fondues — all prepared by the Swiss chef. The decor is basic, but service is attentive and the food well presented.

From Tzaneen, return to the R71 turn-off and turn left towards **Magoebaskloof** and Pietersburg. The road climbs 610 m in 6 km up the beautiful forest-clad Magoebaskloof Pass. At the base of the pass the traveller passes through extensive banana and tea plantations before reaching the forest area. As the road begins to climb, one finds a turn-off to the right for Debengeni Falls. Three and a half kilometres from the turn-off you will find parking area for the falls. This is a popular swimming area and one can also picnic under the trees.

Accommodation

Near the summit the following accommodation is available:
Magoebaskloof Hotel   **TYYY   Tel. (0152222) ask for 82
P.O. Magoebaskloof,
0731   Portfolio of Country Places
Swimming-pool, fishing, tennis, squash, bowls, riding and hiking
The hotel, built on the edge of the escarpment, commands fine views down the valley and over the lowveld, and is surrounded by forest. The rooms are large and comfortable; service in the restaurants is friendly and food of a high standard. The area is especially spectacular during September and October when the azaleas and cherry trees are in full bloom. There are many scenic drives to be enjoyed in this area.
Lakeside Holiday Resort   Tel. (0152222) ask for 53
P.O. Magoebaskloof, 0731   Club Caraville
Laundry, shop, restaurant, swimming-pool, tennis, golf, bowls, squash, wind-surfing, hiking, fishing and boating
This resort is in an idyllic setting on the shores of the lake, surrounded by forest. Accommodation varies from apartments in Troutwaters Inn, sleeping between six and eight people, to chalets sleeping from three to eight, with fully equipped kitchens. All accommodation is self-contained and serviced daily. Caravan and camping sites are all well grassed, level and shady. Ablution blocks are well kept.

Towards Pietersburg the road begins to level out, winding between bolder-strewn koppies. Nineteen kilometres past Haenertsburg is the **Zion City of Moria**. The "city" is identified by a large white star on the hill behind it. Each Easter over three million devotees gather here to worship. Nine kilometres further on is the **University of the North**, attended by the North and South Sotho population groups. The road continues south towards Pietersburg.

PIETERSBURG

The town is an important industrial and educational centre of the northern Transvaal and is known as the "Capital of the North". It was founded in 1886 and named after Commandant General Piet Joubert.

Accommodation

HOTELS **The Ranch Hotel** ***TYYY   Tel. (01521) 7-5377
17 km south of Pietersburg on the N1 (P.O. Box 77, Pietersburg, 0700)   Portfolio of Country Places
Sauna, swimming-pool, tennis and squash
The Ranch is a fine country hotel set in the bushveld amidst well-tended gardens and indigenous trees. Large bedrooms are all comfortably furnished with king-size beds. Suites have their own private courtyards with built in spa-pools. Both restaurants offer romantic intimate dining and good service.
Holiday Inn **TYYY   Tel. (01521) 6584
Vorster Street (P.O. Box 784,
Pietersburg, 0700)   Holiday Inns
Swimming-pool
Like most hotels in the chain, rooms are large and comfortable. But the service and personal attention here is above the normal standard, and the restaurants serve good hearty meals. During the week there is always plenty of action in the bars.

Tourist Information
Pietersburg area telephone code: **(01521)**

South African Tourism Board   Tel. (01521) 3025, Cnr. Vorster and Landdros Marè Streets.

The R71 from Tzaneen by-passes Pietersburg, to join the N1 South towards Potgietersrus, and then continues via Naboomspruit and Nylstroom on to Warmbaths. This 175 km-odd section of road has very little of interest to offer the traveller — it winds its way through savannah grasslands dotted with cattle farms. (The new toll road cuts a few kilometres off the distance and by-passes the towns.)

WARMBATHS

In 1882 the farm on which the springs (and town) are located was bought by the Zuid-Afrikaansche Republiek. The healing powers of the springs had been recognised by the various travellers, including trek parties, who passed through the area long before the town was proclaimed. The town was proclaimed in 1921 and almost immediately the Transvaal Provincial Government began to develop the warm springs, on which the town was proclaimed, as a health and holiday resort. The resort was developed further into one of the world's most advanced spas, when the David Brink Centre was opened in 1979. Today the resort offers a number of spa and health-related activities.

Accommodation

Overvaal Warmbaths   Tel. (015331) 2200
P.O. Box 75, Warmbaths, 0480   Overvaal Resorts
Spa complex, swimming-pools, tennis, wind-surfing, squash,
laundry, electric plugs, shop and restaurant
This magnificent resort complex offers accommodation in self-
contained chalets in garden surroundings, or luxury apartments
within the complex. Caravan and camping sites offer well-
grassed sites scattered amongst trees. The ablution blocks are of
the highest standard. A variety of restaurants provide wholesome meals, from à la carte to take-aways. The spa centre itself
offers a full-time physiotherapist, mud baths, hydrotherapy
baths, massage, sauna, mineral pools, high temperature and cold
plunge pools, a health and fitness centre, and a weight control
course. The massive pool complex offers a supertube slide, wave
pool and warm and cold mineral pools, as well as a lake for
wind-surfing. There is also a game reserve nearby.

From Warmbaths continue on the N1, which becomes a highway
just outside the town, towards Pretoria, and Johannesburg.

Johannesburg

The fortunes of this prosperous young city began just more than a hundred years ago, in 1886, when gold was discovered by George Harrison. Fortune-seekers streamed into the area and tent and shanty towns sprang up all over the place. The population quickly grew to two thousand people, all trying to make a fortune. Surface gold was quickly mined out and prospectors had to start digging deeper to extract the gold. This resulted in more costly operations which many of them could scarcely afford, having spent their fortunes as quickly as they had made them. Slowly larger mining corporations began to buy up their claims and more extensive operations began. Soon a very elegant society of financiers, merchants, and mining magnates established itself in gracious mansions overlooking the vast countryside.

Today the city has a population of over two million and is the industrial heart of southern Africa, as well as one of the richest gold-mining areas in the world. Because Johannesburg is the economic centre of South Africa, public transport radiates from here. The majority of international flights also make Johannesburg their final destination.

Johannesburg's climate is very pleasant, with cool, dry winters and warm summers — cooled down most afternoons by a mid-afternoon thunderstorm. Temperatures range from 0 °C in the early morning to 20 °C during the day in the winter and from 12 °C to 30 °C in mid-summer.

The Johannesburg area is not known for its natural beauty. However, the large population has necessitated the building of many leisure and entertainment complexes. The city itself offers the visitor over two thousand restaurants, fourteen museums, thirty art galleries and fifteen theatres. Tours of the various mining activities are also a great delight to many visitors, and Gold Reef City has been built especially to depict the early mining days of Johannesburg as well as giving the visitor an exciting chance to go underground. Other tours worth doing include a tour of Pretoria's historic buildings, and a trip to Sun City (approximately three-hour's drive from Johannesburg), South Africa's answer to Las Vegas.

Accommodation

HOTELS
De Luxe
Carlton Court   *****TYYY   Tel. (011) 331-8911
Main Street, City Centre (P.O. Box 7709, Johannesburg, 2000)
Swimming-pool
Carlton Court forms part of the Carlton Hotel. This exclusive block of rooms, across the road from the main hotel, offers the height of luxury and elegance. Each room has all the normal fittings plus a jaccuzi in the bathroom. Security and privacy are the number one priority in this exclusive hotel where only residents and their guests are allowed to enjoy the facilities.

Johannesburg Sun and Towers *****TYYY   Tel. (011) 29-7011
Jeppe Street, City Centre,
(P.O. Box 535, Johannesburg, 2000)   Southern Sun
Swimming-pool, sauna, squash, gym and jogging track
Located in the centre of town, this ultra modern de luxe hotel
offers its guests large comfortable rooms and excellent service.
In the Towers section of the hotel, guests are accommodated in
suites. The hotel has a variety of restaurants, including a relatively inexpensive carvery/buffet and superb ethnic Japanese
restaurant, the Suki Hama. The hotel is linked by way of a
pedestrian mall to the major shopping centres in the city centre.
Two features, however, which many guests find disconcerting
in the hotel are that the windows cannot open and that all operations within the room are controlled by a rather complicated
computerised switch panel.

Hotel Braamfontein   ****TYYY   Tel. (011) 403-5740
De Kotze Street, Braamfontein
(P.O. Box 32278, Braamfontein, 2017)
Heated in-door swimming-pool, sauna and squash
A comfortable hotel ideally located for those businessmen with
commitments at the University of the Witwatersrand. All rooms
are, in fact, suites which have been very comfortably furnished.

Sandton Sun   *****TYYY   Tel. (011) 783-8701
Fifth Street, Sandton
(P.O. Box 784902, Sandton, 2146)   Southern Sun
Swimming-pool, gym and sauna
Sandton is fast becoming the business administrative headquarters of South Africa and this hotel is ideally located to
service these needs. Being part of the Sandton City shopping and
office block complex means that a guest staying here need never
leave the complex to do shopping or to attend a business meeting.
Rooms are spacious and very comfortably furnished. The two
most popular restaurants in the hotel are **Chapters,** which is a
very expensive, exclusive French restaurant and the **Buffet**,
which offers good value for money. There is also a pleasant
coffee shop where guests can enjoy a good cup of coffee and
watch the world go by.

The Rosebank Hotel   ****TYYY   Tel. (011) 788-1820
Tyrwhitt Avenue, Rosebank (P.O. Box 52025, Rosebank, 2132)
Swimming-pool
The hotel is situated within two minutes' walk of most of the
Rosebank office blocks as well as the shopping centre. This
pleasant hotel offers comfortable, quiet, but compact rooms.
Service more than measures up to its star ratings and a number
of fine restaurants can be found within the hotel. The **Lien Wah**
Chinese restaurant is one of the finest in Johannesburg (see
page 233).

Medium-Priced   **The Johannesburger**   ***TYYY   Tel. (011) 725-3753
60 Twist Street, Hillbrow (P.O. Box 23566, Joubert Park, 2044)
Swimming-pool
This centrally situated hotel offers excellent value. All rooms
are large and comfortable, while service and food are well above
expectations.

Hillbrow Protea Inn ***TYYY Tel. (011) 643-4911/3
8 Abel Road, Berea, 2198   Protea Holiday Inns

Entertainment at the Thunderdome, Johannesburg

Hot air balloons prepare for an early morning flight over Johannesburg

Diagonal Street, Johannesburg

This is a comfortable unpretentious hotel close to the pulsating heart of Hillbrow.

Holiday Inn Down Town   ***TYYY Tel. (011) 28-1770
88 Plein Street, City Centre
(P.O. Box 11026, Johannesburg, 2000)   Holiday Inns
Swimming-pool, sauna and gym
This hotel is now regarded by many as being on the wrong side of town — mid-way between the city centre and the centre of Hillbrow, but none-the-less it is a fine hotel. It is small and intimate, with superb service. Fine foods is served by the two restaurants. Barnatos restaurant serves some of the best roasts and grills in Johannesburg, while the coffee shop leading to the pool deck offers a very reasonable buffet. A word of warning to unsuspecting travellers: the area is notorius for pick-pockets and bag snatchers.

Mariston   ***TYYY   Tel. (011) 725-4130/9
Cnr. Claim and Koch Streets, Joubert Park
(P.O. Box 23013, Joubert Park, 2044)
Swimming-pool
This is a real value-for-money hotel centrally situated between Hillbrow and the city centre. Rooms are large and comfortable, while service and catering, run with German precision, are well above the standards expected of a hotel of this star rating.

Moulin Rouge   ***TYYY   Tel. (011) 725-4840
Corner Esselen and Claim Street, Hillbrow
(P.O. Box 17283, Hillbrow, 2038)
Although on the expensive side, this well-run hotel nevertheless is well-located in the heart of Hillbrow. Rooms are most comfortable and service is cheerful.

Sunnyside Park Hotel ***TYYY Tel. (011) 643-7226
2 York Road, Parktown, 2193   Southern Sun
Swimming-pool and squash
This comfortable rambling hotel is set in tranquil gardens only five minutes' drive from the city centre. Rates are not low, but service and the standard of catering are very high. The restaurants offer a wide variety of foods and the more intimate ones offer superb service. The various pubs within the hotel serve as meeting places for young executives after a day in the office. Request rooms in the old wing: these are more spacious.

Victoria Hotel **TYYY   Tel. (011) 28-1530
25 Plein Street, City Centre (P.O. Box 2463, Johannesburg, 2000)
Reasonably priced, this old (seventy years) hotel is ideal for those who need to be close to the city centre (very close to the station). Food is good and the bars are always lively, one of which has live entertainment nightly.

Gold Reef City Hotel
see page 245

The Balalaika Protea Hotel ***TYYY
Tel. (011) 884-1400
20 Maud Street, Sandown
(P.O. Box 65327, Benmore, 2010)   Protea Hotels and Inns
Swimming-pool
This rustic country-style hotel offers accommodation in thatched rondavel suites. The hotel oozes all the charm and elegance expected of a country hotel of this rating. Public rooms are well-appointed and there are many pubs and restaurants. An ideal setting for a leisurely stay in Johannesburg.

Sandton Holiday Inn   ***TYYY   Tel. (011) 783-5262
Corner North and Rivonia Road, Sandton
(P.O. Box 781743, Sandown, 2146)   Holiday Inns
Swimming-pool, squash and tennis
One of the new generation Holiday Inns, which has abandoned
the old square, box-shaped buildigs of the past. Rooms are still
large and well appointed with all the normal fittings expected to
be found in a Holiday Inn. The food in the **Grayston** restaurant
is of a very high standard.

Randburg City Lodge   **TYYY   Tel. (011) 706-7800
cnr. Main Road and Peter Place, Randburg
(P.O. Box 423, Cramerview, 2060)
(See Sandton City Lodge.)

Sandton City Lodge   **TYYY   Tel. (011) 884-5300
cnr. Vere and Katherine Streets
(P.O. Box 781643, Sandton, 2146)
Both hotels offer no frills, but very comfortable accommodation,
with an accent on value. They are hard to beat as far as price and
value are concerned, and are ideal for those looking for a tranquil,
comfortable room with a minimum of service.

Indaba Hotel   ***TYYY   Tel. (011) 705-3221
Roughly 15 km north of Sandton on the R511 — the continuation
of the Nicol Highway
(P.O. Box 67129, Bryanston, 2021)   Portfolio of Country Places
Swimming-pool, squash, sauna and tennis
Although this hotel is out in the country it is only 30 minutes'
drive from the city centre and is even closer to Sandton City.
This luxurious country hotel is an ideal place to relax at if you
do not need to be in the city centre, and you have your own
transport. The hotel is set in 36 acres of garden and all rooms
have fine views over the lawns. The **Magaliesberg** restaurant
offers cuisine of international standing with the emphasis on
South African dishes in an intimate atmosphere.

Airport Sun   ***TYYY   Tel. (011) 974-6911
Hulley Road, Isando (Private Bag 5, Jan Smuts Airport, 1620)
Swimming-pool and sauna   Southern Sun
Not a holiday hotel, but ideal for an overnight stop if you have a
connecting plane to catch. Rooms are large and comfortable
while food from the buffet restaurant is good.

Jan Smuts Holiday Inn   ***TYYY Tel. (011) 975-1121
In the airport grounds
(P.O. Box 388, Kempton Park, 1620)   Holiday Inns
Same as above.

Budget   **The Mark Hotel**   **TYYY   Tel. (011) 643-6731
24 O'Reilly Road, Berea (P.O. Box 3882, Johannesburg, 2000)
Swimming-pool
The low tariffs of this no-frills hotel in the heart of flatland,
close to Hillbrow make this a comfortable base for prolonged
stays. All rooms have baths.

New Library   **TYYY   Tel. (011) 832-1551
67 Commissioner Street, Johannesburg, 2001
The New Library is not luxurious, but clean and well run. It is
located in the city centre, which makes it excellent value for
money. Meals and especially pub lunches are good and reasonable. All rooms have bathrooms.

Springbok Hotel   **TYYY   Tel. (011) 337-8336
73 Joubert Street, Johannesburg, 2001

It is close to town and Hillbrow. Rooms are clean and well appointed, all having either a bath or a shower.

Gresham Hotel   *TYYY   Tel. (011) 834-5641

13 Loveday Street, Johannesburg, 2001

Situated in the middle of the business district, this budget hotel supplies all the basic amenities. Pub meals, inclusive of curries, are good value.

Melville Hotel   *TYYY   Tel. (011) 726-6019

20 Main Road, Melville, 2109

This is a basic hotel satisfying the needs of the budget-conscious traveller. Melville has become the home of Johannesburg's creative colony — and this is where you will find them. Meals are pleasant and the pub has a lot of atmosphere as well as live music.

Oribi   *RYYY   Tel. (011) 618-2220

450 Commissioner Street, Kensington, 2094

This hotel is situated in the east overlooking the city. It is a well-run comfortable hotel. All the rooms have their own bathrooms. Food is also more than adequate.

UNGRADED ACCOMMODATION

Guest Houses

Boulevard Guest House   Tel. (011) 642-7491

28 Catherine Avenue, Berea, 2198

This guest house offers comfortable clean rooms at reasonable prices close to town and Hillbrow.

The Pads   Tel. (011) 28-5702/5

295 Smit Street, Joubert Park (P.O. Box 55103, Northlands, 2116)

This is one of the cheapest places in Johannesburg, very close to the city centre and in the heart of Hillbrow.

Youth Hostels and YMCAs

Johannesburg Youth Hostel   Tel. (011) 26-8051

32 Main Street, Townsview, 2190

Situated close to the city centre, this is an ideal place for those on a shoestring budget.

YMCA   Tel. (011) 403-3426

104 Rissik Street, Braamfontein

(P.O. Box 23222, Joubert Park, 2044)

This establishment offers good value for all those under thirty years. Men get first option on accommodation, but women are allowed, especially if accompanied by husbands. It is located within walking distance of the station, the air terminal and town; also on most bus routes. Facilities include a dining room with low price meals, snack bar, TV room, sauna, snooker room, badminton and tennis courts. Accommodation is available in single and double rooms, or in dormitories. Cheaper rates are available for stays longer than one week.

YWCA   Tel. (011) 339-8212

311 Dunwell Road, Braamfontein, 2001

Just across the road from YMCA, this hostel caters for women up to the age of 35. Mostly on a monthly or weekly basis. Doors are locked at midnight.

SELF-CATERING

San Tropez Executive Apartments Tel. (011) 643-4971

43 Van der Merwe Street, Hillbrow, 2000

These apartments are reasonably priced, fully furnished apartments with fully-equipped kitchens — ideal for those who wish to stay for a prolonged period.

The Witberg Executive Apartments
Tel. (011) 642-7451
cnr. Olivia Road and Tudhope Avenue
(P.O. Box 17200, Hillbrow, 2038)
These apartments are situated in the quieter part of Hillbrow,
yet within walking distance of all the action. All apartments are
fully-equipped and furnished. A reception service is located in
the lobby.

CARAVAN PARKS   No caravan parks close to Johannesburg allow tents.
Bezuidenhout Park   Tel. (011) 648-6302
Observatory Road, Dewetshof
(P.O. Box 2824, Johannesburg, 2000)
Laundry, bowls
Neat well-kept park close to the centre of town. All sites are well
grassed.

Restaurants

The list of restaurants below just scratches the surface of the
more than two thousand restaurants in Johannesburg. The
majority have stood the test of time and most have been supplying the same high standard of food and service for a number of
years. For an up-to-date list of restaurants see the *Hello Johannesburg Guide,* put out monthly by **Welcome Johannesburg** (see
address below). Restaurants under the various headings are
divided into those in or close to the city, followed by those
further out of town.

De Luxe   **Chez André**   Tel. 23-3662   Fully licensed
49 Kruis Street, City Centre   French
This is one of the finest restaurants in town, offering a small but
interesting menu. The atmosphere is elegant yet relaxed and
presentation is superb.
De Fistermann   Tel. 23-8006   Wine and malt license
131 Commissioner Street, City Centre   SA traditional
The proprietors have gone to great lengths and have done much
research to find the original recipes for the many delights on
their menu. Fresh fish features prominently on their daily specials
menu.
Dentons   Tel. 331-3827   Fully licensed
125 Fox Street, City Centre   Belgian
Food is of a high standard, prepared in an imaginative and often
unusual way. To complement this the restaurant offers a wide
variety of wines including a large selection of imported wines.
Fat Frank's   Tel. 339-7057   Fully licensed
19 Biccard Street, Braamfontein   Mexican
This restaurant captures the atmosphere of the American deep
south. The food is a blend of Mexican aromas and Southern
ingredients. Many items on the menu have strange names, but
the *Maître d'Hôtel* is very willing to clarify.
Jameson's   Tel. 838-1769   Fully licensed
95A Commissioner Street, City Centre   International
This restaurant has done business from the same premises for
over ninety years. It has an interestingly creative menu ideal for
those who enjoy good service and fine food.
Linger Longer   Tel. 339-7814   Fully licensed
94 Juta Street, Braamfontein   French classical

This is the top restaurant in Johannesburg, specialising in excellent food, attentive service and elegant dining. Not the place for those on diet though, as the exquisite sauces served with many of the dishes are full of mouthwatering kilojoules. A wide variety of wines more than complements the menu.

Pot Luck   Tel. 403-2410   Fully licensed
cnr. Smith and Melle Streets, Braamfontein   French
This elegant restaurant is relatively small but has a changing menu which relies on the freshest produce available.

Scratch Daniels   Tel. 403-3248   Fully licensed
76 Juta Street, Braamfontein   French
This large well-appointed dining-room serves both *table d'hôte* and à la carte menus. Sauces are rich and service is professional.

Town Lobster   Tel. 834-1740   Wine and malt licence
147 Jeppe Street, City Centre   Seafoods
Town Lobster offers a wide variety of excellently prepared fish. The atmosphere is relaxed and service attentive.

Bougainvillia   Tel. 788-4883/5   Fully licensed
Standard Bank Building, Cradock Avenue,
Rosebank   French
This chic well-appointed restaurant maintains a high standard.

Le Français   Tel. 788-8400   Wine and malt
The Mall, Rosebank   French
A wide and adventurous menu is offered with a good selection of daily specials. An added bonus is a selection of mouth-watering soufflés served for dessert.

Les Marquis   Tel. 783-8947   Fully licensed
12 Fredman Drive, Sanddown   French
A grand restaurant which brings the true meaning of classical French cuisine to Sandton. The chef is a master craftsman creating tantalizing dishes with the freshest of ingredients.

The Train   Tel. 805-2906   Fully licensed
Old Pretoria Road, Halfway-House   SA traditional
An unusual restaurant constructed from four converted railway carriages dating from 1920. Inside are gas lamps and polished Burmese teak. The buffet style offers over 100 dishes to choose from, including a wide selection of venison dishes.

Zoo Lake Restaurant   Tel. 646-8807   Fully licensed
Zoo Lake, Parkview   French
Another fine restaurant, offering classicial dining in elegant surroundings with fine views over the lake itself. Definitely not a place for those in a rush. The *Maître d'hôtel* is always more than willing to help.

Medium-priced   **Bella Napoli**   Tel. 642-5062   Fully licensed
31 Pretoria Street, Hillbrow   Italian
This crowded, popular pizzeria also serves a good variety of pasta. A band provides music for dancing.

Gatrile Son and Co.   Tel. 29-0485   Wine and malt
81 De Villiers Street, City Centre   British
A wide variety of typical English foods including steak and kidney pie, oxtail stew, roast beef and Yorkshire pudding are served here.

Golden City Chinese   Tel. 834-5106   Wine and malt
24 Commissioner Street, City Centre   Chinese
Located in the centre of Chinatown, this is a pleasant Cantonese restaurant. The proprietor is always more than happy to prepare special menus if ordered a day or two in advance.

Gramadoelas   Tel. 724-3716   Wine and malt
31 Bok Street, Joubert Park   SA traditional
Located in a reproduced Cape Dutch residence, this restaurant
offers a wide variety of true South African dishes complemented
by some good wines.
Green Oasis   Tel. 648-9202   Not licensed
42 Hunter Street, Yeoville   Vegetarian
This is Johannesburg's oldest vegetarian restaurant, offering a
wide variety of wholesome meals.
Harridans   Tel. 838-6960   Fully licensed
The Market Theatre,
Bree Street, Newtown   South African
A well-run, unpretentious restaurant, ideally situated for patrons
of the Market Theatre. Service is attentive, the atmosphere is
pleasant and servings are reasonably small.
Leipoldts   Tel. 339-2765   Fully licensed
94 Juta Street, Braamfontein   SA traditional
A pleasant restaurant serving an extensive buffet of mouth-
watering South African delicacies.
Mike's Kitchen   Wine and malt   Steakhouse
15 Claim Street, City Centre   Tel. 337-8373
68 Delvers Street, City Centre   Tel. 642-5419
78 Kotze Street, Hillbrow   Tel. 642-5419
Very successful chain of steakhouses concentrating on a wide
selection of salads and good value family grills.
Münchener House   Tel. 403-1835   Fully licensed
11 Biccard Street, Braamfontein   German beer hall
A huge establishment, always noisy and busy —including a live
oompah band. Food is good and helpings are enormous.
Norman's Grill   Tel. 618-1302   Fully licensed
Grand Station Hotel, Jeppe   Seafoods
If prawns and langoustines are to your taste, then this restaurant
is a must. It is very loud, always full and service is impersonal,
but the prawns are scrumptious.
Inn at the Park   Tel. 642-7425   Fully licensed
Park Lane Hotel,
54 Van der Merwe Street, Hillbrow   Buffet
One of the famous Karos carveries, where a wide variety of
well-prepared foods can be enjoyed for a set price.
Rugantino   Tel. 29-9788/9   Fully licensed
6 Twist Street, City Centre   Italian
Authentic, Italian cuisine including a good variety of fresh,
homemade pasta. There are always one or two specials on the
menu and the antepasta table is one of the best in the country.
Trattoria Fiorentina   Tel. 339-3410   Wine and malt
Noswal Hall, cnr. Bertha and Stimans Streets,
Braamfontein   Italian
A well-appointed restaurant serving pleasant Italian foods, inclu-
ding some unusual specialities, such as tripe and liver.
Villa Borghese   Tel. 23-1793   Fully licensed
95 De Villiers Street, City Centre   Italian
This very large restaurant has a dance-floor and offers a good
variety of homemade pasta as well as other Italian delicacies.
Alan's   Tel. 728-5353   Not licensed
232 Louis Botha Avenue,
Orange Grove   South African

Housed in an old Cape Dutch building, this elegant restaurant presents a small, balanced menu which changes periodically. Ingredients are always fresh and include seasonal fish, venison and game birds.

Carvers of Dunkeld   Tel. 788-8804   Not licensed
281 Jan Smuts Avenue, Dunkeld   Carvery
A good old-fashioned carvery offering three roasts and the freshest of vegetables.

Casa Manuel   Tel. 40-5267   Not licensed
108A Corlett Drive, Illovo   Spanish
Apart from good paellas and mouth-watering smoked meats, this restaurant also offers a wide variety of ethnic Spanish dishes. Give the proprietor a day or two's notice and he will prepare for you a special menu catering specifically for your taste.

Cortina   Tel. 788-1284   Fully licensed
Hyde Park Corner, Hyde Park   Italian
One of the most popular Italian restaurants in town, this restaurant serves a wide variety of ethnic Italian dishes. Reservations are essential.

The Courier   Tel. 702-1050   Not licensed
Dahlia Road, Kyalami   Continental
Renowned for its Sunday lunch buffet, this restaurant also serves a good à la carte menu during the week.

Freddies Tavern   Tel. 726-3602   Not licensed
8 Main Road, Melville   Continental
A small, seasonal restaurant. Delights include a good selection of game dishes.

Front Page   Tel. 726-1917   Fully licensed
10 Main Road, Melville   Steakhouse
The decor, like the restaurant's name, is from the newspaper industry, with old style printing covering the walls and the menu printed on newspaper. The quality of the food is high.

The Herbert Baker   Tel. 726-6253   Fully licensed
5 Winchester Road, Parktown   South African
Situated in a fine old house surrounded by beautiful gardens, this pleasant restaurant is open from breakfast until late in the evening. Pub lunches and Sunday family buffets are also served here.

L'Escargots   Tel. 726-5411   Not licensed
85 4th Avenue, Melville   French/Seafood
The restaurant has a country kitchen atmosphere. Food has a distinctive Mauritian flavour, with the accent on fish dishes.

Lien Wah Chinese   Tel. 788-1820   Fully licensed
Rosebank Hotel,
Tyrwhitt Avenue, Rosebank   Chinese
One of the finest Cantonese restaurants in South Africa, offering attentive service and pleasant atmosphere. Speciality dishes will be served if ordered beforehand.

Lobster Tavern   Tel. 787-4017   Wine and malt
83 Sanlam Centre, Randburg   Seafood/Greek
A wide variety of fresh fish, displayed on ice, is superbly prepared in traditional Greek brick ovens.

Meo Patacca   Tel. 880-2442/3   Fully licensed
20 Chaplin Road, Illovo   Italian
A well-run Italian restaurant serving a good variety of authentic dishes, including daily specials and a superb antepasta table.

Nino da Genova   Tel. 726-3801   Not licensed
4A 7th Street, Melville   Italian
A loud, busy, friendly, Italian restaurant serving a wide variety
of Italian dishes, including a big selection of daily specials.

Sharani   Tel. 836-4486/8   Fully licensed
Oriental Plaza, Fordsburg   Indian halal
Located on the first floor in the Plaza, this ethnic restaurant
offers a wide variety of well-presented Indian halal dishes.

Turn 'n Tender   Tel. 440-6357   Wine and malt
127 Greenway, Greenside   Steakhouse
High standards and good service set this steakhouse above
many others. Food is prepared slightly differently with an accent
on good sauces.

Budget   **Café Zürich**   Tel. 725-2730   Not licensed
Nedbank Plaza,
Pretoria Street, Hillbrow   Coffee shop
This is a pleasant place to watch the world go by while enjoying
a good cup of coffee, snack or cheap three-course meal, or perhaps
even a game of chess or backgammon.

Golden Peacock   Tel. 836-4986   Not licensed
Oriental Plaza, Fordsburg   Indian
Most days see long queues outside this restaurant, all lining up
to buy their tasty samoosas and curry pies. Inside simple curries
accompanied by sambals are served.

Gold Rush   Tel. 331-1725   Not licensed
Garlicks, Carlton Centre   Breakfasts and lunches
This clean restaurant serves hearty breakfasts and a carvery
lunch, as well as daily specials.

Hotel School of South Africa
Tel. 403-2858   Fully licensed
123 Smit Street, Braamfontein   International
High quality food and superb service are the hallmark of this
training school. The reason for the low costs here is that, as an
educational institution, it is not allowed to make a profit. Booking
is essential.

La Bella Italiana   Tel. 331-7803   Wine and malt
46 Von Wielligh Street, City Centre   Italian
Pizzas and simple pastas are served in a Mediterranean atmosphere.

Marialva   Tel. 23-4415   Not licensed
104 Kerk Street, City Centre   Portuguese
This is a simple Portuguese restaurant with a small menu, open
from breakfast.

Marisqueira   Tel. 23-2646   Wine and malt
77 Plein Street, City Centre   Portuguese
The Marisqueira comprises a rowdy beer hall with a small
simple restaurant next door. Service is not fantastic but meals
are hearty.

Nisha's   Tel. 724-2512   Not licensed
High Point, Hillbrow   Curries
This is a small, clean restaurant serving a variety of good curries.

Roshika   Tel. 838-1485   Fully licensed
Oriental Plaza, Fordsburg   Indian
Genuine Indian curries served in typical oriental surroundings.

Village Main Hotel Pub
Tel. 337-8887   Fully licensed
Cnr. Anderson and Goud Streets,
City Centre   Pub Meals
One of the busiest and most successful old pubs in town.
Waverley Hotel Pub   Tel. 834-3428   Fully licensed
79 President Street, City Centre   Pub lunches
Good, wholesome pub food.
White Horse Hotel Pub   Tel. 331-9815   Fully licensed
Marshall Street, City Centre   Pub lunches
Wholesome pub meals.
Vera's Kitchen   Tel. 725-4555   Not licensed
37 Kotze Street, Hillbrow   Carvery/German
Cheap buffet and daily specials.
Rose Garden   Tel. 788-1920   Not licensed
Garlicks, The Mall, Rosebank   Buffet
Excellent value, hot and cold buffet meals.

Nightlife

THEATRE   Johannesburg has a large number of theatres, ranging from huge
opera houses to intimate experimental theatres. A full list of
daily performances can be found in the daily press and booked
through Computicket, Tel. (011) 28-3040.
Alexander Theatre   Tel 339-7514, 36 Stiemens Road, Braam-
fontein
Seats 550 and has a bar in the foyer.
Alhambra Theatre   Tel. 402-7726, 61 Beit Street, Doornfontein
Seats 370 for mostly drama and musical shows. It is the oldest
theatre in Johannesburg.
The Leonard Rayne Theatre (same complex as Alhambra)
Seats 160 plus 34 upper seats.
Andre Huguenet Theatre   Tel. 402-7726, 14 Kapteijn Street,
Hillbrow
This modern threatre seats 400 and has a full bar.
Civic Theatre Complex   Tel. 339-8324, Loveday Street, Braam-
fontein
Seats up to 1 100 people. Mainly ballet. The complex also has a
very good restaurant.
Intimate Theatre   Tel. 403-1563, YMCA Building, Rissik Street,
Braamfontein
Mainly children's theatre seating up to 200.
La Parisienne Theatre and Restaurant   Tel. 725-5620, Happiness
House, Rissik Street, Braamfontein
Theatre seating (100 seats) is in the form of terrace booths.
Mainly comedy shows and musicals.
Market Theatre Complex   Tel. 832-1641, Cnr. Bree and Wolhuter
Streets, City Centre
This very interesting complex was constructed within the old
Johannesburg market buildings. It comprises a number of
theatres, as well as an art gallery, bar where live jazz music is
performed and a very good restaurant. Theatres include:
   The Market Theatre, seating 430
   The Laager at the Market, seating 54 — mainly experimental
      theatre
   Upstairs at the Market, seating 150
   The Old Market Restaurant, seating 70

The Warehouse at the Market, seating 300 in a bistro bar which serves Italian food on a self-service basis. Performances are mainly musical.

The Windybrow   Tel. 724-3301, Cnr. Nugget and Pieterson Streets, Hillbrow

Theatre consists of Adcock-Ingram Auditorium and Dalro Theatre.

Wits Theatre   Tel. 716-4051, University of Witwatersrand, Station Street, Braamfontein

Seating 360, this theatre presents mainly University productions.

MUSICAL ENTERTAINMENT

Live

Johannesburg has a number of pubs and other venues where live entertainment can be enjoyed. Many of them support South African bands playing their own compositions, while others have "cover bands" (bands which play the latest hits or golden oldies). For a full list see the local papers. Most venues are open in the evenings from Tuesday to Saturday.

Bentleys   Tel. 726-5100, Milpark Holiday Inn, Empire Road, Auckland park

Mainly cover bands with a bit of humour thrown in.

Bonanza Bar   Tel. 28-1530, Victoria Hotel, Plein Street, City Centre

The Cotton Club   Tel. 789-4938, 220 Hendrik Verwoerd Drive, Sandton

Music and cabaret enjoyed by diners.

Chelsea Underground   Tel. 642-2860, Catherine Avenue, Hillbrow

Supports South African bands playing original music.

Jaggers   Tel. 788-1718, Mutual Square, Rosebank

Supports mainly South African groups playing original rock.

Jamesons   Tel. 836-6002, 95A Commissioner Street, City Centre

Presents a wide spectrum of original South African rock music.

King of Clubs   Tel. 331-6727

Supports mainly local black bands.

Pullman   Tel. 783-5262, Sandton Holiday Inn, Rivonia Road, Sandton

Rosy O'Grady   Tel. 494-4100, Gold Reef City

Live bands and can-can dancers.

Solly's Saloon   Tel. 788-1820, Rosebank Hotel, Tyrwhitt Avenue, Rosebank

Spats   Tel. 783-8701, Sandton Sun, Fifth Street, Sandton

Thunderdome   Tel. 23-8788, Cnr. Claim and Noord Streets, City Centre

The biggest venue in Johannesburg, supporting local bands. Open till very late with disco, restaurants and bars.

Quavers   Tel. 728-1652, Norwood Hypermarket Complex, Norwood

Jazz

The Transvaal Jazz Club   Tel. (012) 323-2957

Jameson's   Tel. 836-6002, 95A Commissioner Street, City Centre

Kippies Musician Bar   Tel. 832-1641, Market Theatre, Cnr. Bree and Wolhuter Streets, City Centre

Plum Crazy   Tel. 23-0441, Criterion Place, Cnr. Rissik and Jeppe Streets, City Centre

Sunday jazz night.

Prohibition   Tel. 726-8400, 14 Main Road, Melville

Quavers Tel. 728-1652, Norwood Hypermarket Complex, Norwood
Sunday jazz night.
Rumours Tel. 648-4605, Rocky Street, Yeoville
Roxy Rhythm Bar Tel. 726-6019, Melville Hotel, Main Road, Melville

Classical/orchestral Most classical concerts can be booked or enquired about through Computicket, Tel. 28-3040. The main venues are:
Johannesburg City Hall Tel. 337-2727, Rissik Street, City Centre
The Linder Auditorium Tel. 642-7373, Johannesburg College of Education, 27 St. Andrew Road, Parktown
Windybrow Tel. 724-3301, Cnr. Nugget and Peterson Streets, Hillbrow
PACT Music and lunchtime concerts.
Civic Theatre Tel. 339-8324, Loveday Street, Braamfontein
Classical Guitar Society of South Africa Tel. 788-5732. Evening concerts are at various venues.
The National Symphonic Orchestra of the SABC Tel. 714-2735. Performs at various venues throughout the city.

Discos **Peppermint Park** Tel. 725-4840, Moulin Rouge Hotel, Cnr. Claim and Esselen Streets, Hillbrow
Plumb Crazy Tel. 23-0441, Criterion Place, Cnr. Rissik and Jeppe Streets, City Centre
This disco also houses a late-night restaurant.
Thunderdome Tel. 23-8788, Cnr. Claim and Noord Streets, City Centre
The largest disco in Johannesburg offering a variety of special functions, laser shows and live bands late at night.

Dinner-dancing **Clay Oven** Tel. 706-3186   Fully licensed
Cnr. Old Pretoria and Witkoppen Roads,
Rivonia   Greek
Cabaret and Greek dancing on Friday and Saturday nights.
Athens by Night Tel. 643-7892   Fully licensed
Nedbank Hill, Cnr. Kotze and Catherine Streets, Hillbrow Greek
Greek music and dancing till late at night.
Coimbra Tel. 29-4276   Fully licensed
Cnr. Troye and President Streets   Portuguese
This establishment serves genuine Portuguese food and specialises in seafoods, especially prawns.
252 Tavern Tel. 23-9451   Fully licensed
252 Jeppe Street, City Centre   Swiss
This restaurant offers good Swiss food and live band. There is a cover-charge.
No. 58 Tel. 642-0243   Fully licensed
58 Pretoria Street, Hillbrow   Seafood
Mozambique Tel. 23-5022   Fully licensed
78 Noord Street, City Centre   Portuguese
Pleasant restaurant serving wholesome Portuguese dishes, including prawns.
Mundo Portugês Tel. 402-7536   Fully licensed
Nedbank City East, 120 End Street,
City Centre   Portuguese
Friendly Portuguese restaurant.
Thatchers Tel. 884-1400   Fully licensed
Balalaika Hotel, Maud Street,
Sandown   International
Dancing Friday and Saturday nights.

Useful addresses and telephone numbers
Johannesburg area telephone code: **(011)**

TOURIST INFORMATION

Welcome Johannesburg   Tel. 29-4961/5, Ground Floor, Markade Building, 84 Pritchard Street, City Centre
South African Tourism Board   Tel. 331-5241, 46th Floor, Carlton Centre, City Centre (P.O. Box 1094, Johannesburg, 2000)
South African Tourism Board   Tel. 970-1669, International Arrivals Hall, Jan Smuts Airport

TRANSPORT

Jan Smuts is the major international airport into South Africa, and most international and domestic flights arrive and depart from here.

Airline reservations

Air Botswana,   Tel. 975-3614, 303 Nedbank Centre, Jan Smuts Avenue, Randburg
Air Malawi,   Tel. 834-2171, Nedbank Mall, 145 Commissioner Street, City Centre
Air Mauritius,   Tel. 331-1918, Kine Centre, Commissioner Street, City Centre
Air Zimbabwe,   Tel. 331-1541, Upper Shopping Level, Carlton Centre, City Centre
Alitalia,   Tel. 28-5980, Sanlam Centre, 14th Floor, Jeppe Street, City Centre
Bop Air,   Tel. 339-2314, Braamfontein Hotel, De Korte Street, Braamfontein
British Airways,   Tel. 331-0011, Nedbank Mall, 145 Commissioner Street, City Centre
Court Republic Helicopters,   Tel. 827-8907, Rand Airport
Commercial Airlines,   Tel. 331-5975, Zambezi House, 44 Von Wielligh Street, City Centre
El Al,   Tel. 337-1717, National Board House, 94 Pritchard Street, City Centre
Inter Air,   Tel. 827-9804, P.O. Box 46, Rand Airport, 1419
Iberia Airlines,   Tel. 331-0611, Suite 2012, Carlton Centre, City Centre
KLM,   Tel. 643-6671, 11 Wellington Road, Parktown
Lufthansa,   Tel. 643-6851, 87 Rissik Street, Johannesburg
Luxavia,   Tel. 833-7900, New Street South, City Centre
Magnum Airlines,   Tel. 973-3841, Bonaero Drive, Bonaero Park, Jan Smuts Airport
Olympic,   Tel. 836-4631, 116 Marshall Street, City Centre
Royal Swazi National Airways,   Tel. 331-9467, 130 Main Street, City Centre
Sabena,   Tel. 331-8166, 25th Floor, Carlton Centre, City Centre
South African Airways,   Tel. 28-1728, Wolmarans Street, Braamfontein
Swiss Air,   Tel. 832-3221, Swiss House, 86 Main Street, City Centre
TAP,   Tel. 337-3832, Sanlam Centre, Jeppe Street, City Centre
United Air,   Tel. 331-1163, Rennie House, Ameshoff Street, Braamfontein

Airport Enquiries

Jan Smuts:
Arrivals/Departures   Tel. 975-9963
Other   Tel. 978-3171
Lost Property   Tel. 978-5571 (International)
Tel. 978-5671 (Domestic)

Airport Transfers

There are two ways of getting into Johannesburg or Pretoria from the airport: by taxi or by airport bus. The bus is, of course, a fraction of the price of the taxi, but a taxi gets you directly to your final destination, while the Johannesburg bus take you to the railway station (Rotunda).

The airport bus leaves from the entrance of the international arrivals section of Jan Smuts Airport as well as from the South African Airways Rotunda terminus in Leyds Street (close to Johannesburg Station) every half hour from 05h00 to 22h00.
Enquiries   Tel. 774-4197

Bus Services

City Services
Enquiries Office   Tel. 836-2061, Market Street (south side of the City Hall)
Timetables, route maps and coupons for special savings or daily unlimited off-peak travel cards can be obtained from these offices.
Regional Services
Johannesburg/Pretoria   Tel. 786-8400. The bus departs from the corner of Commissioner and Kruis Streets, in Johannesburg and transports passengers to the Central Station in Pretoria.
Inter-city
From Johannesburg a number of inter-city routes radiate in all directions. Most reservations can be made through Computicket (Tel. 28-3040). Companies running these routes include:
Garden Line Transport (to the Garden Route) (See page 118)
Greyhound   Tel. 374-3692/4 (countrywide)
Intercity   Tel. 28-3040 (countrywide)
Mainliner   Tel. 28-2040 (To Windhoek)
Translux   Tel. 774-4504
Transcity   Tel. 774-3926

Coach Tours

The following companies offer tours of Johannesburg city, Pretoria and environs:
Springbok Atlas Safaris   Tel. 28-5866
Soweto Tours   Tel. 932-0000
Tour-Rite   Tel. 616-5544
Wildlife Safaris   Tel. 337-1619

Car Hire

Action Car Hire   Tel. 648-9173, P.O. Box 27782, Yeoville, 2143
Avis   Tel. 331-8631, 118 Main Street, City Centre
Budget   Tel. 331-3631, Carlton Centre, 130 Main Street, City Centre
Dorset   Tel. 614-1177/8, 4A Darras Centre, Kitchener Avenue, Kensington
Imperial Car Rental   Tel. 29-7011, Small Street, City Centre
Protea   Tel. 402-6328, 99 Beit Street, Doornfontein
Swan   Tel. 974-8967, Cnr. Skietlood and Latei Streets, Isando

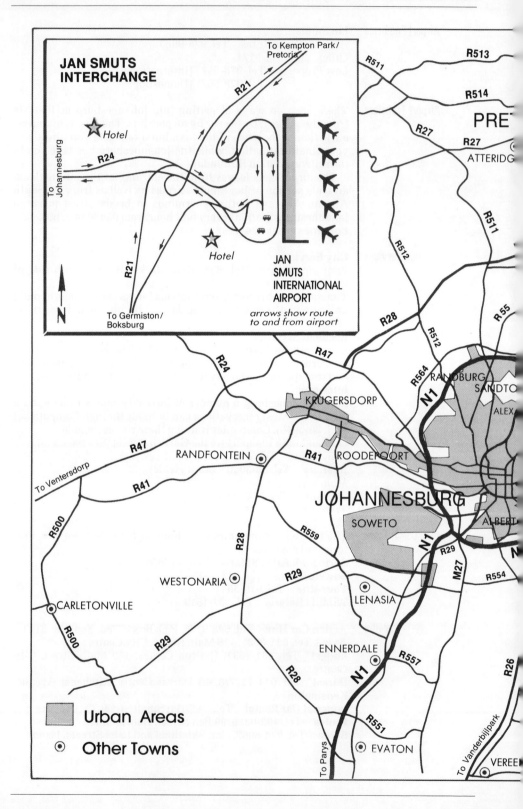

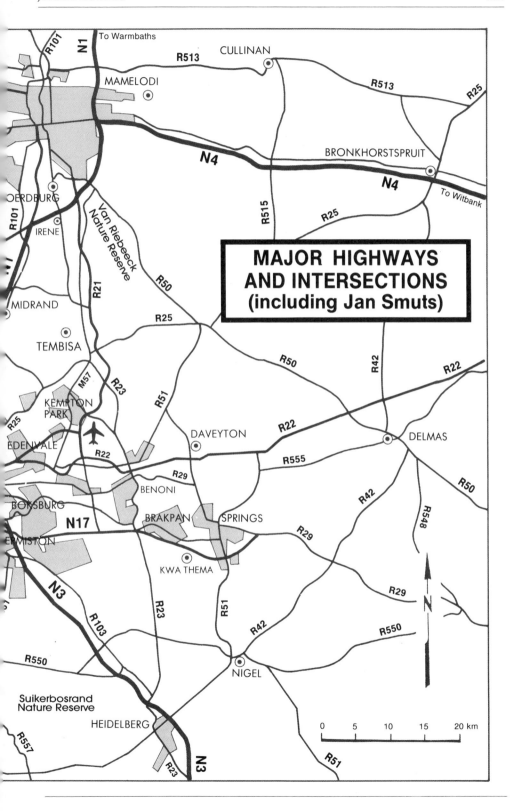

MAJOR HIGHWAYS
AND INTERSECTIONS
(including Jan Smuts)

Camper Hire **Auto Deutsch Mobile Homes,** Tel. 659-1214, P.O. Box 4305, Randburg, 2125
Campers Corner, Tel. 787-9105, 357 Jan Smuts Avenue, Craighall Park, 2196

Taxis Taxis cannot be hailed in Johannesburg. There are, however, ranks outside many of the de luxe hotels. Alternatively contact the Taxi Bureau, Tel. 337-5858/63.

Rail **Information** Tel. 774-4957
Reservations Tel. 774-4128
Fares Tel. 773-8640/1
The Blue Train Tel. 774-3929

EMERGENCY NUMBERS **Ambulance** Tel. 999
Automobile Association Tel. 726-4230
Chemist Tel. 725-2222 (Kings Rondom Building, 42 Wolmarans Street, Joubert Park)
Fire Brigade Tel. 998
General Hospital Tel. 643-0111
Police Tel. 1-0111
Time Tel. 1026
Weather Tel. (012) 21-9621

Sightseeing

THE CITY CENTRE Sadly enough, Johannesburg city centre is not the safest place to stroll around by oneself anymore, because muggers and pickpockets operate on the streets. It is advisable for anybody who wishes to walk through the city centre to take the normal precautions — avoid dark alleys, do not carry purses, shoulder bags or expensive camera equipment, and do not walk around alone. For those who would like a city tour, contact **Welcome Johannesburg.** Places of interest in the city include:

Carlton Centre and Panorama, Tel. 331-2892, one of the major downtown shopping centres and office blocks, and also one of the highest buildings in Johannesburg. From the **Observation Deck** on the fiftieth floor (a fee is charged to reach it) one has a wonderful view of Johannesburg. Also on this deck is the light and sound show **A Day in Johannesburg** which is open daily between 09h00 and 23h00.

The **Africana Museum,** Tel. 836-3787, is located in Market Street. This interesting museum depicts, among other things, the history of South Africa with an emphasis on Johannesburg's birth and growth. It is open on weekdays between 09h00 and 17h30, on Saturdays between 09h00 and 17h00, and on Sundays and public holidays between 14h00 and 17h30.

Diagonal Street, between Market and Pritchard Streets, houses a row of small shops offering a wide variety of traditional African goods. This street is a fine example of a melting pot of the First and Third Worlds. Small shops spill out onto the pavement, offering curries, herbs, fruit, clothing and traditional medicines. One of the best-known herbalists, worth visiting, is number 14. On the other side of the street is an ultra-modern glass building (office blocks); and the Stock Exchange, Tel. 833-6580, is on the north end of Diagonal Street. There is a public gallery in the exchange and tours are conducted during weekdays at 11h00 and 14h30. Trading hours on weekdays are between 08h30 and 16h30.

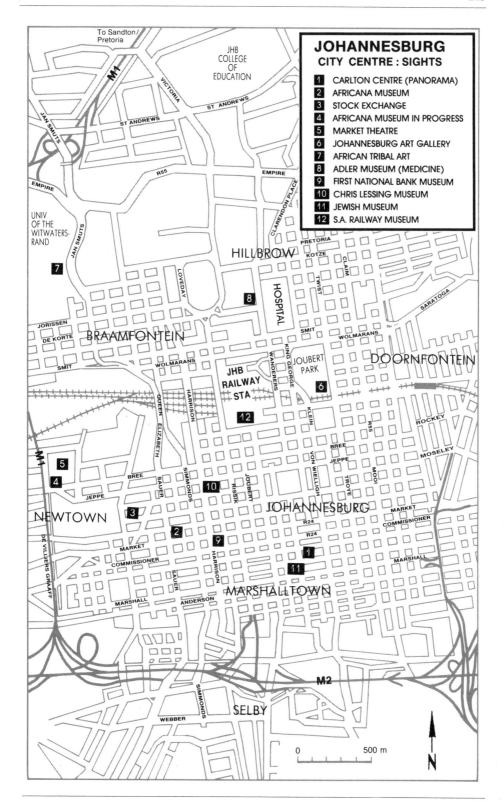

JOHANNESBURG
CITY CENTRE : SIGHTS

1 CARLTON CENTRE (PANORAMA)
2 AFRICANA MUSEUM
3 STOCK EXCHANGE
4 AFRICANA MUSEUM IN PROGRESS
5 MARKET THEATRE
6 JOHANNESBURG ART GALLERY
7 AFRICAN TRIBAL ART
8 ADLER MUSEUM (MEDICINE)
9 FIRST NATIONAL BANK MUSEUM
10 CHRIS LESSING MUSEUM
11 JEWISH MUSEUM
12 S.A. RAILWAY MUSEUM

Africana Museum in Progress, Tel. 836-8482, is located in the old Market Building in Bree Street and has a fascinating display of the development of the different ethnic groups of Southern Africa. It is open on weekdays between 09h00 and 17h30, on Saturdays between 09h00 and 17h00, and Sundays and public holidays between 14h00 and 17h30. **The Market Theatre** itself is the restored old Johannesburg market which has been turned into a number of theatres, an art gallery, and a restaurant and pub. While in the area it is worth taking a stroll around the theatre complex. (On the parade opposite the theatre a fascinating fleamarket is held every Saturday.)

Johannesburg Art Gallery, Tel. 725-3180, in Klein Street, Joubert Park, houses a collection of international works. Gallery tours are conducted on Wednesdays at 10h30 and Saturdays at 15h00 and the gallery is open from Tuesdays to Sundays from 10h00 to 17h00.

SPECIALIST MUSEUMS **African Tribal Art,** Tel. 716-3632, in the Gertrude Posel Gallery, Senate House, Wits University (entrance from Jorissen Street extension), depicts various African artforms. Telephone above number for appointment to view.

The **Adler Museum of the History of Medicine,** Tel. 724-3634, is on the premises of the South African Institute for Medical Research, on Hospital Hill. This fascinating museum depicts the history of all branches of medicine practised in Southern Africa, including African herbalism. It is open on weekdays from 10h00 to 16h00.

Barclays Bank Museum, Tel. 836-5887, 90 Market Street. The museum depicts banking history since 1838. (As Barclays Bank has been renamed First National Bank, the name of this museum might also change, but exhibits and location remain the same.) It is open on weekdays between 09h00 and 16h00, and on Saturdays between 09h00 and 12h30.

The **Bernberg Museum of Costume,** Tel. 646-0716, is on the corner of Jan Smuts Avenue and Duncombe Road in Forest Town. Period costumes from the 18th to the 20th centuries are displayed here from Monday to Saturday between 09h00 and 13h00, and 14h00 to 16h30, and Sundays and public holidays between 14h00 and 16h30.

The **Chris Lessing Boxing Museum,** Tel. 834-3088, in the Old Mutual Centre, corner of Kerk and Harrison Streets, depicts the history of boxing in South Africa on weekdays from 09h00 to 13h00 and 14h00 to 16h30.

The **James Hall Museum of Transport,** Tel. 26-7147, Pioneer Park, Rosettenville Road has a wide collection of historical modes of transport used in South Africa. It is open from Monday to Saturday from 09h00 to 17h30, and on Sundays and public holidays between 14h00 and 17h30.

The **Jewish Museum,** Tel. 331-0331, in Sheffield House, corner of Kruis and Main Streets depicts the history of Judaism from 1920 to the present day and houses a wide variety of ceremonial artifacts. It is open from Monday to Friday from 09h00 to 13h00 and 14h00 to 16h30.

The **Kleinjukskei Vintage Car Museum,** Tel. 704-1204, Witkoppen Road, North Johannesburg, has the largest collection of vintage cars, including a wide variety of Fords, in South Africa. It is open from Wednesdays to Sundays and on public holidays from 10h00 to 17h00.

The **South African Museum of Military History,** Tel. 646-2000, is located at the east end of the zoo. A wide variety of military equipment and memorabilia are displayed here, including equipment from the Boer War, two world wars and the present terrorist skirmishes. It is open daily between 09h00 and 16h30.

The **South African Railway Museum,** Tel. 773-9114, Station Concourse, De Villiers Street. A large number of old locomotives and a model railway are displayed on weekdays between 09h00 and 16h00.

The **South African Airforce Museum,** Tel. 659-1014, located at Lenasia Airport, has a wide range of exhibits tracing South African aviation history. It is open on weekdays from 08h30 to 16h00.

FURTHER AFIELD   **George Harrison Park,** Tel. 836-3787, located about 3 km out of town on the Main Reef Road (continuation of Commissioner Street), is the site of the first discovery of gold. Two claims have been preserved and a 10-stamp battery mill, which was used for crushing ore, can be seen here. Bluegum trees, planted for timber in the mines during early workings still stand in plantations around this area.

Gold Reef City, Tel. 494-4100, (Private Bag 1890, Gold Reef City, 2159) 6 km from Johannesburg, off the N1 south towards Vanderbijlpark. This fascinating "city" has been rebuilt to depict Johannesburg at the turn of the century. Features include a number of pubs and restaurants, theatre, old brewery, goldsmith, hotel, traditional dancing, gold pouring, underground tours, Victorian fun-fair and steam train.

Gold Reef City Hotel ****TYYY Tel. (011) 494-4200
P.O. Box 61, Gold Reef City, 2159   Southern Sun
This charming hotel is situated within the complex. The hotel consists of three different buildings: the hotel itself with 27 rooms, four superior rooms and two suites, the Balmoral with eight rooms, and Market Heights, with two de luxe rooms and two penthouse suites. All rooms and suites are furnished in antique furniture with big brass beds, and cast-iron baths. This is an ideal place for a honeymoon. (There is an interdenominational church within the complex.)

There are also a number of shops in the complex which offer good value gold jewellery pieces and a few antiques. Give yourself at least half a day to explore the whole complex, which is open 7 days a week, from 09h00 to 22h00.

Mine Dancing, Tel. 838-8211, Chamber of Mines, takes place on every second and fourth Sunday of the month. This exciting traditional tribal dancing takes the form of a contest between various mines and costumes and dancing are of a high standard. Performances begin at 09h30. Reservations should be made at least a week in advance.

Gold Mine Tours, Tel. 838-8211, Chamber of Mines. A full-day tour of a working gold mine is organised three times a week. This includes going underground (approximately 2 hours), viewing the gold pouring and training facilities. Transport and lunch are included in the cost of this tour. It is a long day (07h00 to 17h00) and the tour is restricted to people over 18 years old who have energy for a lot of walking.

The Herbert Baker Walk (Signposts showing the route are located on the corner of Jan Smuts Avenue and Sherborne Road, Parktown.) Sir Herbert Baker, an English architect, born in Kent

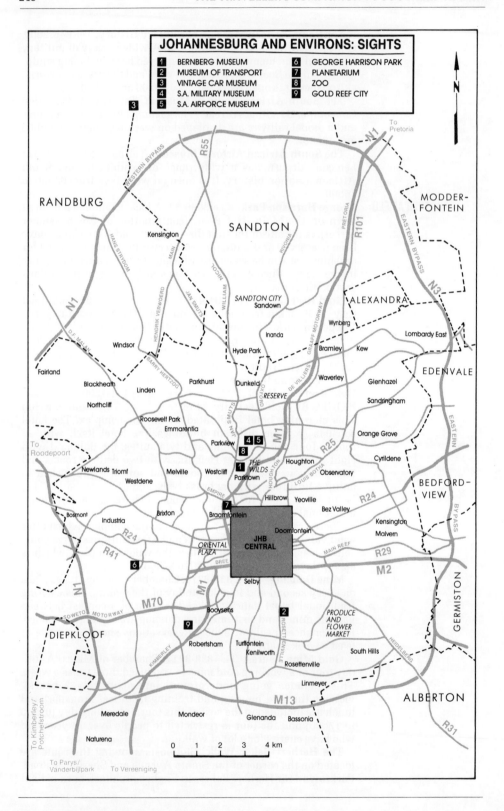

JOHANNESBURG AND ENVIRONS: SIGHTS

1. BERNBERG MUSEUM
2. MUSEUM OF TRANSPORT
3. VINTAGE CAR MUSEUM
4. S.A. MILITARY MUSEUM
5. S.A. AIRFORCE MUSEUM
6. GEORGE HARRISON PARK
7. PLANETARIUM
8. ZOO
9. GOLD REEF CITY

in 1862, settled in the Cape at the age of 30. Lord Milner invited him to Johannesburg at the end of the century and here he developed a characteristic style of architecture, with steeply pitched tile roofs, high bricked chimneys, stone walls with wooden window-frames and small windows. Most of these houses were built in grand colonial tradition on the north ridge overlooking the vast plains below. Many of these houses still stand today, although some have been converted into offices. The walk past a number of these houses takes approximately one hour.

The Planetarium, Tel. 716-3199, in Yale Road, Braamfontein, offers a variety of programmes on different aspects of astronomy. Performances on Fridays at 20h00, Saturdays at 15h00 and Sundays at 16h00 in English and Saturdays at 20h00 in Afrikaans.

The **Musicial Fountains,** Tel. 777-1111, at Pioneer Park, Wemmer Pan, Rosettenville. The multi-coloured fountains are synchronised to popular tunes. The display takes place from September to March between 19h30 and 21h00 and April to June from 18h30 to 20h00.

Santarama Miniland, Tel. 26-8800, in Pioneer Park, is a miniature city of scale models of many of South Africa's more impressive buildings as well as a miniature train, a replica of Cape Town Castle, Kimberley's big hole and Van Riebeeck's ship, the Drommedaris. It is open daily between 10h00 and 17h00.

The **Johannesburg Zoological Gardens,** Tel. 646-2000, in Jan Smuts Avenue, Parkview, has over 3 000 species of mammals, birds and reptiles on 55 ha of ground. Within the grounds are also the South African Military Museum (see museums) and the open-air **Museum of South African Rock Art.** The zoo is open daily between 08h30 and 17h00.

The **Johannesburg Botanical Gardens,** Tel. 782-7064, in Thomas Bowler Avenue, Emmarentia, consists of beautifully laid out rose gardens with over 4 000 roses, a herb garden and exotic trees. It is open daily from sunrise to sunset.

The **Wilds,** Tel. 777-1111, in Houghton Drive, Houghton, is an 18 ha park laid out over two rocky ridges and supporting a wide variety of indigenous plants. The area can be unsafe and visitors are advised to tour in groups.

The **Transvaal Snake Park,** Tel. 805-3116, at Halfway House (north of Johannesburg), has a large variety of African snakes. Snakes are milked on weekdays at 11h00 and 15h00; on Saturdays at 11h00, 14h00, 15h00 and 16h00; and Sundays and public holidays hourly from 11h00 to 16h00.

The **Lippizaner Stallions,** Tel. 702-2103, located at the South African National Equestrian Centre in Dahlia Road, Kyalami, are a team of white stallions which perform in the style of the renowned Spanish riding school in Vienna. Performances take place on Sundays and guests should be seated by 10h40. Bookings can be made through Computicket (Tel. 28-3040).

Soweto (South Western Townships) is the largest black city in South Africa, covering an area of 95 km^2, with a population of over one million inhabitants. An informative tour of this city can be organised through Soweto Tours, Tel. 932-0000 ext. 2020.

The **Heia Safaris Mzumba Dance Display,** Tel. 659-1022/5, is held every Sunday at this resort, 40 km north of Johannesburg.

The day starts with a traditional South African braai, followed by a pulsating performance of ancient legends and ethnic dancing.

Steam Train Trips,   Tel. 795-2356. The Railway Preservation Society of South Africa organises return trips to various destinations on Sundays. Watch local press or contact them for details.

(See also trips from Johannesburg on page 251.)

Shopping

There are a number of large shopping complexes in and around Johannesburg. They sell a variety of goods including supermarket products, specialist clothing and curios. These large complexes include the **Carlton Centre** in downtown Johannesburg, the **Rosebank Shopping Complex** in Rosebank, **Sandton City** in Sandton and the **Oriental Plaza** in Main Road, Fordsburg. The Oriental Plaza is a specialised centre created for the large number of resettled Indian shopkeepers in Johannesburg. Shops specialise in both Eastern and Western merchanise and many shopkeepers are open to bargaining on prices.

MARKETS   **The Artists' Market** takes place on the first weekend of every month at the Zoo Lake in Jan Smuts Avenue. It is an open-air arts and crafts market.

The **Antique Market,** Tel. 646-4211, is located in the lower level of the Parkview Shopping Centre in Parkview and has a wide variety of antiques, brass, books and china on sale. The market is open on Saturdays between 09h00 and 13h00.

The **Flea Market,** Tel. 832-1641, is located on the Mary Fitzgerald Square in front of the Market Theatre (Cnr. of Bree and Wolhuter Streets). This market has a wide variety of unusual odds and ends on sale, including a good selection of hand-made shoes and clothing, beads and junk. It takes place every Saturday between 09h00 and 13h00.

The **Flower and Produce Market** of Johannesburg, Tel. 613-4011, is located in Marjorie Street, City Deep. This is one of the largest markets in Africa and although strictly a wholesale market, smaller quantities may be bought. It is interesting just to walk around and see the various produce on sale, while listening to the intense auctioneering taking place. It is open on weekdays between 06h00 and 11h00.

The **Organic Flea Market,** Tel. 706-3671, is held at Michael Mount Waldorf School, Kulross Road, Bryanston. It is a country market which takes place in the fresh air and sells organically grown fruit, vegetables, herbs and spices, plus a wide variety of home-crafts and antiques. It takes place every Thursday and Saturday between 09h00 and 13h00.

The **Village Flea Market,** located in Pretoria Street, Hillbrow, features forty-odd shops selling a variety of goods ranging from second-hand books to records, clothing and leather.

JEWELLERY   As Johannesburg is the centre of the mining industry in South Africa, it is only natural that it should have a wide variety of good jewellers. The following shops offer duty-free products to all international tourists holding foreign passports:

Diamond Discount Co.,   Tel. 29-5373, National Board House, 94 Pritchard Street, City Centre

J. Fieldman Jewellers,   Tel. 337-5810, 291 Bree Street, City Centre
Messias African City,   Tel. 29-0022, 100 Eloff Street, City Centre
Mervis Bros.,   Tel. 29-9811, 123 Commissioner Street, City Centre
Binyan Diamonds,   Tel. 29-1756, Republic Building, Cnr. Noord and Quartz Streets, City Centre
Tanur,   Tel. 331-8381, Shop 3, Upper Level, Carlton Centre, City Centre
Tanur,   Tel. 783-7191, Upper level, Fountain Court, Sandton City

There are also a variety of other specialist shops in Johannesburg.

CURIOS   **Totem-Meneghilli Gallery,**   Tel. 29-4891, Medical Centre, 209 Jeppe Street, City Centre
Primitive Arts and Antiques,   34 Mutual Square, 169 Oxford Road, Rosebank
Indaba Curios,   Tel. 783-6301, Shop U7, Sandton City
Campers Craft,   Tel. 716-3114, Senate House, University of the Witwatersrand — specialists in ethnic artwork

WOVEN GOODS   **Hilmond,**   Tel. 331-1868, Shop 169, Carlton Centre, City Centre — specialising in hand-woven rugs, tapestries and materials

CAMPING AND HIKING EQUIPMENT   **Camp & Climb,**   Tel. 725-6483, 76 Juta Street, Braamfontein
Drifters Adventure Centre,   Tel. 783-9200, Upper Level, Sandton City — they also hire out equipment and have a second-hand section
Henry's Canvas,   Tel. 788-3202, Mutual Square, Rosebank
M.E. Outdoor Stores,   Tel. 836-7372, Cnr. Harrison and Pritchard Streets, City Centre
Nature Ventures,   Tel. 725-5726, 40 Kotze Street, Hillbrow
Outdoor Living,   Tel. 787-7702, Sanlam Centre, Randburg — they also specialise in equipment hiring
Safrics,   Tel. 337-7917, 54 Kruis Street, City Centre

Outdoor Activities

Cricket is controlled by the Transvaal Cricket Council, Tel. 788-1008, and takes place throughout the city from club to international level. Wanderers cricket ground is the most popular venue for provincial and international matches.

Rugby is controlled by the Transvaal Rugby Football Union, Tel. 402-2960, and has a wide following, with the home side being Transvaal. Provincial and international matches take place at Ellis Park Stadium.

Soccer has a very wide following, especially among the black population of Johannesburg. For a list of current venues contact the national Soccer League, Tel. 29-2971.

PARTICIPATION SPORTS   **Archery** Tel. 26-2989. The *Zoo Lake Club* welcomes visitors and also offers coaching and club equipment for hire to would-be archers.

Bowls (*Southern Transvaal Bowling Association*, Tel. 23-0271). Visitors are more than welcome at most of the the bowling greens in Johannesburg.

Aero-sports (see also Aero-Club page 281) are very popular. As telephone numbers constantly change, it is best to contact the Aero Club for any information.

Gliding, although not cheap, is an exciting sport. The *Witwatersrand Gliding Trust*, Tel. 615-2461, is the closest club to Johannesburg. They offer lessons and hire out equipment. A list of other clubs can be obtained from the Aero Club.

The Hot Air Ballooning Club of Johannesburg is the largest in South Africa. Rental can be arranged through the *Aero Sport Club. Balloon Safaris*, Tel. 705-3201/3, offer an exciting morning's flying (inclusive of a scrumptious champagne breakfast) for all those who wish to experience the thrills of ballooning.

Power flying training can be arranged with *Grand Central Flying School*, Tel. 805-3141, *Lanseria Flight School*, Tel. 659-1213, and *Rand Flight Centre*, Tel. 827-3505. To obtain a licence one is required to have a minimum of forty flying hours, fifteen of which are solo.

Parachuting training can be organised through *Drifters* (see page 292). Most clubs (see page 282) hire out equipment and welcome visitors.

Golf. The *Transvaal Golf Union*, Tel. 640-3714, will supply any interested visitors with a list of clubs which welcome visitors. The *Huddle Park Club*, Club Street, Linksfield, Tel. 640-2748, is a municipal club which is open to the public.

Hiking is organised by the *Johannesburg Hiking Club*, Tel. 643-4437. Visitors are welcome.

Horse-riding schools and stables are located mainly to the north of Johannesburg. *The Transvaal Horse Society*, Tel. 702-1657, will supply telephone numbers of stables to those who are interested.

Ice-skating. The *Carlton Skyrink*, Tel. 331-2641, is located on top of the Carlton Centre car park in the city centre. It is open on Mondays, Wednesdays, Fridays and Saturdays from 11h00 to 17h00; on Tuesdays from 14h00 to 17h00; on Sundays from 14h30 to 17h00 and Saturdays and Sundays from 17h30 to 22h30.

Squash courts are to be found all over Johannesburg and many are open to visitors. Off-peak times (usually between 09h00 and 16h00) are normally cheaper than before and after working hours. Courts include the *Hillbrow Squash Centre*, Tel. 642-5101, and the *Joubert Park Courts*, Tel. 725-3002, close to the city centre. The *Squash Rackets Association of South Africa*, Tel. 883-4390, are happy to supply a full list of courts available.

Tennis clubs are mainly private, but the *Southern Transvaal Tennis Association*, Tel. 614-1419, will supply a list of clubs which welcome visitors, especially during the week.

Ten Pin Bowling has become very popular in Johannesburg and in the rest of South Africa. Alleys are located at:
Ponte Bowl, Tel. 725-6147, entrance Lily Avenue, Berea
Northcliff Bowl, Tel. 782-5216, Northcliff Shopping Centre, Cnr. Milner and D.F. Malan Drive
Broken City Bowl, Tel. 864-5272, Hennie Alberts Street, Brackenhurst

Trips from Johannesburg

Although there are very few places of scenic interest, the mining establishments, historical sights, architectural highlights and entertainment centres are worth visiting. There are three interesting trips from Johannesburg — Cullinan Diamond Mine, 40 km east of Pretoria; Pretoria, the administrative capital of South Africa; and Sun City, South Africa's answer to Las Vegas. Cullinan and Pretoria can be incorporated into one day for those pressed for time, especially if the 09h30 tour is taken at Cullinan.

CULLINAN

To reach this quaint mining town, take the N1 highway towards Pretoria, continue towards Pietersburg (still on the N1); when the N4 is reached, take the Witbank offramp and head east, turning off approximately 26 km along the highway at the Cullinan offramp (onto the R515). Cullinan is a further 15 km away (see map on page 252).

Cullinan grew up around the diamond mine. Many of the old turn-of-the-century houses still stand. The mine itself, the Premier Diamond Mine, is located on a huge extinct volcanic pipe, containing what seems to be an inexaustible pit of diamonds. The town gets its name from Thomas Cullinan, who found the world's largest diamond in the mine, on 26 January 1905. The diamond had a mass of 3 106 carats and measured 127 mm in width (5 inches). It was sold to the Transvaal government, who presented it to King Edward VII. The stone was cut, in Amsterdam, over a two-year period into the 530 carat Star of Africa, now in the sceptre of the Crown Jewels, the 317 carat Lesser Star of Africa, set in the Imperial State Crown, seven other large stones, and 96 lesser stones. For tours of the mine telephone (01213) 30050 for bookings. Tours are offered from Tuesday to Friday at 09h30 to 11h00. From Cullinan either return to Johannesburg, or take the R513 to Pretoria.

PRETORIA

The administrative capital of South Africa and seat of provincial administration of the Transvaal, this city has a population of over three-quarters of a million. In October, the city is transformed into a lilac wonderworld as the jacarandas lining the streets come into bloom. The city is warmer than Johannesburg, with summer temperatures reaching as high as 35 °C.

The city was founded in 1855 on the banks of the Apies River by Martinus W. Pretorius, and named after his father, Andries Pretorius. Between 1860 and 1910 the city was the headquarters and capital of the Zuid-Afrikaansche Republiek. The town was laid out in a rectangular shape with wide streets in which ox-

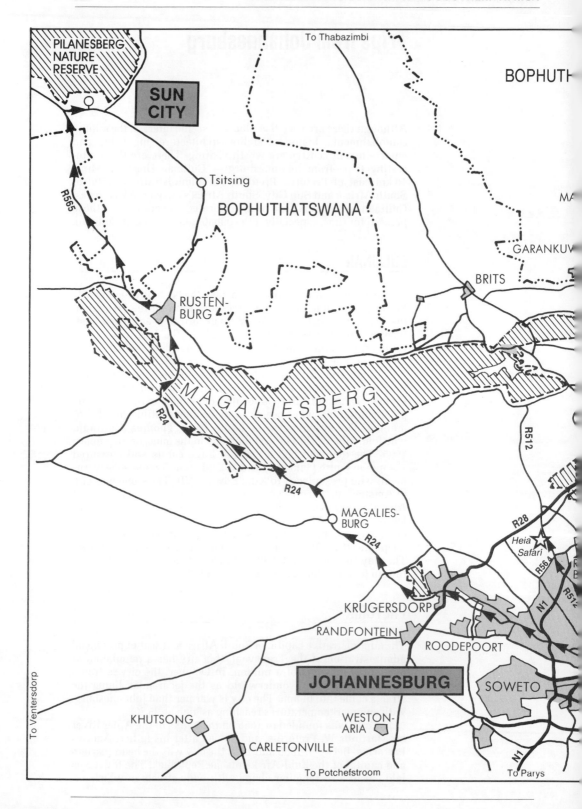

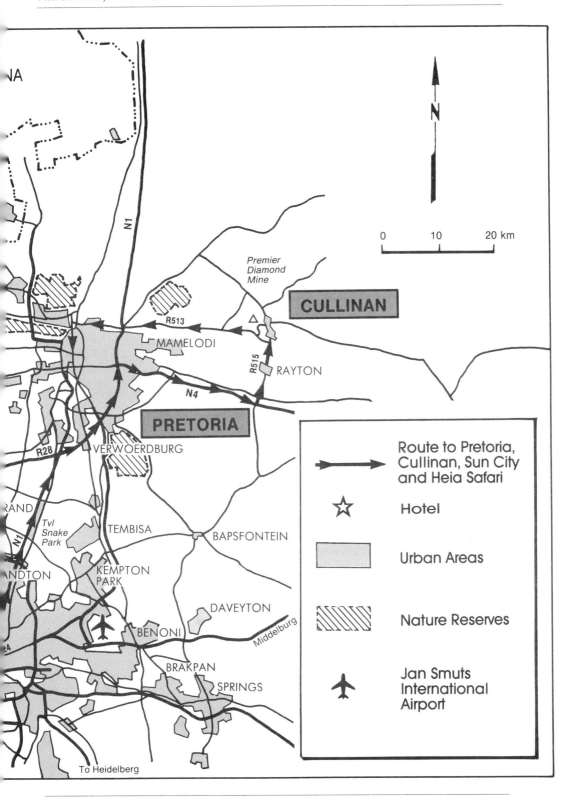

drawn wagons could turn. Today these original streets are a confusing system of one-way streets.

The city boasts two universities, the Pretoria University and the University of South Africa, as well as a number of scientific institutes such as the Council for Scientific and Industrial Research (CSIR), the South African Bureau of Standards (SABS) and Onderstepoort Veterinarian Research Institute.

Accommodation

HOTELS
Burgerspark Hotel ****TYYY   Tel. (012) 28-6570
Minnaar Street
(P.O. Box 2301, Pretoria, 0001)   Southern Sun
Swimming-pool
This is the most expensive hotel in town. It is located in a quiet suburb, close to a park. Rooms are comfortable.

Boulevard Hotel ***TYYY   Tel. (012) 26-4806/ 26-5231
186 Struben Street (P.O. Box 425, Pretoria, 0001)
Swimming-pool
The accommodation is comfortable, and the food is good, especially the pub lunches.

Holiday Inn ***TYYY   Tel. (012) 341-1571
Cnr. Church and Beatrix Streets
(P.O. Box 40694, Arcadia, 0007)   Holiday Inns
Swimming-pool
This is a large, modern hotel with all the usual features. This hotel is ideally situated for those who have business at the Union Buildings.

Karos Manhattan ***TYYY   Tel. (012) 28-6061
247 Scheiding Street
(P.O. Box 26212, Arcadia, 0007)   Karos Hotels
Swimming-pool and squash
This hotel is professionally run and has well-appointed rooms. Their buffet lunch is the best value for money in town.

The Farm Inn ***TYYY   Tel. (012) 87-1612
Lynnwood Road, Die Wilgers
(P.O. Box 71702, Die Wilgers, 00041)
Swimming-pool, riding, hiking
This is a very well-appointed hotel, located just outside the city (just off the N4 to Witbank). Rooms and grounds are large, and the food is good.

Protea Hof ***TYYY   Tel. (012) 28-6900
Cnr. Pretorius and Van der Walt Streets, (P.O. Box 2323, Pretoria, 0002)   Protea Hotels and Inns
A central hotel, ideal for those who have business in the city centre. The rooms that do not face the street, are quiet.

Hamsin **TYYY   Tel. (012) 42-5154/9
675 Pretorius Street, Arcadia, 0083
This large, friendly, well-run hotel is on the lower end of the price scale, and is centrally situated.

New Union **TYYY   Tel. (012) 42-5001
573 Church Street-East (P.O. Box 1337, Pretoria, 0001)
The New Union is a comfortable hotel with well-appointed rooms. Their pub offers the best lunches in town.

Eaton Hall *R   Tel. (012) 28-7232
266 Visagie Street, Pretoria, 0002

This is a very comfortable residential hotel catering mainly for those on longer stays.
Nido *RYYY   Tel. (012) 42-3006
230 Hamilton Street, Arcadia, 0083
Another residential hotel which is clean and comfortable.

OTHER ACCOMMODATION

Malvern House   Tel. (012) 42-5322
575 Schoeman Street, Arcadia, 0083
Pleasant accommodation is offered in fully-furnished flats, rondavels or rooms. Dinner, bed and breakfast tariffs are reasonable.

CARAVAN PARKS

Fountains Valley Caravan Park   Tel. (012) 44-7131
P.O. Box 1454, Pretoria, 0001
Electric plugs, laundry, restaurant, swimming-pool and tennis
Situated on the southern outskirts of town this park offers well-grassed and treed stands.

Restaurants

Asterix Steakhouse
Tel. 47-7532   Wine and malt licence
426 Roderick Street, Lynnwood   Steakhouse
This restaurant offers a small menu with the emphasis on quality.
Belvedere   Tel. 28-6570   Fully licensed
Burgerspark Hotel, Van der Walt and Minnaar Streets   Carvery
This pleasant, value-for-money carvery and buffet allows one to eat as much as you want for a set price.
Böhmerwald   Tel. 26-7658   Fully licensed
85 Paul Kruger Street   German
This pleasant German restaurant serves typical German dishes.
Cynthia's Restaurant   Tel. 46-3220/9   Fully licensed
Maroelana Centre, Maroelana Street,
Hazelwood   International
This restaurant serves good food and has a high standard of service and pleasant decor.
State Theatre Restaurant
Tel. 26-3191/26-3110   Fully licensed
State Theatre, Church Street   French
This surprisingly good restaurant is ideally located for those who would like to enjoy a pre- or post-theatre dinner in elegant surroundings.
Godfather Steakhouse
Tel. 663-1859   Wine and malt licence
Verwoerdburgstad   Steaks only
Some of the best steaks in Pretoria are served here.
Lombardy   Tel. 87-1284   Fully licensed
Lynnwood Road Extension   International
Lombardy is one of the most expensive and grandest restaurants in Pretoria. Many of the business community and senior civil servants do their entertaining here. Food is good, and the wine list is excellent; but service is often poor.
Mike's Kitchen   Tel. 87-3291   Wine and malt
Willow Centre, Rossouw Street,
Willows Ext. 9.   Steakhouse
The usual good quality steakhouse menu and excellent salad bar are the order of the day.

Oude Kaap   Tel. 21-9318/28-6900   Fully licensed
Proteahof, cnr. Van der Walt and
Pretorius Streets   Carvery
This is a good quality value-for-money carvery with a wide
selection of foods.
Pannevis Restaurant   Tel. 42-4094   Fully licensed
South of Pretoria in the Fountain Valley complex above Toulouse
Restaurant   Buffet/traditional South African
A wide variety of interesting South African dishes are served
here.
Plaaskombuis   Tel. 26-8136   Not licensed
Standard Bank Centre   Coffee Shop
Simple farm lunches and stews are specialities here — at realistic
prices.
Rockerfeller 555   Tel. 28-6061   Fully licensed
Manhatten Hotel, 247 Scheiding Street   Carvery
This is one of the best carveries in town and offers a wide
variety of dishes at a set price, which makes this the ideal choice
for those with a big appetite and small budget.
Viktor's   Tel. 26-8282   Wine and malt
446 Church Street   Portuguese
Small exclusive restaurant which is well run, serving ethnic
Portuguese dishes.
Waterfalls Restaurant   Tel. 26-6155   Fully licensed
29 Nedbank Plaza, cnr. Church and
Beatrix Streets   Steakhouse
This well-run restaurant serves standard steaks and well-pre-
pared seafood dishes.

Useful addresses and telephone numbers
Pretoria area telephone code: **(012)**

TOURIST INFORMATION   **Pretoria Information Bureau**,   Tel. 21-2461, Munitoria, cnr. Ver-
meulen and Van der Walt Streets
South African Tourism Board,   Tel. 28-7154, Nedbank Plaza,
Beatrix Street, Arcadia

TRANSPORT
Airlines   **Reservations**,   Tel. 294-3051 (International)
                                294-2222 (Domestic)
Busses   **Airport bus**,   Tel. 26-7028, depart from De Bruyn Park Building,
Andries Street
Municipal busses,   Tel. 28-3562 ext. 2221
Car Hire   **Avis**,   Tel. 323-0871, Merion Building, Bosman Street
Budget,   Tel. 323-3149, Andries Street (between Proes and
Struben Streets)
Imperial,   Tel. 28-1991, 186 Struben Street
Taxis   **Mini**   Tel. 26-6401
Rixi   Tel. 26-9595
Safari   Tel. 26-6401
Rail   **Reservations**   Tel. 294-2401 (Blue Train) 294-2684
Information   Tel. 294-2007

OTHER   **Ambulance**   Tel. 26-0111
Chemist   Tel. 26-8430 (emergency) Pretoria Medical Depot, 326
Church Street

Hospital Tel. 21-3211
Police Tel. 21-0111

Sightseeing

(See map on page 258)

The places mentioned below are discussed in the sequence in which they will be approached from Cullinan or Johannesburg. From Cullinan take the R513 for Pretoria. At Derdepoort Road turn left towards Silverton, and then left again at the T-junction into Pretoria Road.

From Johannesburg take the N1 towards Pretoria. Branch off towards Pietersburg. Then take the N4 highway towards Witbank. Take the first off-ramp towards Meyerspark.

The Pioneer Open-air Museum, Tel. 83-2171, on the banks of the Moreletta Spruit, is a reconstructed pioneer farmyard around a thatched cottage. It is open daily from 09h00 to 17h00.

From here, continue west (towards town) in Pretoria Street, passing the **Pretoria National Botanical Gardens,** Tel. 86-1165, in Cussionia Avenue. The 77 ha of gardens contain indigenous plants from all over South Africa, grouped according to their climatic region, all clearly marked. It is open on weekdays from 06h00 to 18h00.

Continue along Pretoria Street. It becomes Church Street, which is 26 km long, and is one of the longest straight streets in the world. It passes a number of government minister's houses, including the residence of the State President, Bryntirion.

The Union Buildings, located on Meintjies Kop, are the administrative headquarters of the government. They command a fine view of the city, with large terraced, floral gardens stretching down the hill. The red sandstone building was designed by Sir Herbert Baker and completed in 1913.

The Pretoria Art Museum, Tel. 44-4271, in Johann Street, Arcadia Park, houses a wide selection of South African artists' work, including Pierneef, Frans Oerder and Anton van Wouw. It is open from Tuesday to Saturday from 10h00 to 17h00 and on Sundays from 13h00 to 18h00.

Once you have reached the city centre, park in the parking garage in Pretorius Street (see map) and walk to the following:

The State Theatre, Tel. 21-9440, in Church Street, is one of the most impressive modern theatre complexes in South Africa. Tours are conducted on Wednesdays at 09h30 and 14h30, and Fridays at 09h30.

Church Square, on the intersection of Church and Paul Kruger Streets, is regarded as the city centre. Its centre is marked by Anton van Wouw's statue of President Paul Kruger. On the south side, the square resembles London's Trafalgar Square and on the north side it resembles the Palace de la Concorde in Paris. Buildings surrounding the square include the **Old Raadsaal**, built in early Italian Renaissance style. It was the seat of government of the old Zuid-Afrikaansche Republiek; and the **Palace of Justice**, which was completed just before the Boer War and used as a temporary military hospital during the war. Today it houses the Transvaal Division of the Supreme Court.

The Pierneef Museum, Tel. 323-1419, in Vermeulen Street, is housed in a restored late nineteenth century house. The exhibits

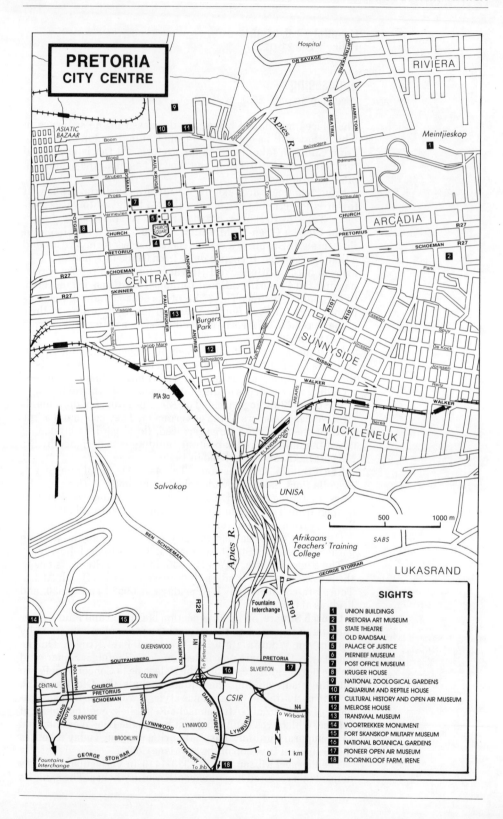

PRETORIA CITY CENTRE

SIGHTS

1 UNION BUILDINGS
2 PRETORIA ART MUSEUM
3 STATE THEATRE
4 OLD RAADSAAL
5 PALACE OF JUSTICE
6 PIERNEEF MUSEUM
7 POST OFFICE MUSEUM
8 KRUGER HOUSE
9 NATIONAL ZOOLOGICAL GARDENS
10 AQUARIUM AND REPTILE HOUSE
11 CULTURAL HISTORY AND OPEN AIR MUSEUM
12 MELROSE HOUSE
13 TRANSVAAL MUSEUM
14 VOORTREKKER MONUMENT
15 FORT SKANSKOP MILITARY MUSEUM
16 NATIONAL BOTANICAL GARDENS
17 PIONEER OPEN AIR MUSEUM
18 DOORNKLOOF FARM, IRENE

Shining shoes outside the Johannesburg Sun

The Houses of Parliament, Pretoria

Historic cottages in the diamond mining town of Cullinan

The salad bar and carvery of a local hotel

represent various aspects of the artists career (1904 to 1957). It is open from Monday to Friday from 08h00 to 16h30.

The Post Office Museum, Tel. 293-1066, on the corner of Bosman and Proes Streets, depicts the history and development of communication in South Africa. It is open from Monday to Friday from 09h00 to 16h00 and on Saturdays from 09h00 to 12h00.

From here, continue by car to **Kruger House,** Tel. 26-9172, at 60 Church Street. This modest house contains the personal belongings of President Paul Kruger, who lived here from 1883 to 1900, and gives a unique insight into that period in history. It is open on weekdays from 07h00 to 16h30 and on Saturdays, Sundays and public holidays from 11h00 to 16h30.

The National Zoological Gardens, Tel. 28-3265, in Boom Street, are one of the largest of their kind in the world. Over 3 500 animal species are found here, and a cable-car transports visitors to various lookout points. Also within the complex is an **Aquarium and Reptile House.** The zoo is open daily from 08h00 to 17h30 (winter) and 08h00 to 18h00 (summer). Seals are fed at 11h00 and 15h00, while carnivores are fed at 15h30.

Within the vicinity of the museum are located a number of **handicraft stalls** where local handicrafts can be bought, and the **National Cultural History and Open-Air Museum,** Tel. 323-3128. The museum features collections of rock engravings and archaeological items and is open on weekdays from 08h00 to 16h30 and on Saturdays, Sundays and public holidays from 11h00 to 16h30.

Melrose House, Tel. 26-7893, 275 Jacob Maré Street, is a beautiful example of Victorian architecture. The house was built for George Heys in 1884. The peace treaty of Vereeniging, which ended the Anglo-Boer War, was signed in the house in 1902. It houses the furniture used by the Heys family and is open from Tuesday to Saturday from 10h00 to 17h00 and on Sundays from 13h00 to 18h30.

The **Transvaal Museum of Natural History,** Tel. 28-7387, and **Geological Survey,** Tel. 28-4230, adjoin each other in Paul Kruger Street. The Natural History Museum houses a *Life's Genesis* exhibition, depicting evolution, and the *Austin Roberts Bird Hall* containing a comprehensive collection of South African birds. The **Geological Survey** houses a comprehensive collection of South African rocks, including precious and semi-precious stones. Both are open from Monday to Saturday from 09h00 to 17h00 and on Sundays and public holidays from 11h00 to 17h00.

The **Voortrekker Monument**, Tel. 26-6770, 6 km south of Pretoria. This huge monument commemorates the Great Trek and depicts the trials and tribulations of the Voortrekkers. A ray of sun falls directly on the words, "We for thee South Africa," (from the National Anthem) at 12h00 on December 16. There are 260 steps leading up to the dome, where a splendid view of the surroundings can be enjoyed. The museum contains an impressive collection of tapestries. Open from Monday to Saturday from 09h00 to 16h45; Sundays and public holidays from 14h00 to 16h45.

Fort Skanskop Military Museum, Tel. 71-5560, located close to the Voortrekker Monument, was built to defend Pretoria's southern entrance, but was never used for this purpose. Today it houses a collection of military memorabilia from Voortrekker times to the end of the Anglo-Boer War in 1902. It is open daily from 10h00 to 15h30.

Shopping

CLOTHING **Nina's Silk Dress Fabrics**, Tel. 48-8374, Shop 35A, Menlyn Park Centre
Eastique Eastern Fashions, Tel. 44-6276, Shop 8, **The Village**, 33 Esselen Street, Sunnyside

GEMS AND NICK-NACKS **Pretoria Diamond Cutting Works** (Pty.) Ltd., Tel. 42-3100, 221 Esselen Street, Sunnyside
Pretoria Wholesale Jewellers, Tel. 21-9571, 330 Struben Street
Claude V. Malan Stamp and Coin Dealer, Tel. 21-5062, 48 Polleys Arcade, Pretoria Central

CURIOS **The Bushman Shop**, Tel 21-9207, Trust Bank Building, Central Street, Pretoria
Tribal Gifts, Tel. 26-6413, 14 Bureau Lane, Pretoria Central

SPECIALITY SHOPS **Pakwells Leather Craft**, Tel. 21-7391, 274 Pretorius Street, City Centre
Kraft Studio Pottery, Tel. 323-8897, SAAU Building, Schoeman Street, City Centre
Swazi Basket Market, Tel. 21-6270, Shop 36, Sanlam Centre, 252 Andries Street, City Centre

Sun City

Sun City, Bophuthatswana's answer to Las Vegas, was erected in virgin bush, to become one of southern Africa's major pleasure resorts. The resort boasts a wide variety of leisure activities from casino, to golf, to water-sport, to international entertainment. The complex is located on the edge of the Pilansberg National Park, the fourth largest park in southern Africa. Three hotels are located in the resort.

To reach the resort, either fly from Johannesburg with **Bop Air** (Tel. 339-2314), go by coach, book through Computicket, Tel. 28-3040, or drive. To reach the resort by car, take the R24 from Johannesburg via Krugersdorp and Magaliesberg to Rustenburg. From Rustenburg follow the signs to Sun City — on the Thabazimbi Road. (See map on page 252).

HOTELS   **Cascades**   Tel. (014651) 2-1000
P.O. Box 7, Sun City,
Bophuthatswana   Sun International
The most upmarket of the three hotels, this pleasant hotel has exterior lifts overlooking the pools, golf-course and lake. The restaurants in the hotel are all good. It is also the closest hotel to the superbowl, where stars like Frank Sinatra and Queen have appeared.
Sun City Hotel   Tel. (014651) 2-1000
P.O. Box 7, Sun City,
Bophuthatswana   Sun International
A very large and comfortable hotel, where the casino, follies theatre, slot machines, disco, movie houses, and many other activities are located. Rooms are large and comfortable.
Cabanas   (address and telephone number as above)
Simple family accommodation to suit the more budget-conscious is offered here.

The resort golf course was designed by Gary Player and is rated as one of the best on the subcontinent. Every other sport is also catered for, and each of the three hotels has its own swimming-pool.

THE PILANESBERG NATIONAL PARK

The park is the fourth largest game park in southern Africa and covers an area of 5 000 km². It has over 8 500 head of game including elephant, leopard, rhino (both black and white), buffalo, hippo and a large variety of antelope.

To reach the Manyane Gate, head towards Mogwase from Sun City. All overnight visitors must book in by 16h30. The park is open from 05h30 to 19h00 (April to August) and 05h00 to 20h00 (September to March). Reservations can be made through: The Reservations Officer, Pilanesberg National Park, P.O. Box 1201, Mogwase, 0302, Bophuthatswana, Tel. (014652) 2405 or 2329, Tlx 4046 (BP).

Accommodation

All tented camps comprise a carpeted concrete base on which
the tents are pitched. Each has two beds (with optional third),
bedding and chairs and table. Guests need to bring eating and
cooking utensils.

Kwa Maritane   Tel (014651) 2-1820

This is a luxury hotel and timeshare complex located within the
park. The hotel offers visitors the use of an excellently positioned
hide overlooking a waterhole.

Tshukudu Chalets

This is a small luxurious camp overlooking the valley and a
waterhole. A total of eight people can be accommodated in the
four thatched rondavels, each with its own bathroom *en suite*.
All meals are included in the tariff.

Mankwe Bush Camp

The Mankwe Bush Camp is the largest of the tented camps
(twenty tents in all) and is located in the centre of the park,
overlooking the Mankwe Dam.

Kololo

This four-tent bush camp is positioned on top of a hill and
provides a magnificent view of the surrounding countryside.
Gas and refrigeration facilities are available. The camp is usually
hired out as a unit to a single party.

Metswedi

Metswedi is a more luxurious four-tent bush camp (compared
with Kololo) with a fully equipped kitchen and two bathrooms.
From the lounge-dining room a fine view of the waterhole next
to the camp can be enjoyed.

Manyane

This is the main camp in the park comprising of a tented camp
and caravan park. The caravan park is rated as one of the best in
southern Africa, with well laid-out sites and clean ablution
blocks. All sites have electric power and braai areas. The camp
also has a licensed restaurant and bar plus a well stocked licensed
grocery and curio store. There are two swimming-pools in the
complex. The camp is open around the clock, which enables the
guests to enjoy the night activities at Sun City.

The Wilderness Leadership School (see page 293) offers exciting
weekend hiking trails through the park, where guests sleep
under the stars and learn about the ways of the bush from
experienced armed rangers.

   Game drives in open vehicles can be organised through the
entertainment desk at Sun City and at Kwa Maritane.

Namibia

This fascinating country, located on the west coast of the subcontinent, between the latitudes 18° and 28° south, covers over 824 269 km². The coastline — some 1 400 km — is a desert. The sea generates large mistbanks, which move inland, thus supplying the desert flora and fauna with the delicate precipitation needed to sustain growth. The northern reaches of the territory supports savannah grasslands, and is the home of a wide variety of wildlife. Much of the wildlife has also adapted well to the desert areas. The sparsely populated country (total population 1,1 million) is also rich in minerals, especially diamonds, uranium and semi-precious stones.

The first Europeans to venture into the country were mainly explorers from the Cape — although Diego Cáo landed on the coast in 1486 to erect a cross at Cape Cross. In 1878 Britain annexed the coastal islands and Walvis Bay for strategic reasons — Walvis Bay was the only potential harbour along the entire coastline. In 1884 Germany placed the territory under its protection, dispatching a colonial force, the Schutztruppe, in 1890, to maintain law in the region. With them came many immigrants who slowly expanded their influence. With the outbreak of World War I, South African troops (allied to the UK) under the leadership of General L. Botha, occupied the territory, and in 1915 the Schutztruppe surrendered. After the war, South West Africa was ceded to South Africa, as a Protectorate, by the League of Nations.

Namibia will gain full independence during 1989. Namibia has a variety of ethnic groups: the Ovambo, Kavango, Herero (known for their magnificent dress), Damara, European, Nama and San. Apart from the various indigenous languages spoken, German, English or Afrikaans are understood by the majority of the population.

The country experiences a wide fluctuation in temperature: days are hot and dry, with temperatures often reaching over 40 °C while night temperatures can drop below zero. Along the coast is an ever present fog bank, which keeps temperatures relatively cool. Inland areas have two rainy seasons: a short one between October and December; and a longer season from mid-January to April, when thunder storms frequently occur.

A wide variety of exciting surprises meets the tourist travelling through the country. The tour below has been compiled to give a good feel of the surroundings. It takes the tourist from Windhoek, the capital and location of the international airport, to the coast at Swakopmund, through fascinating desert landscapes. From here the route runs along the coast, before swinging back inland towards the magnificent Etosha National Park, which is truly one of the most splendid parks on the subcontinent. From here the route traces its way back to Windhoek. Accommodation, although not usually of a five-star quality, is more than adequate. Food is basic, consisting mainly of grills (meat, fish and chicken) — the best restaurants are usually in the hotels. Local

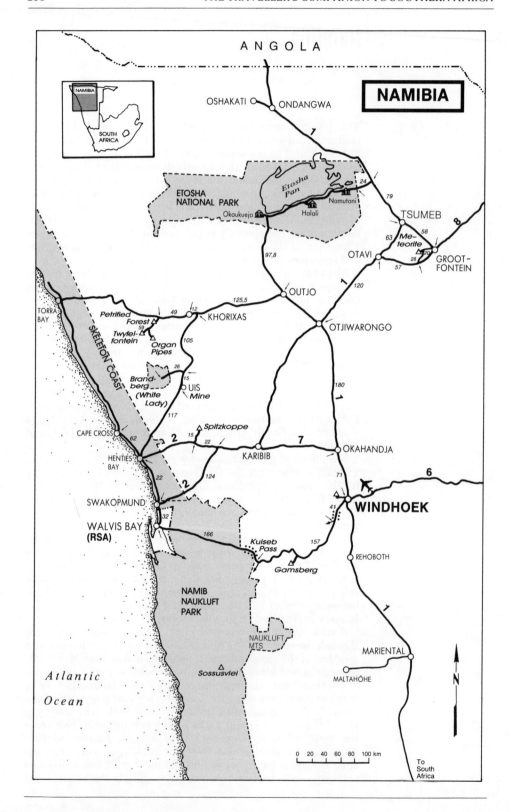

beer is very good, and is an ideal way of satisfying a thirst built up during the day. For those who prefer non-alcoholic beverages *Rock Shandy* is the perfect drink. All accommodation in Namibia is graded from nil to three stars. The symbol YYY means that the hotel is fully licensed, while YY means that only the restaurant is licensed. As accommodation is limited, it is always advisable to reserve, and absolutely necessary during holiday seasons. Roads are not tarred and dirt roads should be approached with extra caution.

WINDHOEK

The capital city of the country with a population of just over 100 000, Windhoek is the principal administrative and economic centre of the country. The first European settlers arrived in 1890 together with the Schutztruppe. They were attracted by the hot springs and water found here. Much of the old colonial German architecture is still standing in the town and a casual drive through the town and suburbs is worthwhile.

Accommodation

HOTELS

Hotel Safari   ***TYYY Tel. (061) 3-8560
Republic Road, 4 km south of Windhoek
(P.O. Box 3900, Windhoek)
Air-conditioning, swimming-pool and fridge
Although located out of town, this is nonetheless one of the finest hotels in Windhoek. Rooms are large and comfortable, and food is above average.

Kalahari Sands Hotel   ***TYYY Tel. (061) 3-6900
Kaiser Street (P.O. Box 2254, Windhoek)   Sun International
Air-conditioning, swimming-pool
This hotel is centrally located, close to all shops and banks. It is a large hotel with more than adequate facilities. The Moringa Room, on the top floor of the hotel, offers dinner-dancing.

Continental Hotel   **TYYY Tel. (061) 3-7293
Kaiser Street (P.O. Box 977, Windhoek)
Air-conditioning
Although noisy, this fine hotel is well located and popular with locals as a meeting place. Food is good and rooms are clean.

Hotel Fürstenhof   **TYYY Tel. (061) 3-7380
4 Romberg Street (P.O. Box 747, Windhoek)
Air-conditioning
Central location and good pricing makes this a pleasant hotel for overnighting.

Hotel Thüringer Hof   **TYYY Tel. (061) 22-6031
Kaiser Street (P.O. Box 112, Windhoek)
Air-conditioning
This is one of the best hotels in town and is very reasonable. Rooms are comfortable, service attentive and food good.

PENSIONS

Privat Pension Berger   *TYY Tel. (061) 22-8660
100 Jan Jonker Street (P.O. Box 5836, Windhoek)
Swimming-pool
Although it is not the cheapest, it certainly is the best in town.

Privat Pension d'Avignon   *TYY Tel. (061) 22-2218
6 Romberg Street (P.O. Box 5836, Windhoek)
Swimming-pool
This very centrally located pension is comfortable and offers good food.

GUEST FARMS   **Gästefarm Elisenheim**   **TYYY Tel. (061) 6-4429
P.O. Box 3016, Windhoek
Swimming-pool, horse-riding, hiking, game-viewing
Situated just 15 km north of Windhoek, this simple but pleasant farm offers visitors an ideal location in which to relax.

CAMPING   **Safari**   Tel. (061) 3-8560
Republic Road, 4 km south of Windhoek
(P.O. Box 3900, Windhoek)
This is the only camp site close to Windhoek which offers basic amenities and caravans for hire.

GAME PARKS   **Daan Viljoen Game Park**   Tel. (061) 3-6975
Private Bag 13267, Windhoek
Swimming-pool and restaurant
Located 24 km west of Windhoek, this park contains a wide variety of game, especially antelope. Guests are accommodated in bungalows with fridges and hot plates. Camp sites are also available.

Useful addresses and telephone numbers
Windhoek area telephone code: **(061)**

TOURIST INFORMATION   **Namibian Publicity and Tourism Association,**
Tel. 22-8160, Municipal Building, 196 Neser Street
(P.O. Box 1848, Windhoek)
Directorate of Trade and Tourism,   Tel. 22-6571, Trust Bank Building, cnr. Kaiser and Jan Meinert Streets
(Private Box 13297, Windhoek)
Department of Nature Conservation and Recreational Resorts,
Tel. 3-6975, Kaiser Street — next to the Post Office (Private Box 13267, Windhoek)

TRANSPORT
Airlines   **Namib Air**, Tel. 3-8220, P.O. Box 731, Windhoek
SAA, Tel. 2-7688, Carl List House, Cnr. Kaiser and Pieter Muller Streets, Windhoek
Hire and Fly,   Tel. 3-1317, P.O. Box 30320, Windhoek

Inter-city buses   **Mainliner**,   Tel. 6-3211, P.O. Box 5673, Windhoek (between Johannesburg, Cape Town and Windhoek — book in South Africa through Computicket, Tel. (011) 28-2040)

Coach tours   **SAR Travel**,   Tel. 298-2532, P.O. Box 415, Windhoek
Skeleton Coast Safaris,   Tel. 3-7567, P.O. Box 20373, Windhoek
Springbok Atlas Safaris,   Tel. 22-4252, P.O. Box 2058, Windhoek
SWA Safaris,   Tel. 3-7567, P.O. Box 20373, Windhoek
Toko Safaris,   Tel. 22-5539, P.O. Box 5017, Windhoek

Car and camper hire	**Avis**, Tel. 3-3166, P.O. Box 2057, Windhoek **Budget**, Tel. 22-8720, P.O. Box 1754, Windhoek **Economy Camper Hire**, Tel. 3-3451, P.O. Box 20274, Windhoek **Trip Car Hire**, Tel. 3-6880, P.O. Box 100, Windhoek **Zimmermann Garage**, Tel. 3-7146, P.O. Box 2672, Windhoek
Taxi	Tel. 3-7070
Rail	*Reservations and enquiries*, Tel. 22-7364

Hunting

SWA Professional Hunters and Guides Association, P.O. Box 11291, Klein Windhoek
Anvo Hunting Safaris,   Tel. 3-7560/2, P.O. Box 21301, Windhoek

Shopping

Two major items worth buying while in Namibia are jewellery — including semi-precious stones — and skins.

JEWELLERY AND SEMI-PRECIOUS STONES	**House of gems**, Tel. 22-5202, 131 Stübel Street, Windhoek **Cheetah Souvenirs**, Tel. 22-7853, 242 Kaiser Street, Windhoek **Adrian**, Tel. 22-5501, Hepworth Arcade, Kaiser Street, Windhoek **Omatako Curio**, Tel. 22-4803, Hepworth Arcade, Kaiser Street, Windhoek
SKINS AND LEATHER GOODS	**Pelzhaus Huber**, Tel. 22-7453, Cnr. Kaizer and Görig Streets, Windhoek

After leaving Windhoek, head south on the dual road towards the RSA. Just out of town is the sign for **Walvis Bay via Gamsberg**. Turn right onto this road, and a further 10 km along you will reach the dirt road. From here the dirt road stretches over 350 km, through some of the most spectacular desert scenery, including two magnificent mountain passes, as well as the **Namib-Naukluft Park**. A few notes of caution:
- Maintain low speeds (below 80 km/hour) as the dirt is very slippery, even during the dry season.
- Leave early in the morning and plan to spend most of the day on the road.
- Make sure that you have a full tank of petrol as there are no fuel stations (or settlements) along the way.
- Carry extra drinking water and food with you in case of emergencies.
- Be wary of sand drifts across the road, especially in sandstorms.

As the road winds its way west, so the land becomes more barren, until the first pass, the Gamsberg Pass is reached. This pass twists through the Gamsberg Mountains and ends on the plateau below. From here the **Namib-Naukluft Park** is entered (stay on main roads if you have no deviation permits). No fee is required to enter the park. Continuing further, the road winds down the barren **Kuiseb Pass,** through the river bed, and onto the desert floor. Take your time along these passes and on the road to Walvis Bay, as a lot of game such as gemsbok, springbok and ostrich can be seen if you are cautious.

Once you reach Walvis Bay continue on to Swakopmund or stay in Walvis Bay. The port of Walvis Bay is part of South Africa. It is slightly industrial with no beaches, while Swakopmund has more of a seaside resort atmosphere with good fishing and pleasant bathing beaches.

WALVIS BAY

Walvis Bay is a perfect harbour, created on the delta of the Kuiseb River. (Today the river does not actively reach the sea, but sinks into the Namib Desert, which acts as a natural reservoir. It supplies the water needs of Swakopmund, Walvis Bay and the mining communities.)

The first known European to land in the area was Bartholomeu Dias — on 8 December 1487. He named it the *Bay of Our Lady Immaculate*, and the barren coast *Sands of Hell*. The first charts named the coast *Praia das Sardinhas* (Coast of Sardines), in recognition of the vast shoals of sardines found off the coast. This name was replaced with *Bahia das Baleias* (Bay of Whales). This is the name that eventually stuck.

During the seventeenth century, many ships were attracted to the coast by the rich finds of whales, seals and guano, but none discovered the most valuable treasure of all, diamonds. These lay scattered on the beaches to the south, just waiting to be found. (The first diamond was discovered in 1907 by August Stauch in a sand embankment. By 1914, R17-million worth of stones had been found; and today they make up an important part of Namibia's industry: R350-million worth of stones are produced a year). In 1793 Walvis Bay was annexed by Holland. On the British occupation of the Cape in 1795, Walvis Bay was also annexed, but no official settlement or representation was established. By 1844 the first traders established themselves here, and for the next thirty-odd years the law was left mostly up to the locals, who had a terrible job, with warring local tribes, gun runners, smugglers and cattle thieves. Representation was made to the Cape Government, but they found little of interest in the territory. On 12 March 1878, however, Commander R.C. Dyer formally annexed the area of 750 km² around the bay.

Today the territory still belongs to South Africa. The fringes of the bay are rich in birdlife, including flamingo and pelican, and a drive around its fringes is more than rewarding for bird lovers.

Accommodation

Flamingo Hotel   *TYYY Tel. (0642) 3011
Seventh Street (P.O. Box 30, Walvis Bay)
This is a comfortable hotel, with clean, neat rooms and low prices.
Municipal Caravan Park   ** Tel. (0642) 5981
Electric power
This is by far the best park in the area, and the only one recommended for those planning to camp along the coast and who want a bit of comfort.

Restaurants

Atlantic Hotel Restaurant Tel. 2811, in Seventh Street
This is one of the best restaurants in town, serving mainly grills
of various kinds.

Useful addresses and telephone numbers

Permits for the **Namib-Naukluft Park** are obtainable from the
following service stations: Troost Transport, 121 Tenth Street;
Namib-Ford, Thirteenth Street

AIRLINES   **Namib Air**   Tel. 5806

CAR HIRE   **Avis**   Tel. 5935, P.O. Box 758, Walvis Bay (also 4-wheel drive
vehicles)
Taxis   Tel. 2568
Rail   **Reservations and enquiries**   Tel. 8226

The 32 km of tar road, linking Walvis Bay to Swakopmund, runs
along the coast. It has towering sand dunes on the one side.
Fishing is very popular along the coast, as is bathing and wind-
surfing at various points.

SWAKOPMUND

Swakopmund is a pleasant seaside resort located at the mouth
of the Swakop River. The town started off as a harbour in the
1890s. It was used by the Germans, who had annexed the territory, and needed a harbour.

Although no natural harbour exists here, a reasonable anchorage is offered off the coast. Goods and passengers were brought
ashore in surf boats. At the turn of the century it was found that
this method had become inadequate, and the construction of a
solid iron pier began. With the outbreak of the World War I, and
South Africa's take-over of the territory, Walvis Bay became the
territory's harbour, and Swakopmund bacame a peaceful seaside
village. The next boom came to the town in 1973 when the **Rös-
sing Uranium Mine** was started approximately 1 500 of the mine personnel
and their families. Because of the town's importance as a seaside
resort, a number of good hotels are found here, and it is thus
worthwhile making this a base for a few days.

Accommodation

HOTELS   **Hansa Hotel** ***TYYY Tel. (0641) 311
Roon Street (P.O. Box 44, Swakopmund)
This hotel is rated by many as one of the best hotels in Namibia.
It is located in the centre of town, but within walking distance of
all amenities. Rooms are spacious and service is excellent. The
food is very good as well.

Hotel Europa-Hof **TYYY Tel. (0641) 5898
Lazarett Street (P.O. Box 1333, Swakopmund)
This is a clean and comfortable hotel with all the usual amenities, close to the beach.
Strand Hotel **TYYY Tel. (0641) 315
P.O. Box 20, Swakopmund
This very well-run hotel is the closest to the beach. It offers well-appointed rooms, friendly service and some of the best continental food in town.
Dig By See *T Tel. (0641) 4130
4 Brücken Street (P.O. Box 1530, Swakopmund)
This is a cheap, clean hotel for budget-conscious travellers.
Hotel Jay Jay's Restaurant YY Tel. (0641) 2909
8 Brücken Street (P.O. Box 835, Swakopmund)
For those travellers on a shoe-string budget, this is the place to stay. Rooms are very clean, service is friendly and the food is good.

PENSIONS **Pension Rapmund** *TYY Tel. (0641) 2035
6 Bismarck Street (P.O. Box 425, Swakopmund)
This pleasant pension offers homely accommodation at realistic prices. Apart from the regular rooms the pension also has five self-contained flats for hire.

SELF-CATERING **Swakopmund Rest-Camp** Tel. (0641) 2588
Swakop Street (Private Box 5017, Swakopmund)
This basic camp offers bungalow accommodation. Bungalows are equipped with stoves, fridges and bedding, but not cooking utensils or cutlery and crockery. (At the time of writing it was found that the B-type bungalows were suitable only for those on the most limited budgets.)

CAMPING **Mile 4** Tel. (0641) 4221
Six kilometres north of Swakopmund
(P.O. Box 3452, Swakopmund)
A very basic, very big park with no grassed sites, north of the town. Popular in season with the fishing fraternity.

Restaurants

Burghotel Nonidas Restaurant Tel. 4544
Ten kilometres east of Swakopmund
Good basic food at realistic prices.
Café Anton Tel. 2419
Pension Schweizerhaus, on Bismarck Street
Located on the street level of the above pension, this European style café offers the finest pastries and cakes in town. A must for those with a sweet tooth.
Hansa Hotel Restaurant Tel. 311
Roon Street
A fine restaurant with a large and diverse menu offering a good choice of continental dishes and some venison specials.
Strand Hotel Restaurant Tel. 315
A perfect venue for a night's dining out on the beachfront. Food is mainly continental, with a few good fish and venison dishes.

Western Saloon   Tel. 5395
8 Molcke Street
A pleasant "action bar" serving good quality grills and fresh oysters.

Useful addresses and telephone numbers

TOURIST INFORMATION

Town Clerk,   Tel. 2411 Garnison Street
(P.O. Box 53, Swakopmund)
Department of Nature Conservation,   Tel. 2172, Cnr. Bismarck and Keiser Wilhelm Streets
Permits are also available from *Charley's Desert Tours* and *Hans Kriess Service Station* in the same street.

TRANSPORT
Airlines   **Namib Air**   Tel. 5123, 21 Post Street
Car hire   **Avis**   Tel. 2527, P.O. Box 1216, Swakopmund
Swakopmund Caravan Hire   Tel. 2448, P.O. Box 3497, Swakopmund
Taxi   Tel. 5880
Tours   **Charley's Desert Tours**   Tel. 4341, P.O. Box 1400, Swakopmund
Desert Adventure Safaris   Tel 5413, P.O. Box 339, Swakopmund
Rail   **Reservations and information**   Tel. 328

Tours

Swakopmund is an ideal base from which to reach a number of exciting places of interest. A few days should be put aside for this purpose.

TOWN CENTRE   Here one finds the relics of a bustling German colonial occupation, when Swakopmund was the major port. An ideal way to view them is to zigzag up and down the streets of the town centre (either by car or on foot). Places of interest include the **station building**, the **old prison, Damara Tower** (now part of the library complex), the **museum** (open daily from 10h30 to 12h30 and 16h00 to 18h00), **lighthouse, Moll** (the original harbour), and the **pier** (which is today a pleasant promenade and angling site).

DAY TOURS   **Cape Cross Seal Reserve** is located 134 km from Swakopmund. To reach the reserve, head north along the coast towards Henties Bay, and then on toward Terrace Bay. The turn-off for Cape Cross is found 127 km from Swakopmund. The reserve was established to protect the breeding colony of Cape Fur Seals, *Arctocephalus pusillus pusillus,* which number between 80 000 and 100 000. These seals do not migrate, but move from colony to colony along the coast between southern Angola and Algoa Bay (Port Elizabeth).
Cape Cross is also of historic interest, being the first place on the Namibian coast on which the Portuguese explorers set foot. In 1486 Diego Cáo erected a cross here in honour of John I of Portugal. He also died here and was buried nearby. A replica of the cross has been erected on the site. The reserve is open daily from 16 December to the end of February between 08h00 and 17h00. From March to the end of June it is open on Saturday,

Sunday and public holidays between 08h00 and 17h00, and from July to December it is open on Wednesdays between 12h00 and 16h00.

The Namib-Naukluft Park (see map on page 273) is the largest of Namibia's nature conservation areas, covering an area of over 23 000 km². It was established in 1979 by combining the Namib Desert Park and the Naukluft Mountain Zebra Park, thus creating a park with many different geological features and eco-systems — including barren mountain ranges, grass, gypsum and quartz plains, and towering sand dunes, as well as an abundance of game.

The Namib Desert is one of the oldest deserts in the world. The area covered by this tour stretches south of the Swakop River from the coast of Walvis Bay, to the eastern border of the park. Herds of springbok, gemsbok, mountain zebra and ostrich roam the plains. Also of immense interest is the *Welwitschia Mirabilis*, a prehistoric plant which has adapted to desert conditions, obtaining moisture from fog.

To reach this area, drive out of town for 3,8 km towards Usakop and Windhoek, and then branch off to the right onto the dirt road (just after the **Martin Luther Monument**) at the signposts for the **Namib Park. Valley of the moon landscape**, the first place reached, is a fascinating area of totally barren hills stretching into the distance. **Welwitschia Plains**, reached next, are barren plains dotted with these fascinating plants. Close by is a primitive camp site. At **Bloedkoppie** there are a number of quiver trees. From here the road leads south, passing a number of water holes, where herds of game are frequently spotted. This tour is a full day's drive, and visitors are advised to depart early in the morning, taking adequate water and food (plus a full tank of fuel). Permits are needed and can be obtained at the addresses on page 271.

The Spitzkoppe (158 km from Swakopmund) are a group of volcanic mountains which rise from the arid desert plain to a height of 1 829 m. The area has a number of interesting plants and rock formations as well as a number of rock paintings. One can barter for semi-precious stones at the village. To reach the Spitzkoppe head for Karibib and Windhoek. Turn left onto a dirt road 124 km from Swakopmund, and drive towards Henties Bay and Uis (D1918). Turn right towards the Spitzkoppe (D3716), 22 km further on. The Spitzkoppe are 15 km further on.

On departure from Swakopmund, head for Henties Bay, along the coast, then swing inland across the desert towards Uis. One kilometre before Uis is reached, swing left towards Kamanjab. Fifteen kilometres along this road is the turn-off for the bushmen painting known as the **White Lady of the Brandberg**, 26 km from the turn-off. To reach the painting from the car park, walk up the river bed into the mountains, following the occasional white arrow. This is a good 20-minute strenuous walk. Brandberg is the highest range of mountains in the country, reaching a height of 2 579 m at their highest point. The White Lady painting is one of many found in the region. It was first thought to depict a lady of Egyptian or Cretan origin, but subsequent theories maintain that it protrays a young man dabbed with white clay for a ceremony. The frieze was made about 16 000 years ago.

From here return to the main road, and continue for a further

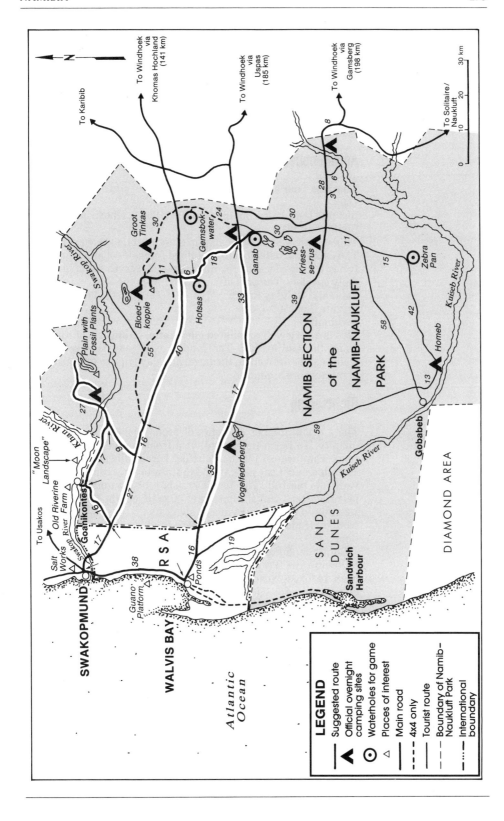

105 km up to the Khorixas intersection — from here Khorixas is a further 12 km.

KHORIXAS

This is the capital town of Damaraland and is an ideal base from which to explore the area.

Accommodation

Khorixas Tourist Camp　**TYY Tel. (0020) and ask for Khorixas 1502
Just less than 12 km out of town (P.O. Box 2, Khorixas)
Swimming-pool
This very pleasant rest camp is situated 11,8 km west of town. The camp consists of self-contained bungalows and camp sites. It has a very pleasant restaurant which serves basic grills and daily specials. The pool offers a relief from the heat.
Bambatsi Holiday Ranch　***TYYY Tel. (06542) 1104
Private Bag 2566, Outjo
Swimming-pool
This is a very well-appointed guest farm, 45 km east of Khorixas, along the Outjo road. The food is good and service homely. Game can be viewed on the farm, and day trips to various places of interest are organised.

Sightseeing

There are a number of sights of archaeological interest in the vicinity. To reach them head west from town on the **Torrabaai** road. The turn-off for the **Petrified Forest** (the sign reads "Versteendewoud") car park is 48 km from town. From the car park walk up the hill. The forest consists of a number of broken petrified tree trunks, some up to 30 m in length. They are about 200 million years old. Evidence suggests that they were uprooted from their place of origin and deposited here during some great flood.

Continue along the Torrabaai road from the petrified forest, following the **Twyfelfontein** signpost. Once the car park has been reached, head up the hill, following the path (there is usually a guide). The rocks on the hill contain a treasure of rock drawings and paintings, reputed to be the largest of their kind in Africa. They depict a large variety of animals.

Go back 7 km and turn right towards **Burnt Mountain** (Verbrandeberg). The mountain slopes are dead, and void of any vegetation. Rocks are coloured in shades of red and purple, giving a feeling of total desolation. In the river bed, just before the mountain, are the geological formations known as the **Organ Pipes**, a mass of vertical basalt slabs. From here return to Khorixas.

From Khorixas head east towards Outjo. The road passes through cattle farming country. The landscape is dotted with mopani trees. The only place of interest along the way, is a Shell petrol station, on the right hand side of the road, 24 km from the cross-

There is much colonial German architecture to be seen in Windhoek

The Valley of the Moon in the Namib Park

A donkey cart in the harshness of Damaraland

A herd of elephants approach the Aroe waterhole in the Etosha National Park

roads. The **pumps** at the petrol station were once hand-operated, but the proprietor has now fixed a plow seat behind the pumps and connected them to a bicycle peddling mechanism.

Continue to Outjo.

OUTJO

This rural town serves mainly the farming community in the vicinity.

Accommodation

Hotel Etosha *TYYYY Tel. (06542) 26
Otavi Road (P.O. Box 31, Outjo)
This basic hotel has clean rooms and is perfect for an overnight stop. It is also half the price of the other hotel in town, the Onduri.
Municipal Rest Camp Tel. (06542) 13
Two kilometres out of town on the Otjiwarongo Road
P.O. Box 51, Outjo
A basic camp with both bungalows (four-beds, fridge and stove) and camp sites.

Restaurants

Hotel Onduri Restaurant Tel. 14
Etosha Road
This basic restaurant serves large plates of food at very realistic prices.

There are two curio shops specialising in the semi-precious stones of the area in the town.

From Outjo head north for 98 km towards Etosha.

ETOSHA NATIONAL PARK

(See map on page 276)

This magnificent game park covers 22 270 km², ranging from dense mopani bush to large open grass plains, with the Etosha Pan at its centre. The park is the home of great herds of animals and it is not uncommon to see herds of over a hundred elephant or zebra at one time. The pan, a huge shallow depression in the ground, is dry and silvery white for most of the year, but during the rainy season the plain sometimes becomes 1 m deep. It then becomes the home of large numbers of waterfowl. The largest antelope found in the park is the eland, and the smallest is the damara dik-dik. The park also has lion, cheetah and leopard. Lion, especially, are often spotted. Bird life is prolific, with over 325 recorded species.

In 1851 the first recorded explorers, Sir Francis Galton and Charles Anderson, visited the region. Fifty years later the German colony established a police outpost on the south-east bank of the pan to control the spread of rinderpest, a cattle disease. The fort was called Namutoni. The fort was destroyed in 1904 during a battle between the troops and the local Ovambo. A new

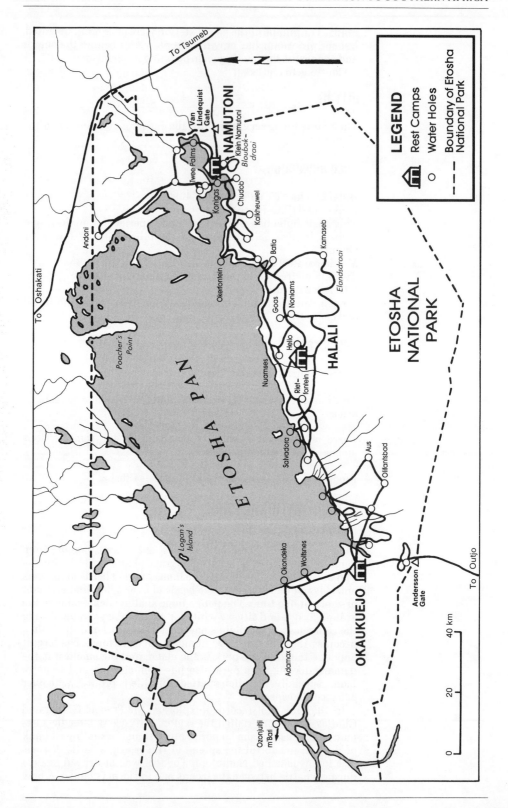

fort was built, but deserted in 1912. The year 1907 saw the area around the pan being declared a game reserve. In 1952 the park was further developed for visitors.

The average rainfall in the park is 400 mm, falling between November and April. During this time roads become muddy and mosquitoes are common (only Namutoni camp is then open). During summer, temperatures often climb above 35 °C. The cooler winters are occasionally below 10 °C in July.

Accommodation

All accommodation can be booked through: The Directorate of Nature Conservation, Tel. (061) 36975, Telex 0908-3180, Private Bag 13267, Windhoek, 9000.

All admission fees can be paid at Namutoni or Okaukuejo. Guests need to be in their camps between sunset and sunrise. All camps have a shop, restaurant, petrol station and swimming-pool, and bedding is supplied. (Bus quarters referred to below are so named as they usually accommodate tourists on coach tours. They are basically a row of rooms constructed and fitted out in the same style as general hotel accommodation.) Restaurant hours are from 07h00 to 08h30, 12h00 to 13h30, and 18h00 to 20h30.

Okaukuejo is the administrative camp of the park, well located on the south-west point of the pan. Accommodation includes two- to four-bedded bungalows (four-bed has two rooms) with fridges, hot-plates, bathrooms, bus quarters (two beds) with bathroom and four-bedded tents as well as caravan and camping facilities. From the camp a number of interesting drives can be undertaken but the most worthwhile from a game point of view is the Okondeka Waterhole. At Sprokieswoud, a forest of *Moringa Ovalifolia* stands, like an erotic surrealist sculpture of half buried humans, with their legs in the air. One of the most rewarding activities is to spend the day at the waterhole at the camp watching the various animal herds come down to drink.

Halali is located midway between the other two camps. Accommodation includes camp sites, two-roomed four-bedded bungalows with wash basins, bus quarters with bathrooms, dormitories (ten beds) or two-bedded joining rooms with toilets and wash basins, and four-bedded tents. Waterholes worthwhile visiting in the area of the camp include Rietfontein, Nuamses, Helio and Goas. It is best to spend a few hours at the waterholes waiting for the game to come and drink.

Namutoni was the first camp in the park to be constructed and is the most impressive. The original fort has been converted into rooms where guests can spend the night. A short distance away are the other facilities. Accommodation consists of two- and four-bedded rooms with bathrooms (four-bedded rooms also have fridges and stoves); two- and three-bedded rooms with wash basins; two-bedded bus quarters with bathrooms; mobile homes with three rooms and four beds, fridges, hot-plates and bathrooms; and camping facilities. Waterholes worth visiting in the area include Kalkheuwel, Chudop, Klein Namutoni, Twee Palms and Aroe.

On Bloubokdraai the shy damara dik-dik is often seen, especially early in the morning. The slower you drive, the more chance there is of spotting them.

From Etosha it is nearly a straight run back to Windhoek, but there are a few interesting places along the way. Head for Tsumeb, 103 km from the park.

TSUMEB

With a population of 17 000, Tsumeb is the most important mining town in Namibia. The mine produces a wide variety of minerals (184 different minerals, ten of which occur nowhere else in the world) including copper, lead, zinc, silver and a wide variety of crystals and gemstones. A good collection of specimens are exhibited in the town's museum (open from Monday to Friday from 09h00 to 12h00 and 15h00 to 18h00, and on Saturdays from 15h00 to 18h00).

Accommodation

Minen Hotel **TYYY Tel. (0671) 3071
Post Street (P.O. Box 244, Tsumeb)
An unassuming, but friendly, pleasant hotel in the city centre. The restaurant is especially good with the best steaks in the country.
La Rochelle Guest Farm **TYYY Tel. (0678) 11013
P.O. Box 194, Tsumeb
Swimming-pool
A superb guest farm 35 km north of town on the Tsintsabis Road which offers game viewing and hunting.

From Tsumeb there is a choice of two routes: direct to Otavi (63 km), or via the Hoba Meteorite near Grootfontein (162 km). To reach the meteorite site, head for Grootfontein. After 58 km turn right at the signpost, onto a gravel road. The meteorite turn-off is a further 20 km.

The **meteorite**, located on the Hoba farm, is regarded as the largest metal meteorite ever found. It weighs about 54 000 kg and consists of 82 per cent iron, 16 per cent nickel and traces of cobalt, copper and chromium.

Continue for 4,5 km along the dirt road, before turning right (no sign). A further 24 km on you reach the tar road for Otavi.

From Otavi continue on to Otjiwarongo. In the vicinity (50 km away on the Karibib road) is the Mount Etjo Safari Lodge.
Mount Etjo Safari Lodge **TYYY Tel. (06532) 1602
P.O. Box 81, Kalkfeld
Swimming-pool
This resort is renowned in central Namibia as it abounds with a wide variety of game. Drives in open vehicles are arranged and guests also have a choice of well-positioned hides. Food is well above average.

From Otjiwarongo continue on to Okahandja and then on to Windhoek, the end of the tour.

PART 3

Useful Addresses and Information

Outdoor Activities

Active participation in sport is the recreational pursuit of most South Africans. There are still vast open spaces where a number of recreational activities can be enjoyed. Many hours of sunshine every day result in the great outdoors being enjoyed to the full.

Below is a list of the national bodies of many of the sports represented in South Africa.

TEAM SPORTS

CRICKET
The South African Cricket Union, Tel. (011) 880-2810, P.O. Box 55009, Northlands, Johannesburg, 2116. One of the most popular summer spectator team sports watched in South Africa. A number of events take place, the most exciting being between the provincial teams. Matches include a day/night series, one-day series and three/four-day series.

FOOTBALL/
SOCCER
The National Soccer League, Tel. (011) 29-2971, Commercial Centre, 251 Bree Street, Johannesburg, 2001. Soccer has one of the largest followings of all team sports in South Africa, and many matches are played to capacity crowds.

POLO
The South African Polo Association, P.O. Box 42, Pietermaritzburg, 3200. Polo is most popular in Natal.

RUGBY
The South African Rugby Board, Tel. (021) 685-3038, P.O. Box 99, Newlands, 7725. Rugby is followed by a large number of people, and many turn out to watch top matches. A number of matches take place, the most exciting being between the provincial teams on most Saturday afternoons during the season. At the time of writing the major teams are the Free State, Transvaal, Northern Transvaal and Western Province.

BOWLS
The South African Bowling Association, Tel. (011) 788-0005, P.O. Box 47177, Parklands, 2121. There are 760 clubs and more than 1 300 greens in South Africa, many open to visitors. Woods are available for hire at several clubs.

INDIVIDUAL SPORTS

AEROSPORT
The Aero Club of South Africa, Tel. (011) 805-3106, P.O. Box 1993, Halfway House, 1685. The club is affiliated to the FAI as well as the CIA, and has a number of subsections, all of which can be contacted through the club.

Gliding
Over twenty clubs exist in South Africa, which is regarded by many to have some of the best unspoilt sites in the world. Temporary membership and rental facilities exist at several clubs. An FAI Certificate with a minimum qualification of a

Silver C licence is needed before being able to fly in South Africa. Two popular clubs near Johannesburg are **White Wings Soaring Centre**, Tel. (01601) 5988, P.O. Box 640, Parys, 9585 and **The Witwatersrand Gliding Trust**, Tel. (011) 615-2461, P.O. Box 6875, Johannesburg, 2000.

Hang-gliding Equipment is not readily available for hire, although various schools do have their own equipment for training. **Drifters** (see page 292) offer hang-gliding lessons.

There are a number of exciting sites in South Africa and flights longer than 200 km are not uncommon. Licensing is required to fly at all sites and enquiries should be made through the subsection.

Hot-air ballooning The largest club is in Johannesburg, but others exist in Durban, Cape Town and Windhoek. Rental facilities are available through the subsections. **Balloon Safaris**, Tel. (011) 705-3201/3, P.O. Box 67, Randburg, 2125, offer balloon safaris from one morning to seven days long. Their morning safaris are an ideal way of getting acquainted with the sport.

Parachuting Clubs with training facilities exist throughout South Africa. Also contact **Drifters** (see page 292).

Power flying Rental and charter facilities exist at many of the clubs in South Africa, where one can train. A minimum of forty flying hours is needed for a pilot's licence.

ARCHERY **The South African National Archery Association**, Tel. (021) 47-4180, P.O. Box 120, Constantia, 7848. They are a friendly bunch of people who welcome guests at the various venues.

CANOEING **South African Canoe Federation**,   Tel. (02353) 733, P.O. Box 5, McGregor, 6708. Various forms of canoeing are practised competitively, including white water, slalom, sprint and long distance. Some clubs also have canoes for hire. The two premier canoeing events in South Africa are the **Berg River Marathon** (see Paarl) and the **Duzi Canoe Marathon** (see Durban). **Trailblazers, Afro Ventures Safaris** and **Drifters** (see page 292) all offer organised canoe safaris on various rivers in Southern Africa.

CYCLING **The Pedal Power Foundation of South Africa**, Tel. (021) 96-4044, P.O. Box 6503, Roggebaai, 8012. The foundation co-ordinates activities and will also help groups or individuals in planning routes. They also hire bicycles for touring in South Africa.

FISHING **South African Anglers' Union**,   Tel. (011) 726-5000, 26 Douglas Street, Horizon View, Roodepoort, 1725. Given South Africa's long stretch of coastline as well as numerous rivers and dams, angling is a popular pastime. **Drifters** offer a wide variety of fishing trips (see page 292). Subsections include:

Freshwater (course) Fishing **The South African Freshwater Angling Association**, Tel. (016) 22-1552, P.O. Box 700, Vereeniging, 1930. Access to private areas can be gained only by prior arrangement, but permission to fish in public waters is not necessary. Licences are, however, necessary, and can be obtained from local clubs, fishing shops, magistrate's offices and the Receiver of Revenue. Licences are not transferable between provinces. Most popular fish caught are carp, eel, yellowfish, catfish and tiger fish in the Transvaal; yellowfish, carp, black bass and tilopia in Natal; and carp, tilopia and whitefish in the Cape.

Trout-fishing This is controlled by the various departments of Nature Conservation in South Africa. They are:
The Transvaal Nature Conservation Directorate, Tel. (012) 201-2361, Private Bag X209, Pretoria, 0001
The Natal Game and Fish Preservation Board, Tel. (0331) 5-1221, P.O. Box 662, Pietermaritzburg, 3200
The Cape Department of Nature and Environmental Conservation, Tel. (021) 45-0227, P.O. Box 9086, Cape Town, 8000
Licences, obtained from the same places as for course fishing, and prescribed tackle are compulsory.
Favourite areas include **Pilgrim's Rest, Graskop, Sabie, Lydenburg** and **Machadodorp** in the Transvaal; the **Drakensberg** escarpment in Natal; and **Stellenbosch, Paarl** and **King Williams Town** in the Cape. Brown and rainbow trout are caught at most sites.

Rock and surf angling **The South African Rock and Surf Angling Association,** Tel. (021) 219-2629, 28 Silverleaf Avenue, Wynberg, Cape Town, 7800. South Africa's extensive coastline offers numerous, excellent opportunities to those who enjoy rock or surf fishing. Licences are required and can be obtained from the receiver of revenue offices. There are restrictions on the number, size and season in which fish may be caught. For further information contact either **Natal Fisheries Licensing Board** or **Cape Nature and Environmental Conservation Directorate** (see addresses under trout fishing).

Game-fishing **The South African Ski-Boat, Light Tackle and Game Fishing Association,** Tel. (021) 96-2714, P.O. Box 4191, Cape Town, 8000. **South African Game Fishing Association,** Tel. (011) 53-1847, P.O. Box 723, Bedfordview, 2008. There are a number of launch sites along the coast (see relevant coastal towns) and boats and tackle can be hired at a number of places. The most popular times of the year are:
— November to April for sail fish and marlin off the Natal Coast;
— June for a number of game fish during Natal's sardine run;
— Tuna (Albocone) in October and snoek in autumn and winter in the Cape.
Companies specialising in excellent fishing tours are **Garden Route Tours** (see page 118), **M. Flanagan Associates, McFarlane Safaris** and **Drifters** (see page 292).

GOLF **The South African Golf Union**, Tel. (021) 46-7585, P.O. Box 1537, Cape Town, 8000. Golf is extremely popular in South Africa and a large number of fine courses exist, even in the more remote areas. Most clubs welcome visitors during the week and kit is available for hire at many clubs.

HIKING **The Hiking Federation of South Africa (HIFSA),** Tel. (012) 46-7562, P.O. Box 17247, Groenkloof, Pretoria, 0027. HIFSA represents the interests of ramblers, hikers and back-packers in South

Africa. A large variety of exciting and exhilirating hikes exist within the country and can be organised individually through the **National Parks Board,** the **Natal Parks Board** or the **Directorate of Forestry**; or in groups through **Drifters, McFarlane Safaris, Trailblazers** and the **Wilderness Leadership School.** The **South African Tourism Board** brings out an informative guide of the various South African hiking trails.

MOUNTAINEERING

The Mountain Club of South Africa, Tel. (021) 45-3412, 97 Hatfield Road, Gardens, Cape Town, 8001. The most popular faces in South Africa are located in the Drakensberg, Western Cape and Magaliesberg (near Johannesburg). Visitors are always welcome on climbs. **Trailblazers** will organise tours.

HORSE-RIDING

The South African National Equestrian Federation, Tel. (011) 706-4508, P.O. Box 69414, Bryanston, 2021.
Various holiday resorts have riding facilities, and there are also a number of stables located throughout South Africa. **Trailblazers** offer an exciting 4-day trail into Lesotho.

HUNTING

The Professional Hunters' Association of South Africa, Tel. (011) 783-0920, P.O. Box 781175, Sandton, 2146. Hunting these days is very conservation-conscious and the above association makes sure that professional ethics are adhered to. They and the South African Tourism Board will be able to supply a full list of registered operators. Contact also **M. Flanagan Associates** (see page 292).

SQUASH

The Squash Rackets Association of South Africa, Tel. (011) 883-4390, P.O. Box 783033, Sandton, 2146.
Many resorts and recreational centres within South Africa have facilities where visitors are welcome.

SURFING

South African Surfriders' Association, Tel. (0391) 2-1150, P.O. Box 617, Umtentweni, 4235. South Africa's coastline offers some of the finest surfing locations in the world. Each year in July, the **International Gunston 500** takes place in Durban, where the top international surfers can be seen in action. Other popular locations include Cape Town, Victoria Bay, Jeffrey's Bay and East London.

TENNIS

The South African Tennis Union, Tel. (011) 402-3580, P.O. Box 2211, Johannesburg, 2000. South Africa's climate allows tennis to be played all year round. Many resorts have their own courts and a number of clubs are open to visitors.

UNDER-WATER SPORTS

The South African Under-Water Union (SAUU), Tel. (021) 69-8531, P.O. Box 201, Rondebosch, 7700. The most popular areas in South Africa are the **Cape Peninsula and Southern Cape** (spring and autumn), and **Sudwana Bay** (mid winter) north of Durban. **Storms River Mouth** offers an exciting under-water trail (see page 129). Equipment can be hired from shops in Johannesburg, Cape Town and Durban (see relevant sections)), on production of recognised qualification certificates. **Spearfishing** is also popular. In Natal permits are required. It is illegal to spearfish with scuba equipment.

WIND-SURFING **The South African Wind-Surfing Class Association,** Tel. (011) 726-7076, Private Box X16, Auckland Park, 2006. Apart from a number of inland venues, the Cape coast is the most popular venue for events. Equipment can be hired through **Wind-Surfing Africa** in Johannesburg.

Useful addresses and telephone numbers

Accommodation

HOTELS **Holiday Inns**   Tel. (011) 883-2200   Tlx: 442-2246
P.O. Box 4280, Johannesburg, 2000
Karos Hotels   Tel. (011) 643-8052   Tlx: 43-1161
P.O. Box 17136, Hillbrow, 2083
Kondotel Inns   Tel. (031) 37-4222   Tlx: 62-2381
P.O. Box 10305, Marine Parade, Durban, 4046
Namib Sun Hotels   Tel. (061) 3-3145   Tlx: 0908-3138
P.O. Box 2862, Windhoek, 9000
Portfolio of Country Places   Tel. (011) 788-1258/9 Tlx: 42-7194
Shop 5E, Mutual Square, 169 Oxford Road, Rosebank, 2196
Private Hotels of Northern Transvaal   Tel. (015236) 2-0100
Tlx: 32-1831
P.O. Box 544, Tzaneen, 0850
Protea Hotels and Inns   Tel. (021) 419-5320   Tlx: 52-0031
P.O. Box 2936, Cape Town, 8000
Selected Hotels (Pty) Ltd.   Tel. (011) 706-5956
Tlx: 42-7515
P.O. Box 98146, Sloane Park, Sandton, 2152
Southern Sun Hotels   Tel. (011) 883-2200
Tlx: 42-3923
P.O. Box 5083, Johannesburg, 2000
Sun International   Tel. (011) 783-8750   Tlx: 42-7427
P.O. Box 784487, Sandton, 2146

OTHER **Bed and Breakfast (Pty) Ltd.**   Tel. (011) 726-6915 Tlx: 4-25800
P.O. Box 31124, Braamfontein, 2017
Club Caraville   Tel. (031) 701-4156   Tlx: 62-4573
P.O. Box 139, Sarnia, 3615
National Caravan Club of South Africa
Tel. (011) 789-3202
P.O. Box 50580, Randburg, 2125
National Parks Board   See Nature Conservation
Natal Parks Board   See Nature Conservation
Overvaal Resorts   Tel. (012) 26-4906   Tlx: 32-2195
P.O. Box 3046, Pretoria, 0001
South African Youth Hostels Association
Tel. (021) 419-1853
P.O. Box 4402, Cape Town, 8000
YMCA National Office   Tel. (011) 724-4541
104 Rissik Street, Johannesburg, 2001
YWCA National Office   Tel. (011) 339-8212
408 Dunwell House, 35 Jorissen Street, Braamfontein, Johannesburg, 2001

Foreign diplomatic missions

Argentina
Pretoria (Embassy)   Tel. (012) 48-4288/9
130 Stella Street, Waterkloof
Cape Town (Embassy)   Tel. (021) 323-8051/2
Anglo American Life Centre, 8 Riebeeck Street

Australia
Pretoria (Embassy)   Tel. (012) 3-7051/2
3rd Floor, Standard Bank Chambers, Church Square
Cape Town (Consulate)   Tel. (021) 22-1576
1001 Colonial Mutual Building, 106 Adderley Street

Austria
Pretoria (Embassy)   Tel. (012) 323-1020/3001/0032
10th Floor, Apollo Centre, 405 Church Street
Cape Town (Consulate)   Tel. (021) 21-1440/1
1012 Cape Town Centre, Heerengracht

Belgium
Pretoria (Embassy)   Tel. (012) 44-3201
275 Pomona Street, Muckleneuk
Johannesburg (Consulate-General)
Tel. (011) 724-5358/9
Heerengracht Building, Cnr. De Korte and Melle Streets, Braam-
fontein
Cape Town (Consulate-General) Tel. (021) 22-5535/6
Southern House, 52 St. George's Street

Brazil
Pretoria (Embassy)   Tel. (012) 43-5559
182 Balmoral Avenue, Arcadia

Canada
Pretoria (Embassy)   Tel. (012) 28-7062
Nedbank Plaza, Cnr. Church and Beatrix Streets, Arcadia
Cape Town (Embassy)   Tel. (021) 23-5240
16th Floor, Reserve Bank Building, 30 Hout Street

Chile
Pretoria (Embassy and Consulate-General)
Tel. (012) 26-9387/8/9
7th Floor, Merino Building, Cnr. Bosman and Pretoria Streets
Cape Town (Consulate-General)   Tel. (021) 21-2344
Heerengracht Tower, 7th Floor, Cape Town Centre Building,
Suite H712.

China (Republic)
Pretoria (Embassy)   Tel. (012) 21-8661/2/3
11th Floor, Old Mutual Centre, 167 Andries Street
Johannesburg (Consulate-General)
Tel. (011) 29-4334/5
4th Floor, Standard Bank Galleries, Cnr. Eloff and Market Streets
Cape Town (Consulate-General) Tel. (021) 21-4267/8
7th Floor, Cape Town Centre, Main Tower, Foreshore

Denmark
Johannesburg (Consulate-General) Tel. (011) 33-6052
Suite 2907, Carlton Centre, Commissioner Street

Finland
Pretoria (Legation)   Tel. (012) 42-7140/1
171 Esselen Street, Sunnyside

France
Pretoria (Embassy)   Tel. (012) 43-5564/5
807 George Avenue, Arcadia
Johannesburg (Consulate-General)
Tel. (011) 21-3468/9
15th Floor, Kine Centre, Cnr. Kruis and Commissioner Streets
Cape Town (Consulate)   Tel. (021) 21-5617
1003 Cape Town Centre, Heerengracht

Germany (Federal Republic)
Pretoria (Embassy)   Tel. (012) 43-5931/2/3/4
180 Blackwood Street, Arcadia
Johannesburg (Consulate-General) Tel. (011) 725-1519
Community Centre of the German Lutheran Church, 5th Floor,
16 Kaptein Street, Hillbrow
Cape Town (Consulate-General)   Tel. (021) 24-2410
825 St. Martini Gardens, Queen Victoria Street
Durban (Consulate)   Tel. (031) 32-5677
1522 15th Floor, 320 West Street

Greece
Pretoria (Embassy)   Tel. (012) 43-7351/2
995 Pretorius Street
Johannesburg (Consulate-General)
Tel. (011) 836-7214/5
116 Marshall Street
Cape Town (Consulate)   Tel. (021) 43-7066/5847
17th Floor, Reserve Bank Building, 30 Hout Street

Israel
Pretoria (Embassy)   Tel. (012) 26-9008/9
Apollo Centre, 405 Church Street

Italy
Pretoria (Embassy)   Tel. (012) 43-5541/2/3/4
796 George Avenue, Arcadia
Cape Town (Consulate)   Tel (021) 23-5157/8
2 Grey's Pass, Gardens
Johannesburg (Consulate-General) Tel. (011) 29-5217
2015 Sanlam Centre, 20th Floor, Suite 2015, Jeppe Street
Durban (Consulate)   Tel. (031) 6-4107
12th Floor, Santam Building, Broad Street

Japan
Pretoria (Consulate-General)   Tel. (012) 21-9561/2
1st Floor, Prudential Assurance Building, 28 Church Square

The Netherlands
Pretoria (Embassy)   Tel. (012) 21-9311/2/3/4/5/6
1st Floor, Netherlands Bank Building, Cnr. Church and Andries Streets
Johannesburg (Consulate-General)
Tel. (011) 93-9011/2/3
11th Floor, Nedbank Corner, 96 Jorissen Street, Braamfontein
Cape Town (Consulate-General)
Tel. (021) 21-5660/1/2
100 Strand Street

Portugal
Pretoria (Embassy)   Tel. (012) 42-7120/1/2
599 Leyds Street, Muckleneuk
Johannesburg (Consulate-General) Tel. (011) 838-5311
7 Rissik Street
Cape Town (Consulate-General)   Tel. (021) 24-1454
417 Atkinson House, Strand Street
Durban (Consulate)   Tel. (031) 31-8293/4
16th Floor, 320 West Street
Windhoek (Consulate)   Tel. (061) 2-8736
P.O. Box 443

Spain
Pretoria (Embassy)   Tel. (012) 21-7761
1st Floor, Anglo American Life Centre, Cnr. Andries and Vermeulen Streets
Cape Town (Consulate-General)   Tel. (021) 25-1468
19 African Eagle Centre, 2 St. George's Street

Sweden
Pretoria (Legation)   Tel. (012) 21-1050
The Old Mutual Centre, 167 Andries Street
Cape Town (Legation)   Tel. (021) 25-3988/9
Ovenstone House, 3rd Floor, 8 St. George's Street

Switzerland
Pretoria (Embassy)   Tel. (012) 43-7788/9
818 George Avenue, Arcadia
Johannesburg (Consulate-General)
Tel. (011) 838-5102/3
2nd Floor, Swiss House, 86 Main Street
Cape Town (Consulate)   Tel. (021) 21-7633
9th Floor, Mobil House, Hans Strijdom Avenue, Roggebaai

Transkei
Pretoria (Embassy)   Tel. (012) 21-5626/7/8/9
Du Toit Street
Johannesburg (Consulate-General) Tel. (011) 331-7688
Kariba House, 164 Commissioner Street
Durban (Consulate)   Tel. (031) 304-5748
320 Commercial City, 40 Commercial Road
Port Elizabeth (Consulate)   Tel. (041) 54-2224/5
1st Floor, Capital Building, 545 Main Street
Cape Town (Consulate)   Tel. (021) 21-7582/3
2nd and 3rd Floor, Vadas Building, 42 Strand Street

United Kingdom of Great Britain and Northern Ireland
Pretoria (Embassy)   Tel. (012) 43-3121
"Greystoke", 6 Hill Street
Johannesburg (Consulate-General) Tel. (011) 331-8161
5th Floor, Nedbank Mall, 145-147 Commissioner Street
Cape Town (Consulate-General)   Tel. (021) 25-3670
Anglo American Centre, 2 St. George's Street
Durban (Consulate)   Tel. (031) 31-3131
712 Barclays Bank Building, Cnr. Smith and Field Streets

United States of America
Pretoria (Embassy)   Tel. (012) 28-4266
7th Floor, Thibault House, 225 Pretorius Street
Johannesburg (Consulate-General)
Tel. (011) 331-1681/3
11th Floor, Kine Centre, Commissioner Street
Cape Town (Consulate-General)   Tel. (021) 46-7720
4th Floor, Broadway Industries Centre, Heerengracht, Foreshore
Durban (Consulate-General)   Tel. (031) 32-4737/8/9
29th Floor, Durban Bay House, 333 Smith Street

Zimbabwe
Johannesburg   Tel. (011) 838-2157
10th Floor, Sanlam Building, 63 Commissioner Street, Marshall-
town

Nature Conservation

**Cape Province Department of Nature and Environment Conser-
vation**   Tel. (021) 45-0227
P.O. Box 659, Cape Town, 8000
Natal Parks Board   Tel. (0331) 5-1514   Tlx: 6-43481
P.O. Box 662, Pietermaritzburg, 3200
Transvaal Nature Conservation Division
Tel. (012) 28-0349
Private Box X209, Pretoria, 0001
Directorate of Forestry   Tel. (012) 299-2632
Private Bag X447, Pretoria, 0001
National Hiking Way Board   Tel. (012) 323-7526
Private Bag X447, Pretoria, 0001
National Parks Board   Head office: Tel. (012) 343-1991
Tlx: 32-1324
P.O. Box 787, Pretoria, 0001
643 Leyds Street, Muckleneuk
Regional offices:
Cape Town Tel. (021) 419-5365
Tlx: 52-1506
P.O. Box 7400, Roggebaai, 8012
Picbel Arcade, Strand Street
George Tel. (0441) 74-6924/5
Tlx: 52-4901
P.O. Box 774, George, 6503
38 Courtenay Street, George
Namibian Directorate of Nature Conservation
Tel. (061) 3-6975   Tlx: 0908-3180
Private Bag 13267, Windhoek 9000

Wildlife Society of South Africa
Tel. (011) 782-4716/7
P.O. Box 44189, Linden, 2104

Tourist Promotion Organisations

Bop Tour (Bophuthatswana)   Tel. (01401) 81-2666 Tlx: (0937) 3176BP
P.O. Box 5442, Mmbatho, 8681
Ciskei Tourist Board   Tel. (0401) 9-1190
Tlx: 25-0795
P.O. Box 56, Bisho, Republic of Ciskei
Southern Africa Regional Tourism Organisation Council (SARTOC)   Tel. (011) 886-1020
Tlx: 4-24222 S.A.
P.O. Box 48405, Roosevelt Park, 2129, Johannesburg
Represents Lesotho, Malawi, South Africa and Swaziland
South African Tourism Board (SATOUR)
Tel. (012) 47-1131   Tlx: 32-0457 S.A.
Private Bag X164, Pretoria, 0001
(See also various cities for regional offices.)
Namibian Directorate of Trade and Tourism
Tel. (061) 22-6572   Tlx: 0908-487 W.K.
Private Bag 13297, Windhoek, SWA/Namibia
Transkei National Tourism Board   Tel. (0471) 2-5191
Private Bag X5029, Umtata, Republic of Transkei
Venda Tourism   Tel. (015581) 2-1131   Tlx: 32-2682
P.O. Box 9, Sibasa, 0970, Republic of Venda

Transport

AIRLINES TRANS-CONTINENTAL

(See relevant sections in Johannesburg, Cape Town and Durban.)
South African Airways (SAA)
Tel. (011) 773-6618   Tlx: 42-5020
P.O. Box 7778, Johannesburg, 2000

AIRLINES – INTERNAL AND NEIGHBOURING COUNTRIES

Air Botswana   Tel. (019231) 35-2812   Tlx: 2413 BD
P.O. Box 92, Gaborone, Botswana
Air Cape   Tel. (021) 934-0344   Tlx: 52-0246
P.O. Box D.F. Malan Airport, Cape Town, 7525
Balloon Safaris   Tel. (011) 705-3201/3   Tlx: 427075
P.O. Box 67, Randburg, 2125
City Air   Tel. (031) 42-2136   Tlx: 62-4470
P.O. Box 32468, Mobeni, 4060, Durban
Comair   Tel. (011) 973-2911   Tlx: 42-8878
P.O. Box 7015, Bonaero Park, 1622
Magnum Airlines   Tel. (011) 973-2941   Tlx: 42-9040
P.O. Jan Smuts Airport, 1627
Namib air   Tel. (061) 3-8220   Tlx: 5090-8657
P.O. Box 731, Windhoek, SWA/Namibia, 9000
South African Airways (see above)

CAR HIRE

African Self-Drive Safaris   Tel. (011) 802-2282
Tlx: 4-24582
P.O. Box 39859, Bramley, 2018 — Fully equipped land-rovers
Avis Rent-A-Car   Tel. (011) 974-2571   Tlx: 42-8888
P.O. Box 221, Isando, 1600
Budget Rent-A-Car   Tel. (011) 484-4072
Tlx: 43-0130
P.O. Box 51351, Readene, 2192
Imperial Car Rental   Tel. (011) 337-6100
Tlx: 48-7536
P.O. Box 260177, Excom, 2023

INTER-CITY COACHES

Greyhound Inter-City   Tel. (011) 762-2544
Tlx: 42-0492
P.O. Box 57, Krugersdorp, 1740
(See also individual towns and cities.)

TRAIN SERVICES

See individual towns and cities for addresses.

TOUR OPERATORS

(See individual regions of regional and city tours.)
Afro Ventures Safaris   Tel. (011) 789-1078/9
Tlx: 42-5604
P.O. Box 2339, Randburg, 2125
Operating in South Africa, Botswana, Namibia and Zimbabwe.
Includes budget and 2-week drive camping safaris.
Drifters   Tel. (011) 673-7012   Tlx: 42-5046
P.O. Box 48434, Roosevelt Park, 2129
Outdoor adventure specialists including hiking, holiday camps,
hang-gliding, canoeing, fishing, pony-trekking, scuba and sky-
diving tours in southern Africa.
Grosvenor Tours   Tel. (021) 23-0428   Tlx: 52-2240
219 Bree Street, Cape Town, 8001
Guaranteed weekly departures throughout South Africa.
Karibu Safaris   Tel. (031) 83-9774   Tlx: 623026
P.O. Box 35196, Northway, 4065
Outdoor safaris to Botswana, Zimbabwe, Namibia, Malawi and
Zaïre.
M. Flanagan Associates, Hunting Tel. (012) 661-1371 Tlx:
32-1531
18 Seafern Park, 18 Fouche Street, Pierre van Ryneveld Park,
Verwoerdburg 0140
Hunting and fishing specialists
McFarlane Safaris Tel. (011) 331-9671 Tlx: 48-2172
CC Box 99050, Carlton Centre, Johannesburg, 2000
Wide range of safaris in Transvaal and Natal including walking,
fishing and photographic.
Springbok Atlas Safaris Tel. (021) 45-5468
Tlx: 52-7912
P.O. Box 115, Cape Town, 8000
Large fleet of coaches with regular guided tours throughout
South Africa and Namibia.
TFC Tours Southern Africa   Tel. (011) 331-0631 Tlx: 48-6981
P.O. Box 9874, Johannesburg, 2000
Wide range of scheduled tour departures throughout South Africa.

Trailblazers   Tel. (011) 724-5198
P.O. Box 18692, Hillbrow, 2038
Offer a wide variety of hiking, pony-trekking and canoeing safaris in South Africa and Lesotho.
Wilderness Leadership Schools   Tel. (011) 782-1613
P.O. Box 87230, Houghton, 2041
Organise small group trails to wilderness areas in South Africa.
Wilderness Safaris   Tel. (011) 884-1458/9
Tlx: 4-28642
P.O. Box 651171, Benmore, 2010
Operating quality safaris into Botswana, Namibia, Malawi and Zimbabwe. Includes budget camping safaris.
Wildlife Expeditions   Tel. (011) 53-1814
P.O. Box 645, Bedfordview, 2008
Small groups on trails in game areas including Botswana.

If you have any suggestions or ideas to improve subsequent editions of this guide, kindly forward these to:
    Mike Crewe-Brown
    The Traveller's Companion to southern Africa
    PO Box 846
    Fourways
    2055

Index

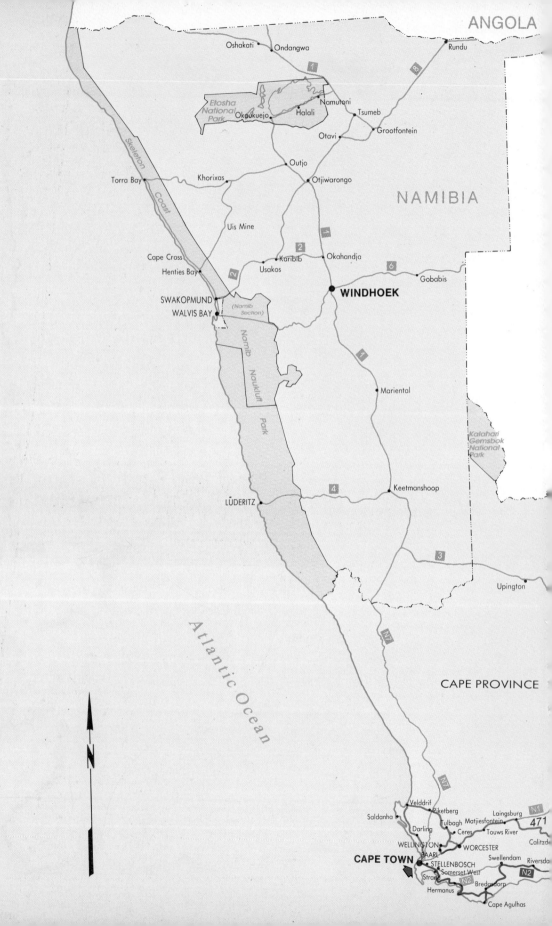